Evading the Patronage Trap

Evading the Patronage Trap

Interest Representation in Mexico

BRIAN PALMER-RUBIN

University of Michigan Press
Ann Arbor

Published in the United States of America by the
University of Michigan Press
Manufactured in the United States of America
Printed on acid-free paper
First published August 2022

A CIP catalog record for this book is available from the British Library.

Library of Congress Cataloging-in-Publication data has been applied for.
ISBN 978-0-472-07544-7 (hardcover : alk. paper)
ISBN 978-0-472-05544-9 (paper : alk. paper)
ISBN 978-0-472-90287-3 (OA)

DOI: https://doi.org/10.3998/mpub.12132850

An electronic version of this book is freely available, thanks in part to the support of libraries working with Knowledge Unlatched (KU). KU is a collaborative initiative designed to make high quality books Open Access for the public good. More information about the initiative and links to the Open Access version can be found at www.knowledgeunlatched.org.

The University of Michigan Press's open access publishing program is made possible thanks to additional funding from the University of Michigan Office of the Provost and the generous support of contributing libraries.

CONTENTS

Appendices

Digital materials related to this title can be found on the Fulcrum platform via the following citable URL https://doi.org/10.3998/mpub.12132850

ABBREVIATIONS

ABM	Asociación de Bancos de México (Association of Mexican Banks)
AD	Acción Democrática (Democratic Action, Venezuela)
AMIS	Asociación Mexicana de Instituciones de Seguros (Mexican Association of Insurance Institutions)
ANAGSA	Aseguradora Nacional Agrícola y Ganadera (National Agricultural Insurance Agency)
ANEC	Asociación Nacional de Empresas Comercializadoras de Productores del Campo (National Association of Commercializing Firms of Rural Producers)
ANIT	Asociación Nacional de la Industria de la Transformación (National Association of the Industry of Transformation)
APRA	Alianza Popular Revolucionaria Americana (American Popular Revolutionary Alliance, Peru)
ARIC	Asociación Rural de Interés Colectivo (Rural Collective Interest Association)
BANRURAL	Banco Nacional de Crédito Rural (National Rural Credit Bank)
BJP	Bharatiya Janata Party (India)
CAJ	Consejo Agropecuario de Jalisco (Jalisco Agricultural Council)
CANACINTRA	Cámara Nacional de la Industria de Transformación (National Chamber of the Industry of Transformation)
CANACO	Cámara Nacional de Comercio (National Chamber of Commerce)
CANACOPE	Cámara Nacional de Comercio en Pequeño (National Chamber of Small Commerce)

CANIETI	Cámara Nacional de la Industria Electrónica de Telecomunicaciones y Tecnologías de la Información (National Chamber of the Electronic Telecommunications Industry and Information Technologies)
CANIRAC	Cámara Nacional de la Industria de Restaurantes y Alimentos Condimentados (National Chamber for the Restaurant and Prepared-Foods Sector)
CAREINTRA	Cámara Regional de la Industria de Transformación del Estado de Jalisco (Regional Chamber of the Industry of Transformation of the State of Jalisco)
CCC	Central Campesina Cardenista (Cardenista Peasant Central)
CCE	Consejo Coordinador Empresarial (Business Coordinating Council)
CCENI	Consejo Consultivo Estratégico de Negociaciones Internacionales (Strategic Consultative Council for International Negotiations)
CCI	Central Campesina Independiente (Independent Peasant Central)
CCIJ	Consejo de Cámaras Industriales de Jalisco (Council of Industrial Chambers of Jalisco)
CEPE	Consejo Estatal de Promoción Económica (State Economic Support Council)
CESJAL	Consejo Económico y Social del Estado de Jalisco para el Desarrollo y la Competitividad (Social Council of the State of Jalisco for Development and Competitiveness)
CICEG	Cámara de la Industria del Calzado del Estado de Guanajuato (Chamber of the Footwear Industry of the State of Guanajuato)
CICEJ	Cámara de la Industria del Calzado del Estado de Jalisco (Chamber of the Footwear Industry of the State of Jalisco)
CIOAC	Central Independiente de Obreros and Campesinos (Independent Workers and Peasants Central)
CMHN	Consejo Mexicano de Hombres de Negocios (Mexican Council of Businessmen)
CMIC	Cámara Mexicana de la Industria de la Construcción (Mexican Chamber for the Construction Industry)

CNA	Consejo Nacional Agropecuario (National Agricultural Council)
CNC	Confederación Nacional Campesina (National Peasant Confederation)
CNG	Confederación Nacional Ganadera (National Ranchers Confederation)
CNOP	Confederación Nacional de Organizaciones Populares (National Confederation of Popular Organizations)
CNPA	Confederación Nacional "Plan de Ayala" (National Confederation "Plan de Ayala")
CNTE	Coordinadora Nacional de Trabajadores de la Educación (National Coordinator of Education Workers)
COCOCAM	Consejo Consultivo de Organizaciones Campesinas de Michoacán (Consultative Council of Michoacán Peasant Organizations)
CODUC	Coalición de Organizaciones Democráticas Urbanas y Campesinas (Coalition of Democratic Urban and Peasant Organizations)
COECE	Coordinadora Empresarial de Comercio Exterior (Business Coordinator for Foreign Trade)
COMAGRO	Comercializadora Agropecuaria de Occidente (Agricultural Commercializing Organization of the West)
CONAIVE	Cámara Nacional de la Industria del Vestido (National Chamber for the Textile Industry)
CONASUPO	Compañia Nacional de Subsistencias Populares (National Company of Popular Subsistence)
CONCAMIN	Confederación de Cámaras Industriales de los Estados Unidos Mexicanos (Confederation of Industrial Chambers of the United States of Mexico)
CONCANACO	Confederación de Cámaras Nacionales de Comercio (Confederation of the National Chambers of Commerce)
CONTAG	Confederacao Nacional dos Trabalhadores na Agricultura (National Confederation of Agricultural Workers, Brazil)
COPARMEX	Confederación Patronal de la República Mexicana (Patronal Confederation of the Mexican Republic)

COPLADEMUN	Comité de Planeación para el Desarrollo Municipal (Planning Committee for Municipal Development)
CPC	Confederación de la Producción y del Comercio (Confederation of Production and of Commerce, Chile)
CROC	Confederación Revolucionaria de Obreros y Campesinos (Revolutionary Confederation of Workers and Peasants)
CTM	Confederación de Trabajadores de México (Confederation of Mexican Workers)
EZLN	Ejercito Zapatista de Liberación Nacional (Zapatista Army of National Liberation)
FA	Frente Amplio (Broad Front, Uruguay)
FARAJAL	Fideicomiso de Apoyo a la Rentabilidad Agrícola de los Productores de Maíz del Estado de Jalisco (Trust in Support of the Agricultural Profitability of Jalisco Corn Producers)
FDN	Frente Democrático Nacional (National Democratic Front)
Fondo PyME	Fondo de Apoyo para la Micro, Pequeña y Mediana Empresa (Support Fund for Micro, Small, and Medium Firms)
FPFV	Frente Popular Francisco Villa (Francisco Villa Popular Front)
INADEM	Instituto Nacional del Emprendedor (National Institute for the Entrepreneur)
ISI	import-substitution industrialization
MAS	Movimiento al Socialismo (Movement to Socialism, Bolivia)
MNR	Movimiento Nacionalista Revolucionario (Revolutionary Nationalist Movement, Bolivia)
MORENA	Movimiento Regeneración Nacional (National Regeneration Movement)
MST	Movimento dos Trabalhadores Rurais Sem Terra (Movement of Landless Rural Workers, Brazil)
MUP	Movimiento Urbano Popular (Urban Popular Movement)

NAFTA	North American Free Trade Agreement
PAN	Partido Acción Nacional (National Action Party)
PJ	Partido Judicialista (Justicialist Party, Argentina)
PLANTAR	Consejo Nacional Acción Rural (National Council for Rural Action)
PNR	Partido Nacional Revolucionario (National Revolutionary Party)
PRD	Partido de la Revolución Democrática (Party of the Democratic Revolution)
PRI	Partido de la Revolución Institucional (Institutional Revolutionary Party)
PROCAMPO	Programa de Apoyos Directos al Campo (Program for Direct Payments to the Countryside)
PROCEDE	Programa de Certificación de Derechos Ejidales y Titulación de Solares Urbanos (Program for Certification of Ejido Land Rights and the Titling of Urban House Plots)
PROGRESA	Programa de Educación, Salud y Alimentación (Program of Education, Health, and Nutrition)
PRONASOL	Programa Nacional de Solidaridad (National Solidarity Program)
PT	Partido dos Trabalhadores (Workers' Party, Brazil)
REDCCAM	Red de Empresas Comercializadoras Campesinas de Michoacán (Network of Peasant Commercializing Firms of Michoacán)
REDMOCAF	Red Mexicana de Organizaciones Campesinas Forestales (Mexican Network of Forest Peasants Organizations)
RN	Renovación Nacional (National Renewal, Chile)
SAGARPA	Secretaría de Agricultura, Ganadería, Desarrollo Rural, Pesca y Alimentación (Ministry of Agriculture, Ranching, Rural Development, Fishing, and Food)
SE	Secretaría de Economía (Ministry of the Economy)
SEDECO	Secretaría de Desarrollo Económico de Estado de México/Michoacán (Ministry of Economic Development of Estado de México/Michoacán)
SEDESOL	Secretaría de Desarrollo Social (Ministry of Social Development)

SEDER	Secretaría de Desarrollo Rural de Estado de México/ Jalisco (Ministry of Rural Development of Estado de México/Jalisco)
SEDRU	Secretaría de Desarrollo Rural de Michoacán (Ministry of Rural Development of Michoacán)
SEPROE	Secretaría de Promoción Económica de Jalisco (Ministry of Economic Promotion of Jalisco)
SIEM	Sistema de Información Empresarial Mexicana (Mexican Business Information System)
SNTE	Sindicato Nacional de Trabajadores de la Educación (National Educational Workers Union)
SPR	Sociedades de Producción Rural (Rural Production Societies)
UCD	Unión Campesina Democrática (Democratic Peasant Union)
UCR	Unión Cívica Radical (Radical Civic Union)
UDI	Unión Democrática Independiente (Independent Democratic Union, Chile)
UGOCM	Unión General de Obreros y Campesinos de México (General Union of Workers and Peasants of Mexico)
UNAM	Universidad Nacional Autónoma de México (National Autonomous University of Mexico)
UNORCA	Unión Nacional de Organizaciones Regionales Campesinas Autónomas (National Union of Regional Autonomous Peasant Organizations)
USMCA	United States–Mexico–Canada Agreement

FIGURES AND TABLES

Figures

Tables

ACKNOWLEDGEMENTS

My intellectual venture at Berkeley was shaped at every step by my mentors, Ruth Berins Collier and David Collier. Ruth has been an adviser extraordinaire, dedicating vast amounts of time to talking through my argument, commenting on my writing, and marveling with me over Mexican politics. I began graduate school with an interest in understanding the ways that marginalized populations organize to wield political influence. Ruth taught me that this was popular-sector interest representation and guided me as I figured out what I wanted to say about it. David encouraged me to pursue answers to important questions in the social and political world and taught me to express my ideas in ways that have resonance. He also pushed me to engage in intellectual communities by collaborating on research, presenting at conferences, and reaching out to scholars.

The other professors on my dissertation committee struck the difficult balance between constructive criticism and encouragement. Paul Pierson, who has a knack for making those little comments that lead to "aha!" moments, helped me see parallels between the structures of interest representation in Latin America and in the United States. Dylan Riley guided me in my interpretation and application of classic social theories. And Jason Wittenberg was a source of wisdom for issues ranging from argumentation to model specification. This project has also benefitted from useful comments and discussions with several other faculty members at Berkeley, including Leo Arriola, Thad Dunning, Peter Evans, Heather Haveman, Alison Post, Steve Vogel, and Nick Ziegler. Harley Shaiken and the team at the Center for Latin American Studies created an extraordinary community of scholars and involved me in opportunities that stoked my passion for Mexican politics, not least of which was the chance to teach a course with Cuauhtémoc Cárdenas. I would like to thank Ing. Cárdenas for generously sharing his time and insights with a green doctoral student, for pointing me to the puzzling questions in Mexican party politics, and for introducing me to several key interview subjects.

At Berkeley, I was privileged to belong to a community of generous Latin Americanists who sustained a culture that values analytical rigor and fellowship in equal measure. Among those that have offered guidance, feedback and support are Ben Allen, Tomás Bril, Tara Buss, Chris Chambers-Ju, Adam Cohon, Tasha Fairfield, Hernan Flom, Candelaria Garay, Eugenia Giraudy, Sam Handlin, Veronica Herrera, Danny Hidalgo, Diana Kapiszewski, Ben Lessing, Lindsay Mayka, Simeon Nichter, Lucas Novaes, Mathias Poertner, Jessica Rich, Andrés Schipani, and Coach Walker. Completion of my dissertation was supported by a squad of writing companions, including Ali Bond, Sara Chatfield, Nina Kelsey, Ben Krupicka, Dan Mattingly, Akasemi Newsome, and Suzanne Scoggins.

At various conferences and workshops, and in informal conversations, several scholars have generously shared contacts, given advice, or commented on portions of this book, including Maria Lorena Cook, Mariela Daby, Gustavo Flores-Macías, Ken Greene, Patrick Heller, Anirudh Krishna, Paul Lagunes, Chappell Lawson, Brian Min, Vicky Murillo, Steven Samford, Ben Ross Schneider, Andrew Schrank, Ken Shadlen, Eduardo Silva, Prerna Singh, Richard Snyder, and Deborah Yashar. Throughout my academic career, Jonathan Fox has been a model of socially engaged scholarship and pointed me in the right direction at several stages of this project.

The field research for this project would not have been possible without grants from the Social Science Research Council and the Inter-American Foundation.

Two great friends, Janice Gallagher and Libby Haight, made field research in Mexico City more feasible and enjoyable, both through their companionship and by putting roofs over my head. Janice was my roommate, sounding board, confidante, and the DJ on my Xochimilco birthday gondola. Libby has been a friend and mentor since she first invited me to work as a research assistant coding access-to-information responses in 2007. In the ensuing years, Libby has taught me a great deal about transparency and rural development policy and introduced me to others like her, whose drive to make things better in Mexico inspired this study.

In Mexico City, several people kindly helped me during the field research and writing stages. I would like to thank Carlos Alba, Isabel García, Tim Kessler, Matilde Luna, Juan Pardinas, Emiliano Shea, and Tim Wright for help with field research. The fabulous faculty at CIDE—especially Rosario

Aguilar, Allyson Benton, Guillermo Cejudo, Juan Fernando Ibarra, María Inclán, Joy Langston, Sandra Ley, Gilles Serra, and Andreas Schedler—and at ITAM—Federico Estévez, Eric Magar, Alejandro Moreno, Juan Pablo Micozzi, Alberto Simpser, and Jeff Weldon—provided useful feedback and advice. Fundar was an ideal institutional affiliation, offering a congenial community of committed advocates and researchers. At Fundar, I would like to thank Cécile Lachenal, Miguel Pulido, Héctor Robles, Ana Joaquina Ruiz, and Renata Terrazas.

Several people helped me with fieldwork *en provincia*. In Michoacán, I would like to thank Enrique Bautista and Héctor Chávez and in Jalisco, Clemente Castañeda, Mario Hueso, Carlos Moreno, and Alfonso Hernández, who introduced me to the most valuable contact of them all. In Estado de México, I thank the Pinzon Kuhn family for their hospitality.

I am grateful to leaders of several organizations for opening their doors to an outsider and for sharing so openly about their activities. In particular, Omar Lando at REDCCAM, Adán Rivera at ANIT, Marco Rodríguez at COCOCAM, Miguel Ángel Rodríguez at CCC-Jalisco, Claudia Serrano at Coparmex-Toluca, and Ana Isabel Solís at CANACO-Guadalajara generously invited me to conduct extended case studies of their organizations. The survey was made possible by the kind support of personnel at four confederation headquarters in Mexico City: Ivan Polanco and Víctor Suárez at ANEC, Santiago Domínguez at CCC, Pedro Pérez at CONCANACO, and Marco Antonio Lara at CANACINTRA. The members of these organizations are too numerous to name, but I have for them the highest gratitude and respect. While I observed organizational dysfunction at times, I was always inspired by the optimism, ingenuity, and civic mindedness in organization members.

I have been lucky to have the help of several talented research assistants. José Manuel de Alba, Kary Chávez, and Daniel Isita turned government data and survey questionnaires into useable datasets. Radamanto Portillo turned out perfect transcriptions of my interviews on short notice. Heather Darrin and Ricardo Morales-Vivero helped with the research and writing stages at Marquette.

The writing phase was facilitated, both intellectually and financially, by a visiting fellowship at the Center for US–Mexican Studies at UCSD, where I received valuable input and support from Maya Duru, Melissa Floca, Micah Gell-Redman, Victor Hernández-Huerta, Gema Kloppe-Santamaría, and Greg Mallinger, among other faculty and fellows.

The difficult transition from dissertation to book manuscript mostly occurred during a fruitful postdoctoral stay at the Ash Center for Democratic Governance at the Harvard Kennedy School, where I benefited from feedback and fellowship from Matthew Baum, Archon Fung, Marshall Ganz, Yanilda González, Sean Gray, Scott Mainwaring, Tarek Massoud, Quinton Mayne, Maya Sen, and Ryan Sheely. I am especially grateful to the Ash Center for hosting a book workshop, where I received concentrated feedback from Ruth Berins Collier, Alberto Díaz-Cayeros, Jorge Domínguez, Candelaria Garay, Fran Hagopian, Steve Levitsky, and Tesalia Rizzo.

At Marquette, the final stages of this project benefitted from mentorship and encouragement by a stellar and generous group of colleagues, especially Lowell Barrington, Noelle Brigden, Barry McCormick, Jessica Rich, Phil Rocco, Duane Swank, and Amber Wichowsky. My passionate students at Marquette have helped me frame my contribution in terms of big questions that matter for people's well-being.

I have been fortunate to work with a professional team at University of Michigan Press, including Elizabeth Demers and Haley Winkle.

Portions of this manuscript were previously published in *Comparative Political Studies*, *World Development*, and the Cambridge University Press edited volume, *The Inclusionary Turn in Contemporary Latin America*. I thank these outlets for permission to use these materials.

This book would not have seen the light of day without my loving and supportive family. Thanks to my mom, dad, and brother for visiting me in Mexico, for asking how this book is going, and for sensing when not to ask. I thank the Unda Gutiérrez family for giving me a home in Mexico and keeping me well fed wherever I am. To my partner-in-life Moniquita I am grateful for building a new home with me five times as this book has inched along in the background. Thank you for all the sacrifice, encouragement, and insight. Our love is my driving force.

This book is dedicated to my dad, Jay Rubin. Having become a dad myself during the decade it took to write this book, I have gained a greater appreciation for everything that he gave me, especially a lifelong urge to explore, understand, and explain. One day my kids will roll their eyes as I retell stories about my world travels, and I'll know that I'm in the best of company.

Introduction

Interest Organizations and Unequal Development in Latin America

Fifteen years ago, the World Bank (2007, 108) attributed disappointing economic performance in many developing countries to the "inequality trap," a vicious cycle linking economic and political inequality. The World Development Report on inequality concluded that "societies prosperous today are so because they have developed more egalitarian distributions of political power, while poor societies often suffer from unbalanced distributions." The World Bank—one of the most influential advocates of the "market-led" economic model in the last century—today has come around to the idea that free markets alone often fail to produce inclusive growth. It has increasingly become apparent that slow growth and sharp contrasts between economic winners and losers in many developing countries are due more to the underrepresentation of non-elite economic interests than to excessive state intervention in markets.

Latin America has long been recognized as the most unequal region in the world (Lustig 2020). Nonetheless, development models in the region have hewed to an oligarchic economic model—masked as a neutral market-led model—and the prospect of economic policies oriented to generate economic opportunity has been off the table for decades. Economic elites manipulate the policymaking process to produce "extractive" economic institutions (Acemoglu, Johnson, and Robinson 2005), which are oriented to funneling rents to themselves rather than spurring innovation or productivity gains or creating good jobs for ordinary citizens. Inclusive development models have been off the agenda for so long that non-elite actors have very few policy alternatives on which to focus their demand-making.

At best, we may point to the success cases of twentieth-century industrialization in East Asia, which featured a much more active role for the state in protecting domestic firms, regulating labor market institutions, and guiding finance (Evans 1995; Johnson 1982). It is not clear that this model would work for Latin America, nor that it is appropriate for the late-industrial age. However, we may extract from these success cases the lesson that large-scale upgrading in models of production requires close coordination between the development bureaucracy and societal stakeholders. In most Latin American countries, such formal institutions of interest representation are sorely lacking. And while economic elites have many avenues through which to influence policy, the demands of non-elites—industrial workers, small-business owners, family farmers, and the massive informal sector—are inchoate and typically go ignored.

This failure of economic interest representation is puzzling in light of significant advances in democratic representation in the region, which may have been expected to empower the masses in development policy. As mid-twentieth-century authoritarian regimes recede into history, procedural democratic institutions have consolidated, affording most citizens a genuine choice at the ballot box. Over the last few decades, elections in the region have become increasingly trustworthy and the rule of law has strengthened. Based on expert assessments of democratic institutions in the region, Mainwaring, Scully, and Cullell (2010, 19) surmised a decade ago that "the period since 1990 has been by far the most democratic in the history of Latin America."

Latin America has also witnessed important innovations in democratic deepening. Every country in the region—save Panama—has passed national laws requiring participatory institutions—"formal institutional spaces that involve citizens or civil society groups in...public policy" (Mayka 2019, 1). These institutional models have improved well-being for marginalized populations (Touchton, Sugiyama, and Wampler 2017; Touchton and Wampler 2014). For example, participatory budgeting—a system that allows inhabitants of urban neighborhoods to determine how to spend a portion of their local budgets—has contributed to a democratic culture of deliberation in Brazil (Baiocchi, Heller, and Silva 2011; Fung and Olin Wright 2003). These models have acquired "best practices" status among multilateral development institutions and have been replicated across five continents (Ganuza and Baiocchi 2012; Mansuri and Rao 2013).

Latin American countries have also expanded social and economic rights by adopting much more inclusive welfare states, which in some cases foster significant societal participation. Social policies have expanded beyond unionized formal-sector workers to also include previous labor market outsiders, such as informal sector workers and the rural poor. Conditional cash transfer programs—devised in the 1990s in Mexico and Brazil—represent a sea change in social policy by delivering benefits to the neediest and have expanded throughout the region (Garay 2016; Pribble 2013). Combined with expansions in old-age pensions and health care, these policies have improved living standards and broadened citizenship rights across the region (Diaz-Cayeros, Estévez, and Magaloni 2016, chaps. 5–6; Hunter and Sugiyama 2014).

Why, despite these advances, have Latin American democracies proven unable to confront the structural inequalities that cripple their economies and leave their masses without opportunity? I contend that we may lay the blame at the feet of these countries' systems of interest representation, which exhibit an exaggerated version of "biased pluralism," a system in which the demands of organizations representing economic elites—especially large corporations—predominate over those that represent the interests of the much more numerous non-elites. The malady of biased pluralism was diagnosed by classic works of American political economy decades ago (Dahl 1961; Lindblom 1977; Schattschneider 1935) and has been revived in recent years (Gilens 2012; Hacker and Pierson 2002; Skocpol and Hertel-Fernandez 2016). These scholars conclude that economic institutions in the United States and other wealthy democracies respond disproportionately to the interests of economic elites, who leverage political connections, campaign contributions, and mobile capital to sway regulatory policy, government contracts, infrastructure, tax breaks, and more.

Undoubtedly, disparities in economic representation are more pronounced in developing countries, where the working classes are yet more prostrate and a dependence on foreign direct investment grants extraordinary power to multinational corporations. Schneider (2013, chap. 5), for instance, attributes the "hierarchical" character of Latin American economies to the weakness of organized labor and fragmentation of the working classes along the formal–informal divide. Large informal sectors—beset by economic vulnerability and challenges to collective action—are certainly partly to blame for the persistence of oligarchic development models (Blofield 2011; Castells and Portes 1989). However, a more inclusive model of sectoral representation—along the lines of Northern European societal corporatism or East Asian developmental states—would not only require a more encompassing and empowered set of institutions to represent *workers*, but would also feature spaces for *non-elite producers*—such as farmers and small-business owners. Organizations representing such producers are uniquely positioned to demand state intervention oriented to generating economic opportunity, as opposed to simply increasing benefits for consumption.

This book focuses on such organizations and develops an account of biased pluralism in developing countries typified by the centrality of patronage—discretionarily allocated state benefits—to popular-sector interest representation. Rather than serving as conduits for demand-making about development models, political parties and interest organizations often broker state subsidies or social programs, augmenting the short-term income of beneficiaries, but doing little to improve their long-term economic prospects. The predominance of patronage (or clientelistic) appeals as the currency of party-voter linkages in Latin America has received considerable attention (Diaz-Cayeros, Estévez, and Magaloni 2016; Kitschelt et al. 2010; Stokes et al. 2013). In contrast, I centrally engage the *demand side* of interest representation, diagnosing the pressures that cause many non-elite interest organizations to specialize in demand-making for patronage rather than the fundamental policies that shape development models.

When organizations become diverted into patronage politics, the economic demands of the masses go unheard in the policies that most affect their lives and, along the way, their economic interests go unrepresented. While experiments in participatory governance have proven to empower marginalized citizens in decision-making processes about spending, they fail to address a vacuum in scaled-up demand-making about development models. And while expansions in social policy have increased benefits for consumption, policies to guide models of production and generate economic opportunity have withered. When it comes to structural components of economic policy—trade agreements, industrial policy, labor policy, infrastructure, and regulation of competition—states lack institutional tools for the incorporation of non-elite stakeholders. Rather, economic representation in neoliberal Latin American has been characterized by a haphazard blend of insulated technocracy, crony capitalism, and populist and clientelist co-option of the lower classes by political elites.

This book traces this disconnect to the failure of organizations to channel citizen interests into economic representation. I focus on non-elite interest organizations—specifically agricultural and small-business associations, but this category also includes labor unions, neighborhood associations, indigenous associations, and many others. These organizations are the key actors with the potential to levy economic policy demands on behalf of non-elites, yet divide into two camps. On the one hand, some organizations engage in *programmatic representation*: translating members' interests into sector-wide policy demands, socializing citizens to identify with sectoral or class interests, and mobilizing these populations in electoral campaigns and protests on behalf of collective interests. Other organizations, however, focus their efforts on *patronage representation*, maximizing their members' share of individualized benefits from the state, typically by entering into clientelistic relationships with political parties. The perseverance of oligarchic capitalism in Latin America generates from the overwhelming proportion of organizations—especially those organizations that represent the most marginal populations—that specialize narrowly in the latter representation model. So what explains why non-elite interest organizations so often fail to offer programmatic representation?

Argument

I argue that these models of representation are explained by the types of relationships that these organizations form downwardly (with their members) and upwardly (with political parties). For interest organizations to confer programmatic representation on their membership base, both the organization and an ideologically aligned political party must converge: the organization with programmatic demands and the party with a programmatic incorporation strategy. For popular-sector organizations and left-wing parties, this convergence is rare. Quite often, one or the other of these actors—or both—is compelled to engage in patronage politics, undermining the potential for programmatic representation. For organizations representing middle-class economic sectors—such as small-business owners—and for right-wing political parties, this convergence on a programmatic representation model is more common, as middle-class organizations tend to be less dependent on state benefits for survival. These *a priori* asymmetries are the prime causes of biased pluralism in developing democracies. The theoretical model has two parts, corresponding to the organization and to the party.

First, I consider organizations' downward ties with their members. Organizations' policy demands are shaped by the strategies that they use to recruit, retain, and mobilize members. Any mass organization must retain a large and active membership to survive. Thus, organizations must address this central collective action challenge before devoting their resources to effecting policy change. Regardless of the stated purpose of an organization, the way that it meets this challenge shapes its policy engagement. I refer to this strategy as the source of its *organizational capacity* and categorize organizations into two groups. Some organizations sustain organizational capacity internally by offering services that encourage members to join and participate in organization activities. Such services may include training programs, legal support, networking opportunities, access to finance and more. By generating their own "selective benefits" (Olson 1965), these organizations maintain a degree of autonomy that allows them to engage in programmatic demand-making and to push back against biased pluralism. For other organizations, selective benefits are externally provided. Most commonly, a state or party patron provides access to individual benefits through sectoral subsidies or social programs that leaders allocate selectively to members to incentivize participation. When organizational capacity is externally provided, the organization becomes dependent on the state or party patron. It lacks the autonomy to engage in programmatic demand-making and becomes specialized in patronage bargaining.

Second, I consider organizations' upward linkages with political parties. Ruling parties typically are willing to reciprocate with patronage benefits if their core organizational allies are focused on patronage demands. In systems where distributive spending is discretionary, the cost is relatively low for a party to favor its electoral allies with these benefits in exchange for campaign support. However, organizations' programmatic demands go unanswered in the absence of a political party that coincides in its preference for a programmatic linkage. Parties stand to benefit by incorporating organizations with which they share policy goals into programmatic policies, as this cements powerful long-term linkages and frees up distributive benefits for allocation to non-core groups. However, not all parties are capable of sustaining programmatic linkages.

I argue that parties' origins shape their future capacity to form either programmatic or patronage-based linkages with interest organizations. Parties that form ties to ideologically aligned organizations before they are able to challenge for elected office go on to incorporate these organizations into programmatic policies once they govern. In contrast, parties that only come into contact with organizations in the midst of challenging for office do not invest in the arduous task of creating programmatic linkages with interest organizations, instead mobilizing these allies opportunistically through patronage.

Where organization and party coincide in a preference for a programmatic or a patronage-based linkage, that outcome becomes self-reinforcing.

Such an outcome is common for organizations representing middle- and upper-class groups, such as business chambers and their right-wing party allies. Thus, in the programmatic equilibrium, the organization develops traits that sustain programmatic representation, such as formal non-partisanship, which allows it to lobby with politicians of all parties; a homogenous membership base, composed of members who engage in the same economic activities and thus share economic policy goals; and norms of internal democracy, which nurture new leaders and hold them accountable to shared goals.

In contrast, where organizations and parties converge on a patronage-based linkage—a common occurrence for organizations representing the popular sector and left-wing parties—the organization becomes ensnared in "the patronage trap," a vicious cycle wherein the organization specializes as a broker for discretionary state benefits and becomes unable to engage in programmatic representation. Such organizations feature oligarchic leadership norms as the leader converts into an indispensable broker for patronage benefits and attract a heterogenous membership base, drawn to short-term private benefits. The ubiquity of the patronage trap for popular-sector interest representation is a key explanation for the extreme mode of biased pluralism that most developing countries exemplify. However, these pressures are not insurmountable and there is much to be learned from non-elite organizations that manage to evade the patronage trap.

Why Programmatic Organizations Matter

The ability of interest organizations to represent non-elite interests in economic policy has important implications for economic development models, the effectiveness of social spending, and the quality of the electoral process. In each of these realms, democracies—and developing democracies in particular—face trenchant obstacles that organizations potentially help overcome. By the same token, however, organizations that fall prey to the patronage trap contribute to the problems of elite bias, inefficient and unfair social spending, and clientelist electoral systems.

First, where non-elite organizations have voice in important policy episodes—e.g., the negotiation of trade agreements, defining priorities for infrastructure investments, regulating markets—they can help counteract upper-class distortions in economic models. Class bias in interest representation has long been a concern of scholarship of advanced democracies

(Lindblom 1977; Schattschneider 1960; Verba, Schlozman, and Brady 1995). While less empirical research exists to uncover biases in poor and middle-income democracies, such as those of Latin America, we might expect the problem to be more pronounced, given their hierarchical economic institutions (Acemoglu, Johnson, and Robinson 2005) and discretionary state institutions (Levitsky and Murillo 2013). And while the rise of technocratic governance in the region was meant to insulate economic policymaking from rent-seeking, the effect has more often led to the severing of channels for popular-sector influence, while elites and corporations continue to enjoy privileged influence through social ties to technocratic elites (Babb 2001; Dargent 2014) or through the threat to disinvest, which confers *de facto* structural power (Fairfield 2015b).

When non-elite groups wield voice in economic policy, they *can* counteract this class distortion, with important consequences for development models and wealth distribution. Scholars of Latin American politics have identified organized non-elite stakeholders as key actors in important reforms of union regulations (Burgess 2004; Cook 2007; Murillo 2001), tax policy (Fairfield 2015a), the welfare state (Garay 2016; Pribble 2013), environmental regulation (Amengual 2016; Hochstetler 2011), minority rights (Paschel 2016; Yashar 2005), and informal-sector labor enforcement (Holland 2015; Hummel 2017). On the other hand, when these organizations' participation in policymaking is geared toward maximizing patronage benefits, engagement with the state can have the perverse result of excluding popular-sector interests (Fox 1994).

Programmatic organizations can also bolster the effectiveness of distributive programs. Programmatic organizations are involved in the design of distributive programs, such as agricultural subsidies or training programs for small businesses, seeking to orient these programs to address the needs of their sector. In contrast, patronage-based organizations typically are concerned only with maximizing the share of these programs that they can control. The discretionary allocation of distributive benefits to promote the electoral prospects of governing parties has been well documented, particularly in the developing world.[1] Scholars of anti-poverty spending have shown how partisan distribution criteria undermine the efficiency of these programs. Yet these scholars have focused their recommendations on the *supply side*, stressing the importance of adopting formula-based criteria to

1. See Golden and Min (2013) for a review.

tie politicians' hands (Diaz-Cayeros, Estévez, and Magaloni 2016, chap. 5; Stokes et al. 2013, chap. 9).[2] In contrast, my findings suggest that *demand* is also largely to blame for persistent misappropriation of these funds. Where organizations approach the state with the central goal of maximizing their share of distributive resources, politicians have little incentive to adopt formula-based distribution criteria. Thus, overturning discretionary norms in distributive politics may require not only reform of state institutions, but also a transformation in the demand-making strategies of the organizations that represent these programs' beneficiaries.

Finally, programmatic organizations play an important role in connecting voters to political parties that align with their policy preferences. Given limited information about party and candidate platforms, voters are not automatically drawn to the parties that best represent their policy preferences or their economic interests (Bartels 1996). Rather, voters, particularly in developing democracies, often support parties based on a variety of other factors, such as the personal traits of the candidate, populist campaign rhetoric, performance evaluations of the incumbent, or vote buying (Arnold and Samuels 2011; Baker and Greene 2015; Kitschelt and Wilkinson 2007; Stokes et al. 2013). Lower-class citizens are particularly vulnerable to non-programmatic voting given greater deficits in information and value derived from electoral handouts (Dixit and Londregan 1996, 1144; Stokes et al. 2013, 158–71). In the last century, social-democratic and labor parties relied on labor unions to do the work of socializing the working class to support parties of the left and mobilizing it in campaigns (Collier and Collier 1991, 41–44; Katznelson 1986). Thus, the decline of unions and other mass popular sector organizations has played a central role in the current crisis of representation in Latin American democracies.

Existing organizations—both those that have held over from the heyday of corporatist mass organizing, as well as those that have emerged in recent decades to represent outsiders—have the potential to fill in this gap. In contrast, when organizations are enmeshed in patronage linkages with political parties, as often occurs with organizations composed of the poorest

2. Conditional cash transfer programs, such as Mexico's PROSPERA (previously PROGRESA and Oportunidades) and Brazil's Bolsa Familia are the poster children for a wave in non-discretionary (formula-based) social spending (De La O 2015; Garay 2016). However, "demand-based" social programs and subsidies remain widespread in Mexico, particularly on the subnational level (Cejudo, Michel, and Sobrino 2017; Garay, Palmer-Rubin, and Poertner 2020; Rizzo 2019).

segments of society, they undermine programmatic party–voter linkages. Voters are encouraged to mobilize on behalf of the party that offers the most private benefits for members, whether or not that party promotes an economic model that stands to benefit them.

Situating the Analysis: From State Corporatism to Neoliberal Pluralism in Latin America

The setting for my analysis is Mexico since the turn of the century, a country with a variety of structures for interest representation in both urban and rural areas. In the twentieth century, Mexico's political system was dominated by a single party, the Institutional Revolutionary Party (PRI). The PRI built sectoral organizations of labor, peasants, and other popular-sector groups. These sectors were incorporated into a corporatist system, wherein they were controlled from above by the party-state, while also receiving financing and organizational resources such as mandatory membership requirements (Collier and Collier 1991, 232–50; Stevens 1977). As in other corporatist Latin American states, this system of interest representation relied on the import-substitution industrialization (ISI) economic model, which granted the state ample margin to invest in privileged economic sectors, regulate trade, and sustain a generous welfare state for labor market insiders (Malloy 1977). From the 1980s onward, Mexico passed through two massive transformations that drastically altered the terms for popular-sector interest representation. First, it embraced the neoliberal orthodoxy of free trade agreements, liberal macroeconomic policy, minimal market intervention, and a thin welfare state (Lustig 1998). Second, Mexico's electoral system opened up. After seven decades of one-party rule at every level of government, opposition parties from the center-left and center-right began to claim important subnational victories in the 1980s and 1990s, culminating in the PRI's loss of the presidency in 2000. The electoral opening introduced space for dissident interest organizations to engage in demand-making outside the PRI's corporatist structure. This history endows Mexico with a wide spectrum of interest organizations, which vary both in the types of relationships that they form with political parties and in the type of policy demands that they levy.

While Mexico offers an ideal context to probe the roots of programmatic and patronage-based modes of interest representation, the dynamics uncovered in this study extend much further. Most broadly, the challenges of organizational maintenance—and the tradeoffs inherent in the decision of linking with an external actor to generate selective benefits—are relevant for mass-membership interest organizations throughout the democratic world. For instance, anarcho-syndicalist labor unions in twentieth-century Western Europe moderated their demands when embedded into social-democratic parties (Przeworski and Sprague 1986). On the party side, the observation that a party's genetic organizational traits shape the ways in which it mobilizes societal allies has been confirmed in research on Western Europe (Mair 1994), post-communist Eastern Europe (Tavits 2013), and Sub-Saharan Africa (Riedl 2014).

The challenges of non-elite interest representation that motivate this book are most pronounced in "patronage democracies" (Chandra 2004), systems in which government actors exercise discretion over the distribution of basic goods and services, and often allocate these benefits under an electoral logic. Many such democracies are found in Latin America, and scholars have widely documented the use of state patronage to mobilize individual voters through clientelistic ties (Diaz-Cayeros, Estévez, and Magaloni 2016; Hidalgo and Nichter 2016; Muñoz 2014; Nichter 2008; Stokes 2005). Patronage politics is also incredibly common in state interactions with interest organizations (Holland and Palmer-Rubin 2015).

While the centrality of patronage to Latin American systems of interest representation has remained a constant over the past century, the dynamics of patronage exchange have changed drastically over the last few decades. Since the 1980s, Latin American states have moved from corporatist systems—which combined heavy doses of economic resources and top-down coercion of interest organizations—to pluralist systems that grant greater autonomy, but less support. Under mid-twentieth-century corporatism, hierarchical and often monopolistic representatives of workers, peasants, and business were embedded in elaborate pacts with ruling parties (Collier and Collier 1991; Lehmbruch and Schmitter 1982). These organizations were granted privileged access to policymaking, government posts for their leaders, as well as economic and organizational inducements such as state subsidies and mandatory-membership statutes. In exchange, the organizations ceded control and accepted regulation by the state, undermining their ability to engage in contentious mobilization or to demand fundamental changes in their countries' economic models. Mexico's post-Revolutionary administrations mobilized the popular sectors in what was perhaps the broadest-reaching, and certainly the most durable, instance of popular-sector incorporation in the region.[3]

As the statist development model was phased out beginning in the 1980s, however, corporatism decayed in Mexico and throughout the region. Unable to sustain the same level of inducements for their allies, former "labor-based" parties weakened ties with mass organizations, relying increasingly on media appeals and clientelist handouts to win elections (Greene 2007; Levitsky 2003; Roberts 2015). As Collier and Handlin (2009b, 48–60) describe, these economic and political transformations in Latin America over the past three decades have led to a decline of the mode of interest representation typified by corporatist union–party linkages (the "union–party hub"), and the emergence of a new pattern. This new interest regime, which they refer to as the "associational network," is composed of a diverse array of interest organizations. These interest organizations include both the formal-sector workers that were incorporated during the previous period, but also more precarious groups such as informal-sector workers, landless peasants, neighborhood associations, and indigenous movements. These organizations are organized less hierarchically than union confederations and execute a wider variety of functions independent of political parties (Collier and Handlin 2009b, 66–73).

While the withdrawal of the state from top-down control of organizations affords greater *autonomy*, the cessation of state subsidies and compulsory membership have left organizations more *precarious* (Collier and Handlin 2009a, 24–29; Kurtz 2004b; Shadlen 2004). Organized interests struggle to secure financial resources, sustain membership rolls, and coordinate in collective activities to pressure the state.[4] Facing these challenges, many organizations turn to external actors—often political parties—which offer material benefits in exchange for campaign support and control over

3. Along with Venezuela, Mexico undertook a "radical populist" mode of incorporation, in which "both the working class and the peasantry were mobilized electorally and organized into functional associations, such as unions, linked to the reformist political movement or party" (Collier and Collier 1991, 196). Unlike Venezuela, where the labor-mobilizing party eventually entered into a pact that ensured alternation among moderate parties, Mexican incorporation spearheaded a coalition of forces that became part and parcel of a one-party dominant regime that monopolized elected office in Mexico until the late twentieth century.

4. A group of studies have identified cases of neo-corporatism under more decentralized and contingent forms of state support (Chartock 2013; Etchemendy 2019; Rich 2019; Rich, Mayka, and Montero 2019).

organizational activities (Garay 2009). However, the prospect of aligning with a political party, as opposed to engaging in other forms of political mobilization, still presents these organizations with a tradeoff between *access* to the levers of power and *autonomy* over demand type and strategies (Collier and Handlin 2009b, 81–91; Fox 1992a). Some organizations, therefore, opt to remain non-partisan, forgoing privileged access to patronage benefits to retain control over demand-making strategies. However, consolidating and surviving as an autonomous interest organization poses the significant challenge of sustaining collective action through organizational resources alone. Organizations that abstain from state patronage must devise services on their own that are sufficiently appealing to attract and retain members. This challenge is rarely met by organizations representing the lower classes.

Parties' approaches to linking with interest organizations have also transformed in the neoliberal era. The decline of organized labor and the ISI model made mass organizing more tenuous for twentieth-century corporatist parties. Former "labor-based parties" navigated this transition with varying levels of success (Burgess and Levitsky 2003). For example, Mexico's PRI and Argentina's Justicialist Party (PJ) persisted in programmatically moderate forms while Peru's American Popular Revolutionary Alliance (APRA) and Venezuela's Democratic Action (AD) became non-competitive party shells. Recent decades have also witnessed the emergence of new electoral vehicles on the left, born out of quite diverse circumstances and with quite different relationships to the organized popular classes. In the 1970s, Brazil's Workers' Party, Brazil (PT) built a national organization on the back of a democratic labor movement and other grassroots movements to fill a vacuum on the left in a country that never had featured a successful labor-based party. In the 1980s, Mexico's Party of the Democratic Revolution (PRD) split off from the dominant party, bringing in urban social movements and dissident peasant associations to occupy the space that the PRI relinquished on the left. In the 2000s, Bolivia's Movement to Socialism (MAS) merged indigenous social movements with corporatist associations inherited from a previous age of radical populism to reach the presidency as the region's only consolidated "movement-party" (Levitsky and Roberts 2011, 11–16). And in Ecuador and Venezuela, party-system collapse opened space for populist leaders to construct personalistic regimes with highly redistributive agendas, but little space for autonomous societal participation.

Right-wing parties in Latin American also take different organizational forms, with consequences for their relationships to organized business. Mexico's main right-wing party, the National Action Party

(PAN), represents an extreme case of an externally mobilized party, which has retained a strong ideological brand and organic ties to core business organizations, even as it moderated to compete in subnational elections in the 1990s and to conquer the presidency in 2000. In this sense, the PAN is relatively unique in the region, as most other prominent right-wing parties are either "authoritarian successors" (Loxton 2015) or were founded as personalistic vehicles, such as the parties of Uribe in Colombia, Fujimori in Peru, and most recently Bolsonaro in Brazil.

These different partisan movements have different uses for interest organizations. While parties today rarely embed organizations to the same degree as under the heyday of corporatism, organizational allies continue to offer parties highly coordinated networks of citizens, capable of mobilizing voters and organizing ground campaigns. However, under the current interest regime, parties often seek much looser ties with organizations than before. These linkages are *intermittent*—lasting for a single election rather that over several elections—and instrumental—based on a negotiated exchange rather than programmatic or ideological affinity (Garay 2009). Particularly where parties are unstable, they often form ties with organizations that last only a single election, and are based on clientelist exchange rather than policy influence (Holland and Palmer-Rubin 2015; Novaes 2018).

Other parties, however, sustain *organic* ties to interest organizations, featuring long-standing linkages based on shared programmatic goals and the nomination of organization leaders to state office and party leadership. Such linkages can help anchor a party brand and signal to voters that the party is favorable to a particular social group (peasants, informal workers, etc.) (Lupu 2013; Poertner 2021). Organic ties to organizations can also help a party build and maintain "activist networks" (Calvo and Murillo 2019), bringing voters into contact with the party, recruiting candidates and sustaining a presence during periods out of office. Since the 1980s, innovative modes of incorporating popular-sector organizations organically into the party have helped the Brazilian PT, Bolivian MAS, and Uruguayan Broad Front (FA) consolidate and sustain electoral success (Anria and Cyr 2017; Bentancur, Rodríguez, and Rosenblatt 2019; Gómez Bruera 2013).

In summation, the neoliberal interest regime poses distinct challenges for the programmatic representation of non-elite interests. Yet organizations have navigated these waters with differing levels of success. Organizations have been left to themselves to devise strategies to sustain collective action and influence economic policy; and have resolved this dilemma in diverse ways—some by reproducing party-dependent patronage ties and others by devising member-service models that allow them to sustain organizational capacity autonomously. National and subnational party organizations have innovated in the types of institutions that they construct to foment programmatic organizational participation in policymaking, while others have turned to organizations as intermediaries though which to mobilize voters with clientelist appeals. This book analyzes the Mexican case to generate and test an explanation for these distinct representation models.

Plan of the Book

This book has eight chapters, broken into three sections. Chapters 1 and 2 lay out the theoretical framework for this study and the historical context. In the first chapter I describe the phenomenon of biased pluralism in Mexico—and in developing democracies more broadly—and present my theoretical framework for explaining variation in representation models. I also present my research design for testing this theory though subnational comparisons of organizations and parties in Mexico. Chapter 2 provides a brief historical overview of interest representation in the agricultural and small-business sectors in Mexico. I begin with the construction of one-party dominance and sectoral corporatism under the PRI in the post-Revolutionary period. In particular, I focus on transitions in Mexico's economic model and in its electoral system that set the stage for the context within which my analysis occurs, the first dozen years of this century, or Mexico's "post-transition" period.

The second and third sections constitute the main empirical analysis, first from the organization's point of view and then from the party's point of view. Part 2 presents evidence showing how the source of organizational capacity shapes the types of policy demands that organizations levy. In Chapter 3, I conceptualize organizational capacity—the ability of an organization to sustain collective action—and illustrate its internal and external variants using case study and survey evidence from organizations in both the small-scale agriculture and small-business sectors. Chapter 4 analyzes the effect of organizational capacity models on demand type in the agricultural sector. Using case study evidence, I show how most dissident peasant organizations found themselves in the patronage trap within the first few years after Mexico's transition as they failed to devise attractive services to sustain organizational capacity internally. However, I also focus attention on affiliates of a confederation of grain producers' cooperatives that has bucked this trend and resultantly retained the capacity to make programmatic demands.

Chapter 5 conducts a parallel analysis for the small-business sector, focusing on chambers of commerce, chambers of industry and affiliates of COPARMEX, the Patronal Confederation of the Mexican Republic. Contrary to the lower-class peasant sector, most small-business organizations sustain an internal organizational capacity model, based on the provision of consulting, training, and networking services for members. As a result, the majority of these organizations evade dependence on party patrons and establish themselves as influential voices in the policy areas that most affect their sectors. I do, however, identify exceptional cases, particularly among chambers of industry, the sector most adversely affected by the globalized development model. These organizations' inability to react to the revocation of mandatory membership requirements led them to become dependent on state subsidies, and resultantly to neglect to participate in arenas for programmatic representation. Analysis of survey data in both Chapters 4 and 5 supports qualitative findings. For organizations in both sectors, the diversity of resource flows and the number of services that organizations offer to members—traits of internally generated organizational capacity—are positively associated with the breadth of mobilization strategies and, ultimately, with the degree of programmatic demand-making.

Part 3 analyzes the party side of the story, explaining why Mexico's former opposition parties (PAN and PRD), once in office, sometimes seek to incorporate organizational allies into spaces for programmatic representation and other times opt to mobilize organizations narrowly through patronage exchange. I find that these divergent incorporation models are due to two factors: the founding traits of state-level party organizations and the degree of electoral competition that they face. In Chapter 6 I analyze the left-wing PRD, founded in 1989. In most states where this party has governed, its dominant strain was formed from a rift within the PRI and led by politicians that aspired to immediate electoral victory. As a result, the PRD failed to establish long-term programmatic ties to ideologically aligned organizations, such as dissident peasant associations, instead reproducing PRI-style clientelistic ties. The state of Michoacán is an exception as in this state the PRD organization was most institutionalized and societally rooted prior to the PRD's 2001 gubernatorial victory. As a result, PRD governors in Michoacán invested in the construction of authentic spaces for peasant representation in rural development policy.

Chapter 7 analyzes the right-wing PAN, which featured a quite distinct trajectory from the PRD. Formed in 1939 as an ideologically rooted yet electorally non-competitive party, the PAN established organic ties to organized business during its lengthy exile from elected office. Once the PAN began to win gubernatorial elections in the 1990s, these ties allowed the party to capitalize on the reputation and campaign resources of business organizations without having to engage them in patronage linkages. In-depth analysis of Jalisco, where the PAN governed for three terms from 1995 to 2012, reveals the measures that these administrations undertook to consolidate spaces for the state's powerful business organizations to influence economic policies, such as infrastructure investments, regulation of informal commerce, and tax policy. Analysis of data from a small-business subsidy program demonstrates that only when PAN governments establish dominance in a state—a rare phenomenon—do they choose to favor small-business organizations with distributive spending. Under conditions of competitive elections, PAN governments instead channel these funds to types of spending oriented to attract swing constituencies.

Finally, Chapter 8 concludes the book. In this chapter I speak to the broader implications of my findings and issue a call for more research on interest organizations and productionist economic policies, especially at the subnational level. I also address the external validity of my findings, applying my framework to two types of organizations in Mexico (urban popular movements in Mexico City and indigenous associations in Chiapas), as well as the Brazilian landless movement and organized business in Chile. I conclude by discussing the implications of my findings for interest representation in Mexico and Latin America in the coming decades.

PART 1

Situating the Analysis

CHAPTER 1

Analytical Approach to Organizations and Policy Representation

This book offers an explanation for representational inequality in Mexico based on an analysis of organizations representing two non-elite economic sectors: small-business owners and small-scale farmers. I find that small-business organizations—representing a middle-class constituency—tend to offer a higher level of programmatic representation than lower-class peasant organizations. I do, however, find significant variation *within* each of these sectors, suggesting that class is not wholly determinative of representation models. While the deck is stacked against them, organizations representing the lower classes can gain voice in economic policy if they devise strategies to sustain collective action autonomously and count on electoral allies willing to build institutions to incorporate them into programmatic policies.

Mexico is not the only country where the transition to a market-led economic model produced a bifurcated economy. Recent studies situated in Latin America, Eastern Europe, and South Asia have similarly traced linkages between economic liberalization and "hierarchical," "oligarchical," or "predatory" economies (Cameron 2021; Markus 2015; Naseemullah 2016; Schneider 2013). In all of these cases, elite economic interests' superior policy power is exercised through both formal and informal channels. For every consultative council offering space for business owners to opine on the policy of the day, big business wields power through dozens of instances of informal lobbying, exchange of favors, and threats to disinvest.

Class bias in economic policy is by no means unique to late industrializing economies either. Classic scholarship on interest group politics in the United States and Europe attributed policy outcomes favoring elite interests to the outside influence enjoyed by business and the wealthy

(Dahl 1982; Lindblom 1977; Schattschneider 1960). These studies rejected the conclusions of Madisonian pluralism and its twentieth-century exponents (Dahl 1961; Truman 1951), who argued that competition between organized interests would produce policies that respond equally to the interests of all segments of society. Instead, the record has shown that capitalist democracy has more often than not produced "biased pluralism" (Gilens and Page 2014). By funding lobbying, donating to campaigns, or threatening to take their investments elsewhere, elite interests push for policies that strengthen the profitability of their economic ventures, therein regenerating yet more wealth. Recent literature on the United States confirms that the outsized influence of economic elites in policymaking persists and has expanded in recent decades with the decline of unions, weakening of the regulatory state, and relaxing of limits on campaign contributions, among other trends (Baumgartner et al. 2009; Gilens 2012; Grossmann 2012; Hacker and Pierson 2010; Schlozman, Verba, and Brady 2012; Skocpol and Hertel-Fernandez 2016).

Organizations representing lower-and middle-class groups, such as small business, farmers, or blue-collar workers, can level the playing field when they mobilize large numbers of citizens in contentious movements or behind left-wing parties, as illustrated in research on welfare expansion in Western Europe (Esping-Andersen 1990; Korpi 1983) and Latin America (Garay 2016; Huber and Stephens 2012). However, such policy victories are the exception, and non-elite groups typically face trenchant obstacles to remaining politically engaged, owing to the precarious economic positions of their members (Verba, Schlozman, and Brady 1995) and the free-rider problem (Olson 1965). It is hard to convince ordinary people to contribute to a political cause when this participation draws on scarce economic resources and when those who do not contribute can still enjoy the benefits. Poor rural populations are particularly difficult to organize given their geographical dispersion and economic marginality (Bates 1981; Kurtz 2004a).

Popular-sector interest organizations such as labor unions, peasant associations, and neighborhood councils proliferate in the developing world, yet the underrepresentation of lower-class interests is perhaps more pronounced than in rich democracies due to two factors. First, poverty and economic informality produce vast segments of the population that are so economically precarious as to lack political knowledge or an inclination to political participation, exacerbating obstacles to collective action (Boulding and Holzner 2015; Dunning 2009). Second, patronage—the discretionary allocation of particularistic state benefits, such as subsidies, jobs, or social programs—is often the central currency of political engagement for popular-sector organizations (Auerbach 2017; Grindle 2007; Palmer-Rubin 2019). These two traits combine to produce a scenario in which organizations that might otherwise push for policies that generate economic opportunity for the lower and middle classes instead focus their efforts on electoral campaigns for political parties, which in turn face little incentive to respond to the economic interests of these groups.

As I illustrate in this book, however, significant variation does exist in models of representation, even among organizations representing the same economic sectors in the same country. In semi-institutionalized democracies such as Mexico, it is quite easy to find interest organizations that focus their energies on *patronage brokerage*. These organizations narrow their policy participation to bargaining for discretionarily allocated benefits such as subsidies for small capital investments or access to anti-poverty programs. Patronage politics is particularly common among organizations representing the poor, such as peasants or urban slum dwellers. However, even in the most precarious of economic sectors, some organizations sustain *programmatic representation*, influencing policies that shape the conditions for sectoral competitiveness, including regulatory policy, trade policy, infrastructure, and the adoption of rule-based sectoral support programs.

To date we lack a satisfying explanation for this variation. The closest approximation comes from studies of party–voter linkages, which analyze the electoral determinants of programmatic and patronage politics (Diaz-Cayeros, Estévez, and Magaloni 2016; Hagopian forthcoming; Keefer 2007; Kitschelt 2000; Shefter 1977). This literature typically turns to regime-or party-level factors that shape the *supply side* of programmatic and patronage politics, such as bureaucratic professionalization or democratic immaturity. To the extent that scholars address the demand side, they focus on social class, arguing that the poor are prone to selling their vote for handouts from the state or a party because they enjoy a higher marginal utility from these patronage goods than do upper-income groups (Calvo and Murillo 2004, 743–45; Dixit and Londregan 1996, 1144; Stokes et al. 2013, 158–71). As I document, patronage politics is certainly rampant among the Mexican poor. However, it is unclear that the same factors that drive individual citizens' policy demands work equally as well for collective actors—and class-based explanations fail to explain variation in models of representation among organizations that represent the same social groups in the same country.

Thus, by placing the focus on organizations, the first contribution of this book is to elucidate the demand side of programmatic and patronage politics. Given that individual economic actors (i.e., farmers and business owners) have interests that correspond to both programmatic policies and patronage benefits, *how do the organizations that represent these actors filter their interests into demands for policymaking?*

My answer to this question has to do with the internal traits of organizations. As opposed to elite interests, which wield power through economic might and personal connections to politicians, non-elite organizations' power rests in their ability to mobilize large numbers of members. Therefore, *organizational capacity*, the ability to recruit, retain, and mobilize members, is the lifeblood of these organizations. When organizations fail to generate organizational capacity internally, they often turn to patronage ties with political parties to access the resources that they need to survive. And while the economic benefits that flow from these relationships can sustain a large and active organization, a specialization in patronage politics makes organizations ill-equipped to make programmatic demands. In contrast, organizations that are able to sustain this capacity internally by offering desirable services to members—such as training activities or participation in a cooperative enterprise—retain the autonomy to make programmatic demands.

However, the presence of programmatically oriented organizations is not sufficient to produce programmatic representation. Thus, the second contribution of this book is to explain the factors that lead political elites—centrally ruling political parties—to incorporate interest organizations into programmatic and patronage politics. In the absence of state actors interested in building institutions for organizations to have voice in the policymaking process, programmatic demands fall on deaf ears. By analyzing the linkages formed between interest organizations and political parties, I address a second question: Given the types of demands that organizations settle on, *how are these demands translated into policy representation?*

Responding to this second question compels me to analyze how the traits of party organizations and electoral competition produce incentives for political parties to construct distinct types of linkages with interest organizations. Parties may build institutions to incorporate organizations into programmatic policy or institutions to mobilize organizational allies through patronage brokerage. Offering a caveat to existing literature that documents the decline of mass-based parties (Katz and Mair 1995; Levitsky 2003), I find that political parties today do, in fact, stand much to gain from forming long-standing linkages with ideologically aligned interest organizations. Incorporating organizational allies into party leadership and economic policy strengthens citizens' partisan attachments (Poertner 2021), reinforces the party "brand" (Lupu 2014), and supplies loyal "activist networks" (Calvo and Murillo 2019) even when out of office. The ability of organizations to incorporate core organizations in this way, however, is shaped by "genetic traits" (Panebianco 1988) of parties that derive from their founding trajectories. Parties that develop as electoral outsiders generate organizational institutions conducive to promoting the participation of ideological activists in party leadership and in governing. In contrast, "insider" parties—formed with access to state largesse and a primary goal of winning elections in the short term—neglect to invest in such institutions, instead deploying allied organizations as patronage machines. Parties cannot form long-term linkages with non-core organizations, but sometimes do incorporate them into short-term patronage ties in the context of a single election if (1) an electoral threat poses an incentive to broaden the party's coalition, and (2) programmatic ties to core organizations allow the party to deviate patronage resources to non-core organizations without running the risk of core organizations defecting.

Ultimately the demand-making strategies of interest organizations and the incorporation strategies of political parties interact to produce distinct outcomes for policy representation. Only where both organization and party converge on a preference for programmatic politics does this mode of representation prevail. In Mexico at least, the conditions that favor this convergence—autonomous organizations and an externally mobilized party—are characteristic of middle-class organizations (such as small business) and the center-right party (the National Action Party, PAN). Among organizations representing lower-class economic groups, such as small-scale farmers, it is much more common to find a narrow preoccupation with the brokerage of state handouts, a fate that I refer to as "the patronage trap." This scenario derives from the challenges that these organizations face to sustain collective action as well as the founding trajectory of the main center-left party (the Party of the Democratic Revolution, PRD). Important exceptions do exist, however. My research uncovers several cases of lower-class peasant organizations that sustain programmatic representation by independently generating selective benefits and linking programmatically with subnational party organizations. Conversely, I find examples of middle-class small-business organizations that fail to sustain organizational capacity internally or succumb to pressures of co-optation and therefore find themselves caught in the patronage trap.

Conceptualizing Programmatic and Patronage Representation

This book seeks to explain variation in organizational representation models. I distinguish between *programmatic* and *patronage* models of representation, which differ in terms of the "scope of interests" (Schmitter 1974, 96) that an organization represents. An organization may narrowly pursue the interests of its leader or members; or it may act on behalf of broader segments of the population, such as its economic sector or geographic community. At the broadest (i.e., most programmatic) level, the organization is a representative of its social class. While (patronage-based) organizations that narrowly represent the interests of members can do much to improve their quality of life, organizations must be on the broader side of this spectrum to effect change in the macro-level policies that shape economic competitiveness for economic sectors.

My conceptualization of representation models draws on a variety of literatures concerned with demand-making and policy representation. Research on organized labor asks why some unions make demands on behalf of unionized workers (the union wage) and others on behalf of the working class more broadly (the social wage) (Iversen 1999; Mares 2006; Streeck and Hassel 2003).[1] Similarly, studies of social movements have been concerned with the displacement of "transformative" goals for demands that are specific to the survival of the organization—a fate that they attribute to bureaucratization (Katsiaficas 2006; Piven and Cloward 1979, 34–37; Staggenborg 1988). Outside the realm of organizations, the distinction made in the party–voter linkage literature between programmatic and clientelistic ties turns on whether the voter supports a candidate

1. A classic literature concerned with internal democracy in labor unions shows how leadership entrenchment and co-optation causes unions to abandon even the interests of members in furthering the political prospects of leaders (Lipset, Trow, and Coleman 1956; Voss and Sherman 2000). In PRI-dominated Mexico, the co-optation of union leaders by the party-state, making them more responsive to the party and their own political prospects than the interests of the base, became known as *charrismo* (Collier and Collier 1991, 413–15; Snodgrass 2014).

in exchange for "selective material incentives" or in response to "packages of policies" whose consequences benefit the voter only indirectly (Kitschelt 2000, 849–50).[2]

In the case of economic interest organizations, an ordering of the scope of beneficiaries begins with the interests of the organization itself, then expands to the organization's members, the immediate community in which the organization operates, the sector, and the class group. In Figure 1.1, the innermost circles—shaded in black—represent the patronage arena, including policies that allocate disaggregable material benefits that stand to benefit only the organization itself or its members. Beyond this patronage core, demands can be considered programmatic. The next two circles represent demands for club goods, public goods, or regulatory policy that benefit populations that extend beyond the organization. Such populations may be quite limited, such as the community within which the organization

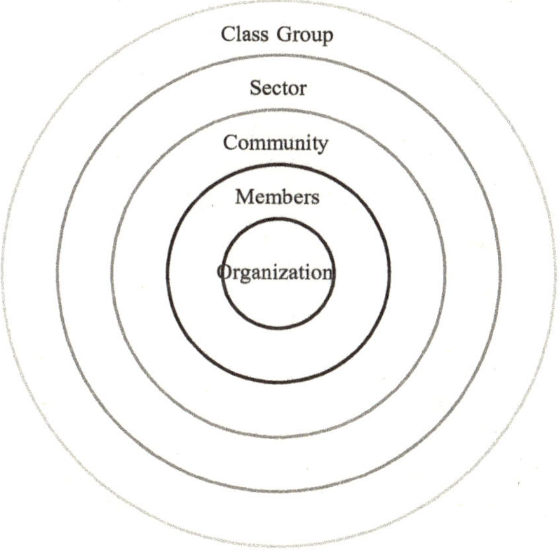

Figure 1.1 Scope of Interests for Economic Interest Organizations
Source: Author.

2. The formal political economy literature makes a distinction between "general interest" and "special interest" policies. However, existing studies are more concerned with explaining the policymaking dynamics within each of these arenas rather than how interest groups divide their political resources between them. For example, see Persson and Tabellini (2002, chaps. 6–7).

operates, or quite large, such as all firms in a given sector. The largest circle—in the lightest shade of grey—represents policies that affect the class group to which the organization pertains. Policies in this category have redistributive consequences that affect many members of society such as tax policy, land reform, or social entitlements.

Owing to the essential nature of organizational survival and recruitment, all non-elite organizations have an interest in pursuing policies in the innermost circles—representing the interests of the organization itself and of its members—as these policies generate benefits that can be used to fund organizational activities or incentivize members to join and participate. In fact, all organizations observed in this study actually do pursue such policies to some degree. However, some organizations are limited to *patronage representation*, while others also devote significant resources to *programmatic representation*, whose scope of interests extends beyond their membership base. To illustrate the types of demands that correspond to each of these circles I take the hypothetical example of an organization of small-scale corn farmers. Table 1.1 lays out the populations that correspond to each type of demand and examples of benefits that would satisfy each demand.

Classifying a given policy demand as programmatic or patronage requires considering not only the type of policy—as in Lowi's (1964) canonical distinction between distributive, regulatory and redistributive policy areas—but also the criteria that determine the policy's effect. In line with Stokes et al. (2013, 6–18), I evaluate whether the implementation of the policy in

Table 1.1 Examples of Organizational Demands by Scope of Interests

Beneficiaries	Who Stands to Benefit	Examples of Benefits
Organization	A local organization of small-scale corn farmers	Grant for organizational activities; compulsory membership requirement
Members	All or many members of the organization	Subsidies for members; favorable resolution of land disputes for members
Community	The region where the organization operates	Local infrastructure, such as irrigation technology or storage facilities
Sector	All small-scale corn farmers	Adoption of subsidy program targeted to corn farmers; government buying program favoring small-scale farmers
Class Group	All small-scale farmers, rural poor	Adoption of broad-based subsidy program or welfare program; land reform

question follows programmatic or non-programmatic criteria.[3] Analyzing distributive policies, Stokes et al. define two requirements for programmatic distribution: (1) rules of distribution are public; and (2) publicized rules shape actual distribution. In violating these principles, patronage representation concerns policies and benefits that are discretionarily targeted to the organization and its members. And programmatic representation concerns policies that may generate benefits for the organization in question but will typically also generate benefits for many actors outside the organization.

In theory, any type of policy can be discretionarily manipulated as patronage; however, distributive programs are much more often the currency of patronage politics than infrastructure or regulatory policy. In practice, my operationalization of representation models sets a low bar for programmatic demands: demands must generate some benefits that extend beyond the organization and its members. In most cases of programmatic representation that I find, the organization's demands are mainly local, such as a chamber of commerce that demands greater regulation of informal street vending or a peasant organization that demands that the state government adopt formulas for allocating subsidies that favor small-scale producers. I here walk through the different policy areas most common to the sectoral interest organizations analyzed, offering examples of programmatic and patronage variants.

Distributive programs produce disaggregable benefits, including cash transfers or in-kind benefits, such as school vouchers, farm tools, or food stamps. They also include payments directly to the organization. Distributive policies are quite common in the two sectors under study, including agricultural subsidies, housing programs, and small-business subsidies or consulting services. Due to their individual nature, the allocation of these policies is often manipulated by politicians to generate patronage benefits for individual citizens and for organizations. Such discretionary implementation operates outside of formal program rules, which in the Mexican case usually stipulate formula-based qualification and application criteria. Eager to maximize their share of these material benefits, interest organizations

3. Stokes et al. further distinguish on the basis of conditionality. I do not build conditionality into the operationalization of this variable, and thus use the term *patronage* rather than *clientelism*, which is by definition contingent on political support (Kitschelt and Wilkinson 2007, 10–12). However, patronage benefits are certainly *amenable* to clientelist politics, which aptly describes the dynamic for most organizations in the patronage trap.

commonly negotiate with politicians for special treatment in the allocation of these benefits (Garay, Palmer-Rubin, and Poertner 2020). On the other hand, demand-making about distributive programs can be programmatic when it concerns the adoption of new programs or the modification of the formulas that formally govern allocation. Likewise, modifications to tax policy—a frequent demand of business chambers—are programmatic, unless demands concern special exemptions for individual firms.

Infrastructure, in contrast, is almost always classified as a programmatic demand because it generates non-excludable public or club goods, classifying under the outer three rings of Figure 1.1. Agricultural organizations typically demand investment in irrigation systems, rural roads, or storage facilities. Business organizations demand cleaner and safer public spaces, roads, parking, and public transportation. A potential exception to the classification of infrastructure as programmatic are cases of very local club goods that may come under the control of organizations—e.g., an irrigation system that operates only in a small town or an industrial park overseen by a business chamber.

Regulatory policy, similarly, is almost always programmatic, as it concerns policies that affect broad classes of citizens. In the agriculture sector, common demands for regulatory policy correspond to land tenure governance, environmental standards, and genetically modified crops. Business chambers frequently make demands about regulation of informal commerce, intellectual property, labor law, and permitting. Any of these modes of regulatory policy can be manipulated as patronage in the final implementation stage, such as overlooking a permitting violation for a business or express processing of a rural land claim. The organizations studied rarely voice demands for such special treatment; however, they do advertise to members their ability to help navigate regulatory processes.

A final category—which may be called *political issues*—always falls under the rubric of programmatic demands. These are demands concerning macroeconomic policy that affects the sector (trade agreements, financial reform) or democratic institutions (transparency, corruption, electoral).

Taking individual agricultural and business organizations as the unit of analysis, I observe the degree to which each organization engages in programmatic and patronage models of representation. An organization can be described as offering programmatic representation if some substantial proportion of its political activity corresponds to policies that affect the organization's sector, such as regulatory policy, infrastructure, and the adoption or reform of sectoral support programs. Programmatic representation varies substantially in degree above this threshold. The ideal type of a programmatic organization—typified by the Jalisco branch of COPARMEX in this book—resembles societal corporatism (Schmitter 1974): *routinized* (as opposed to intermittent) participation of organizational representatives in *high-level* policy discussions, in a way that *exercises legitimate influence* over agenda setting or outcomes. Programmatic representation may occur through formal mechanisms that guarantee organizational input, such as consultative councils, or through informal access to decision makers.

I use two strategies to empirically evaluate an organization's degree of programmatic representation: First, I analyze qualitative evidence such as in-depth interviews with organization leaders and bureaucrats and observations of organization participation in policymaking. Second, I analyze multiple indicators from a survey of organizations, including the level of bureaucrat or politician with whom the organization communicates (secretary, under-secretary, program director, etc.), the frequency of contact between the organization and the ministry, and the stage in the policy process in which the organization participates (agenda setting, policy design, policy modification, and policy implementation).

Patronage representation concerns the degree to which the organization is involved in the discretionary allocation of the benefits that are generated by distributive programs, or more rarely by infrastructure and regulatory policy. Given the rareness of the latter and the ubiquity of the former, my measurement of patronage representation simply observes the actual share of subsidies or other distributive benefits that the organization receives or brokers. In interviews and surveys, I ask organization representatives about the frequency with which they have applied to distributive programs and how many applications have been accepted. I also analyze data on small-business subsidies that indicate the organizations that receive or mediate these.

Argument: Organizational Demands and Party Incorporation

My explanation for distinct modes of representation consists of three elements, as illustrated in Figure 1.2. First, organizations adopt a mode of demand-making, centering on programmatic or patronage demands. Second, political parties develop strategies for incorporating interest organizations in either programmatic or patronage policymaking. Third,

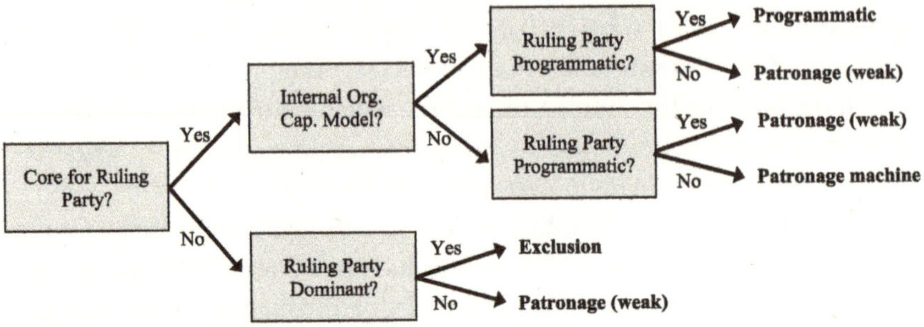

Figure 1.2 Causal Model
Source: Author.

parties and organizations enter into linkages, based on the interaction of their preferences, producing either programmatic or patronage-based representation.

Step One: Determinants of Organizations' Demands

An organization's demands are the policy changes that the organization seeks to bring about through its political activities (e.g., electoral mobilization, protests, lobbying). These demands can either concern programmatic policies—those that affect the sector within which the organization operates—or patronage—discretionary distributive programs. The central determinant of programmatic versus patronage demands is the organization's model for achieving *organizational capacity*, the ability to recruit, retain, and mobilize members. Maintaining organizational capacity is the central factor in survival for any mass membership organization, as it enables mobilization in protest, electoral campaigns, or any other form of political activity. Such capacity furthers both the interests of the leader, whose stature increases with membership size, and the base, which derives benefits from the policy clout that a large membership affords. The source of this capacity shapes demand-making. When an organization is able to maintain an active membership autonomously it may turn its attention to external goals, such as influencing programmatic policies. However, organizations that are unable to achieve collective action autonomously are prone to prioritize demands for patronage, which the leader can repurpose as selective benefits to incentivize member participation.

The source of organizational capacity is reflected in two traits. First, organizations achieve collective action by offering "selective benefits," which provide members with individual incentive to participate (Clark and Wilson 1961; Olson 1965). However, not all selective benefits are equivalent. Some organizations generate these benefits on their own by offering services such as training programs, legal support, or participation in a cooperative enterprise. These organizations can be said to generate organizational capacity internally. For other organizations, selective benefits are externally provided. Most commonly, a state or party patron provides access to disaggregable benefits that leaders allocate selectively to incentivize participation.

Second, organizations require financial resources to cover basic expenses, such as hiring staff, renting headquarters, and hosting activities. While self-financing through member dues is one way that organizations generate capacity internally, this option is often off the table for organizations representing the poor. Alternatively, organizations may secure diverse sources of financial resources—including multiple donors or generating revenue from the sale of services or goods—therein reducing vulnerability to withdrawal of any particular source (Cress and Snow 1996; McCarthy and Zald 1977).

Organizations that generate organizational capacity internally are positioned to lobby a broad spectrum of political actors and to select mobilization strategies that are appropriate to further their policy goals. Such organizations may combine participation in consultative institutions, direct contact with bureaucrats and politicians of all parties, and pressure tactics such as protest and media campaigns. Internally generated organizational capacity and programmatic demand-making are common for business organizations in Mexico. Most of these organizations are able to fund themselves through member dues and generate selective benefits by offering training, consulting, and networking services. With some exceptions, nonpartisanship is the norm for business associations, which place a priority on maintaining strong relationships with politicians of all parties and tend to be frequent participants in state development planning institutions.

In contrast, when organizations depend on a state or party actor to generate organizational capacity, their political participation is more constrained. Patronage benefits can be very effective for achieving collective action and patronage-based linkages with political parties are likely to be available for organizations that are minimally operational. Over time, this brokerage role spurs a growth in membership and can produce a thriving organization. Dependence on an external actor for resources, however, comes at the price of ceding power to that actor (Emerson 1962; Pfeffer and Salancik 2003). It follows that when an organization depends on a political party for financing and selective benefits the party patron can leverage the threat of withdrawing these benefits to exercise control over the organization's structure and activities. Thus, when organizational capacity is externally provided, organizations limit their political engagement to electoral campaigns on behalf of the affiliated party, either at party leaders' behest or because mobilizing electorally displaces other modes of participation. As the organization becomes specialized as an electoral vehicle, its demand-making capacity is limited to pressing for a greater share of patronage.

This mode of demand-making is common for peasant organizations, which typically struggle to remain afloat with internal resources alone. Many such organizations specialize in the brokerage of discretionary state programs, such as subsidies for agricultural inputs or housing. Affiliated to political parties across the electoral spectrum, when these organizations mobilize politically, it is either in electoral campaigns for their partisan allies or as reprisals against government ministries that fail to follow through on promised patronage benefits.

While my theory concentrates less on the *sources* of distinct organizational models aside from social class, I do observe common traits of organizations that adopt strategies for generating organizational capacity internally. First, such organizations were typically formed independently of ruling political parties. Much as political parties founded with access to the state tend to develop patronage-based models of mobilization (Shefter 1977), interest organizations founded with ties to ruling political parties tend to adopt member recruitment strategies based on the intermediation of patronage. Thus, the National Peasant Confederation (CNC), which was formed from within Mexico's dominant party, never had to develop its own sources of organizational capacity because it counted on steady flows of patronage from the PRI during the first several decades of its existence. In contrast, COPARMEX, a business association founded in 1929 in opposition to the PRI, was forced to devise its own sources of selective benefits and did so by organizing networking events and offering legal representation for businesses in employment disputes.

Step Two: Determinants of Party Incorporation Strategies

The second step in explaining representation models corresponds to ruling parties' approaches to incorporating organizations in policymaking. On a smaller scale, and in a more fragmented fashion, this policy incorporation bears resemblance to twentieth-century labor incorporation (Collier and Collier 1991), in that it shapes both the political activation of interest organizations as well as the type and level of their policy representation.[4] And just as under corporatism (Collier and Collier 1979; Lehmbruch and Schmitter 1982), party ties to interest organizations today entail exchange-based linkage relationships, which vary in the type of benefits exchanged each way and the degree of control that the state or party holds over the organizational ally.

In my analysis, the state actors who execute this policy incorporation include governors and other politicians representing the ruling party in a given state.[5] Parties' main incorporation strategies correspond to "core" organizations—those that are organizationally embedded in the party and/or share programmatic goals. Parties may have programmatic or patronage incorporation strategies for core organizations. However, parties also adopt strategies for short-term—and typically patronage-based—incorporation of non-core organizations.

Parties' incorporation strategies are shaped by two factors. First, parties' founding trajectories determine the long-term capacity of the party to incorporate core organizations into programmatic linkages or to deploy these organizations as patronage brokers. For instance, rules for electing party leaders may be more or less conducive to incorporating organizations into the party organically and nominating their leaders for elected office. And the degree of societal penetration of the party organization strengthens its capacity to identify and co-opt societal organizations with patronage ties. Second, the degree of electoral competition faced by the ruling party alters

---

4. Recent studies have described organizational and partisan expressions during Latin America's post-2000 "left turn" as a second instance of incorporation (Rossi 2017; Rossi and Silva 2018). I use the term in a much more limited way to refer to the strategies of individual political parties to build linkages with individual interest organizations.

5. This is not to say that parties out of office are unable to form electoral linkages with interest organizations or to make efforts to facilitate their participation in public policy. However, given that the governor and the ministries that she controls drive both programmatic participation (e.g., the operation of consultative councils) and patronage participation (e.g., the disbursement of distributive programs), the actions of the ruling party are highly determinative of the degree of representation afforded by an organization in both policy areas. This tendency is especially pronounced in Mexican state politics, where policymaking authority is tilted drastically in favor of the executive branch (Lawson 2000).

the short-term incentives to enter into different types of linkages with non-core organizations. Only when parties face electoral competition do they have an incentive to broaden their electoral coalition by engaging non-core organizations in patronage-based linkages.[6]

Electoral strategies differ between the PRI and the former opposition parties, the center-right PAN and center-left PRD. As an ideologically nebulous patronage-based party with extensive roots in society, the PRI's optimal strategy for linkages with popular-sector organizations is based almost entirely on the allocation of patronage. Where it remained electorally dominant at the time of research, the PRI's goal was simply to bolster its sectoral organizations, which serve as clientelistic machines for the party. While the PRI's cronyistic economic policies on the macro level often conflict with the economic interests of these sectoral organizations' popular-sector members, I classify these organizations as core for the PRI because they are so deeply embedded in the party and depend on the party for organizational resources. Consistent patronage flows sustain these organizations' "endogenous loyalty" (Diaz-Cayeros, Estévez, and Magaloni 2016) and forestall their defection to opposition parties. Deeply embedded in the patronage trap, these organizations remain loyal to this party as long as benefits persist. When the PRI faces an electoral threat from another party, however, it may choose to divide patronage benefits between its core organizations and unaffiliated groups, with the goal of co-opting the latter and broadening the party's electoral coalition.

In contrast, the PAN and PRD face a more complex set of goals, combining programmatic and patronage-based linkages in a *segmented incorporation strategy* (Luna 2010). In practically every state where these parties governed in the period under study, they faced an electoral threat from the PRI.[7] Thus, they were forced to devise strategies to expand linkages beyond

---

6. Gibson (1996) defines a party's "core constituencies" in terms of individual voters as the segment of the party's electoral coalition that provides ideological and financial resources and helps define the party's identity for voters. My description of "core" and "non-core" organizations is related, in that I refer to those organizations that share programmatic goals with the party and/or have overlapping memberships.

7. During the period under study (prior to the emergence of MORENA (the National Regeneration Movement) as a national political force), the possible exceptions were Guanajuato for the PAN and Mexico City for the PRD, states where each of these parties dominated electoral politics for over a decade. In these states, the ruling parties are free to behave like the PRI, focusing on patronage ties to core organizations.

the core organizations that are predisposed to support them. Furthermore, these parties do not count on the same "activist networks" (Calvo and Murillo 2019) as the PRI and are therefore at a disadvantage in distributing patronage. The optimal strategy for these newly governing parties after winning office in previously PRI-dominated states is to combine two types of linkages: (1) programmatic incorporation of core organizations consolidates these organizations' role in the party and capitalizes on the organization's reputation and resources; (2) short-term patronage linkages with non-core organizations expand the coalition at election time.

Parties' ability to combine these two types of linkages is constrained by their organizational traits. Parties only are equipped to incorporate core organizations programmatically where the party organization takes a long view of party building, having been formed as an "externally mobilized" party several years before party alternation. Thus, my argument aligns with Shefter (1977, 1994), who argues that "internally mobilized parties," those born with access to state resources, build organizations to engage in patronage politics while "externally mobilized parties," those formed outside of government, develop stronger programmatic identities to mobilize ideologically motivated activists.

The PAN conforms to the externally mobilized type in most states, as well as nationally. This party survived over five decades as a non-competitive protest party before competing successfully in elections in the 1990s. Most of its state-level organizations persisted with the same leadership structures over time and were closely tied to business organizations whose leaders held prominent positions in the party. Therefore, the PAN is at an advantage in pursuing a segmented incorporation strategy. With the organized business community firmly aligned with the party through programmatic linkages, PAN administrations can allocate patronage strategically at election time to co-opt non-core groups. This strategy is yet more feasible for the PAN because core business organizations are usually self-sustaining through dues and member services and do not demand patronage as a condition for supporting the party.

In contrast, the PRD exhibits subnational variation in its organizational traits, conforming to the internally mobilized type in most states. On the national level, the PRD formed as a hybrid between these two party models, combining defecting insiders from the PRI regime with outsiders such as dissident interest organizations and minor leftist parties. However, the party was a major player in electoral politics from its very founding, and electoral professionalists who prioritized short-term electoral victory came to dominate the organization very quickly. In most states where the PRD has governed, it has embraced defecting PRIistas as gubernatorial candidates with name recognition and personal patronage networks, but without organic ties to the parties' long-term organizational allies. These leadership structures did not have space to incorporate organization leaders as major actors in the party and thus opted to mobilize them opportunistically as clientelistic machines through linkages that are renegotiated from election to election. The state where the PRD comes closest to an externally mobilized party is Michoacán, where the party endured twelve years between its founding and its first gubernatorial victory, sustaining the same leadership structure throughout this period. This state may be the exception that proves the rule, as it is the best example of a case where party leadership sought to incorporate dissident rural organizations programmatically through an innovative peasant consultative council.

Step Three: Party–Organization Linkages and Policy Representation

Organizations' policy representation—my dependent variable—results from the interaction between an organization's mode of demand-making and a political party's mode of incorporation. For organizations that are core for the ruling party (upper half of Figure 1.2), this interaction takes place through a party–organization linkage, an exchange relationship in which both party and organization contribute resources that are of value to the other. For programmatic participation to take place, both the party and organization must converge with a preference for a programmatic linkage. That is, preferences for programmatic linkages by both actors are individually necessary and jointly sufficient causes for programmatic representation. Similarly, for patronage-seeking organizations to achieve a high degree of patronage representation, there must be a party with control over these resources willing to allocate them to the organization. Such conditions produce patronage machines, wherein a political party deploys the organization as a clientelistic network. The other two scenarios, where only one of the organization or the party favors programmatic linkages, are less stable, and tend to drift into weak or intermittent patronage arrangements.

Where parties and core organizations converge in their preferences for program or patronage, organizations specialize in patronage brokerage or programmatic demand-making and parties consolidate institutions to perpetuate these representation models. Institutionalized cases of programmatic representation include business chambers embedded in the PAN, particularly in states such as Jalisco and Guanajuato where this party has governed over multiple terms. In such states, business organization leaders are often elected to office under the party label, and these organizations enjoy extraordinary access to policymaking through participation in consultative councils and informal contact with elected politicians. An example of a consolidated patronage machine is the CNC, the PRI's peasant wing, which specializes in clientelistic mobilization in elections and the allocation of discretionary distributive programs funneled from governments under the control of PRI politicians.

Outcomes are less stable where party and core organizations differ in their linkage preferences, and these outcomes tend to drift into contingent patronage exchange. Where the ruling party is patronage-oriented and the organization sustains programmatic demands, organizations adopt a principled autonomy, criticizing the government for its corrupt practices without participating in any significant way in policy. Such is the case of many programmatic leftist organizations (e.g., peasants, indigenous, or neighborhood associations) operating in states where the PRD is mainly patronage oriented. However, maintaining this abstinence from patronage politics demands an extreme level of discipline when the administration offers patronage benefits in exchange for electoral support. Quite often, during a period of weakness, the organization gives in to the pressures of co-optation and forms a patronage-based alliance with the ruling party.[8]

The opposite scenario, where the organization has patronage demands and the ruling party favors programmatic incorporation also leads to an outcome of weak patronage representation. This situation emerges for many patronage-seeking agricultural organizations in Michoacán. PRD administrations in this state have attempted to incorporate peasant organizations programmatically into rural development policy. The few peasant organizations that share a programmatic orientation make effective use of participatory institutions, orienting the rural budget to the needs of small-scale grain farmers. However, for the majority of peasant organizations, which struggle with organizational maintenance and are

8. The EZLN (the Zapatista Army of National Liberation) in Chiapas is an important exception, having stayed out of electoral politics rather than enter into an alliance with this state's highly patronage-oriented PRD.

predisposed to look to the state as a source of handouts, programmatic demand-making is out of the question. Given control over distributive programs and a captive segment of organizations eager to mobilize in elections in exchange for these benefits, very few politicians in patronage democracies such as Mexico resist the temptation to construct patronage linkages, even if the party may have preferred to construct more durable programmatic linkages.

Finally, in scenarios where the organization is not core for the ruling party (lower half of Figure 1.2), programmatic incorporation is entirely off the table. When the ruling party is dominant, it will simply exclude these organizations from all forms of politics. In the cases under study, this is exemplified by the Estado de México, where a dominant PRI administration closes off spaces for non-PRI embedded business and peasants to engage in any area of policymaking. Where ruling parties face an electoral challenge, they may reach out to non-core organizations with contingent patronage appeals, resulting in a weak patronage form of representation, whether or not the organization is oriented to patronage. Such is the fate of peasant organizations in PAN-governed Jalisco and business organizations in PRD-governed Michoacán.

Mechanisms of Change and Reproduction in Representation Models

My explanation for these contrasting representation models is path dependent, as organizations can only change "paths" quite infrequently, and these paths have "increasing returns" (Pierson 2000) locking organizations into one of the two types. The opportunity to build new programmatic linkages occurs only during quite rare periods of institutional change. Mexico's transitional period discussed in Chapter 2—featuring a change in the economic model, the tearing down of corporatist supports for interest organizations, and the onset of electoral competition—constitutes such an upheaval.[9] In the aftermath of these transitions, parties and organizations forged new linkage models. Where a programmatic incorporation model prevailed, such a mode of participation tended to persist as long as the leading figures of the party that forged these linkages retain some degree of power in the

9. The 2018 election of Andrés Manuel López Obrador to the presidency and the concomitant decline of Mexico's stable three-party system potentially represents another such transformative moment.

state. Programmatic participation generates pressures of reproduction as members are socialized to broader issues facing the sector and the organization attains a reputation in the political system as an important actor in policymaking.

This path dependence is asymmetric, however, as the forces of reproduction are even stronger for the patronage representation model, resulting in what I refer to as *the patronage trap* (Palmer-Rubin 2019). When organizations adopt norms of patronage brokerage to sustain organizational capacity, it is all but impossible for them to revert to the internal production of selective benefits. Leaders enjoy the privileged position that comes from brokering patronage benefits, members become socialized to prefer patronage benefits over programmatic change, and future recruitment draws a diverse group of members without shared programmatic goals. Parties that otherwise may have been interested in incorporating the organization programmatically neglect to do so given the organization's reputation as a patronage broker. Many organizations tied to the PRD solidified such patronage representation models during the aftermath of the transition, while PRI-affiliated organizations—such as the CNC—carried over the patronage legacy from before the transition. Other organizations emerged from the transition in one of the unstable modes of weak patronage representation. In many of these cases, it was a matter of time before the organization passed through a rough patch in sustaining organizational capacity or a politician came into power with a generous enough offer of patronage to convert the organization to a patronage broker.

Alternative Explanations

I here discuss alternative explanations for variation in representation models. I consider three variables that may be hypothesized to shape organizational demand for program versus patronage (class, interest alignment, and leadership) and three alternative explanations for supply of patronage or spaces for programmatic influence (ideology, party alignment, policy design). With the exception of class—which is a key antecedent variable tilting the field against programmatic representation for lower-class organizations—I argue that these variables either exercise little influence over the outcome or are endogenous to the causal process laid out above.

Organization: Class

The most important alternative explanation for this study is social class, a variable that has been deployed to explain individuals' programmatic and distributive demands. In my argument, the social class of an organization's membership base determines the level of risk that the organization will fall into the patronage trap. Class may establish resource and membership conditions that shape an organization's options for generating capacity. Organizations that represent the poor are vulnerable to budget constraints and demobilization owing to their potential members' inability to contribute financially and disinclination to civic participation (Holzner 2007; Kurtz 2004a; Verba, Schlozman, and Brady 1995). The poor are also more likely to join an organization in pursuit of handouts than middle-class citizens, who may be drawn to the social networks or prestige that the organization offers (Wilson 1974, 56–77). However, organizations are not simply passive aggregators of members' self-interest, and may socialize members to pursue broader goals. Thus, in contrast to the implication in the party-linkage literature that class determines demand type, I argue that class is but one of several traits that shape the options that organizations have for generating organizational capacity, which is the key factor that sets them on programmatic or distributive paths. Organizations representing lower-class populations can evade a patronage orientation and levy programmatic demands if they generate organizational capacity internally; and middle-class organizations that fail to do so may restrict their demands to the patronage realm.

Organization: Leadership

Another competing explanation has to do with organizational leadership. Perhaps organizations that are fortunate to have altruistic or well-informed leaders adopt a programmatic mode of representation while organizations whose leaders are focused on their own wealth and career prospects are more vulnerable to the patronage trap. I find that leadership practices are better understood as a consequence of an organization's mode of demand-making rather than as the exogenous "luck of the draw." In line with scholarship on endogenous leadership (Ahlquist and Levi 2011, 14–15), I argue that organizations that focus narrowly on patronage extraction tend to attract and promote leaders that seek monetary rents and are skilled at brokerage. In contrast, organizations with high levels of member solidarity and collective consciousness *produce* leaders with the skills and motivation to reinforce an orientation to the common good (Andrews et al. 2010). In this way, the presence of an oligarchic leader prioritizing rent extraction is an element that reproduces the patronage equilibrium rather than an explanatory factor that causes organizations to specialize in patronage demands. Similarly, leaders who rotate frequently and are held accountable to collective goals reinforce the programmatic equilibrium.

Organization: Interest Alignment

Preference homogeneity (alternatively referred to as "interest alignment") among members has also been identified as a factor increasing organizations' ability to mobilize behind collective goals (Moe 1981; Offe and Wiesenthal 1980; Olson 1965). Again, I show that this organizational trait fails to independently account for differences in demand-making, for two reasons. First, the membership pool drawn to an organization is shaped by the incentives offered. For instance, an organization offering productive benefits, such as training in crop production methods, attracts a more homogeneous membership of producers of those crops, whereas organizations that mediate state handouts attract a more diverse—and, thus, more difficult to coordinate—membership. Second, once inside an organization, member preferences are induced by organizational norms (Moe 1981, 537–38). Programmatic organizations generate collective consciousness, and patronage-based organizations reinforce particularism in members (Palmer-Rubin, Garay, and Poertner 2021).

Party: Ideology

On the supply side of program and patronage, we may ask what traits of political parties make them more prone to prefer one or the other of these linkage strategies. I have argued that a party's electoral goals at its founding determine the path-dependent linkages that it seeks to form with core organizations. These founding traits cut across the ideological spectrum, predicting that Mexico's right-wing PAN and Brazil's left-wing PT—both non-competitive outsiders at their founding—would incorporate core organizations programmatically. An alternative prediction is that a party's ideology explains its approach to organizational linkages. Such an account would posit that the PAN resorts to patronage politics with its core organizations less than other parties in Mexico because of its core principles that reject patronage politics. Similarly, Weitz-Shapiro (2012) shows that political parties targeting middle-class voters in Argentina abstain from patronage politics so as not to alienate their party base. Important counterexamples exist, however. Chile's UDI and India's BJP are prominent right-wing parties that rely on patronage-based linkages with non-core poor constituencies to maintain an electoral coalition (Luna 2010; Thachil 2014). Furthermore, an account based on ideology does little to explain subnational variation in PRD governments across Mexico or the PRI's combination of a technocratic neoliberal ideology and extreme patronage orientation.

Party: State–Federal Alignment

Another factor that may explain the supply of patronage on the state level is the party alignment between the governor and president. Existing research from Brazil would lead us to expect that the federal government would permit *greater* discretion in allocating distributive benefits to states governed by copartisans, who are likely to deploy these resources in line with party goals (Bueno 2018). This logic might lead us to expect a greater use of patronage in Jalisco and other PAN-governed states than by PRD- and PRI-governed states during the presidency of PANista Felipe Calderón. While such discretion may have been afforded to PAN-governed states, these do not reflect a higher share of patronage spending, likely because the PAN and its business allies are simply more oriented to programmatic linkages than other parties and organizations.

State: Policy Design

A final alternative explanation for the supply of patronage is the design of sectoral support programs. These distributive programs (particularly in rural areas) are often designed (intentionally or not) to be prone to being used as patronage. Thus, perhaps even a program-oriented state government may unwittingly find itself engaging organizations in patronage politics. The ample margin for patronage-based discretion in the allocation of distributive programs is an ongoing problem in Mexico (Cejudo and Zedillo Ortega 2015; Garay, Palmer-Rubin, and Poertner 2020). Perhaps the higher degree of patronage politics for peasant organizations is attributable to a more discretionary design for rural support programs. This may very well be true, although it would not account for variation *among* peasant organizations (e.g., REDCCAM (Network of Peasant Commercializing Firms of Michoacán) vs. CCC (Cardenista Peasant Central) in Michoacán). This observation does, however, raise an interesting puzzle: The PAN stood little to gain from overseeing a highly decentralized set of distributive programs for rural areas, given its lack of clientelistic networks in the countryside, yet these programs persisted throughout the twelve years of the Fox and Calderón administrations. More broadly, the patronage trap is certainly a more common problem in countries that permit a large degree of discretion in distributive spending, suggesting a limit to the generalizability of the present argument.

Research Design

My research design deploys the subnational comparative method (Snyder 2001b), analyzing variation across Mexican states and economic sectors, while also controlling for a host of structural and institutional factors that remain constant throughout Mexico. Thus, key similarities between all cases include Mexico's corporatist history—and the emergence of dissident interest organizations from outside this corporatist structure; a history of one-party dominance—and the opposition parties that emerged to confront it; and the types of programmatic and distributive policies that the organizations may seek to influence. Most crucially, the choice of these two sectors allows me to analyze the allocation of "federalized" subsidy programs for the agricultural and small-business sectors. These two programs—Alianza para el Campo and Fondo PyME, respectively—operate under rules of operation established by federal government agencies, but are jointly funded and administered by federal and state government agents. Thus, they offer an ideal framework within which to analyze the participation of subnational interest organizations in distributive politics.

The unit of analysis for this study is the organization. Within this framework, I make comparisons across economic sectors (peasant vs. small-business), across individual organizations within those sectors, across Mexican states, and across Mexico's three major political parties. Table 1.2 summarizes the four different types of comparisons conducted in the study, along with the variables that vary across them and the corresponding cases.

Table 1.2 Comparisons and Cases Analyzed in Study

Comparison	Variables	Cases
Sectors	Class, corporatist history	Small-scale agriculture, small business
Organizations	Party alignment, mode of generating organizational capacity	Agriculture: CNC, CCC, ANEC Business: COPARMEX, CANACO, CANACINTRA
States	Party in power, electoral competition	Estado de México, Jalisco, Michoacán
Parties	Founding traits, ideology	PRI, PAN, PRD

First, I develop my explanation for contrasting representation models with controlled comparisons of eighteen organizations—the three largest organizations in each of the small-business and agricultural sectors in each of three Mexican states. I observed routine organization meetings, encounters with government and party figures, and participation in campaign events and protest. These observations revealed the motivations that brought members to organizations, as well as the dynamics regarding leader selection and decision-making. I also interviewed organization leaders, the party personnel with whom they interact, and personnel at state development ministries that allocate benefits to these organizations. I conducted over 100 interviews, mainly from 2011 to 2013, with additional follow-up interviews in the subsequent years. Information from these sources offers insights into the diverse strategies pursued by organizations to influence economic policy and the ways that partisan actors build ties with these organizations in furtherance of their policy and electoral goals.

I complement qualitative findings with two types of quantitative data, oriented to testing hypotheses across all Mexican states. I conducted an original survey of organizations in the small-scale agriculture and small-business sectors in 2012. This novel survey was designed to measure three categories of organizational traits: (1) *internal structures*, including the sources of financial resources, member recruitment, leadership selection, and decision-making; (2) *modes of state engagement*, including contract with politicians, bureaucrats, party leaders, and as well as pressure tactics, such as protest and media campaigns; and (3) *policy demands*, including demands for programmatic policies, such as regulatory policy or infrastructure, as well as access to distributive programs. Finally, I test hypotheses about parties' organization-linkage strategies on an original dataset of small-business subsidies. This analysis allows me to observe how state governments controlled by the three major parties involve interest organizations in distributive spending as the degree of electoral competition varies.

Sectors and Organizations

The overarching comparison is between two large non-elite economic sectors, small-scale agriculture and small business. These both classify as non-elite in the sense that they rely on power in numbers to wield political power as opposed to large corporations—national or transnational—that influence policy through control of capital and personal connections in the upper echelons of politics. These two sectors vary between each other in two theoretically relevant ways. First, organizations of small-scale agricultural producers (or peasants) represent among the most vulnerable of populations, with high levels of poverty and extreme obstacles to collective action. In contrast, organizations of small-business owner, if not an elite type of interest, are a middle-class group with significantly greater financial, human, and social capital to draw on.[10] Second, as I discuss in detail in the Chapter 2, these two sectors were both grouped into peak-level corporatist organizations by the state in the aftermath of the Mexican Revolution, albeit through quite different modes of corporatism; the peasant sector (the CNC) was thoroughly incorporated into the ruling party, while the Chambers of Commerce and Industry were formally non-partisan and enjoyed relatively greater autonomy from the party-state.[11]

In addition to these theoretically relevant traits, the agricultural and small-business sectors are important subjects of analysis given their large contributions to employment and Mexico's economic production. Mexico's economy relies much more heavily on business, and particularly on the manufacturing sector, than on agricultural production, as shown in Figure 1.3. In 2013, manufacturing production totaled 7.4 trillion pesos (roughly 489 billion dollars), or 27.6 percent of GDP. Services and

---

10. Portes and Hoffman (2003, 44–50) characterize agricultural laborers as members of the proletariat and micro-entrepreneurs as belonging to the petty bourgeoisie.

11. As Schneider (2002) discusses, big business interests were particularly well organized in the twentieth century, through a variety of voluntary encompassing organizations that are larger, more numerous, and more active than their counterparts in other Latin American countries.

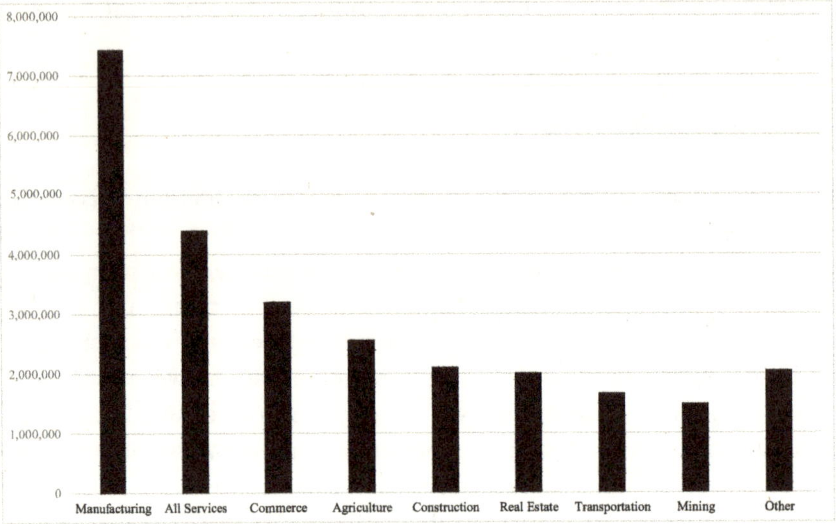

Figure 1.3 Sectoral Production in Mexico (millions of pesos), 2013
Note: Data taken from México en Cifras, Instituto Nacional de Estadística y Geografía (https://www.inegi.org.mx/). Amounts shown in millions of 2013 Mexican pesos. The food processing industry is grouped with agriculture. The "other" category includes Energy, Media, and Government.

commerce totaled 7.6 trillion pesos (28.3 percent of GDP), while agriculture constituted 2.6 trillion pesos (9.5 percent of GDP).

In terms of total employment, however, the tertiary sector (composed of commerce and services) accounts for over half of Mexican jobs (Figure 1.4). The secondary sector (composed of manufacturing, construction, and extractive industries, accounts for 21.8 percent of jobs, and agricultural production (the primary sector) composes 11.6 percent of jobs. It is important to note that these data exclude the informal economy, which is estimated to account for roughly 25 percent of GDP and employ close to 60 percent of the working population.[12] These labor market "outsiders" struggle to organize and perhaps enjoy less representation in productionist economic policy than even peasants (Collier and Palmer-Rubin 2021).

Finally, as shown in Figure 1.5, the vast majority of Mexicans employed in the secondary and tertiary sectors work in microenterprises or small

12. Zúñiga, Juan Antonio. "La economía informal contribuye con 26% del PIB, revela estudio del Inegi," *La Jornada*, July 31, 2014.

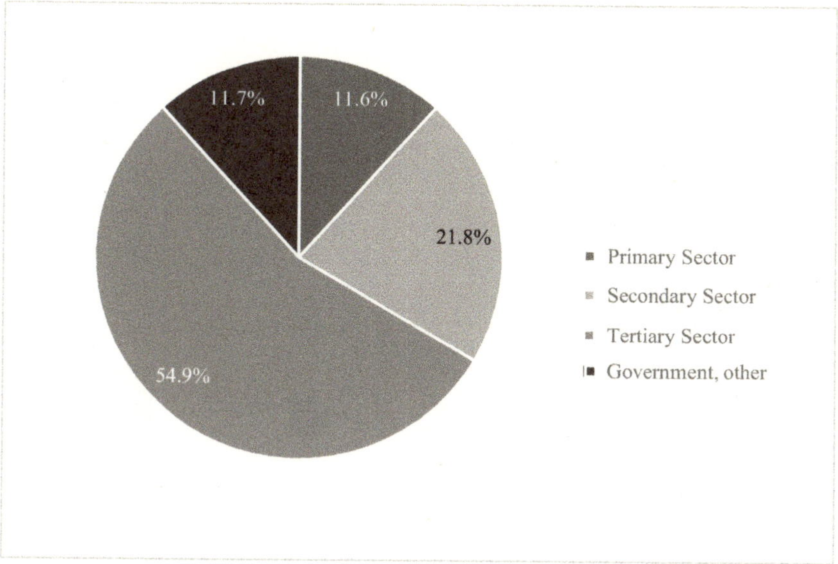

Figure 1.4 Mexican Employment by Sector, 2015
Note: N = 49,806,064 (total formally employed population). Data taken from the Encuesta Nacional de Ocupación y Empleo, Instituto Nacional de Estadística y Geografía (https://www.inegi.org.mx/programas/enoe/15ymas/) and correspond to the first quarter of 2015. Primary sector refers to agricultural production; secondary sector refers to manufacturing, construction, and extractive industries; and tertiary sector refers to commerce and services.

firms.[13] Altogether, 27.2 million Mexicans work in these two sizes of firms (73.9 percent of the secondary and tertiary sectors combined), with 19.8 million working in microenterprises of fewer than ten employees, many of which are self-operated family businesses.

From these data, we can draw two main conclusions. First, while agriculture takes a back seat to the industrial and commercial sectors, both in terms of economic production and employment, we can still say that both of these sectors are core components of the Mexican economy. Second, the

13. The Mexican statistical bureau defines micro-enterprises as those with ten or fewer employees; small firms as those with 11–50 employees in the industrial and service sectors and 11–30 employees in the commercial sector; medium firms as those with 51–250 employees in the industrial sector, 31–100 employees in the commercial sector, and 51–100 employees in the service sector; and large firms as those with over 250 in the industrial sector and over 100 in the commercial and service sectors. See: https://www.inegi.org.mx/contenidos/programas/ce/2009/doc/micronegocios.pdf.

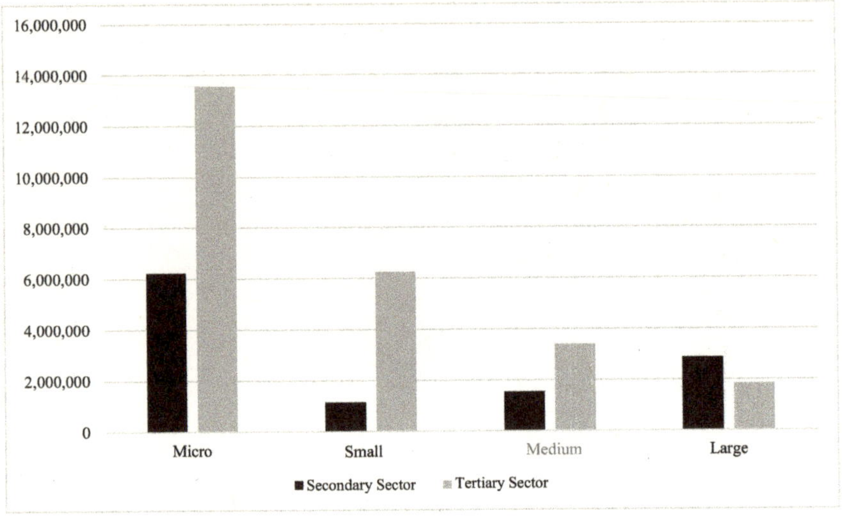

Figure 1.5 Mexican Employment in Secondary and Tertiary Sectors by Size of Establishment, 2015

Note: N = 36,734,293 (total population formally employed in secondary and tertiary sectors). Data taken from the Encuesta Nacional de Ocupación y Empleo, Instituto Nacional de Estadística y Geografía (https://www.inegi.org.mx/programas/enoe/15ymas/) and correspond to the first quarter of 2015.

vast majority (33.7 million or 67.6 percent) of citizens formally considered to be employed in Mexico labor in agriculture or micro to small-sized firms, the types of economic establishments that are typically disadvantaged in economic policy compared with large corporate interests. Thus, the ability of organizations assembling these economic establishments to represent their interests in economic policy is of fundamental importance.

Within each of these two sectors, I analyze both qualitative and original statistical data on a variety of organizations belonging to distinct confederations.[14] Ethnographic case studies and controlled comparisons of eighteen organizations allow me to generate explanations for variations in

14. Not all of agglomerations of these organizations have federative structures or use the term "confederation" to describe their peak-level structures. Of the six major groups analyzed three have federative structures (COPARMEX, CONCANACO (the Confederation of the National Chambers of Commerce), CNC), two describe themselves as a central (CCC) or singular chamber (CANACINTRA (National Chamber of the Industry of Transformation)) with local affiliates, and one uses the term "network" (ANEC). For simplicity's sake, I refer to all of these peak-level structures as confederations throughout this book.

demand type and elucidate the feedback mechanisms, having to do with leadership and membership traits, that cause organizations to remain in the patronage trap or the programmatic equilibrium. Within-case process tracing allows me to establish the "causal chain" variables and detect feedback effects pertaining to the programmatic and patronage equilibria (George and Bennett 2005, 205–32). In particular, I analyze organizational development over time to refute alternative explanations for organizational demands having to do with leadership, member homogeneity, and partisan alignment. Statistical analysis of original survey data with roughly 100 business and agriculture organizations across all thirty-one Mexican states allow me to more broadly test explanations for variation in policy demands and mode of representation.

Research in the agricultural sector focused on state-level organizations belonging to three confederations: the CNC, the long-time peasant sector of the PRI and two dissident confederations (CCC and ANEC). While both of these latter confederations espouse similar goals for rural development policy and were founded in rejection of the PRI's coercive rural corporatism, they followed quite distinct paths in the 2000s, as CCC affiliates came to rely on patronage from the PRD to sustain organizational capacity while ANEC affiliates maintained an internally generated organizational capacity model based on the operation of grain cooperatives.

The differences are subtler between the business confederations analyzed. For instance, all three have formal rules against party alignment. Nonetheless, these three confederations reflect meaningfully distinct histories of state engagement and organizational capacity models. COPARMEX is the complete opposite of the CNC, as it was founded in opposition to the PRI's corporatist system and established an internally generated organizational capacity model from the start. In contrast, confederations of chambers of commerce (CONCANACO) and industry (CANACINTRA) were formed from above by the post-Revolutionary state. While these confederations were formally autonomous from the state, they benefitted from mandatory membership requirements for the greater part of the twentieth century and were only forced to devise organizational capacity models upon the 1997 revocation of this policy.

States and Parties

The second type of comparison in this project is across three states, one governed by each of Mexico's main political parties at the time of research.

Mexico's three main parties vary both in their founding trajectories and ideologies. These parties, the PAN, PRI, and PRD, can be arrayed from right to left on economic development policy goals with differing preferences for interest organization participation. The PRI was constructed in the aftermath of the Mexican Revolution and dominated electoral politics for the greater part of the twentieth century.[15] While this party's hold on power was in large part constructed through corporatist pacts with interest organizations of all economic sectors, in the 1980s it undertook a transition to technocratic policymaking and clientelistic appeals to voters, often brokered through sectoral organizations embedded in the party structure. During the breakdown of one-party dominance in the 1980s and 1990s, the PAN and PRD, opposition parties from the right and left, respectively, secured electoral victories in many states. The electoral transition culminated in the PAN's presidential victory in 2000. State-level PRI administrations that faced electoral threats from the PAN or PRD often responded both by increasing inducements for core sectoral organizations to forestall defection and by co-opting non-core organizations with patronage appeals. However, in the handful of states where the PRI had yet to face an electoral threat at the time of research, it excluded non-core organizations from policymaking. Where former opposition parties won electoral office, they faced an ongoing electoral threat from the PRI and the dual challenges of consolidating a party base among core organizations while reaching out to non-core organizations to broaden their electoral appeal in ensuing elections.

The state cases under study are Estado de México, Jalisco, and Michoacán, all situated in central-western Mexico. These states were governed by the PRI, PAN, and PRD, respectively at the onset of my field research in 2011, as shown in Figure 1.6. In Estado de México, the PRI maintained electoral dominance and was thus free to focus its incorporation strategy on core organizations, without the need to broaden to non-core groups. In the latter two states, opposition parties unseated the PRI, the PAN in Jalisco in 1995 and the PRD in Michoacán in 2001. These administrations were charged

15. The first version of this party organization, formed in 1929, was the National Revolutionary Party (Partido Nacional Revolutionario, PNR). In 1938, the Cárdenas administration incorporated four sectoral organizations into the party, creating the mass-based party structure that persisted and renaming it the Party of the Mexican Revolution (Partido de la Revolución Mexicana, PRM). These sectors were constituted by hierarchical confederations of labor, rural, military, and popular organizations. In 1946, the Ávila Camacho administration recast the PRM as the PRI and the military sector was removed.

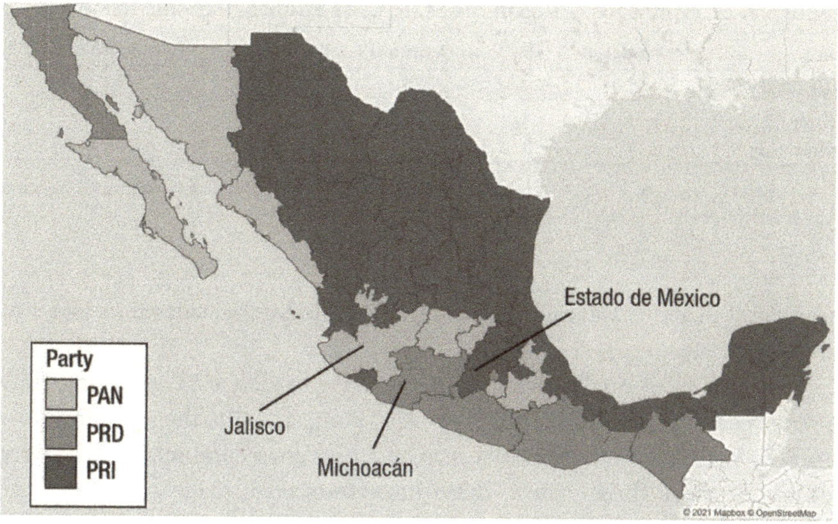

Figure 1.6 Mexican States by Ruling Party, 2011
Source: Author.

with consolidating ties to their base while at the same time broadening their support among non-core groups to secure re-election in the face of persistent challenges by the PRI.[16] These two states can be classified as among the most successful cases of opposition-party consolidation, as Jalisco was ruled for three consecutive terms by the PAN from 1995 to 2012, while three out of four elected governors of Michoacán post-2001 were PRD affiliates.

The further logic for selecting these three states was to control for certain geographic and economic factors. As shown in Table 1.3, each of these three states is quite large, all ranking in the top ten in population. Furthermore, each of these three states is an important site both of urban businesses and agricultural production. Estado de México, Jalisco, and Michoacán rank second, fourth, and thirteenth, respectively, in GDP. Jalisco and Michoacán have the largest agricultural sectors in the country, with Estado de México coming in at ninth. Estado de México and Jalisco are both among the top

16. In 2012, PRI candidates unseated both the PRD in Michoacán and the PAN in Jalisco. In both cases, however, PRI rule lasted only one term. In the 2015 election, the PRD reclaimed the governorship in Michoacán, and in 2018 a candidate aligned with Movimiento Ciudadano unseated the PRI in Jalisco. On the national level, the 2018 and 2021 elections drastically shook up the electoral map and today MORENA holds sixteen out of thirty-two governorships, including Michoacán.

Table 1.3 Economic Activities in the State Case Studies, Ranking in Mexico

State	Population	GDP	Agricultural GDP	Industrial GDP	Services GDP
Estado de México	1	2	9	2	2
Jalisco	4	4	1	4	4
Michoacán	9	13	2	22	9

Note: Data taken from PIB por Entidad Federativa, Instituto Nacional de Estadística y Geografía (https://www.inegi.org.mx/programas/pibent/2013/).

four states in industrial and services GDP, while Michoacán ranks lower in these activities.

I employ both qualitative and quantitative evidence in analyzing state governments under these three parties. First, as with the organizations studied, many of my inferences rely on interviews conducted with party leaders in these three states. These interviews were oriented to uncover historical processes that created and sustained party organizational traits and strategies for forming linkages with interest organizations. I test these arguments about party strategies through a statistical analysis of a small-business support program called Fondo PyME. This is a "federalized" subsidy, meaning that it is designed and largely funded by the federal government's Ministry of the Economy, but administered by state governments. Thus, this program offers a standardized institutional framework that permits a controlled cross-state comparison of distributive spending. I use these data to test my argument about the effect of electoral competition on governments' incorporation strategies.

CHAPTER 2

Structures of Sectoral Representation in Mexico's Transition

The 2018 negotiation of the United States–Mexico–Canada Agreement (USMCA)—the replacement for the North American Free Trade Agreement (NAFTA)—offered a glaring example of representational bias in Mexican economic policy. The Mexican delegation's priorities centered on sustaining export markets for large Mexican firms and consolidating Mexico's position as a site for foreign-based multinational corporations to employ cheap labor. Much lower down the list of priorities: wages and working conditions for industrial workers; the profitability of small businesses; and the expansion of economic opportunity in Mexico's impoverished and violence-stricken countryside.

These priorities are perhaps not surprising once we consider who had a seat at the bargaining table. The Strategic Consultative Council for International Negotiations (CCENI) was constituted as a space for sectoral representatives to offer input to Mexico's negotiating delegation. The members of this council mirrored Mexico's Business Coordinating Council, a group of peak-level business associations. The CCENI's president was a textile magnate, whose firm exports most of its products to the United States. Absent were representatives of non-elite interests: labor unions, small-business owners, or small-scale farmers. Thus, while the average factory worker earns about 20 dollars a day, the Mexican negotiating delegation fought *against* a joint proposal by U.S. and Mexican labor groups to increase the factories' minimum wages.[1] And as the Trump administration instigated a trade war in 2018, the Mexican government

1. See Lawder (2018).

chose to retaliate against U.S. corn exporters by importing corn from Argentina and Brazil rather than promoting domestic production by small-scale farmers.[2]

Where were Mexico's famously powerful labor unions and peasant associations when these important decisions were being made? After all, Mexico was the country that executed the most wide-reaching and durable incorporation of these popular-sector interest organizations in the twentieth century (Collier and Collier 1991, chap. 5). In USMCA negotiations, corporatist sectoral associations embedded in the ruling party—the formerly dominant PRI—toed the party line. These nationwide confederations have long acted as electoral vehicles for their leaders rather than as representatives of working-class interests. The largest PRI-affiliated labor confederation only took notice of the reform when threatened by the possibility of competition for members from U.S.-based unions expanding into Mexico.[3] "Dissident" labor and rural organizations, those that traditionally opposed the PRI during its twentieth-century period of dominance, were either brushed aside by the negotiation team[4] or consumed with the short-term goals of extracting government subsidies, unable to muster much of a fight to push for a new approach to the trade agreement.[5]

In this chapter, I provide the historical context to explain how Mexico's political-economic system shifted from state-led development—with state-embedded labor and peasant associations—to today's oligarchic market-led model. I trace the consequences of this transition for collective action among organizations in the agricultural and small-business sectors. My central argument is path dependent, as I show that many organizations' structures for policy representation were "locked in" to either a programmatic or patronage model during critical junctures defined by the demise of corporatism and the onset of party alternation. The exceptions are popular-sector organizations that emerged from the transition with a programmatic orientation. For these organizations, ongoing programmatic representation was fragile, requiring constant vigilance against co-optation in the face of resource deficiencies and threats to collective action. This chapter lays out the antecedent conditions that shaped how this transitional period unfolded.

---

2. See Huffstutter and Barrera (2018)
3. See Pilar Martinez (2017).
4. Suárez, Carrera, Víctor. "TPP + TLCAN = RIP," *La Jornada del Campo*, January 16, 2016.
5. See Rodriguez (2017).

At the end of the twentieth century, two transitions converged to shape the context for organizational representation in sectoral economic policy. (1) The transition from an interventionist economic model to a market-led model fundamentally altered the *resources* available to economic interest organizations and the role of the state in their operations. Organizations responded to this economic transition by devising new organizational capacity models, either internal (based on autonomous service delivery) or external (based on the intermediation of patronage). (2) The onset of electoral competition after several decades of one-party dominance offered organizations *new interlocutors* with whom to lobby for programmatic policies or enter into patronage relationships. These newly competitive, former opposition parties (the PAN on the right and PRD on the left) differed greatly in their organizational structures and consequently in their strategies for incorporating interest organizations into the party and into policymaking. The PRD also exhibited significant subnational variation, resulting in distinct incorporation strategies across the different states where it governed.

The Situation Today: Biased Pluralism in Mexico

Since the demise of the import-substitution industrialization paradigm in the 1970s, Mexico's development strategy has focused on attracting foreign capital and bolstering the export capacity of large corporations in strategic industries such as agribusiness, telecommunications, and tourism (Kurtz 2004a; Levy 2010; Shadlen 2004). While certain export-oriented industries have flourished, domestic small business and small-scale agriculture have been the losers of the economic transition. Leather and textile industries have contracted under competition from Chinese exporters (Truett and Truett 2010). Independent *tiendas de abarrotes* (grocery stores) and *tlalpalerías* (hardware stores) have buckled in the face of competition from the likes of Walmart and Home Depot.

Prospects for economic opportunity in the countryside have arguably suffered the most. Small-scale corn production—once the most common vocation in Mexico—has long ceased to be a viable pursuit for families in the face of the dumping of highly subsidized and industrially produced U.S. corn (Wise 2010). A previous agricultural regime that sustained a stable—if meager—standard of living for grain producers through subsidized inputs and price guarantees was torn down in the latter part of the 1990s. In its place, neoliberal governments have successively adopted piecemeal distributive programs oriented to alleviate poverty rather than bolster production (Fox and Haight 2010b). Farmers are left to their own devices if they seek sustain their rural lifestyles by improving crop yields or transitioning to higher value crops. And most of the rural interest organizations that purport to resist the large-producer bias in Mexico's rural development model are either locked out of policymaking spaces or too consumed with the immediate survival of the organization to devote attention to demands on behalf of their sector.

The new economic model has failed to produce the widespread prosperity that was promised as the justification for these "growing pains." The neoliberal period has been distinguished by low economic growth, whose benefits accrued mostly to those at the top.[6] After growth rates of over 3 percent from the 1930s through the 1970s, per capita GDP growth in Mexico has averaged less than 1 percent since 1980. Prior to the COVID-19 crisis—which exacerbated poverty—53 percent of Mexicans lived in poverty, the same proportion as in 1992, while the wealth of Mexico's sixteen billionaires grew more than fivefold during that period.[7] According to some observers who supported liberalization in the 1990s, Mexico erred in pursuing rapid and unfettered globalization, without complementing it with a strategy to promote new economic activities that produced high-productivity employment. As a result, Mexico's economy has become increasingly "bifurcated" between "a small number of technologically advanced, globally competitive winners, and a growing segment of firms, particularly in services and retail trade, that serve as the residual source of employment" (Levy and Rodrik 2017).

What has been striking is the degree to which this transition's losers—who may have pushed for a more inclusive development model—have been silenced. The dismissal of popular-sector interests takes on a

6. It is far beyond the scope of this book to evaluate successes and missteps in Mexico's economic liberalization of the 1980s and 1990s. There certainly have been positive developments, such as the absence of severe economic crisis over the past quarter century (Marichal 2013, chap. 5), a welcome streak of non-calamity after successive bouts of recession and hyperinflation. Mexico's middle class is generally content with the post-NAFTA boom in cheap consumer goods (Baker 2003) and wages have increased substantially for factory workers in Mexico's northern states (Hanson 2003).

7. See: Estevez (2017); Hernández (2015); Levy and Rodrik (2017); CONEVAL, "Evolución de las Dimensiones de la Pobreza, 1990–2014."

couple of variants. On the one hand, proponents of economic liberalization argue that empowering these groups politically would send Mexico back to the bad old days of excessive and arbitrary intervention in the economy in the pre-neoliberal period.[8] On the other hand, elite actors point with disdain at those labor unions, peasant associations, and other popular-sector organizations that are oligarchic, corrupt, or clientelistic, claiming that Mexican civil society is simply too rotten to confer legitimate representation.[9] Both of these arguments follow the not particularly democratic logic that non-elite interests have the "wrong" demands and that policymaking should thus should thus be left in the hands of experts who "know what's best" for Mexico.

The result of this dismissal is that in technocratic and international circles, what passes as "Mexican civil society" is usually restricted to elite groups, such as the business owners that consulted on NAFTA or Mexicanos Primero, the NGO founded by billionaire Emilio Azcárraga to promote education reform.[10] Meanwhile, Mexico has lagged well behind its neighbors in developing participatory institutions that might have amplified popular-sector voice in policy (Hevia de la Jara and Isunza Vera 2012; Zaremberg 2012).[11] This exclusion of organized interests has had detrimental consequences for policy outcomes. The incorporation of stakeholders in the design, implementation, and oversight of economic policy through inclusive democratic institutions has long been recognized as indispensable to tailor policies to social needs, ensure societal buy-in,

8. Similar criticisms have been levied from the business community against current left-wing president López Obrador, comparing him to former presidents Echeverría and López Portillo who oversaw budget deficits, devaluations, and economic crises in the 1970s and 1980s. See, for example: "Mexico's business chiefs urge voters to shun Amlo," *Financial Times*, May 30, 2018.

9. For a discussion of this dismissal of Mexican civil society, see Ackerman (2018).

10. López Obrador derisively refers to these groups as *fifi* (posh) civil society. Elite civil society and thinktanks certainly have their place in the political sphere, but should not be mistaken for the organizations that represent distinct societal interests, such as business, labor, environmentalists, feminists, etc. For a reflections on the oligarchization of Mexican civil society through the PRI's state corporatism and big business, see Morales (2018).

11. Amidst overall mediocre results and a failure to institutionalization, comparative studies identify some variation in the degree of empowerment offered by municipal councils in Mexico. See Fox and Aranda (1996) for a study of rural development councils in Oaxaca and Montambeault's (2011) analysis of urban participatory institutions.

and hold policymakers accountable (Acemoglu, Johnson, and Robinson 2005; Evans 1995; Fukuyama 2001; Ostrom 1996). Particularly for countries passing through economic transformations, as did Mexico beginning in the 1980s, societal participation serves as a "meta-institution" to guide the adoption of new market institutions and build new opportunities for those whose livelihoods are threatened by the new economic model (Rodrik 2008, chap. 5).

Furthermore, when non-elite voices are silenced, economic policy reflects a consensus among elites to preserve their privileged status. How else to explain why Mexico's tax rate is a third of that in similar middle-income countries such as Argentina, Brazil, and Turkey, while close to half of Mexico's wealth is concentrated in the top 1 percent? And how else to explain why Mexico's minimum wage as a proportion of average salaries was the lowest in Latin America in 2018, before López Obrador entered office?[12] What would the core elements of Mexican economic policy look like if, instead of dismissing organized interests, reformers tried to promote and expand on the "pockets of excellence,"[13] those organizations that have the potential to offer programmatic voice to non-elite economic interests?

The Big Picture: From State Corporatism to Biased Pluralism

One century ago, it may have been difficult to predict that Mexico would be notable for the political *exclusion* of popular-sector interests. In the aftermath of the Mexican Revolution (1910–1917), the incoming regime established a unique brand of electoral dominance that was distinguished by the incorporation of societal interests into the ruling party through corporatist sectoral organizations. Mexico's popular incorporation was the most complete in the region, as Venezuela's Democratic Action (AD) party was the only other major populist party in the region to incorporate both

12. On Mexican tax policy in comparative perspective, see Unda Gutiérrez (2015). On wealth inequality in Mexico, see: Hernandez (2015). On minimum wage comparisons, see ILO (2018, p. 49).

13. I borrow this idea from a series of works that identified rare autonomous and capable industrial bureaucracies in Latin American developmental states (Bersch, Praça, and Taylor 2017; Evans 1999; Geddes 1994; Schneider 1999). Like these works, my hope is that by identifying the few success cases amidst a sea of rent-seeking, we may glean strategies to expand these successful models.

labor and the peasantry; others were limited solely to labor (Collier and Collier 1991, 196–270).[14] Mexico's peasants were incorporated into the ruling party through the CNC. In contrast, corporatist ties to business were constructed through state-created confederations of chambers of commerce and industry, which were mandated to be non-partisan. The relationship between the one-party state and these associations can be described as state corporatist, in which peak-level confederations were "created by and kept as auxiliary and dependent organs of the state, which founded its legitimacy and effective functioning on other bases" (Schmitter 1974, 102–03).[15] Through these corporatist ties, organizations enjoyed significant "inducements"—state subsidy, mandatory membership, and political representation through nominations of leaders to legislative office—while also being subject to sharp "constraints"—limitations on the their internal governance and demand-making (Collier and Collier 1979). However, top-down coercion was less complete in the business sector, as chambers enjoyed greater autonomy owing to their position outside the party, yet still exercised influence over economic policy through their sizable structural power (Schneider 2004, 60–66).

During the 1980s and especially the 1990s, this corporatist system unraveled, and interest organizations were forced to devise new strategies to sustain collective action. Traditional corporatist organizations—such as the CNC and business chambers belonging to CONCANACO and CANACINTRA—were most adversely affected during the transition because corporatist benefits that sustained collective action and access to policymaking were withdrawn with the threat of disappearing entirely if the PRI was defeated. Dissident organizations—such as COPARMEX and dozens of peasant associations—had never enjoyed access to patronage benefits or state support for membership. COPARMEX had long prior established strategies for sustaining organizational capacity internally, having taken an oppositional stance to the PRI since the organization's founding in

14. Bolivia's Revolutionary Nationalist Party (MNR) attempted a similar process of incorporating labor and peasant organizations following the 1952 Revolution. This process was aborted, however, with the 1964 military coup of René Barrientos (Hylton and Thomson 2007, chap. 6).

15. In a departure from Schmitter's definition, which describes union confederations under state corporatism as "non-competitive," the PRI-affiliated labor sector was made up of several distinction confederations that did compete with each other for members.

1929. However, the organizational challenge was distinct for dissident social movements and peasant associations that had been formed in the 1980s and 1990s. While these associations had mobilized large numbers of popular-sector citizens during a cycle of large-scale social unrest—the 1985 Mexico City protests, the 1988 presidential election, and the 1994 entry into NAFTA and economic crisis—their ability to sustain an active membership base and routine demand-making following these episodes depended on their consolidation of new models of organizational capacity.

The six confederations that constitute the focus of this study responded to these transitions differently, entering into the period of party alternation having either devised a sustainable model of internal organizational capacity, based on the provision of valuable services to members, or having failed to do so, and thus vulnerable to entering into patronage-based ties in order to sustain collective action. Table 2.1 shows the pre-transition and post-transition organizational capacity models for the six confederations that constitute the core of this study.

Among the six confederations, the CNC and COPARMEX represent ideal types of patronage-based and programmatic organizations, respectively; and their organizational trajectories are mirror images of each other. As the long-time peasant sectoral organization for the patronage-based PRI regime, the CNC was founded with an external organizational capacity model and would sustain this orientation through the transition. Even in states where the PRI has lost the governorship, the CNC relies on the brokerage of discretionary distributive benefits to sustain collective action. In contrast, COPARMEX was founded with an internal organizational capacity model without access to state patronage given its oppositional character and strong norms against partisanship. Even when the PAN—a natural ally for COPARMEX—won gubernatorial elections in the 1990s

Table 2.1 Organizational Capacity Models, Pre- and Post-Transition

Confederation	Year of Founding	Pre-Transition Model	Post-Transition Model
Agriculture			
CNC	1938	External	External
CCC	1988	Internal	External
ANEC	1995	Internal	Internal
Business			
COPARMEX	1929	Internal	Internal
CONCANACO	1917	Mixed	Internal
CANACINTRA	1941	Mixed	Mixed

and the presidency in 2000, COPARMEX affiliates remained steadfast in their internal organizational capacity model, incentivizing member participation by offering training, consulting, and network services and remaining as non-partisan voices in economic policy.

While CNC and COPARMEX reflect stasis in organizational models through the transition, the remainder of the organizations were presented with mandates (or opportunities) to modify their organizational capacity models. Given the examples set by the CNC and COPARMEX, there were pressures for these other organizations to replicate their models. Thus, in states where the PRD took office, the path of least resistance was for dissident agricultural organizations and their party allies to mimic the patronage-based repertoire for their sector pre-established by the PRI and the CNC. Most CCC affiliates did fall prey to this tendency and turned to patronage brokerage as their mode of sustaining collective action. In contrast, organizations belonging to ANEC explicitly avoided it, designing an internal organizational capacity model based on the operation of grain cooperatives and training activities that improved the productive capacity of their members.

Chambers of commerce and industry passed through organizational trajectories that were slightly more varied. Peak confederations of chambers for these two sectors were established in 1917, immediately after the Revolution. While these confederations had been incorporated into the PRI's corporatist system—most importantly through the granting of mandatory membership requirements—they were not organized inside the party, which was formally devoted to representing working people and not capital (Collier and Collier 1991, chap. 5). The 1997 revocation of mandatory membership forced chambers to devise new organizational capacity models. The vast majority of chambers of commerce (CONCANACO affiliates) followed in the path of COPARMEX by turning to a member service model to sustain an active membership. Chambers of industrial firms, in contrast, representing a sector that had faced harder times in the economic transition, had mixed success in reinventing themselves in this way, and several of these chambers came to rely on state subsidies to remain afloat.

Economic crisis and reform also spurred a transformation in Mexico's political party system. Denied state funds by privatizations and austerity reforms, the PRI shifted away from a corporatist sectoral model—capable of co-opting opposition activists—to a clientelist catch-all party, that had to resort to fraud to win elections (Greene 2007, chap. 7). Opposition parties on the left (PRD) and on the right (PAN) capitalized on this opening to challenge the PRI in elections. While the electoral transition reached its climax with the 2000 presidential victory of the PAN's Vicente Fox, these opposition parties had chipped away at subnational PRI rule with gubernatorial victories as early as 1989. By 2000, PAN and PRD governors had defeated the PRI in fourteen states.

The three parties' postures towards interest organizations varied markedly after the transition. During the 1990s, the PRI marginalized its sectoral organizations in the party. Thus, the party-incorporated CNC experienced a reduction in its access to national policymaking, while retaining its role as a patronage network. During these years, business chambers suffered cutbacks in corporatist supports and saw their role in economic policymaking supplanted by big business. However, the PAN's presidential administrations (2000–2012) courted chambers and other business organizations by offering electoral and ministerial posts to business leaders and creating small-business support programs that operated through these organizations. As an externally mobilized party with long-standing ties to organized business based on overlapping membership and shared policy goals, PAN administrations prioritized the programmatic incorporation of these organizations in economic policy. The PRD on the national level took up the mantle of small-scale farmers by forging alliances with dissident rural organizations and promoting an anti-free trade agenda and the reinvigoration of state support for the countryside. However, the PRD's commitment to programmatic incorporation of core organizations was sharply limited by its electoral-professional orientation and immediate need to mobilize ground campaigns, leading it to build patronage ties with the majority of dissident peasant organizations.

Rural Organizing During PRI Hegemony

Mexico's post-Revolutionary state embarked on a massive project of incorporating popular sectors into the ruling party, which was organized into three sectoral confederations by President Lázaro Cárdenas in 1938 (Hardy 1984, 27–32) corresponding to labor, peasants, and the military.[16] The CNC,

16. Each of these sectors is composed of various national confederations, but labor was dominated by the Mexican Workers' Confederation (CTM), and the peasant sector by the National Peasant Confederation (CNC). Ávila Camacho, Cárdenas'

the largest component of the rural sector, had a pyramidal structure whose geographic base was the *ejido*. These collective landholdings of peasants (with private appropriation) were created and governed by article 27 of the 1917 Constitution, which promised agrarian reform in line with demands of the Revolution's agrarian movement. However, redistribution of land was not accomplished on a large scale until Cárdenas' presidential term (1934–1940), through a process that served both to economically empower Mexico's peasantry and create institutions of social control of the countryside (Collier and Collier 1991, 232–36).

Subsequent administrations departed from Cárdenas' rural populism, vastly reducing the scale of land redistribution and promoting the interests of the relatively better-off rural smallholders over those of landless peasants and *ejidatarios*.[17] Weakened as an agent in land claims, the CNC shifted to intermediating state agricultural supports as its main appeal to peasants.[18] During the period of important-substitution industrialization (1940s to 1970s), however, the interests of smallholder farmers were subordinated to those of the growing urban working class. While the state instituted a series of programs to guarantee a basic standard of peasant profitability—including a centralized buying operation with price guarantees (CONASUPO), subsidized credit for farmers (BANRURAL), and subsidized crop insurance (ANAGSA)—post-Cárdenas administrations privileged larger, more productive producers and neglected to invest in the irrigation systems, storage and transportation infrastructure, and production machinery that would provide for the competitiveness of the peasant sector (Gordillo 1988, 32–68; Hewitt de Alcántara 2007).[19]

---

successor, modified the sectoral structure, removing the military sector and replacing it with the National Confederation of Popular Organizations (CNOP), a residual and mostly middle-class sector, including state-employee unions, small landholders, and others.

17. For instance, Ávila Camacho increased the size of landholdings that were considered small (and thus immune from expropriation), to 200 hectares and introduced the *amparo* for landholders, a legal process to forestall expropriation (Hardy 1984, 80–81).

18. Objecting to the CNC's perceived conciliatory posture regarding these changes, a faction broke off in 1947, eventually joining labor factions departing the CTM in the General Union of Workers and Peasants of Mexico (UGOCM) (Hardy 1984, 34-36). UGOCM has since broken into multiple factions, the largest of which (UGOCM-Jacinto López) reintegrated into the PRI's peasant sector in 1976.

19. CONASUPO stands for Compañia Nacional de Subsistencias Populares (National Company of Popular Subsistence). BANRURAL stands for Banco

Discontent with these failings came to a head in dissident rural movements in the 1960s and 1970s, leading to the fragmentation of peasant organizations, as the Independent Peasant Central (CCI) and Independent Workers and Peasants Central (CIOAC) broke off from the CNC (Hardy 1984, 36–46). The CNC persisted, however, as the weakest of the PRI's sectors, yet still quite privileged as the central brokerage outfit through which Mexico's peasants accessed supports doled out by the one-party dominant state. Splinter organizations—like UGOCM, CCI, and CIOAC—either were co-opted by later PRI administrations to operate as patronage networks within the peasant sector, but outside the CNC; or were forced to survive in the absence of state supports.

Business-State Ties during PRI Hegemony

The incorporation of business chambers into the PRI's post-Revolutionary corporatist system was more immediate, yet less restrictive than the case of the peasants. In 1917, during the wind-down of the Revolution, Venustiano Carranza's administration adopted a Law of Chambers that set the basis for the establishment of two confederations of business chambers—the CONCANACO and the CONCAMIN (Confederation of Industrial Chambers of the United States of Mexico).[20] In a context where the economic elite were threatened by the 1917 Constitution's promise of agrarian reform and extension of union organizing rights, these confederations were designed as peak-level consultative bodies to provide for the representation of private-sector interests in economic policy (Juárez González 1989, 259–62). Reforms to the Law of Chambers in 1936 and 1941 established mandatory

Nacional de Crédito Rural (National Rural Credit Bank). ANAGSA stands for Aseguradora Nacional Agrícola y Ganadera (National Agricultural Insurance Agency). For a summary of the various government programs that supported peasant production under ISI, see Fox (1992b, 88–116) and Grindle (1977).

20. CONCANACO has a two-level structure, consisting of local chambers of commerce (of which there are today 254) and the national confederation. CONCAMIN is a looser confederation of both national and local chambers, both industry-wide and sector-specific. Today the largest national organization of industrial firms is CANACINTRA, formed in 1941 from within CONCAMIN and today with delegations in every state, except Jalisco and Nuevo León, which have regional industrial chambers (Shadlen 2004, chap. 2).

membership requirements, compelled all chambers of commerce and industry to incorporate into CONCANACO and CONCAMIN, and required that business organizations be non-partisan (Alcázar 1970; Luna 1995, 78–79; Schneider 2004, 60–66). The post-Revolutionary reforms organized chambers into peak-level structures, securing a mass membership, while also facilitating engagement with—and control by—the national government.[21] However, business organizations were never incorporated into the PRI as were unions and peasants, and thus enjoyed considerably greater autonomy over their mobilization strategies.

Throughout the twentieth century, ties between these chambers and the state served the dual purposes of channeling business demands and securing private-sector sanction for economic policies. If CONCANACO and CONCAMIN were initially conciliatory with the state—evidenced in their acquiescence to the establishment of the income tax in 1924—their rapport with PRI administrations ebbed and flowed throughout the twentieth century. State–business relations were particularly antagonistic during Cárdenas' presidency, owing to his promotion of union organizing, agrarian reform, and expropriations of foreign-owned businesses (Camp 1989, 19–21). This discontent found expression in the formation of two powerful organizations designed to defend business interests: COPARMEX, an organization of employers formed in 1929 by businessmen in the northern industrial city of Monterrey; and the PAN, a right-wing political party founded in 1939 through a coalition of business owners and Catholic intellectuals (Juárez González 1989, 265–70; Loaeza 1999, 105–12; Mizrahi 2003, 17–22).

As an organization mainly representing small industrial firms and quite dependent on state support, CANACINTRA represented the opposite end of the spectrum, prioritizing a friendly relationship with the state, even amidst economic policies biased in favor of large firms. CANACINTRA was founded in 1941 by Mexico City industrialists to represent a variety of industrial sectors that did not have their own sector-specific chambers already. Unique among CONCAMIN affiliates, this left CANACINTRA as a catchall chamber, composed mainly of small and medium-sized firms that were excluded from state industrial policies that favored

21. The Mexico City Chamber of Commerce, founded in 1874, was the most important precursor of business organizing in Mexico and chambers were constituted in several other cities in the pre-Revolutionary period (Juárez González 1989, 256).

large-scale manufacturers (King 1970; Story 2014). CANACINTRA's appeal to members relied on its role as intermediary for particularistic state contracts, financing, and subsidies and its membership grew rapidly in the post-war period, reaching nearly 12,000 firms in 1960 and 56,000 in 1979 (Shadlen 2004, chap. 2). Large in membership, but relatively meager in economic weight, CANACINTRA's political influence depended on maintaining a massive membership and chamber leadership constantly lobbied the state to enforce mandatory membership and prohibit the creation of new chambers that would compete for members. Combined with the state-dependent nature of most of its affiliated firms, CANACINTRA thus came to be the most accommodationist of the major chambers, refraining from criticizing industrial policies that favored large firms or political cronies.

Business–state harmony was the norm during post-Cárdenas administrations until the 1970s, when chambers began to publicly oppose economic policies of populist PRI governments. In 1975 CONCANACO and CONCAMIN joined the Business Coordinating Council (CCE), along with COPARMEX and other business organizations,[22] establishing a united opposition to policies by the Echeverría (1970–1976) and López Portillo (1976–1982) governments that were threatening to business interests, including the promotion of a peak labor organization, land expropriations, and the nationalization of the banking sector (Camp 1989, 25–29; Collier 1992, 93–97). While subsequent PRI administrations embraced a market-led growth model—reflected in Mexico's 1994 entry into NAFTA—large businesses were the prime beneficiaries, and small-business organizations were increasingly marginalized from governing coalitions. Shadlen (2004, 99–100) describes the position of the Salinas administration (1988–1994) thusly: "'Economic modernization' and the broader program of integration implied by NAFTA meant that the owners and managers of Mexico's largest firms came to be regarded in an almost heroic light, as the crusaders leading Mexico's insertion into the 'First World.'"

22. Other founding members of the CCE include the Mexican Association of Insurance Institutions (AMIS), Mexican Council of Businessmen (CMHN), National Agricultural Council (CNA), and Association of Mexican Banks (ABM). All but CONCANACO, CONCAMIN, and COPARMEX are elite, big-business led groups, most prominently the CMHN, analogous to the Business Roundtable in the United States.

The Shifting Rural Development Paradigm and Consequences for Rural Organizing

By the 1990s, the shifting rural development policy landscape led the CNC to transform from the core corporatist intermediary in a highly regulated and subsidized agricultural system to an informal broker for subsidies and social programs in a liberalized system. This transition was produced by three central policy changes: a transformation in state agricultural supports, the privatization of *ejido* land, and Mexico's embracing of global agricultural markets. The liberalized rural development framework reduced the financial resources available to the CNC and, most troublingly, revoked its most valuable organizational resource—the captive membership afforded by the *ejido* system. At the same time, the advent of multi-party competition raised the possibility of further limitations on access to state benefits if the party patron were to lose office. Despite these challenges, the CNC persisted in a weakened state as a clientelist broker of discretionary distributive programs, channeled to the organization through PRI politicians. At the same time, this environment opened space for a new generation of dissident rural organizations to engage in demand-making through the newly pluralist system and also to intermediate patronage benefits, especially in states with a strong presence of the PRD.

Transformation in Agricultural Supports

Following the 1982 economic crisis, state agricultural institutions such as CONASUPO and BANRURAL were dismantled, weakening the appeal of the CNC to the peasantry, as it had been the intermediary for these programs (Hewitt de Alcántara 2007, 90–91). These programs were replaced by two new types of support designed to deliver benefits directly to individuals, therein circumventing rural organizations: compensatory subsidies and social development programs. The former were designed to cushion the blow of NAFTA; the largest program of this type was PROCAMPO, a program adopted in 1994 that offered set payments per hectare produced (Fox and Haight 2010b, 17–18).[23] Social-development programs, operated by the

23. PROCAMPO was originally formulated as a temporary measure, set to expire in 2009, fifteen years after entry into NAFTA. However, the Calderón administration chose to continue payments, acknowledging that the small-scale agricultural

Ministry of Social Development (SEDESOL), included PRONASOL during the Salinas administration (1989–1994) and PROGRESA (the Program of Education, Health, and Nutrition, the precursor to Oportunidades and PROSPERA) during Zedillo's presidency (1994–2000). PRONASOL was the overarching structure for a variety of development interventions for marginalized communities, ranging from transportation infrastructure to health clinics, and was notoriously vulnerable to electoral manipulation, as the federal government strategically allocated benefits to preserve subnational PRI rule (Diaz-Cayeros, Estévez, and Magaloni 2016, chap. 4; Molinar Horcasitas and Weldon 1994). Reforms by the Zedillo administration decentralized discretionary support programs while revolutionizing the federal anti-poverty approach through the adoption of the conditional cash-transfer program PROGRESA.[24]

Thus, while state spending in the countryside has remained relatively constant as a percentage of total government spending since the 1980s, the policy goals shifted drastically, from a focus on the productionist logic of supporting agricultural producers to a consumptionist logic of alleviating rural poverty.[25] This shift was continued during PAN administrations. Robles and Ruiz (2012) show that between 2003 and 2012, the "competitiveness" category of rural spending (composed mainly of agricultural subsidies) decreased from 26.4 percent of total rural spending to 20.7 percent (thirty-one billion pesos to fifty-three billion pesos),[26] while social spending increased from 11.0 to 23.9 percent (thirteen billion pesos to seventy-three

---

sector had yet to reach competitiveness and that revocation of these supports would be hugely unpopular (Palmer-Rubin 2010a, 17). While reports certainly exist of the electoral conditioning of PROCAMPO payments, and the role of the CNC in brokering the inclusion of workers on the beneficiary list, the program's operation leaves no space for organizational mediation, as it delivers direct payments to farmers.

24. For broader discussions of PRONASOL and Oportunidades, see Cornelius, Craig, and Fox (1994), Diaz-Cayeros, Estévez and Magaloni (2016) and Hevia de la Jara (2009). For analysis in a comparative context, see De La O (2015) and Garay (2016).

25. See Collier (2015, 7–13) for a discussion of the shift from productionist to consumptionist policies (and demand-making).

26. Absolute spending on agricultural subsidies has increased markedly over the past fifteen years. However, the subsidies for irrigation infrastructure, machinery, and production inputs that expanded under the Fox and Calderón administrations have favored large, export-oriented producers (Fox and Haight 2010b).

billion pesos). Concomitantly, rural households have come to rely much less on farm income and increasingly on government transfers and non-farm income. From 1992 to 2004, the share of total income derived from agricultural production for the typical Mexican household decreased from 37.7 to 17.3 percent, while non-farm income increased from 38.3 to 54.8 percent and transfers from 12.3 to 16.6 percent (Scott 2010, 82).

The technocratic revolution in federal distributive programs, combined with Zedillo's decentralizing reforms, shifted clientelistic rural development policy to the state level. The second-largest agricultural subsidy (after PROCAMPO), Alianza para el Campo (Alliance for the Countryside) is an application-based "federalized" program, requiring potential beneficiaries to design projects and submit them to state-level committees that make funding decisions.[27] While PROCAMPO is relatively immune to electoral manipulation or misappropriation—with notable exceptions[28]—Alianza para el Campo, along with several other subnational subsidy and support programs, provides ample space for discretion (Palmer-Rubin 2010b). These programs reintroduced space for rural organizations to appeal to potential members through their services of designing projects, navigating bureaucratic application processes, and negotiating with ministry personnel. These negotiations, commonly referred to as *gestión*, constitute the central activity of many patronage-oriented organizations (Garay, Palmer-Rubin, and Poertner 2020).[29] While such programs typically are designed for individual farmers or families, they are practically impossible for small-scale producers to access in many states without a politically connected organization leader negotiating on an applicant's behalf.

Alongside this transformation in state support for the countryside, the CNC was confronted with a 1992 agrarian reform that further eroded its

27. The Zedillo administration adopted a variety of federalized rural subsidy programs and grouped them under the rubric of Alianza para el Campo in 1996 (Palmer-Rubin 2010b). These federalized rural subsidies have been reorganized and renamed several times in the years since, yet continue to represent a sizable portion of federal agricultural spending (Robles Berlanga and Ruiz Guerra 2012).

28. The collaborative efforts of Mexican NGO Fundar, the Woodrow Wilson Center, and researchers uncovered several instances of producers receiving PROCAMPO payments that exceeded the yearly maximum, government officials receiving benefits (against program rules), and known drug cartel members. See: Fox and Haight (2010a), Merino (2010), and Cejudo (2012).

29. On the concept and practice of *gestión* in Mexico, see Hilgers (2018) and Rizzo (2020).

role in rural mediation. The reform of article 27 declared that the state no longer was obligated to redistribute land, provided for *ejidatarios* to secure individual ownership, and facilitated private investment in *ejido* land (Cornelius and Myhre 1998; de Janvry, Gordillo, and Sadoulet 1997, 13–22). *Ejido* commissariats were removed from the land tenure process, and new institutions were established to grant land titles through the Program for Certification of Ejido Land Rights and the Titling of Urban House Plots (PROCEDE). A panel survey of *ejidatarios* conducted in 1990 and 1994 (two years before and after the reform) shows that the share of farmers who sought to resolve land issues through *ejido* unions decreased from 10.8 percent to 0.8 percent over this period and that 83.8 percent of farmers reported obtaining only "purely economic benefits" through rural organizations in 1994 (de Janvry, Gordillo, and Sadoulet 1997, 115–21).[30] *Ejidos*—the basic building block of the CNC—were no longer involved in resolving the existential issue of land tenure for farmers. Furthermore, this policy led to the depletion of the CNC's base. Where *ejidatarios* were previously required to reside on and work their land to retain usufructuary rights, now they could sell or rent their land. Thousands of farmers grasped the opportunity to cash out and migrate to cities or to the United States in pursuit of higher paying jobs (de Janvry et al. 2015). At the same time, new organizations such as the CCC began recruiting members in the early 1990s through the promise of helping resolve land disputes and gaining land titles.

The *ejido* reform also undercut the CNC's control over rural supports and investments. While *ejidatarios* previously were limited to state development banks to access finance, new landowners could now (in theory) access capital more easily by using their plots as collateral and contracting with private investors. Furthermore, PRONASOL exacerbated the marginalization of *ejido* unions by channeling benefits through new rural organizational structures called "solidarity committees" rather than through *ejidos*. In short, the CNC transitioned from a monolithic intermediary, formally vested with the responsibility to incorporate peasants into state agricultural support programs to the largest among several actors in the countryside jockeying to extract distributive state benefits for a dwindling peasant population.

30. The celebrated "end" to land redistribution proved to be premature, as a wave of land invasions sparked by the 1994 Zapatista movement eventually pressured the state to grant land to peasant and indigenous populations in southern Mexico.

The third major policy change that affected rural intermediation was Mexico's embracing of global agricultural markets. Mexico's entry into NAFTA in 1994 constituted the climax of the transition to market-led development. While NAFTA is often credited with boosting economic growth and job opportunities in Mexico, particularly in the exploding *maquila* (foreign-owned manufacturing) sector (Hanson 2003; Harrison and Hanson 1999), in the agricultural sector it furthered tilted the playing field against the small-scale farmer. Most threatening was the importation of U.S.-grown corn, the commodity produced by an estimated 75 percent of *ejidatarios* in 1994 (de Janvry, Gordillo, and Sadoulet 1997, 123–25). Mexican imports of basic grains increased 130 percent from 1990 to 2011 (from 7.7 to 17.9 billion tons), while domestic production increased only 11 percent (from 25.4 to 28.3 billion tons) during the same period (Robles Berlanga 2014, 19–20). The dumping of highly subsidized U.S.-grown corn in Mexico is estimated to have caused a 66 percent decline in real prices for Mexican corn producers (Wise 2010, 19–23). Small-scale farmers that have successfully weathered NAFTA have either transitioned to higher-value crops, such as table vegetables, avocados, or coffee or have joined cooperative commercializing outfits that negotiate higher prices for grains and offer training and access to resources to improve yields.[31] Meanwhile, a handful of industrialized rural producers benefitted from the expansion of their consumer base at the same time that the organizations that represent these export-oriented producers—the CNA and CNG (National Ranchers' Confederation)—ascended to the most influential non-state actors in shaping rural development policy through their leadership role in NAFTA negotiations (de Grammont 1996).

In the context of transitions to a liberalized rural development model and multi-party competition, rural organizations fragmented, adopting diverse strategies of collective action and demand-making. One category of organizations specialized in *gestión*, the intermediation of discretionary distributive programs for members. Patronage politics and clientelistic mobilization continued to define the CNC and, as non-agricultural employment has come to predominate in rural areas, only a small percentage of CNC affiliates or representatives are farmers. Similarly, and on a much smaller scale, the

31. Among the rural "winners" of NAFTA, avocado producers in the state of Michoacán stand out. An organization of producers in this state successfully lobbied for a monopoly of avocado exports to the United States.

UCD (Democratic Peasant Union), formed within the PRD in 1989 with an expectation of prompt electoral victory and also specializes in *gestión*.

Other organizations, however, were founded with a concern for the conditions for small-scale agricultural production, providing services to improve the profitability of their members and mobilizing against the withdrawal of the state from support for small-scale production. The CCC, formed in 1988, was initially non-partisan (although favored the PRD), and spearheaded a movement for a new agrarian reform while recruiting members by assisting in land claims (García Ponce 2009, 38–43). And ANEC, formed in 1995, innovated through its cooperative commercializing model, offering support for small-scale farmers to increase yields, access credit, and receive higher and more stable prices for their products (Suárez Carrera 2011).

These two types of groups have come together in episodic large-scale social movements, the largest of which erupted in 2002 under the mantle of El Campo no Aguanta Más (The Countryside Can't Take It Anymore). This movement listed a set of demands oriented to secure the economic sustainability of small-scale farming, including a moratorium on the agricultural terms of NAFTA, the construction of a new state rural financial institution, and an increase in the percent of the federal budget allocated to production supports (Bartra 2007). This movement culminated in an agreement with the Fox administration—the National Agreement for the Countryside (Acuerdo Nacional para el Campo)—which promised to increase budgets for support programs, privileging producer organizations' role as intermediaries. However, the state's refusal to respond to the more transformative demands created a schism in the movement, with several organizations refusing to sign the agreement. Critics claimed that late incorporation of the CNC into negotiations hijacked the movement to push for larger allocations for use in clientelistic strategies while acquiescence to only symbolic gestures by the government in response to the movement's more fundamental demands (Bartra 2007). ANEC and CCC remained in the faction that signed the agreement and, while disappointed in the failure of the movement to produce substantial change in rural development policy, were promised a role in mediating a growing share of compensatory subsidies for small-scale farmers.

Perhaps as much as economic transition, electoral transformation altered the playing field for rural interest organizations. The 1988 presidential election and the ensuing creation of the PRD revived the dissident peasant movement, including both factions of the CNC that had broken off in previous years and long-time outsiders. Discontent with PRI rule, owing to the withdrawal of agricultural supports and this party's practice of controlling and co-opting rural organization, dissident peasant organizations rallied at the possibility of a new interlocutor, many campaigning on behalf of Cuauhtémoc Cárdenas, the presidential candidate in 1988 who would go on the next year to found the PRD.

While only the UCD, formed by PRD operatives, declared an overt party alliance, several formally non-partisan national confederations of rural organizations emerged or revived in the late 1980s and 1990s as PRD allies. Some of the largest included the CCC, CIOAC, ANEC, CNPA (National Confederation "Plan de Ayala"), and UNORCA (National Union of Regional Autonomous Peasant Organizations) (de Grammont and Mackinlay 2006).[32] These confederations pursue a spectrum of political strategies. CIOAC and CNPA, founded in the 1970s, espouse a socialist discourse and once had ties to socialist parties; UNORCA, espoused a vehement non-partisanship at its founding in 1985, yet by 1989 succumbed to co-optation by the CNC (Mackinlay 1996, 201); and the CCC, ANEC, and several others, consolidated in the aftermath of the 1988 election, have some degree of electoral ties to the PRD or other left-wing parties.[33] In the neoliberal environment, however, the programmatic demands of these groups are quite similar, as reflected in their cooperation in the El Campo no Aguanta Más movement.

What has varied—and created confrontations within the peasant movement—is the steadfastness with which these organizations prioritize programmatic goals versus the extraction of distributive benefits. Among national peasant organizations, ANEC is unique in its promotion of a specific economic model—the cooperative commercializing firm—and has several state-level affiliates that combine this productive model with programmatic demand-making (Appendini 2003, 266–69). ANEC has maintained a formal non-partisan stance, although its founder and highest authority has been a member of Congress with the PRD and in 2018 was named an undersecretary in López Obrador's agricultural ministry. CCC is

32. El Barzón is another organization with a large rural presence, but also including middle-class urban elements. This organization emerged following the 1994 economic crisis and peso devaluation, demanding debt forgiveness for farmers and homeowners whose debt obligations were compounded by the crisis (de Grammont 2001).

33. See García Ponce (2009) and Suárez Carrera (2011) on the histories and platforms of the CCC and ANEC, respectively.

the largest dissident rural organization and is most active in delivering agricultural and social-development subsidies to its members, but its involvement in state-level programmatic policies varies by state. The CCC has from its beginnings declared non-partisanship, while often campaigning on behalf of the PRD, However, the CCC departed from its non-partisan stance in 2011, forming an overt alliance with the Nueva Izquierda (New Left) faction of the PRD. The CCC is today affiliated with López Obrador's party, MORENA.

Finally, the CNC has persisted as the PRI's rural sector throughout the period of electoral competition. In states where the PRI has lost the governorship, the CNC has hemorrhaged members, many flocking to dissident groups, particularly if the PRD or MORENA governs. The CNC made a modest comeback under the Peña Nieto administration and, in recent years, has seen factions break off to ally with MORENA. However, the CNC today is much less a representative of smallholder agricultural interests than a rural campaign operation and patronage network for the PRI; unlike dissident organizations, the CNC gave sanction to the 1992 land reform and the agricultural clause of NAFTA (Mackinlay 1996). During the twelve years of national PAN rule—2000–2012—the CNC's clout declined further, without dissolving completely as it maintained a foothold in government through dozens of congressional seats that the PRI grants to CNC leaders. At the same time dissident organizations experienced a marginal increase in their access to state decision makers during the Fox administration. Fox's (perhaps reluctant) openness to working with these groups was evidenced in his willingness to sit down at the negotiating table with the El Campo No Aguanta Más movement. However, the most notable aspect of PAN administrations' rural development policies was the promotion of export-oriented producers capable of competing on international commodity markets, accompanied by a middling attempt to support small producers by subsidizing commercializing cooperatives (Mestries Benquet 2007, 199–205).

Changes in Small-Business Development and Consequences for Organizing

While not as devastating as in the small-scale agricultural sector, free-market reforms introduced new challenges for organizing in the small-business sector as well. Facing the revocation of mandatory membership requirements most business chambers responded by adopting member service model to sustain collective action. Other chambers, however, particularly those representing small industrial firms, came to specialize in the extraction of state subsidies, which had become increasingly prevalent under pro-business PAN presidencies post-2000. Small-business organizations faced lighter headwinds in sustaining collective action through the transition, as the Mexican state sustained modified versions of corporatist supports, particularly during the dozen years of PAN rule.

Market-based reforms introduced economic pressures for Mexican firms. NAFTA and other trade agreements paved the way for multinational corporations that would compete with locally owned firms, while benefitting certain domestic firms that were prepared to offer complementary services, such as transportation and construction and regions that were positioned to invest in manufacturing and high-tech business clusters (Alba Vega 2002; Puga 2004, 217–22). It is not difficult to identify sectors that were adversely affected by the advent of free trade. Traditional industrial sectors, such as textile and shoe manufacturers, have been unable to compete with cheap Chinese imports and small commercial firms have folded in the face of competition from multinational giants like Walmart, Home Depot, and Starbucks.

With privatizations of close to 200 state-owned enterprises with a total value of over 18 billion dollars during the Salinas administration, owners of huge corporations, both domestic and multinational, became the protagonists of Mexico's economy (Puga 2004, 76–80). Where chamber confederations had traditionally been the privileged representatives of business in economic policymaking, big business owners and executives supplanted the chambers under Presidents Salinas and Zedillo. Magnates such as Claudio X. Gonzalez (Kimberly-Clark Mexico), Carlos Slim (TelMex), Emilio Azcárraga (Televisa), and Roberto Servitje (Bimbo)—had the ear of NAFTA negotiators, both through personal relationships and through the CCE, which sided to a greater degree with the export-promoting interests of big business than the protectionist impulses of the chambers. During the Salinas administration, pro-NAFTA elements such as the Business Coordinator for Foreign Trade (COECE) assumed leadership of the CCE (Schneider 2004, 86–88; Shadlen 2004, 92–94). Salinas named González, a former president of the CMHN and CCE, Special Adviser to the President on Economic Issues, formalizing the direct contact with the highest levels of Mexican politics that big business had previously enjoyed only informally.

The organizations most associated with small-business interests, CONCANACO, CANACINTRA, and COPARMEX fell in line with the

CCE's pro-NAFTA posture, receiving only loose promises that the Zedillo administration would pursue policies to help small business transition to a free-market economy. CANACINTRA, which stands outs from other industrial chambers for its concentration of small firms, led the charge in pressing Zedillo to pursue a more active industrial policy to protect and promote small firms that were struggling to compete on international markets (Johnson Ceva 1998, 139–40; Shadlen 2004, 42–43). However, Zedillo's administration was hampered significantly by the 1994 economic crisis, leading to austerity and a focus on macroeconomic stability over promotion of domestic industry. As a result, Zedillo's protectionist measures were small and narrowly defined, such as a tariff on shoe and textile imports that applied only to countries *without* trade agreements with Mexico (Johnson Ceva 1998, 149–50).

Zedillo also delivered a damaging blow to small-business collective action by reforming the Law of Chambers in 1997, removing the mandatory membership requirement, which led to a precipitous decline in chamber membership. This reform came at the behest of both anti-corporatist elements in the new PRI as well as pressure from outsider small-business insurgencies that complained that official chambers had abandoned their interests in acquiescing to NAFTA and that the mandatory membership requirement violated business owners' freedom of association (Puga 2004, 230–34; Shadlen 2004, 103–07). This reform hit CANACINTRA the hardest, which had historically relied the most on state supports to sustain collective action among its precarious small-scale industrialist membership base. Shadlen (2004, 121–22) reports that CANACINTRA's membership fell from nearly 90,000 to 15,000 in 1997, representing only 5 percent of industrial firms. Corporatist support for chambers was not completely withdrawn, however, as the 1997 reform also introduced the Mexican Business Information System (SIEM), a database of firms that Mexican businesses were required to sign up for, at a nominal yearly charge.[34] Chambers were given the exclusive right to sign firms up for the SIEM, keeping one half of the fee themselves, granting a constant source of funding and an entrée to recruit firms as chamber members. Today, many chambers rely on this process as their principal source of funding and in interviews would give the number of SIEM affiliates as their membership base, which was typically two to five times the size of active dues-paying chamber membership.

34. While the Law of Chambers declares SIEM enrollment as mandatory, Ministry of the Economy personnel estimate that over half of Mexican formal-sector firms do not participate, in addition to all informal-sector firms.

Following these reforms, state and federal PAN administrations assiduously courted small-business organizations. The Fox administration (2000–2006) reinvigorated corporatist relationships with business chambers that had decayed during the nadir of PRI rule through the creation of subsidy and training programs that operated through these organizations: the México Emprende (Mexico Entrepreneur) program placed small-business support offices in CONCANACO, CANACINTRA, and COPARMEX affiliates and Fondo PyME—Fox's flagship small-business subsidy program—included a provision allowing business organizations to design and implement projects, often retaining a portion of the benefits themselves. No longer counting on mandatory membership, chambers would now capitalize on these programs to recruit new firms through the promise of subsidized services, participation in conventions, and opportunities to meet politicians.

As a result, the past two decades have witnessed a retrenchment of business organizations as voluntary organizations, no longer as large in membership or as influential in national policymaking as during the mid-century period. Chambers that thrive are those that have placed an emphasis on providing valuable services for their members, such as training, consulting, and networking opportunities, and have established themselves as key opinion leaders in state and local politics.[35] Chambers that have failed to deliver these productive services rely on income from SIEM and broker small-business subsidies from the state or federal government to attract members. Where PAN administrations rule, these organizations are often granted institutional spaces for participation in consultative councils and other participatory institutions at all levels of government. Chambers of commerce commonly press for tighter enforcement of regulations against informal commerce, infrastructure and transportation improvements, and

35. On the other hand, experiments in uniformly small-business organizations have been largely unsuccessful. As Shadlen (2004) details, the National Association of the Industry of Transformation (ANIT), a break-off of CANACINTRA in 1986, experienced initial success in policy battles, claiming credit, for instance, for the revocation of mandatory chamber membership. However, ANIT declined into irrelevance in the 2000s owing to disadvantages in political access and funding compared with CANACINTRA. CANACOPE includes thirty-seven chambers operating in cities that also have National Chambers of Commerce (CANACOs), which typically dwarf CANACOPE in size. CANACOPE affiliates belong to the CONCANACO, but interviewed personnel at the confederation headquarters say that CANACOPE chambers typically participate very little.

transparency in government contracting. While more precarious, chambers of industry encourage investment in industrial parks and active industrial policies to promote domestic production.[36] Chamber leaders typically enjoy direct access to governors and cabinet members and are often nominated to run for executive office.

COPARMEX, in contrast, is known to be more autonomous and critical of government action. Since its initiation as an agent of employers' interests in labor matters, COPARMEX has broadened its mandate to promote policies identified as central to democratic strengthening and economic growth, positioning the confederation as the preeminent national civil society organization speaking on behalf of the private sector and a natural ally to the PAN (albeit without a formal alliance). The national confederation and subnational delegations issue statements and commission studies concerning macroeconomic policy, education, security, and transparency reforms. While COPARMEX is non-partisan, state delegations frequently organize debates among candidates, election-monitoring initiatives, and get-out-the vote campaigns. Without the benefit of SIEM, COPARMEX branches—of which there are eighty-two nationwide—tend to have smaller memberships than CONCANACO and CANACINTRA members. Recruitment is achieved instead by offering training and consulting—often subsidized by México Emprende and Fondo PyME—and through the organization's prestige as a shaper of public opinion and policy actor.

New Party Organizations and Incorporation Strategies for Business and Rural Organizations

The dual transitions not only affected the organizational arena; they also had important consequences for the electoral arena. Simultaneously with its

36. In addition to the umbrella confederations of industry and commerce, Mexico has a variety of sector-specific chambers such as the National Chamber for the Textile Industry (Cámara Nacional de la Industria del Vestido, CONAIVE), the Mexican Chamber for the Construction Industry (Cámara Mexicana de la Industria de la Construcción, CMIC), and the National Chamber for the Restaurant and Prepared-Foods Sector (Cámara Nacional de la Industria de Restaurantes y Alimentos Condimentados, CANIRAC), all of which are members of CONCAMIN. These chambers also benefit from the SIEM system, and are occasional intermediaries of Fondo PyME projects, but they are not members of the CCE and their advocacy efforts are typically limited to sector-specific policies.

embracing of a free-market economic model, the PRI underwent a reform of its organizational structure and electoral strategies, while the PAN and PRD claimed important subnational victories and introduced multi-party competition on the national and subnational levels. These shifts had important implications for the ways that these three parties relate with interest organizations that belong to their core and non-core constituencies. For the PRI, core organizations are those that belong to its sectoral organizations—the CNC in the case of this study. While these popular-sector sectoral organizations ceased sharing programmatic goals with the PRI once this party transitioned to a market-led model, they continued to be organizationally incorporated into the party. Through the transition, the PRI came to rely less on its sectoral organizations for campaigning, while still deploying these as patronage networks. Core organizations for the former opposition parties are those organizations that share programmatic goals and/or have an overlapping membership with the parties. These organizations—small-business for the PAN and dissident agriculture for the PRD—may or may not have formal alliances with the party. Newly governing PAN and PRD administrations varied in the degree to which they sought to solidify programmatic ties with core organizations and/or constructed linkages with both core and non-core groups through patronage appeals.

During the Salinas and Zedillo administrations (1988–2000), the PRI undertook reforms, both to its formal party statutes and to its informal practices of leadership selection, with the goal of modernizing the party and retaining the electoral upper hand in the face of increasing electoral threats from the PAN and PRD. The first of these was to shift from an electoral mass mobilizing party—based on sectoral confederations—to a catch-all party, combining mass media appeals with the clientelistic mobilization of voters (Burgess and Levitsky 2003; Greene 2007; Magaloni 2006). The traditional sectors—labor, peasants, and the popular sector—were downplayed within the party. Post-1988 reforms to party statutes allowed for individual party affiliation (membership had previously been solely through the sectors) and transitioned to a geographic party structure, which led to a reduction in nominations to elected office for CNC and other sectoral representatives (Langston 2001, 2017, chap. 7). The technocratic wing of the party had prevailed over the populist wing, much of which departed the party to support Cárdenas in 1988 (Bruhn 1997). The technocrats espoused neoliberal economic principles that conflicted with the programmatic demands of the majority of their sectoral organizations, particularly with the CNC, and were thus eager to weaken these organizations' roles in the party. However,

PRI leaders recognized the value that the CNC offered in mobilizing rural voters, and thus preserved the confederation as a rural electoral operation (Mackinlay 1996).

Another consequence of the PRI's shift away from an organizational base was a transition in the way it dealt with non-core organizations—those that did not belong to its sectoral organizations. While the PRI had historically sought to monopolize the organizational infrastructure—granting privileged access to corporatist organizations in every sector and co-opting and/or repressing dissident groups through the famed "two carrots, then a stick" approach (Smith 1979, 57)—the neoliberal PRI increasingly took to simply ignoring party outsiders. This neglect is perhaps due to the increasing centrality of the mass media for electoral campaigns and lessons learned from public outcry in response to repression of opposition groups, which severely damaged the party's public image in the 1970s and 1980s. Thus, organizations that are not predisposed to support the PRI, such as non-partisan business chambers or dissident peasant organizations, enjoy greater autonomy in PRI-governed states than they did thirty years ago, but also find themselves shut out of policymaking, particularly where the PRI is dominant. However, where the PRI faces electoral threats or is seeking to reclaim power in states that it has lost to the PAN or PRD, it has incentives to co-opt these non-core groups, typically through contingent patronage appeals.

The PAN was founded in 1939 as a classic externally mobilized, programmatic party and was highly successful at incorporating core small-business organizations into programmatic policies once it won gubernatorial and federal elections fifty years later. The period of electoral transition saw the PAN shift from an ideologically committed also-ran, tied to Catholic doctrine and liberal economic principles, to a major competitive party. This party won its first gubernatorial election in 1989, in the state of Baja California. While small-business organizations had historically been wary to associate themselves with a minor "protest" party, the PRI's perceived mishandling of the economy in the 1970s and turn to big business in the 1980s, coupled with the PAN's important gubernatorial victories in the 1990s, paved the way for the construction of new linkages with small business (Middlebrook 2001, 21–24; Wuhs 2010). The urge to win more elections led to a broadening of the party's programmatic agenda and the incursion of "neopanistas," most of whom were prominent businessmen less committed to the party's ideological principles than to the institution of good governance and the defeat of the PRI (Mizrahi 2003, 80–84; Shirk

2005, 98–100).[37] Among these neopanistas were many leaders of business organizations, such as COPARMEX, CONCANACO, and CANACINTRA, who commonly received nominations for elected office and cabinet posts.[38] Integrating business leaders into the party served two functions: quickly building societal ties by associating itself with prestigious and programmatically compatible organizations; and availing administrations of capable administrators, given that, in the 1990s, the PAN was bereft of figures with government experience.

In contrast to the PAN, the PRD was founded with the immediate goal of winning high-level office, and thus did not have the chance to establish organic linkages to core organizations prior to mobilizing its allies in campaigns. The ascendancy of the PRD was much more sudden than the PAN, as this party was born from a split in the PRI in the lead-up to the 1988 presidential election. In this election, Cuauhtémoc Cárdenas (son of Lázaro) broke from the PRI, running for president with a coalition of small leftist parties called the National Democratic Front (Frente Democrático Nacional FDN). After narrowly losing to Carlos Salinas—in an election infamous for fraud—Cárdenas and his allies registered the PRD as a party, inaugurating the first period of electoral competition in modern Mexico. In the interest arena, the PRD was beset by a tension between its opposition to the PRI's mode of coercive corporatism and the mandate to consolidate ties to the popular-sector organizations that had contributed to the party's rise (Bruhn 1997, 210–27; López Leyva 2007, chap. 4). This tension was exacerbated by the fact that PRD elites had been politically baptized within the PRI and thus were prone to replicate the dominant party's practice of co-optation through patronage ties. And while the PRD's natural allies—urban popular movements, dissident rural organizations, and dissident

---

37. The broadening of the party spurred objections from long-time party figures concerned about the ideological purity of the PAN, a rift that reached its highest point during Fox's presidency, pitting the "foxistas" against the "doctrinarios" (Loaeza 2010, 199–204). The PAN retains safeguards to preserve its right-wing, good governance character, such as a resistance to granting nominations to PRI defectors and the expulsion of party members seen to contradict party principles (Mizrahi 2003, 96–103).

38. COPARMEX in particular has been a springboard for PAN politicians. PAN gubernatorial candidates in the states of Baja California, Chihuahua, Guanajuato, Puebla, Sinaloa, and Sonora were previous COPARMEX presidents, as were two presidential candidates, Manuel Clouthier and Vicente Fox (Mizrahi 2003, 168 n. 15).

union federations—proudly espoused their electoral autonomy—many soon succumbed to clientelist patterns of mobilization, mediated through leaders who had become PRD-embedded brokers (Bruhn 2013; Haber 2013; Hilgers 2008; Holland and Palmer-Rubin 2015, 1208–11). Whether the party seriously pursued a new model of programmatic linkages with these organizations depended on the founding traits of subnational party organizations.

While the PRD's electoral base was concentrated in urban areas, dissident agricultural organizations also constituted core organizations for this party, as they shared a rejection of the neoliberal economic model and a desire for more state intervention in rural development. In a less coherent way than the PAN did with business, the PRD made attempts to consolidate programmatic ties to these organizations, even creating its own *campesino* sector, the UCD. However, programmatic incorporation was obstructed by two factors that were less present in the case of the PAN and business. First, the fragmented and conflictive nature of the PRD's party organization forced rural organizations to form linkages with factions within the party, inserting them into intra-party rivalries and complicating the process of granting concessions and nominations, which were often doled out through contentious intra-party negotiations (Bruhn 1997, 225). Second, many rural organizations such as the UCD were centrally patronage seeking by the time the PRD began winning elections in the early 2000s and thus unprepared and uninterested in collaborating with PRD politicians on a comprehensive model for rural development favoring small-scale farmers (de Grammont and Mackinlay 2006).[39]

In addition to building ties to these core groups, PAN and PRD administrations attempted to create new ties to non-core organizations. This process posed a significant challenge, given that business organizations were ideologically opposed to the PRD's economic principles and dissident agricultural organizations were antagonistic to the right-wing PAN's embracing of neoliberal policies. In response, these parties pursued two strategies. First, they identified or constructed new organizational allies with programmatic alignment in non-core sectors. For instance, the PAN, historically bereft of ties to the countryside, built linkages with export-oriented

39. Similar factors also played out in the PRD's relationships to urban popular movements in Mexico City (Bruhn 2013, 150–52; Hilgers 2008, 142–47). I discuss this additional case in Chapter 8.

large-scale farmers and agribusiness. Second, these parties would reach out to non-core organizations opportunistically with patronage appeals in the lead-up to elections. While the prospect of long-term linkages with non-core organizations on the basis of shared programmatic goals is unrealistic, such short-term arrangements at times proved worthwhile for both party and organization.

Conclusion

This chapter has undertaken a brief historical analysis to lay out two sets of antecedent conditions for the remainder of the analysis. First, I have shown how transitions in Mexico's economic development model and electoral landscape have shaped the interest organizations in the small-scale agricultural sector and small-business sector. The loosening of corporatist ties between the state and the traditionally favored confederations in these sectors—the CNC, CONCANACO, and CONCAMIN—created pressure for these organizations to offer new services to sustain an active membership. Furthermore, economic pressures from the onset of free-market competition increased the precariousness of small-scale farmers and small industry. The CNC, as insiders in the PRI's patronage system, monolithically conformed to an external model of organizational capacity, specializing in the brokerage of patronage benefits allocated by PRI governments. In contrast, confederations of business chambers attempted to weather the transition to voluntary associations by providing consulting and networking services to small firms, while some came to rely on renewed corporatist supports under PAN administrations.

Dissident confederations—those created outside the PRI corporatist system—include COPARMEX and a bevy of peasant associations, such as the CCC and ANEC. With a stable service delivery and programmatic outsider stance since its founding, COPARMEX affiliates have thrived, and have enjoyed improved access to policy under federal and state PAN administrations. In contrast, dissident peasant confederations have followed one of two paths. Some developed internal organizational capacity models based on services that assist peasants in remaining profitable under a market-led rural development model. Others—particularly those formed as insiders to the PRD—recreated CNC-style patronage mediation with this new party.

While the national story is sufficient to explain CNC and COPARMEX affiliates' approach to policy demands, the other four confederations present more significant internal variation. In the next three chapters, I integrate findings from an original survey of these four confederations with field research findings from Estado de México, Jalisco, and Michoacán to explain subnational variation in demand-making strategies. Chapter 3 lays out the two distinct strategies for sustaining organizational capacity in the context of this transition: the internal model, based on offering member services; and the external model, based on patronage brokerage. Chapters 4 and 5 analyze demand-making in the agricultural and small-business sectors, respectively. In these two chapters, I show how those organizations that converted successfully to internal organizational capacity strategies were best positioned to levy programmatic demands on behalf of their sectors.

In this chapter I have also shown how transitions in party organizations have modified the routine ways in which the three major parties of Mexico's democratic transition engage with interest organizations in the electoral and policymaking spheres. As the PRI embraced neoliberalism and confronted electoral challenges from the left and right, it subordinated corporatist ties to its sectoral base organizations such as the CNC and engaged in the selective co-optation of non-core groups with targeted patronage benefits, especially when facing an electoral threat. In contrast, PAN and PRD state-level administrations have attempted to consolidate ties to core organizations—small-business and dissident agriculture, respectively—and to incorporate these organizations into institutions for programmatic policy deliberation. This process has been less smooth for the PRD, which has struggled with internal factions and a middling commitment to programmatic engagement with core allies. In Chapters 6 and 7, I continue my analysis of the parties' incorporation strategies, showing how founding traits of state-level party organizations interacted with core organizations' demand-making strategies to yield different outcomes for sectoral representation.

PART 2

Demand Formation in Organizations

CHAPTER 3

Organizational Capacity

The CCC and ANEC are two of the largest rural organizations in Mexico. These organizations were founded in the 1980s and 1990s in opposition to the PRI's coercive rural corporatism and narrow favoritism of the CNC and other insiders with subsidies. The CCC and ANEC have participated together in large-scale protests, demanding a reversal of market-based reforms to rural development policy. Yet today, these two organizations' paths have diverged significantly.

Most affiliates of the CCC are *organizaciones de gestión.* This term is well-known among rural organizations and more broadly in Mexican civil society to refer to organizations that specialize in the brokerage of government programs.[1] Even though rules of application for these programs—such as subsidies for agricultural inputs, small-business investments, or housing materials—usually stipulate no role for organizational representatives, CCC affiliates specialize in delivering these benefits to members. In fact, the promise of helping members gain these government benefits is their central tool for recruiting, retaining, and mobilizing members. *Gestión* services provided by organizations are comprehensive. These organizations: (1) select and

1. In Mexico—as in many semi-institutionalized democracies—discretion in the allocation of distributive programs is commonplace. What is perhaps distinctive about the Mexican case is that many of these programs are formally subject to quite technocratic rules and formula-based processes for evaluating applications, based on the quality of the projects proposed, the deservingness of the applicant, and the program's target population. Nonetheless, in practice, these programs are often allocated according to partisan criteria; highly bureaucratic application procedures serve to filter unwanted applicants (Cejudo, Lugo, and Michel 2018; Garay, Palmer-Rubin, and Poertner 2020; Rizzo 2019).

rank the beneficiaries whom they will aid; (2) design the projects, often asking for identical amounts of funding for identical investments across dozens of applications; (3) communicate to development ministry personnel which projects come from their members, and in what priority they should be funded; (4) negotiate with politicians for a greater number of "their" applications to be funded; (5) organize sit-ins and protests to pressure politicians to follow through on their promises; (6) deliver the benefits (reserving a commission for the organization); and (7) publicize these programs and their success in accessing them though festive events.

Given how successful the CCC is at delivering these benefits ("*bajar recursos*" or "bringing down resources" to use the common language), it is not surprising that they are one of the largest organizations in rural Mexico and wield substantial political power. Yet this mode of sustaining collective action—which I refer to as *externally generated organizational capacity*—has consequences for the organization's ability to represent its members in policymaking. The leaders become firmly entrenched in their positions, monopolizing the *gestión* process and converting into brokers who control and coerce members through the power derived from control of these benefits. The organizational model attracts and reinforces a self-interested membership, who view the organization through the short-term lens of personal consumption rather than long-term goals of improving economic conditions for their sector. And the organization becomes dependent on the political party that favors it in the allocation of distributive programs, ceding autonomy over its goals and strategies and sacrificing legitimacy in the eyes of other parties.

ANEC is another rural confederation that operates according to completely different norms. Where the CCC specializes in delivering benefits for *consumption*, ANEC brings members together to participate in joint activities of *production*. ANEC affiliates' main attraction to members is the operation of a cooperative that collectively negotiates higher prices for corn, wheat, and other grains that members produce. ANEC additionally helps members access loans and insurance and operates training programs to help members increase yields and diversify to incorporate higher value crops.

This organizational model—which I refer to as *internally generated organizational capacity*—produces a quite distinct set of dynamics than those that are found in *organizaciones de gestión*. ANEC attracts a membership base that is more homogenous in their economic positions and policy interests—small and medium-sized grain farmers eager to improve their production conditions. And through participation in the cooperative and other organization activities, they generate a collective consciousness, viewing their well-being according to collective goals that correspond to small-scale grain farmers. Members remain in the organization for a long time, building capacity and rotating through leadership. And without dependence on any party for patronage benefits, the organization eschews partisanship, retaining autonomy to interact with politicians of all parties and to combine insider tactics (such as lobbying) with outsider tactics (like protest or media campaigns).

Both of these organizations are thriving, with a growing and active membership and substantial political power. In other words, both organizations have *high levels* of organizational capacity. Yet *the way* that they sustain this capacity varies markedly.

This chapter conceptualizes organizational capacity and explains the origins of these contrasting (i.e., internal vs. external) organizational capacity models in the Mexican agricultural and small-business sectors. This constitutes the first step in a causal process that explains the types of policy demands that interest organizations make; and ultimately how these organizations represent their sectors in economic policymaking. Chapters 4 and 5 show how organizational capacity models shape *demand-making* in these two sectors, respectively. Within each of the business and agriculture sectors in Mexico, there are some organizations that levy *programmatic* demands—which respond to the interests of their sector—and others that strive instead to maximize *patronage* benefits for members. I argue that the source of organizational capacity is the key factor that differentiates programmatic from patronage-oriented organizations. In the last part of this book (Chapters 6 and 7), I show how these demands interact with ruling parties' incorporation strategies to produce different *models of representation*.

The remainder of this chapter is composed of four sections. The first section conceptualizes organizational capacity and its internal and external variants. I also describe the four paths for organizations in this study, which vary based on their organizational capacity models before and after the neoliberal transition. The second section uses data from my original survey of interest organizations to depict overall variation between organizational capacity models for organizations in the agricultural and small-business sectors. The following two sections analyze qualitative evidence pertaining to organizations in the agricultural and small-business sectors. Case studies draw on evidence from three Mexican states with distinct electoral trajectories at the time of research: Jalisco, Michoacán, and Estado de México. In the rural sector, organizations reacted to the demise of corporatism, which favored the CNC with benefits and closed off avenues for dissident groups to access state benefits. Peasant organizations responded to changing patterns of electoral competition on the state level to devise models for organizational capacity based either on service delivery or patronage brokerage. Business organizations also responded to the demise of corporatism—expressed most drastically in the revocation of mandatory membership requirements for chambers—by opting either to devise services for local businesses or to specialize in the brokerage of small-business subsidy programs offered by state and federal PAN governments.

Conceptualizing Organizational Capacity

Before turning their attention to any external pursuits, such as demands for policy, organizations must solve their existential problem of sustaining an active membership. In the words of James Q. Wilson (1974, 10), "(w)hatever else organizations seek, they seek to survive. To survive they must somehow convince their members that membership is worthwhile." As shown in Table 3.1, organizations can be sorted into two models for generating organizational capacity, the ability to recruit, retain, and mobilize members. First, some organizations generate organizational capacity internally by offering desirable services that serve as selective benefits for members. For example, a rural organization may offer training programs to improve crop yields or a business organization may organize conventions in which affiliated businesses can participate and meet clients. Other organizations' organizational capacity is externally provided. In these cases, the organization acts as an intermediary for benefits provided by an outside actor. In "patronage democracies" (Chandra 2004), such as Mexico, discretionary distributive programs managed by the state often function as such external benefits.

These two models of organizational capacity have consequences for the types of policy demands that the organization makes, as shown in Table 3.1. Organizations that generate organizational capacity internally tend to make programmatic demands and organizations whose organizational capacity is externally provided tend to be limited to patronage demands. As I elaborate on in Chapters 4 and 5, the organizational capacity model shapes demand-making through three mechanisms, having to do with effects on members, on leadership, and on the organization's orientation to the state. Here I briefly elaborate on these three mechanisms.

Table 3.1 Models of Organizational Capacity

	Membership	Leadership	State Engagement	Type of Demands
Internally Generated	Homogeneous	Democratic	Autonomous, multi-faceted	Programmatic
Externally Provided	Heterogeneous	Oligarchic	Dependent brokerage	Patronage

Source: Author's original survey.

First, organizations with internally generated organizational capacity tend to have a more homogeneous membership with a stronger collective consciousness. Because non-elite organizations typically cannot afford to give away costly benefits for consumption such as subsidies or machinery, internally generated services often take on a productive character; that is, they help their members transition to more profitable economic activities. These productive benefits tend to attract a homogeneous group of members that engage in the productive activity in question. Additionally, through participation in the productive activities of the organization, members become socialized to value the collective goals of their sector rather than their narrow personal goals.[2] Participation in these collective enterprises can broaden members' social networks, create collective identities, and engender norms of reciprocity (Andrews et al. 2010; Putnam, Leonardi, and Nanetti 1994). In contrast, organizations that fail to sustain organizational capacity internally, and thus rely on externally provided benefits, attract a more heterogeneous membership that is drawn to broadly appealing types of benefits for consumption that these organizations broker, such as cash subsidies or building materials. These one-off benefits do little to keep members in the organization and may even socialize members to view civic engagement through the lens of personal benefit rather than collective goals (Palmer-Rubin, Garay, and Poertner 2021).

Second, internally generated organizational capacity lends itself to norms of internal democracy and leadership accountability. All organizations are prone to pressures of oligarchization (Michels 1915). Yet these pressures are not felt *equally* in all organizations. Organizations that rely on external resources to sustain organizational capacity are most vulnerable to oligarchic

2. Where these collective goals correspond to the interests of a social class, such socialization approaches what can be described as "class formation" (Katznelson and Zolberg 1986; Przeworski 1986, chap. 2).

pressures because bargaining for these benefits requires that a representative act as a broker for the organization. Such patronage brokers often come to prioritize sustaining their leadership positions—and the political and economic benefits that come with them—over the goals of the base, and thus endeavor to make themselves indispensable (Fox 1992a; Holland and Palmer-Rubin 2015; Stokes et al. 2013). In contrast, where organizations generate their own resources and services through cooperative activities, leaders are developed from within, share power horizontally, and rotate frequently (Han 2014).

The final mechanism connecting organizational capacity to demand-making has to do with the organization's orientation to the state. Internally generated organizational capacity bestows on the organization autonomy in its state engagement, allowing it to engage in contentious action and lobbying with politicians of all parties. In contrast, externally provided benefits typically come with strings attached that limit organizations to mobilize in campaign events on behalf of the party patron to the exclusion of other modes of state engagement. Where organizations depend on political parties, they become restricted in both the types of demands that they can make and the ways in which they can level those demands (Fox 1992a; Garay 2009). These limits come from several causes: the party ally coerces the organization to abandon transformative demands and obstructive mobilization tactics; the organization voluntarily ceases external modes of mobilization to avoid asking too much of members already asked to mobilize electorally; or opposition party figures cease taking the organization seriously once it attains a reputation as a patronage broker for another party.

In addition to depicting variation between these two organizational capacity models, this chapter takes a step back to explain how organizations sort into these two models in the first place. I show that the origins of distinct organizational models have to do with the conditions at the organization's founding, namely whether they were founded during a period with an electoral ally in power and, if not, whether they adopted a sustainable type of internally generated benefit. Combining these two factors, four pathways of organizational capacity can be defined, as shown in Table 3.2: (1) organizations founded with an externally provided model and sustaining this model; (2) organizations founded with an internally generated model and sustaining this model; (3) organizations founded with an internally generated model and transitioning to an externally provided model over time; and (4) organizations founded with an externally provided model and shifting to an internally generated model after state benefits are withdrawn.

Table 3.2 Organizational Capacity Pathways

Founding	Ending	Ally in Power at Founding?	Sustainable benefits model?	Cases
Internal	Internal	No	Yes	ANEC, COPARMEX
Internal	External	No	No	CCC
External	External	Yes	No	CNC, CANACINTRA
External	Internal	Yes	Yes	CONCANACO

Source: Author's original survey.

Organizations that are founded with an ally in power—or the expectation thereof—are prone to establish an externally provided model, as they expect be in a position to broker benefits from the state. Such organizations are likely to thrive as intermediaries of state benefits as long as the ally remains in power and continues to funnel benefits to the organization leader. This has been the fate of the CNC; even as the PRI has lost the presidency and several governorships, this party has enjoyed enough control over discretionary funds to consistently reward allied CNC affiliates with subsidies. Organizations that adopt this external mode of organizational capacity rarely, if ever, revert to an internally provided model.

An exception are some business chambers, particularly chambers of commerce (CONCANACO affiliates) that benefitted from legally mandated mandatory chamber membership to sustain collective action until 1997. These chambers constitute a hybrid case because many were in the practice of offering services to their members during this period yet can be said to have had a largely external model of organizational capacity given the importance of corporatist policies to sustain a membership base. When the mandatory membership requirement was revoked, however, these business chambers had to redouble their emphasis on service delivery, and many chambers were successful at sustaining a vibrant membership through the operation of conventions, training, consulting, legal aid, and other services.

Organizations that were founded without an ally in power were forced to generate their own membership incentives from the start. Lacking external funding, these incentives often take the form of productive services in which the organization itself holds training activities, operates a cooperative, or delivers benefits that otherwise improve the productive potential of members. Where such benefits successfully offer long-term incentives for members to participate—as in the operation of a cooperative—this model is sustainable. An example of such a case is ANEC, a national-level network of grain cooperatives. Founded in 1995 as a vehemently non-partisan organization, ANEC's central appeal to members was the ability to help them improve their productivity, and to be more profitable through participation in a cooperative that negotiates higher prices for and offers access to finance and insurance.

However, where the success of internally generated benefits in sustaining collective action is exhausted, organizations may convert to an external orientation. Such was the plight of several rural organizations that focused on negotiating land claims in 1980s and 1990s Mexico, later finding that their members were no longer interested in participating in a peasant organization because they had sold their land and/or ceased agricultural production. Such organizations shifted to patronage brokerage as a mode of sustaining a membership. This chapter focuses on the largest of such organizations, the CCC. The greater the amount of time that passes from the organization's founding to the entry of a party ally into government, the more likely that organizations will have confronted such a crisis and undergone this transition to an external model.

Cross-Sectoral Comparison in Organizational Capacity Models

An original survey of organizations in the agricultural and small-business sectors conducted in 2012 and 2013 allows me to measure several aspects of organizational activity, including their organizational capacity models. Survey respondents were leaders of state and local affiliates of four confederations: CANACINTRA and CONCANACO in the business sector and ANEC and CCC in the peasant sector. These confederations were chosen to maximize within-confederation variation across representation models, facilitating controlled comparisons. Thus, excluded from the survey were COPARMEX—a uniformly programmatic confederation—and CNC—a uniformly patronage-seeking confederation. In this section I use survey data to describe the overall variation between the agricultural and small-business sectors and the two confederations within each of these sectors that participated in the survey. In the following two chapters I employ these data in multivariate analyses to test the relationship between organizational capacity and demand type.

My quantitative metric of organizational capacity models is made up of two indicators: the diversity of resource flows and the diversity of services offered to members. First, to conduct activities or provide services that appeal to members, organizations require financial resources. While it is difficult to establish an objective amount of funding that is sufficient for an organization, the diversity of an organization's funding sources is an observable trait that reflects an organization's financial autonomy. An organization that counts on several funding sources is less vulnerable to the withdrawal of any single source. The *Resource Flows* variable analyzed is measured as a count of the number of sources of funds, from a list of five categories: membership fees, donations from the confederation, commissions for mediating subsidies, payments for services, and other lucrative activities.

A second indicator of organizational capacity is the diversity of *Member Services* that organizations offer to their members. Organizations typically must offer selective benefits to recruit, retain, and mobilize members and, as organizations offer a wider variety of services, they are better positioned to sustain collective action by responding to the economic needs of members. This variable is measured as a count of the number of different services offered to members, from a list of five categories: consulting or project design, access to credit, helping access government programs, legal aid (such as help in resolving land or employment conflict), and other services. To the extent that organizations offer more of these services, they can be said to generate organizational capacity internally.

Figure 3.1 illustrates the mean and standard deviations of five-point indices of each of these two dimensions for organizations that participated in the survey, grouped by confederation. Overall, these data reveal little cross-sector or cross-confederation variation in means. Mean number of resources are between two and three for organizations in all confederations. And representatives of agricultural organizations reported offering roughly four different services while business chambers reported offering about three services.

I offer two notes for interpreting these data. First, the most notable variation on each of these indicators is actually *within* rather than *across* confederations as reflected in the wide bands showing standard deviations. This suggests that much of the cause for these distinctions generates from specific traits of individual organizations rather than sectoral trends or practices imparted by confederation leadership. Second, an important qualifier to these figures is that they reflect whether a given organization has engaged in the form of fundraising or service delivery in question *at all* in the year prior to the survey. Thus, the survey does not provide evidence to distinguish intensity, such as whether a given revenue source accounts for a large or insignificant portion of the budget, or whether a given service was a central element of the organization's activities. Furthermore, social

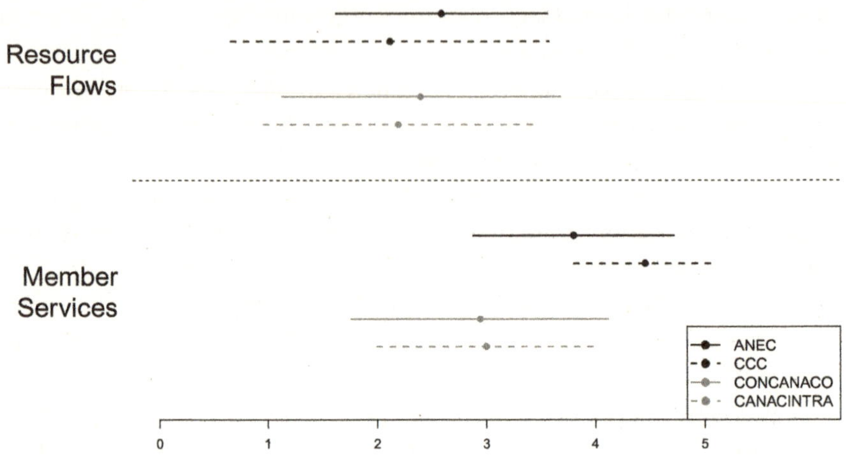

Figure 3.1 Cross-Confederation Comparison in Resource Flows and Member Services
Source: Author's original survey.
Note: Points represent mean number of positive responses for organizations on five-point questions and bars reflect standard deviations.

desirability bias may certainly have caused respondents to overreport these activities. Such bias would cast doubt on overall averages but is unlikely to affect rankings of organizations within confederations or sectors.

The following two tables break down the components of the resource and services indices for each of the four confederations. These data reveal three central observations about organizational capacity in these two sectors. (1) Business organizations have an advantage in generating resources given that their membership base is made up of middle-class citizens capable of paying dues. (2) However, within-sector variation is more notable than across-sector variation, suggesting that these two sectors' differing social class positions are not wholly determinative of differing organizational capacity models. (3) Practically all organizations participate to some degree in the brokerage of distributive programs as a tactic to generate resources and attract members; the key variation relates to their ability to *also* generate resources and collective action internally, thus evading dependence on state resources.

I proceed by analyzing the sources of organizations' financial resources. As shown in Table 3.3, none of the agricultural organizations reported collecting membership fees, while over three-quarters of business organizations report doing so. For some agricultural organizations, this negative response may

Table 3.3 Resource Flows Across the Four Confederations

	Agriculture			Business		
	CCC (N = 25)	ANEC (N = 11)	All Ag. Org's (N = 36)	CANA-CINTRA (N = 14)	CON-CANACO (N = 53)	All Bus. Org's (N = 67)
Membership Fees	0%	0%	0%	78.6%	77.4%	77.6%
Donations from Confed.	16%	45.5%	25.0%	7.1%	34.0%	28.4%
Commission for Subsidies	40%	27.3%	36.1%	28.6%	26.4%	26.9%
Payments for Services	76%	90.9%	80.6%	50.0%	52.8%	52.2%
Other Lucrative Activity	16%	36.4%	22.2%	57.1%	52.8%	53.7%
Mean Number of Sources	2.2	2.6	2.3	2.2	2.4	2.4

Source: Author's original survey.

be technically true, while in reality they do ask for nominal voluntary donations from members.[3] In any case, agricultural organizations are unable to sustain operational expenses through dues alone and most representatives interviewed reported that their main source of revenue was a commission charged for subsidies acquired for members or a percentage of proceeds from a cooperative. Of the other resources listed in Table 3.3, charging a commission for subsidies represents the most external form of revenue, as it is contingent on state agencies approving applications for organization members for whom the organization has advocated. Thirty-six percent of agricultural organizations generate revenue in this way, with a slightly higher percentage of CCC affiliates (40 percent) than ANEC affiliates (27 percent). In contrast, ANEC affiliates were more likely than CCC affiliates to engage in each of the other three modes of fundraising—donations from the confederation, payments for services, and other lucrative activities (such as operating a cooperative). These latter two signify internally generated resources and bestow financial autonomy on the organization.

3. Both of the CCC affiliates interviewed and described below reported requesting a "voluntary contribution" of twenty pesos per month to cover operational expenses (Interviews, Carlos González, Secretary-General, CCC-Michoacán, December 14, 2011; Miguel Ángel Rodríguez, Secretary-General, CCC-Jalisco, June 6, 2012).

Moving to the business sector, there is very little difference in the average amount and types of resource flows reported by CANACINTRA and CONCANACO chambers. (Further data in Chapters 4 and 5 explores the significant within-confederation variation.) The only sizeable distinction is that chambers of commerce (CONCANACO affiliates) receive funding from the confederation at a much higher rate than industrial chambers (CANACINTRA affiliates), likely due to the distinct structures of these two confederations. CONCANACO is more decentralized, while CANACINTRA affiliates delegate more responsibilities (such as lobbying, producing newsletters, organizing events) to the central organization in Mexico City.

Chambers belonging to these two confederations average between two and three sources of funding, similar to agricultural organizations. However, the largest contrast that emerges between business chambers and agricultural organizations is that the most common source of funding for the former are payments for services while the most common source of funding for business organizations are membership fees. These fees take on two different forms. First, all business chambers receive some portion of their fees as commission for enrolling local businesses in the SIEM.[4] These yearly payments vary based on the size of the business from 100 to 670 pesos (about 6–40 dollars). Half of the SIEM fee accrues to the enrolling chamber. In addition to SIEM fees, organizations have an additional chamber membership, with yearly fees ranging from 2,000 to 5,000 pesos (about 120–300 dollars). While membership practices vary widely among chambers, it is common for roughly 10–20 percent of SIEM enrollees to also be chamber members.

Roughly similar proportions of agricultural organizations and business chambers report accepting commissions from subsidies, while a higher percentage of agricultural organizations report payments for services (81 percent vs. 52 percent reported in Table 3.3). As mentioned above, for agricultural organizations, these services often take the form of designing projects to apply for government programs. Finally, business organizations engage in "other lucrative activities" at higher rates—over

4. In practice, the extent to which chambers emphasize the SIEM varies drastically. Some chambers have made this process their central organizational goal—hiring personnel with the express purpose of recruiting businesses door-to-door—while at the other extreme some chamber reported encouraging local businesses to defy this imposition.

Table 3.4 Member Services Across the Four Confederations

	Agriculture			Business		
	CCC (N = 25)	ANEC (N = 11)	All Ag. Org's (N = 36)	CANA-CINTRA (N = 16)	CON-CANACO (N = 58)	All Bus. Org's (N = 74)
Consulting, Project Design	100%	90.9%	97.2%	56.3%	53.4%	54.1%
Access to Credit	88%	72.7%	83.3%	62.5%	48.3%	51.4%
Access Gov. Programs	100%	90.9%	97.2%	100%	86.2%	89.2%
Legal Aid	96%	45.5%	80.6%	12.5%	29.3%	25.7%
Other Services	56%	63.6%	58.3%	62.5%	72.4%	70.3%
Mean Number of Services	4.6	3.6	4.2	2.9	2.9	2.9

Source: Author's original survey.

50 percent, compared to 22 percent in the agricultural sector. As high-profile public-facing entities, business chambers are often positioned in their communities to organize events or offer services to tourists, such as the Mariachi Festival in Guadalajara. In contrast, agricultural organizations are much more exclusively linked to their members. Where they operate some lucrative activity, it regards commercializing their members' agricultural products.

The second dimension of organizational capacity is *Member Services*. As shown in Table 3.4, agricultural organizations actually report offering a larger number of services to members on average than small-business chambers, again selecting from a list of five categories of services (4.2 vs. 2.9). The areas where agricultural organizations stand out in particular are in "consulting and project design" and "access to credit." Both of these services could plausibly be related to the process of applying to government subsidies for benefits. This type of service is obviously central to the organizational capacity model for narrowly patronage-oriented organizations, yet, as I describe below in the cases of ANEC, CONCANACO, and COPARMEX, is often an important service offered by organizations that also offer ample services themselves, such as consulting or the operation of a cooperative. An organization has an external organizational capacity model if it relies narrowly on brokerage of these programs to recruit, retain, and mobilize members.

Data from the agricultural sector reveal little differentiation between CCC and ANEC affiliates in the services offered to members. Organizations in both confederations reported offering a majority of the services mentioned, although I lack a measure of the quality of these services or the share of membership that enjoy them. In contrast to Resource Flows, where ANEC affiliates' sources of funds were on average slightly more diverse than CCC affiliates, the latter affiliates average one point *higher* on the five-point count measure of Member Services (4.6 vs. 3.6). The biggest contrast shows up in the legal aid category—most typically related to land disputes. All but one of the CCC affiliates offer this service versus fewer than half of ANEC affiliates.

The focus on dispute resolution for the CCC has to do with the policy environment at this confederation's forming in 1989. The *ejido* system persisted yet was soon to be disrupted by the 1992 PROCEDE agrarian reform, which introduced a mechanism by which *ejidatarios* (collective landholders) could acquire individual titles to their land plots. One of the CCC's main appeals to potential members in this period was helping navigate the bureaucratic process to gain these titles.[5] This service was very successful for recruitment, but less useful for retention, as beneficiaries would cease attending organization events once they had their land title in hand, often selling or renting their land and leaving the countryside altogether.[6] This challenge encouraged the leadership to transition to a *gestión* model—helping members gain access to state funds or subsidized credit to invest in their property. In contrast, ANEC was formed in 1995, when the central preoccupation of small-scale farmers had moved from land tenure to productivity in the face of NAFTA, which introduced cheap imported grains from the U.S. market. ANEC affiliates' central service of operating cooperatives serve as a continuous inducement to members, generating ongoing ties to the organization and norms of collaboration.

Overall, we may highlight two main findings in the cross-sectoral comparison of organizational capacity models. First, agricultural organizations commonly (but not universally) rely on service delivery and *gestión* of government programs to generate income while business organizations sustain themselves through member dues and by offering services to the public. Second, agricultural organizations report offering a greater variety

5. Interview, Santiago Dominguez Luna, Secretary of Organization, Central Campesina Cardenista, July 14, 2012.

6. Dosh (2009) describes this dilemma as the "security trap": organizations specializing in land claims lose their appeal to members once they gain land titles. As a solution to this trap, Dosh argues that organizations can remain active through the integration of a non-material agenda.

of services than business organizations, although three of these—project design, access to credit, and access to government programs—are associated with intermediation of state benefits. In the following two chapters, I will revisit these indicators of organizational capacity models, employing them as explanatory variables to account for individual organizations' demand-making models.

The remainder of this chapter illustrates these two modes of generating organizational capacity qualitatively and traces the roots of this variation in the founding trajectories of the four confederations analyzed. I also discuss two confederations that lack internal variation: COPARMEX, a business organization that is universally devoted to the internally generated model across all subnational affiliates observed; and the CNC, the PRI's peasant confederation that is wholly devoted to mediating patronage for its party's electoral ends.

Organizational Capacity in the Peasant Sector

The CNC operates as a pyramidal hierarchy of brokers, specializing in the intermediation of state benefits and the mobilization of rural populations to attend rallies and vote for the PRI. This monolith of rural organizing in twentieth-century Mexico is the archetype of externally provided organizational capacity, relying on state patronage benefits for its survival. In addition to the CNC, most states count on a large number of "dissident" organizations, promising to remain closer to the needs of farmers rather than elected politicians. These dissident organizations followed two quite distinct paths. Some experienced a brief period of "outsider" activism, participating in widespread protests against neoliberal reforms in agricultural markets in the 1990s and early 2000s, but soon thereafter reproduced CNC-style patronage politics with parties of the left. Other organizations constructed autonomous institutions for delivering services that were valuable to small-scale farmers, such as processing land claims, operating cooperatives, and offering training in production techniques. These latter organizations are the rare success cases for rural collective action that have sustained an internally generated organizational capacity model over the long term.

This section uses case study evidence to illustrate variation between the internal and external modes of generating organizational capacity and traces how dissident peasant organizations fell into one camp or the other. Recall that the overall contrast between ANEC and the CCC presented above with survey data revealed that ANEC affiliates tend to have slightly greater diversity of resource flows, while organizations belonging to both confederations report providing a wide variety of services to members. Case studies, however, add an important caveat to this latter finding. While many organizations report that they provide productive services, in their routine operation some of these organizations focus much more on patronage brokerage, thus exhibiting an external model of organizational capacity.

Case studies illustrate two paths that produce organizations with an external organizational capacity model. First, some organizations adopt this model at their founding due to immediate access to patronage through political allies, or the expectation thereof. Other organizations began with an internal model, which later decayed as the services offered became obsolete, leading the organization to convert to the external model. The key trait of organizations that sustained an internal model is that these services offered ongoing *productive* benefits, helping members remain profitable in Mexico's neoliberal economy.

I proceed by walking through the organizational capacity models for organizations belonging to these three confederations (CNC, CCC, ANEC) in three different Mexican states (Jalisco, Michoacán, Estado de México). These cases conform to one of three paths, as depicted in Table 3.2: (1) organizations founded with an external organizational capacity model and sustaining this model (CNC); (2) organizations founded with an internal model, but shifting to an external model over time due to the exhaustion of member services (CCC); and (3) organizations that were founded with an internal model and sustained this model (ANEC). (As noted above, the fourth possibility—from external to internal—has no corresponding cases in the agricultural sector.)

These case studies come from three Mexican states that presented contrasting conditions for rural organizations during Mexico's economic and democratic transitions. Michoacán was the strongest state for the left-wing PRD, offering the hope of increased policy access and patronage benefits to this state's dozens of dissident rural groups beginning in the early 1990s (although the PRD did not win the governorship until 2001). In Jalisco the PAN displaced the PRI in 1995, bringing into power a right-wing party without ties to peasant organizations. In Estado de México, the

PRI remained dominant at the time of data collection, granting inordinate power to the CNC and offering little space for dissident agricultural organizations in either programmatic policy or patronage.

CNC: Clientelist Brokerage under PRI Hegemony and Multi-Party Competition

The first category of organization includes those that were founded with access to patronage—or the expectation thereof—and therefore adopted externally generated organizational capacity models. The paradigmatic case in this category is the CNC. The CNC has an eighty-year history, going back to the 1930s land reform, and was founded inside the PRI as the privileged representative of the peasant sector in the dominant party's corporatist system. While the type and level of inducements enjoyed by CNC base organizations transformed drastically during Mexico's neoliberal turn—as described in Chapter 2—it has consistently retained a membership model based on the intermediation of benefits allocated from PRI politicians. The CNC thrives in states governed by the PRI. Yet as the Jalisco and Michoacán cases illustrate, state-level CNC organizations can get by in non-PRI governed states, albeit on tighter budgets, through patronage benefits allocated through national power structures or negotiated by PRI representatives in Congress.

The CNC in Estado de México serves as something of a throwback, illustrating how this organization dominated rural patronage—government benefits, government appointments—during the heyday of PRI dominance. Today, the CNC is less a representative of agricultural interests as it is the PRI's rural clientelist machine (de Grammont and Mackinlay 2009; Larreguy, Marshall, and Querubín 2016). Typically about 10 percent of the PRI's delegation in Mexico's lower house (the 500-seat Chamber of Deputies) are formally allocated seats to the CNC (Langston 2017, 147) although any PRI Congress member representing a rural district may claim a CNC tie.[7]

---

7. The CNC reported having eighty-five federal deputies in the 2009–2012 legislature, over one-third of the PRI's bench and 17 percent of the entire chamber (Interview, Vicente Estrada, Secretary of Political Operations, CNC-Michoacán, January 26, 2012).

In Estado de México, the CNC claims roughly 500,000 members, the largest number of any state.[8] These members are organized in a pyramidal structure that has at its base the *ejidos*, collective landholdings created during the 1930s land reform. This structure serves as the conduit for the government benefits that operate as the lifeblood of the CNC. Edgar Castillo, the president of the CNC in Estado de México, reported that base-level organizational brokers—operating in all of the state's 125 municipalities—recruit members by promising subsidies. Word of mouth spreads quickly about local leaders who control large numbers of government benefits. Higher-level *dirigentes* (leaders) negotiate with party and government personnel for these discretionary distributive programs. The exchange of these handouts for political support cascades down the chain of command and those who prove capable of mobilizing more voters are rewarded with a larger share. In the July 2018 national elections, Castillo claimed that the organization mobilized 230,000 voters in Estado de México alone through this process.

Given PRI dominance, dissident agricultural organizations are considerably rarer and weaker in Estado de México than in other states, as avenues for both programmatic influence and patronage intermediation are closed off. Those that persist do so either by offering services such as operating a cooperative or by relying on patronage benefits negotiated with the national government by confederation leadership in Mexico City.[9] These organizations are quite small, however, as rural populations have little incentive to align themselves with organizations that are antagonistic to the dominant party.

In states that have passed through party alternation—and particularly when the PRI is out of office—the CNC's role in mediating benefits is significantly diminished. Nonetheless, the organization persists through its brokerage of discretionary distributive programs and sustains a structure that allows it to return to a privileged brokerage role once the PRI reclaims power. Interviewed leaders of the CNC in Jalisco and Michoacán reported

8. Interview, Edgar Castillo Martínez, President, CNC-Estado de México, June 28, 2018. CNC membership numbers are notoriously inflated given the common practice of counting any residents of *ejidos* as members, even those who are inactive in the organization, have ceased producing crops, or have emigrated or passed away. In any case, the CNC is by far the largest rural organization in Estado de México, and probably is in all states.

9. Interview, David Juárez Piña, Secretary of Rural Development, CCC-Toluca, June 26, 2018.

sizeable losses of membership during these two states' multiple terms of opposition party rule.[10] A representative of the Michoacán CNC lamented, "governments that are not on our side have tried to make us disappear because we are the organization most committed to the ideological issues and productive issues in favor of our members."[11] In 2011, after sixteen years of PAN rule, Jalisco's CNC president estimated that the organization had lost 75 percent of its members since the last PRI governor. However, when the PRI reclaimed the governorship in Michoacán and Jalisco in 2012 and 2011, respectively, membership rebounded. Throughout this entire period, the CNC remained by far the largest rural organization in these states.

These two states also reflect a more collaborative approach by the CNC, which opens itself to participation in institutions alongside dissident organizations and lobbies opposition-party leaders, without abandoning their identity as a PRI partisan organization. According to Vicente Estrada, representative of the CNC in Michoacán, the organization joined this state's Peasant Consultative Council—dominated by PRD-affiliated dissident groups—with the objective of participating in broader initiatives on behalf of the state's rural poor. The CNC in Michoacán persisted, however, in negotiating for benefits outside this chamber, capitalizing on its political connections to PRI Congress members at the state and federal level. According to Estrada, while roughly 75 percent of the CNC's applications for agricultural subsidies operated by the state government were approved under PRI governors, fewer than 30 percent were funded under PRD governors from 2001 to 2011.

Aside from the CNC, the other organizations that exhibit this consistent reliance on externally provided organizational capacity are certain dissident peasant groups that were founded with close ties to the PRD and with the expectation that this party would claim electoral victory in their state in the near term. The clearest such example is the UCD in the state of Michoacán. The UCD was formed by Cristóbal Arías, the first PRD senator from Michoacán and a close associate of Cuauhtémoc Cárdenas and was defeated in the 1992 gubernatorial election. In the UCD, Arías

10. Interviews, Gabriel Ponce Miranda, President, CNC-Jalisco, November 8, 2011; Vicente Estrada.

11. Interview, Vicente Estrada. "Los gobiernos que no son afines a nosotros han tratado de desaparecernos porque somos la organización que más les pelean la cuestión ideológica y la cuestión productiva para nuestros agremiados."

attempted to bring together several groups of dissident peasants—many CNC defectors—into a single left-wing rural political organization that would serve as a counterbalance to the CNC in the state. This initiative failed to realize its promise, however, due to a refusal on the part of the leaders of these individual dissident organizations to cede control over their base operations. According to Arías, "they preferred to hold onto their little groups, their clienteles and the deals that they were able to make with rural government agencies than form a single larger force, capable of confronting the rural situation."[12] The twelve-year lapse until the PRD finally won the governorship in 2001 left these organizations in the cold, and by the time Lázaro Cárdenas Batel—the first PRD governor of Michoacán—assumed power, many were defunct or shadows of their previous size.

CCC and Exhausted Dissidents: From Activism and Land Claims to Patronage Brokerage

A second category of organization contains those that began with an internally generated organizational capacity model, but over time shifted to a dependence on patronage. This is the dominant tendency for CCC affiliates, as well as many other rural confederations such as CNPA, CIOAC, and UGOCM that were founded as outsiders during PRI hegemony, but are today wholly dependent on state benefits to sustain membership. The CCC was founded in 1988 as electorally autonomous, but with an affinity to the PRD. In its earliest years, the CCC was centrally engaged in providing services to the most vulnerable rural producers who lacked representation by the CNC, including managing land claims and resolving land disputes. The organization found its initial approach difficult to maintain as it was designed to resolve a principal concern for the early 1990s—land disputes—but not to provide benefits relevant to post-NAFTA production. Eventually, the CCC on the national level underwent a transition to an externally provided model, mediating state benefits for the rural poor under PRD governors.

---

12. Interview, Cristóbal Arías Solís, UCD founder, December 15, 2011. "Prefirieron ellos quedarse con sus pequeños agrupamientos, sus clientelas y sus gestiones que hacían ante las dependencias oficial del sector agropecuario, de tener una gran fuerza, una sola capaz de confrontar la problemática rural."

As the cases below illustrate, the form that the organization takes varies between states with a strong presence of the PRD, such as Michoacán, and states where the PRD is weak, such as Jalisco. In the former case, the CCC approaches the case of the UCD, given its optimism over a PRD victory in the early 1990s and thus expectation of forthcoming patronage benefits soon after its founding. In Jalisco, in contrast, no possibility of PRD rule was on the horizon, and the CCC in this state thus was not formed with the expectation of patronage benefits. A transition to a patronage orientation was wholly attributable to the exhaustion of its initial organizational capacity model and a later reliance on patronage benefits channeled from national leaders.

CCC-Michoacán is a case of an organization that generated its own organizational capacity at its founding, but had shifted to an external model by the time the PRD assumed power in the state in 2001. The Michoacán affiliate was among the founding members of the CCC in 1988, along with a nationwide network of rural leaders eager to counterbalance the CNC and support a new electoral movement on the left (García Ponce 2009). Michoacán—the home state of the PRD's founder, Cuauhtémoc Cárdenas—was a key locus of power. Much like social movements in the national capital, the CCC maintained a formal non-partisan stance at the beginning, participating in Cárdenas' campaign without entering into an official alliance. In the first years, the CCC's main demands revolved around resisting neoliberal reforms, joining with a broader coalition of dissident peasant organizations, several of which had been founded in the 1970s and 1980s and were linked to socialist movements predating the PRD. However, CCC representatives were not party insiders in the PRD, as was the UCD.

After Cárdenas' defeat in the 1988 election and amidst the lack of PRD allies in Michoacán government, the CCC persisted in a model that combined an ideological mobilization of peasants affected by the series of neoliberal transformations of the countryside taking place under the Salinas presidency with the provision of aid in resolving land tenure. This was a key service during the early 1990s, as the Salinas administration instituted PROCEDE, a land reform program that opened space for *ejidatarios* to attain title to their individual land plots. The CCC's success in helping peasants navigate the government infrastructure to acquire land titles was a powerful inducement, but had the drawback of being a discrete benefit that did not incentivize continued participation once the land issue was resolved. PROCEDE claims declined precipitously by the late 1990s and, in the context of NAFTA, the CCC, like many other rural organizations, failed to shift from a model based on navigating rural populations *through* the neoliberal transition to a model of helping them remain profitable as *participants in* neoliberal agricultural markets.

The shift of the rural popular classes to non-agricultural modes of employment prompted CCC-Michoacán to broaden their mandate to appeal to a heterogeneous body of rural laborers and microentrepreneurs. While the state has created several programs to improve livelihoods and support non-agricultural employment in the countryside, these were difficult for the CCC to access throughout the 1990s, as the PRI retained control of the state and federal governments. On the other hand, CCC-Michoacán's shift to the external organizational capacity model became quite successful once the PRD assumed the governorship of Michoacán in 2001.

While many patronage-oriented organizations are small, precarious, and struggle to draw members to meetings or activities, CCC-Michoacán is today large, institutionalized, and capable of mobilizing in large numbers in both electoral and contentious movements. With a membership of approximately 6,000 in 2012, CCC pursued an effective strategy of recruitment based on the promise of organization-mediated subsidies. It has accumulated a heterogeneous membership, made up of producers of several crops (grains, fruits, vegetables) as well as non-producers from rural and semi-urban areas. An estimated 60 percent of members are *ejidatarios*, but many lease their land to others or do not produce.[13] Members find the organization through word of mouth, as others have joined and gained title to land, funding from a rural housing program, or subsidized agricultural inputs. Since these types of benefits are one-off and of broad appeal, the membership is heterogeneous and fleeting, with new members joining frequently, but many members inactive after extracting the benefit that the organization has to offer or struggling to move up Gonzalez's list for support in applying for state benefits.

Like CCC-Michoacán, the Jalisco affiliate offered self-generated benefits at its founding, principally helping rural populations resolve land disputes and gain title to their land. And similarly, as the utility of this service declined, the organization found itself in existential crisis. However, PAN governments in Jalisco did not deliver patronage benefits to the degree that Michoacán's PRD administrations did. With a waning membership, and a scandal in which the leader was accused of embezzling organization

13. COCOCAM, *Fichas Informativas*, p. 122.

funds, the CCC went defunct in Jalisco in 2002. In 2008, it was revived under a leader who embraced the brokerage of state programs, launching an expansion into semi-urban areas in the Guadalajara Metropolitan Zone, based on the provision of housing and subsidies for microenterprises for a non-agricultural membership base. These benefits did not accrue from the Jalisco state government, but rather from the federal government under pressure from the national CCC confederation.

The CCC-Jalisco is an example of a successful patronage-oriented organization, owing to the present leadership's ability to leverage alliances to extract benefits from federal government programs. Its policy demands are limited almost exclusively to maximizing such benefits for its members. The organization leader devotes his energies to *gestión* of subsidies for agricultural inputs, materials for residential housing, or funding for small businesses. This leader—Miguel Ángel Rodríguez, Secretary General of CCC—monopolizes the *gestión* process, as well as the discretion to determine which members receive state benefits mediated by the organization. This authority serves as his main tool to recruit and mobilize members, as he makes clear that active participation in organization activities—including electoral rallies for the affiliated party—will be rewarded with handouts. In interviews, Rodríguez mentions broader policy concerns on behalf of the rural poor, but these demands are unspecific—"greater redistribution" or "more spending in the countryside"—and the organization rarely dedicates significant attention to them.

Recruitment for CCC is based primarily on promises of subsidies. The organization's ability to extract government handouts for its members spreads through word of mouth, leading potential members to approach the organization in hopes of acquiring such resources themselves. At a CCC rally, several members that I interviewed were unabashed in explaining that they were motivated to join and participate in the organization's activities by the promise of individual benefits, such as a new room for their house or free fertilizer from the state government. Referring to a government program that provides housing materials for the rural poor, one woman explained: "El Profe told me that if I participate in rallies and [CCC] assemblies, he'll make sure that I receive support from Vivienda Rural."[14] (Rodríguez is known as "El Profe" to the members of CCC, owing to his prior employment as a teacher.)

---

14. "El Profe me dijo que si me lanzo a los mítines, a las asambleas, que se va a encontrar la forma de bajar un apoyo de Vivienda Rural" (interview, June 6, 2012).

Rodríguez strategically allocates these resources to expand the membership and is proud of the growing ranks of CCC, which have risen from approximately 500 to over 6,000 since Rodríguez entered in 2008. However, this growth in membership has come at the cost of sacrificing organizational coherence. While it began strictly as a peasant association advocating for policies to improve the market position of small-scale farmers, the CCC has grown by incorporating semi-urban populations, many of whom are service-sector workers in the city of Guadalajara, micro-entrepreneurs, or wage laborers. Women, many of whom are wives of agricultural producers, constitute the majority of members and instead of looking to the organization for help to improve agricultural productivity, are interested in social programs that support housing or micro-enterprise investments.

ANEC and Productive Dissidents: The Cooperative Model

The third model of organizations are those that maintained an internally generated organizational capacity model from the start. In the peasant sector, organizations belonging to ANEC constitute the clearest examples, as they operate cooperatives and training activities for small-scale grain farmers. The Network of Peasant Commercializing Firms of Michoacán (REDCCAM) and the Agricultural Commercializing Organization of the West (COMAGRO) are the ANEC affiliates in Michoacán and Jalisco respectively. In comparison with CNC and CCC affiliates that generate organizational capacity externally, ANEC affiliates exhibit different traits in terms of membership, leadership, and relationship to political parties. Their members are homogenous—small and medium-sized corn farmers—and tend to remain in the organization over a long period of time. They are drawn to the productive benefits that the organization offers and come to be concerned with broader issues of rural development through contact with activists in the organization. Their elected leaders rotate frequently, while paid staff play an important role in managing day-to-day operations. And these organizations sustain a steadfast non-partisanship, facilitating the maintenance of a lobbying relationship with all political parties.

REDCCAM, ANEC's affiliate in Michoacán, represents small and medium-sized grain farmers and acts both as a cooperative for commercializing these products as well as an advocate for the interests of its sector in the state of Michoacán. REDCCAM is certainly not disinterested in accessing distributive programs; in fact, one of the main services that it offers to members is designing projects for potential government funding and leaders frequently engage with state bureaucrats regarding subsidy applications. However, these subsidies are limited to productive agricultural supports, as opposed to the wider variety of small business funds, housing programs and other benefits that patronage-oriented organizations trade in. Lamenting the fact that most rural organizations are driven by the self-interested motive of extracting subsidies and propping up their leaders' electoral prospects, an interviewed official in Michoacán's rural development ministry attested that REDCCAM is "one of the only serious producer organizations in the state."[15] REDCCAM members are not immune from temptation to pursue patronage-oriented strategies, however, and only through a carefully cultivated organizational culture and the management of a lucrative grain cooperative has REDCCAM sustained a joint production model of organizational capacity.

In contrast to CCC, which was founded along with the PRD in 1988, REDCCAM was founded in 2004, once the PRD was already in power in the state. As a dissident agricultural organization with a friendly party in office, REDCCAM may have been able to focus its energies on the extraction of benefits, as other COCOCAM members did in the 2000s once the PRD assumed power in the state. However, multiple factors caused REDCCAM to sustain a programmatic orientation and autonomous organizational capacity. First, REDCCAM replicated a cooperative commercializing model devised by its parent organization, ANEC. ANEC's founding in 1998 took place in a context of low electoral prospects of the left, and a vulnerable small-scale grain farming sector in the aftermath of NAFTA passage. The operation of grain cooperatives, paired with capacity building to improve yields, became a model that ANEC imparted, along with requiring non-partisanship. Second, ANEC entered into the political situation in Michoacán at a time that was propitious for programmatic engagement, and when the field was crowded for subsidy extraction. With a clear mandate from ANEC and the advent of the COCOCAM—a new consultative council for peasant organizations, promising to improve policy access—REDCCAM established a rapport with the state government as the most articulate communicator of the needs of small-scale farmers to compete in liberalized agricultural markets.

Recruitment for REDCCAM consists of integrating pre-existing base-level associations of grain producers into the state-level organization. Such

15. "Una de las pocas organizaciones de productores en el estado con seriedad" (interview, Enrique Rojas, Head of Federalized Programs, SEDRU-Michoacán, December 6, 2011).

organizations typically operate in one or a few municipalities, with anywhere from a dozen to 500 members.[16] Today, seventeen associations belong to REDCCAM, totaling approximately 2,000 members. When REDCCAM was founded in 2004, it was made up of ten organizations. According to Omar Lando Estañol, General Director of REDCCAM, five of these organizations were expelled within the first five years because they lacked commitment to the social mission of development of an autonomous grain cooperative and were more interested in extracting subsidies and promoting the political careers of their leaders: "Those five (organizations) were asked to resign because they were uninterested in the productive activities that we were carrying out in the network. They were more interested in their own personal interests—economic and political."[17]

REDCCAM's recruitment strategy is geared to slow growth, carefully adding members that are committed to the goals of the organization, as opposed to a single-minded push to grow the ranks. Recruitment typically operates through word-of-mouth; leaders of local organizations of grain farmers approach REDCCAM if they are interested in taking part in the network's cooperative and other productive activities.[18] These organizations are drawn to REDCCAM for two reasons. First, membership affords the ability to sell products through the cooperative, which generally offers higher and more certain prices for products and reduces their dependence on informal intermediaries. Second, REDCCAM has a staff of technical experts who can help these organizations design projects to access government subsidies, which can be used to buy equipment or agricultural inputs. Potential members must present a case to the executive committee—made up of representatives of all organizations—that they are prepared to participate in the cooperative and committed to its long-term goals. The assembly votes on all membership decisions and new members join for a one-year trial period.

Founded in 1992 by twenty-three organizations, eleven of which were *comisariados ejidales* that had defected from the CNC, COMAGRO grew

---

16. Interview, Omar Lando Estañol, General Director, REDCCAM, December 9, 2011.
17. "Esas cinco (organizaciones) que solicitamos su renuncio porque prácticamente no congeniaron en los objetivos productivos que veníamos llevando a cabo en la Red. Hubo cierta preferencia por ciertos intereses personales—económicos y políticos" (interview, Omar Lando Estañol).
18. Author observation of REDCCAM meetings, December 2011-January 2012, July 2013.

to involve over 60,000 corn farmers in the states of Jalisco, Michoacán, and Nayarit, growing corn and beans on plots averaging four hectares.[19] As with REDCCAM, COMAGRO's recruitment was based on the participation in a joint cooperative venture, first commercializing fertilizer for farmers' consumption, and later commercializing the grains produced by these farmers. COMAGRO was an early adherent to the strategy that ANEC affiliates implemented on a national scale, centering on three pillars to bolster the sustainability of smallholder grain production in neoliberal Mexico: (1) the operation of a cooperative, wherein farmers could join together to purchase capital and inputs and commercialize grains at better prices; (2) offering affordable finance to members through the organization's line of credit; and (3) improvement of crop technologies and the introduction of higher-value products through training and technical support provided by the organization and subsidized by government programs.

COMAGRO emerged in response to the privatization of FERTIMEX, the federal government's fertilizer distributor, and was among the first non-governmental actors in Mexico to commercialize fertilizer imported from the United States (de la Fuente Hernández and Morales Valderrama 1996, 294–98; Rodríguez Gómez and Torres 1994). While COMAGRO assumed a non-partisan political stance, it was at odds with Jalisco's PRI-led government from its founding, as then governor Guillermo Cosío Vidaurri favored a group of investors, including his son, to receive the monopoly on fertilizer storage over COMAGRO and other social groups (Guerrero Anaya 1999, 136–37). Only three years after COMAGRO's founding in 1992, party turnover took place in Jalisco, as the PAN displaced the PRI for the governorship. PAN administrations were not open to patronage bargains with popular-sector organizations, but were eager to support COMAGRO's cooperative model to set an example in contrast to the bulk of dissident peasant associations that the ruling administrations dismissed as clientelist networks for the PRI or the disorganized left. COMAGRO persisted for several years as a productive cooperative enterprise and was in fact one of the founders of ANEC's national confederation.

Internally generated organizational capacity alone was not enough to guarantee the survival of COMAGRO, especially in the face of a state

19. Interview, Antonio Hernández Alarcón, President, Unión de Ejidos de Producción Agropecuaria de la ex-Laguna de Magdalena General Lázaro Cárdenas, November 15, 2011.

administration that came to favor large-scale agribusiness over small-scale grain cooperatives. Falling grain prices, the demise of smallholder subsidies, and the aging of the organization's members led COMAGRO to wither. In 2001, the failure of member organizations to repay loans that had been secured by COMAGRO led to bankruptcy. Several of the member organizations renewed efforts by forming SiCampo (Sociedad Integradora para el Campo, Integrating Society for the Countryside), but the "social" organizations (former *ejidos*) were outnumbered six to four by large grain intermediaries—many of which own large plots of land themselves or which instead buy corn produced by small-scale producers and resell it at a higher value.[20] COMAGRO's organizational model of offering productive services to small-scale farmers eroded completely under the Jalisco's last PAN governor (Emilio González, 2007–2012). The González administration promoted for-profit ventures of larger-scale grain producers. The peasant wing left COMAGRO, with its leaders disappointed with SiCampo's lack of a commitment to rural development and claiming that they can do just as well selling their product to informal intermediaries as through the organization.[21] And the members that remain are all Rural Production Societies (Sociedades de Producción Rural, SPR), for-profit intermediaries rather than small-scale farmers.

Having undergone this conversion, SiCampo is successful in brokering distributive benefits for its entrepreneurial membership. The organization belongs to the Executive Committee of the Trust in Support of the Agricultural Profitability of the Corn Producers of Jalisco (Fideicomiso de Apoyo a la Rentabilidad Agrícola de los Productores de Maíz del Estado de Jalisco, FARAJAL), and SiCampo's head was president of this committee during the last two state administrations.[22] The main responsibility of this body is to disburse subsidies for small-scale corn producers; however, CNC and other organizations have protested that benefits were being concentrated

20. This model reserves a great deal of the surplus value for the entrepreneur, rather than the farmer and, according to Hernández, goes against the principles of ANEC.
21. Interview, Antonio Hernández Alarcón.
22. CAJ (the Jalisco Agricultural Council) is also a permanent member of FARAJAL, which has fallen in line with the PAN administrations' approach to the countryside, declaring as their primary accomplishment on their website "Changing the mentality of the producer to BUSINESSPERSON" ("El cambio de mentalidad en el productor de Agricultor a EMPRESARIO," Source: http://www.farajal.com/quienes-somos/logro-integral).

in the hands of SiCampo and other intermediaries.[23] In addition to this state trust, SiCampo acquires subsidies from a variety of state and federal programs, supporting investments in organizational infrastructure for storage and transportation, training to increase yields, production technology (tractors), and crop insurance.[24] Hernández now complains that, by supporting SiCampo, the state government can give the perception that it is supporting small-scale farmers, without having to really respond to their interests.

The case of COMAGRO underscores the difficulty of sustaining autonomous collective action in the countryside. This should still be considered a success case, however; for over a decade this organization persisted in offering valuable services to its dedicated core of small-scale corn farmers and—as Chapter 4 will show—pushing for rural development policies that favor this segment. This approach proves easier to sustain in the presence of a ruling party that is friendly to the organization, supporting it with occasional funding and opening spaces for access to policymaking. Such was the scenario of REDCCAM in Michoacán, which deftly combined a friendly relationship with PRD governments—and the corresponding economic benefits—with a core model based on internally generated organizational capacity. This model is what has helped REDCCAM avoid the fate of CCC affiliates and other dissident peasant organizations, which have come to rely exclusively on patronage benefits from the state to sustain organizational capacity.

Organizational Capacity in the Small-Business Sector

Compared with the peasant sector, small-business organizations have a relatively easier time sustaining organizational capacity internally, owing to two factors. First, because their members belong to higher socio-economic strata, business associations are able to charge dues. Second, while lower-class peasants may be reticent to participate in an organization that does not offer the immediate promise of economic benefit, small-business owners are more likely to be drawn to non-material benefits, such as networking opportunities. Thus, this project finds a higher rate of internally generated organizational capacity among small-business organizations than among peasant organizations.

---

23. "Denuncian anomalías en Farajal," *Mural*, January 25, 2007.

24. Interview, José Antonio Lisardi, President, Agrícola Ganadera los Suaces (member organization of SiCampo), July 1, 2013.

However, several examples do exist of small-business organizations with external organizational capacity models. The federal government and several state governments sustain small-business subsidy and support programs that formally grant a role for business associations in project design and implementation. Furthermore, business chambers retain the exclusive right to enlist firms in their jurisdictions into the SIEM, a (*de jure* if not *de facto*) mandatory national database of firms, keeping half of the registration fee for themselves. Where business chambers come to depend on these programs for financing and for selective benefits to offer members, they come to resemble the rural model of the *organización de gestión*.

These distributive benefits do not have as long a trajectory in the small-business sector as do agricultural subsidies and other benefits for the rural poor. Rather these benefits constitute a mode of neo-corporatism constructed during PAN presidencies (2000–2012). The advent of these organizational resources followed the neoliberal demise of a corporatist system that supported small-business collective action through mandatory membership requirements for business chambers (Shadlen 2000).

This shift affected organizations differently depending on how they were positioned during the transition. While variation exists within each of the three major confederations of business organizations, they correspond roughly to three distinct models. Chambers of Commerce, belonging to CONCANACO and representing service-sector firms most commonly adopted a service-delivery model, and many continue to thrive with internally provided organizational capacity, offering training, consulting, and organizing conventions among many other high-profile lucrative activities related to tourism and local festivals. In contrast, industrial chambers, mostly belonging to CANACINTRA, found themselves most under threat, as the domestic manufacturing sector has been considerably less dynamic. These chambers were the most vulnerable to adopting an external model of organizational capacity. Finally, COPARMEX affiliates, which never benefitted from mandatory membership requirements at any point in their history, set the example of a service-oriented organization, while also tapping into economic resources that flowed from state-level and federal PAN administrations beginning in the 1990s. Owing to its long-standing internal organizational capacity model, COPARMEX constitutes a mirror-image of the CNC, an organization formed from within a patronage-dominated political system and defined by the intermediation of particularistic economic benefits.

In the remainder of this section, I walk through the three pathways for generating organizational capacity for business organizations. I begin with the path of being founded with internally generated organizational capacity and sustaining it throughout. The archetypal case of this path is COPARMEX, an organization formed as an outsider under PRI dominance in 1929 and sustaining this posture through the democratic transition. I document COPARMEX affiliates in all three states, showing how their organizational capacity models vary little based on the partisanship of the government in power. The other two types correspond to the distinct paths taken by business chambers in the aftermath of the demise of PRI-led corporatism and the rise of the PAN as a potential electoral ally in power. Many business chambers replicated the model of COPARMEX by converting into purveyors of useful services for local businesses. Such was the strategy of many chambers of commerce and exemplified by the Guadalajara Chamber of Commerce, analyzed in detail here. Other organizations came to specialize in the extraction of state benefits made available by PAN governments at the national and subnational level, as in the case of Jalisco's and Michoacán's industrial chambers.

All three paths feature cases from the state of Jalisco (alongside cases from Michoacán and Estado de México as well). In Jalisco, the pro-business PAN held the governorship for three consecutive terms from 1995 to 2012. Nonetheless, the distinct organizational imprints led COPARMEX and CANACO to internal organizational capacity models and the Regional Chamber of the Industry of Transformation of the State of Jalisco (CAREINTRA, Jalisco's industrial chamber) to an external organizational capacity model. However, sectoral distinctions do not align entirely with the distinct paths. I do find chambers of commerce that adopted external organizational capacity models and industrial chambers that approach an internal organizational capacity model.

Notably, externally provided organizational capacity is typically less obviously clientelistic in the business sector than it is in the agricultural sector. Organizations described here as generating organizational capacity externally still formally declare non-partisanship. And while they may orient their activities around maximizing sources of funding and benefits from the state, they do not advertise their central function to members so much in terms of brokering state benefits. As the case of CANACO-Morelia below illustrates, however, they tend to adopt a "transactional" approach to membership, appealing to members with offers of discount cards or other personal benefits unrelated to the chambers' political activity or consulting services—or even with the unspoken threat of repercussions for not submitting to "mandatory" SIEM enrollment.

COPARMEX: A Legacy of Principled Autonomy

COPARMEX constitutes the archetypical case of an organization founded with an internal organizational capacity model. This organization dates back to 1929, the same year as the founding of the PRI (then known as the PNR) and was formed with the explicit goal of representing business interests from outside the PRI's corporatist structure. Thus, the founding model featured several traits that were conducive to internally generated organizational capacity: service delivery, a strict non-partisan stance, and a highly public reputation for principled autonomy.

Despite its non-partisanship, COPARMEX leaders have remained "extremely political" throughout their decades in existence, alternating between collaboration alongside the more institutionalist business chambers and defiant stances against economic policy by PRI administrations. When the PAN began competing seriously in elections in the 1990s, COPARMEX leaders were often granted candidacies or cabinet positions with this party. For example, two former COPARMEX presidents include Manuel Clouthier, the PAN's 1988 presidential candidate, and Carlos Abascal, Minister of Labor and Minister of the Interior under Vicente Fox.

Jalisco's COPARMEX affiliate is one of the most long-standing and prestigious in the country. For the greater part of the twentieth century, it stood alongside the PAN and the Catholic Church in this state as stalwarts of the conservative resistance to PRI dominance (Gómez López 1992; Juárez González 1989). The most important of the services that COPARMEX offered to its members was legal representation in labor disputes. In this way the organization served as a counterweight to the powerful PRI-embedded labor sector.

When the PAN assumed power in 1995, COPARMEX figures were swept into the administration, but these nominations did not threaten the organization's stubborn autonomy. Bureaucrats in charge of PAN administrations' business support programs claim that COPARMEX is an infrequent applicant.[25] COPARMEX representatives concur, and while

25. Interview, Jorge Urdapilleta, General Director, State Council for Economic Promotion (CEPE), October 28, 2011.

they participate in México Emprende—the national small-business subsidy program instituted under the Fox administration—most of the benefits that they offer members are of their own accord and not part of a government support program.[26]

COPARMEX representatives interviewed related that they focused on an organizational capacity model consisting of the delivery of useful services to members. According to the Director of Business, the person in charge of the full suite of business services, many members are initially drawn to the COPARMEX thinking that it is a consulting agency and later decide to join the organization to receive discounts on the wide variety of services and training in such areas as developing a business plan, web design, human resources, advertising, accounting, and legal representation. He said that they need to prove to members that COPARMEX will be useful to them over the long term to give clients of these services reason to join.

Financial benefits for COPARMEX-Jalisco come almost entirely from dues and for enrollment fees for these services. In 2011, yearly dues were 3,200 pesos (about 200 dollars) for firms with fewer than fifteen employees, which make up 90 percent of the total membership of 1,700. These funds are sufficient to sustain a paid staff of over sixty employees, most of whom specialize in delivering services to members. COPARMEX is also quite active in public activities. For example, in the 2012 elections, COPARMEX organized a statewide electoral observation operation, recruiting and training thousands of volunteers throughout the state.

While Jalisco represents a particularly strong and well-established COPARMEX affiliate, the norm for COPARMEX centers in other states is consistently to sustain organizational capacity internally. For instance, at the time of research in Estado de México, COPARMEX was going through a change in leadership following the resignation of its president in the midst of a conflict with other business organization leaders in the state.[27] The new leadership team was focusing on core principles of developing useful member services as a means of growing the membership while cultivating a reputation as an independent voice on behalf of the business community and in favor of good government. According to the incoming Director of

26. Interviews, Juan José González Nuño, Business Manager, COPARMEX-Jalisco, October 26, 2011; José Guadalupe Pérez Mejía, Legal Director, COPARMEX-Jalisco, October 20, 2017.

27. "Sigo siendo presidente de Coparmex: Edgar Cerecero López," *MVT*, December 22, 2011.

COPARMEX-Estado de México, they were beginning with holding monthly breakfasts for business owners, often inviting politicians or other speakers. This type of activity both serves as an opportunity to recruit members and also a space to generate a collective consciousness around the business community in the state.

CONCANACO: Successful Transition to Service Delivery Model

CANACO-Guadalajara represents a case of an organization that benefitted significantly from the PRI's corporatist structure and mandatory membership requirements, while also investing in its own internal organizational strategy model. Upon the Law of Chambers reform, CANACO-Guadalajara had little problem pivoting to an organizational capacity model based on the delivery of services to businessowners. Well prior to the late 1990s, when mandatory membership was revoked and PAN rule initiated in Jalisco, CANACO had already established itself as one of the strongest civil society voices in the state. CANACO representatives joked that citizens often mistake the chamber for a government ministry, given its highly institutionalized nature and lavish headquarters. They also asserted, however, that in its operations it was autonomous and non-partisan.

Today, recruitment for CANACO-Guadalajara capitalizes more on services and networking opportunities than the organization's role as an intermediary for distributive programs. Thus, small- and medium-sized business owners in Guadalajara have ample reason to join the chamber beyond the promise of state benefits. Membership offers discounts for dozens of training and consulting programs, participation in networking events and meetings with politicians, and the use of the chamber's ample facilities.[28]

CANACO-Guadalajara's resources come mainly from member dues, fees for services, as well as public-facing events and services, such as a tourist train to tequila distilleries, a Christmas fair, and the annual Mariachi Festival. The organization represents 45,000 members registered in the SIEM, with around 3,500 who pay an additional membership fee, allowing them to access organization services and discounts. Together, membership and SIEM registration fees accounted for less than

28. Interviews, Erick Herrera Ramírez, Consultant, Centro México Emprende; Ana Isabel Solís, Manager of Strategic Analysis, CANACO-Guadalajara, October 31, 2011.

20 percent of CANACO's eighty million peso (about six million dollar) operating expenses in 2011. The remainder of the resources come mostly from services offered to the public.

Like COPARMEX, the main benefits that CANACO offers to members are training and networking. CANACO-Guadalajara is quite active in managing state programs though its ample México Emprende Center. In 2011 the center set the goal of assisting 1,000 business owners. An initial consultation at the Center would be uncharged, and staff would make recommendations for additional training or services, which could be accessed at a discounted rate by chamber members.

CANACO-Guadalajara has developed a reputation as a preeminent representative of civil society in Jalisco. Politicians of all political parties seek out meetings with chamber leadership during electoral campaigns to present their platforms to membership. Election of leaders follows clearly mandated rules regarding term limits and eligibility and leaders' public pronouncements in the media are consistently related to the needs of the business sector as opposed to extracting benefits for the chamber narrowly.

While CANACO-Guadalajara represents an extreme case of a chamber that flourished through internally generated services and revenue sources, chambers of commerce elsewhere in Mexico had to scramble to a greater degree to configure themselves to remain afloat after the revocation of mandatory membership. CANACO-Morelia is an example of such a case. In 1997, this chamber was not as firmly entrenched in the business community nor as a civil society actor, compared with CANACO-Guadalajara. Also, given that Morelia is a much smaller and more economically depressed city than Guadalajara, the universe of business owners able or willing to pay dues was significantly smaller.

As a result, after the revocation of mandatory membership, CANACO-Morelia placed an overwhelming emphasis on recruiting firms to the SIEM and collecting member fees, which together represent over two-thirds of the chamber's funding. In a much smaller urban area than Guadalajara, CANACO-Morelia has almost the same number of SIEM enrollees (32,000) and even more registered members (4,000). The director of CANACO-Morelia boasted about his innovative approach to recruitment, having written his master's thesis about this strategy.[29] The approach included

29. Interview, Agustín Rebollar Cruz, General Director, CANACO-Morelia, July 5, 2013.

highly publicized festivals to attract new members, offering discount cards for local establishments upon signing up, and contracting several employees working on commission to travel the area on motorcycle to approach businesses about joining. This leader has run the day-to-day operations of the chamber for close to twenty years, and clearly had become indispensable to the organization's organizational capacity model

CANACO-Morelia additionally offers member services—approximately one weekly workshop, with roughly a dozen participants in the average workshop, but these pale in comparison to the number of training activities offered in Guadalajara.[30] And CANACO-Morelia does work to extract distributive benefits for members, but with limited success. A consultant at the chamber's Centro México Emprende estimated that in the two years that he had worked there, they had acquired government subsidies for about one dozen business owners, out of about 200 who had approached with the goal of accessing these programs. Ultimately, I classify CANACO-Morelia as having internally generated organizational capacity given its success in sustaining a large membership through chamber-generated resources—mainly membership fees. However, it represents something of a hybrid case given that it employs service delivery to a much lesser extent than other autonomous business chambers, and thus does not generate the same traits of member solidarity, internal democracy, or reputation as a representative of the business community.

CANACINTRA: Struggling to Adapt and Dependence on the PAN's New Business Corporatism

The final pathway for business organizations corresponds to those that depended on corporatist policies to sustain collective action during the twentieth century and rely today on government funding and *gestión* to remain afloat. This is the most common fate for industrial chambers, which have weathered the onset of the neoliberal economic model in much worse shape than chambers of commerce. The growth of the *maquila* sector and the rapid influx of imported manufacturing goods has decimated small industry, just at the time that these organizations were reeling from the revocation of mandatory membership (Johnson Ceva 1998).

30. Interview, Humberto Ortega, Centro México Emprende Consultant, CANACO-Morelia, December 5, 2011.

Jalisco's industrial chamber, CAREINTRA,[31] offers a notable contrast to this state's COPARMEX and CANACO. The resource disparities are palpable. While each of the latter organizations occupy prominent buildings in upscale neighborhoods of Guadalajara, CAREINTRA'S headquarters are in a middle-class outlying area. Having lost the overwhelming majority of their members and teetered on the brink of bankruptcy, they have sold or rented out three-fourths of their building to local businesses in an effort to raise funds. When offered the opportunity to move to a new LEED-certified building designed to house several business chambers, CAREINTRA eventually declined owing to the expenses associated with replacing furniture.

CAREINTRA only has a membership of about 500 firms and is responsible for 2,200 SIEM affiliations. Financial resources accrue in their entirety from member fees and SIEM enrollment commissions and afford a budget for only limited activities and twelve paid staff. According to CAREINTRA's president, it is quite difficult to get members to actively participate in the organization, which lacks the economic resources or the dynamism to organize a modern high-profile convention for example.[32] CAREINTRA's members tend to be older than those of other chambers, long-time owners of family firms, legacy members of the organization's better days in the twentieth century. The current president, in his forties, was chosen in part to impart a more youthful image for an organization that has attained a reputation for being stuffy and inactive. But this new president faces several challenges.

While CAREINTRA does not have any overt partisan affiliation nor does it depend to a great extent on patronage benefits, it cannot be described as enjoying significant autonomy in its dealings with the state. The chamber has very little direct contact with politicians about policy, delegating such contact to the Consejo de Cámaras Industriales de Jalisco (CCIJ), of which it is a member. The president also lamented finding it difficult to get the attention of the governor, a stark contrast from CANACO-Guadalajara and COPARMEX-Jalisco, whose leaders are in frequent communication with the governor and area mayors.

---

31. CAREINTRA stands for Cámara Regional de la Industria de la Transformación del Estado de Jalisco. Like Nuevo León's industrial chamber CAINTRA, CAREINTRA was formed prior to the creation of CANACINTRA and has remained outside this national industrial chamber. It participates alongside CANACINTRA and CAINTRA in the national umbrella manufacturing Confederation, CONCAMIN.

32. Interview, Juan Alberto Porras Brambila, President, CAREINTRA, October 20, 2017.

Another example of an industrial chamber that has transitioned to an external model is CANACINTRA-Morelia. Since the 1997 Law of Chambers reform and the decline of the manufacturing industry in the state of Michoacán (of which Morelia is the capital), this organization has seen its membership decline, with roughly 1,600 members at the time of the interview.[33] Today, the chamber depends on the SIEM both for financial resources and for membership. The main source of financing for the delegation is the commission that they receive for signing firms up to the SIEM. But at least as important is the opportunity that the SIEM process gives the chamber to pitch CANACINTRA to prospective members. The manager of the Morelia CANACINTRA described the process:

> The first people that have contact with business owners are the SIEM staff, those who go out in the streets and go door to door. That's the first contact that a businessperson has with the people from CANACINTRA. They go with their uniforms, with their credentials, they explain to them what the SIEM is and what the chamber is. That's where we get an influx of members.

Conclusion

This chapter has introduced the concept of organizational capacity, the ability of organizations to recruit, retain, and mobilize members. Organizations sort into two distinct models for generating this capacity: internally generated and externally provided. Organizations that generate this capacity internally do so by providing valuable services to members, typically services that are useful for increasing the profitability of economic activities. The external organizational capacity model pertains to organizations that rely on government resources—such as discretionary distributive programs—for funding and inducements to members. Either of these models can produce a large and thriving organization.

However, a series of organizational traits flow from these different models. First, internally generated organizational capacity tends to attract a homogeneous membership in the same economic sector who come to develop a shared consciousness and collective goals. In contrast, externally

33. Interview, Delia Cárdenas Pedraza, General Manager, CANACINTRA-Morelia, January 26, 2012.

provided organizational capacity produces a fleeting, heterogeneous, and self-interested membership. The internal organizational capacity model promotes internal democracy and capacity building to generate leaders from within, while the external model anoints a leader as the broker for state benefits and this leader concentrates power as he becomes indispensable. Finally, organizations that generate organizational capacity internally enjoy greater autonomy from state actors, retaining the freedom to choose their own policy demands, modes of pursuing their goals, and to communicate with politicians of all parties. In contrast, externally provided organizational capacity produces dependence on a state or party patron, closes off avenues to lobby opposition-party politicians, and harms the organization's prestige as a civil society actor.

This chapter traced the sources of these distinct organizational capacity models in the agricultural and small-business sectors. First, organizations establish internal or external models at their founding, with the latter favored by organizations that were founded in the presence of an ally in government, capable of funneling state benefits to them. However, even organizations founded with internal models can transition to an external model, as the services that they offer to members become obsolete and a party ally assumes elected office.

The next two chapters show how these distinct organizational capacity models produce different types of demand-making. Internally generated organizational capacity is associated with programmatic demands on behalf of the organization's sector, while externally provided organizational capacity leads to narrow patronage demands, seeking to maximize particularistic benefits for members. In Chapter 4, I show how this narrow patronage is quite common in the agricultural sector, but that organizations like ANEC, that generate organizational capacity by offering productive services, become key actors in policymaking in their states. Chapter 5 details demand-making in the small-business sector, showing that while a narrow patronage orientation is rarer than in the agricultural sector, those organizations that fail to offer members valuable productive services are at risk of receding from programmatic demand-making.

CHAPTER 4

Demand-Making for the Lower Classes

Peasant Organizations

Collective action for poor rural populations is notoriously difficult (Bates 1981; Scott 1977). In the Mexican case, peasant organizations face particularly daunting obstacles to programmatic demand-making, given a legacy of rural clientelism and membership base that often looks to the state for particularistic benefits to make ends meet more than as a source of policies to improve their production conditions (Fox 1994; Kurtz 2004a). As a result, many peasant organizations are embedded in patronage ties with political parties that deliver preferential access to discretionary distributive programs in exchange for electoral support. However, other organizations in this lower-class sector evade a patronage orientation and prioritize programmatic demands on behalf of their sector. This chapter explains these divergent models of demand-making.

This variety of modes of demand-making in the countryside is characteristic of interest representation more broadly in post-democratic transition Mexico. Prior to the onset of electoral competition in the 1980s and 1990s, representation in policymaking, particularly for the popular classes, was monopolized by sectoral organizations of the PRI, such as the CNC. The norm was for leaders of these organizations to be co-opted by the ruling party, and to prioritize their role as party broker above the representation of the programmatic interests of their base (Mackinlay 1996). However, the onset of electoral competition opened space for new organizations to form and more faithfully represent their sectors (while the CNC and other party-co-opted organizations persist). Thus, the puzzle is why some of these more recently formed "dissident" organizations—which placed such a high priority on autonomy from patronage-based control from above—would find themselves reproducing this mode of politics.

In this chapter and Chapter 5, I show how the source of organizational capacity—a variable analyzed in Chapter 3—shapes organizations' demands. Those organizations that generate this capacity internally—typically by offering productive services that function as selective benefits—enjoy the autonomy to pursue programmatic policies (e.g., regulatory policy, infrastructure, non-discretionary subsidies) on behalf of the sectors that they represent. Organizations that do not generate such capacity internally often opt to enter into dependent linkages with state or party actors and limit their demands to bargaining for patronage. As discussed in Chapter 3, the ability to generate organizational capacity internally is shaped by the context in which the organization was founded. Specifically, the availability or expectation of patronage benefits at an organization's founding caused it to undervalue the importance of autonomous service delivery for membership maintenance. And some organizations are founded with internally generated organizational capacity models that are exhausted as the services that they offer become obsolete.

Class also plays an important role, as illustrated in the contrast between the lower-class peasant sector analyzed in this chapter and the middle-class small-business sector discussed in Chapter 5. Organizations with a lower-class membership face an uphill battle in sustaining organizational capacity internally, as members are often unable to pay dues and lack the time or civic engagement to engage in the collective activities that generate an ongoing commitment to the organization and its ideals. However, class is not destiny, and these two chapters will detail cases of lower-class peasant organizations that are programmatic and middle-class small-business organizations that are patronage-seeking.

As previewed in Chapter 3, internally generated organizational capacity helps sustain programmatic demand-making in three ways. First, this model offers a sustainable source of selective benefits, therein liberating the organization from dependence on a political party or other external source. Second, the provision of productive benefits attracts a homogenous membership base—composed of those economic actors for whom such benefits are useful—and providing a venue through which those members come to attain a collective consciousness. That is, they come to connect their own circumstances to the broader conditions facing their sectors and identify their interests with the programmatic policies that affect their sector. Third, internally generated organizational capacity guards against pressure of oligarchy, as it helps organizations produce new leaders from within. In contrast, externally generated organizational capacity typically anoints an indispensable leader who monopolizes brokerage of state benefits.

In this chapter, I combine qualitative and quantitative evidence to show that the ability of peasant organizations to generate organizational capacity internally shapes the way that they engage the state and the types of policy demands that they prioritize. I analyze organizations that belong to three nationwide confederations of peasant associations. The first of these, the CNC, has long operated as a patronage broker for the PRI. The other two—ANEC and CCC—are the two largest dissident agricultural confederations in Mexico. While within-sector variation exists in the organizational capacity models and demand-making strategies for affiliates of ANEC and CCC, the former tend to persist in internally generated organizational capacity and have become leaders in making programmatic demands on behalf of small-scale grain producers. In contrast, CCC affiliates typically generate organizational capacity from external sources and specialize in the intermediation of patronage.

This chapter proceeds in three sections. First, I operationalize programmatic and patronage-based demand-making for the peasant sector, displaying survey data to depict variation in organizational capacity models for organizations belonging to the CCC and ANEC. I then trace qualitative case studies of programmatic and patronage-based agricultural organizations, showing how differences in the source of organizational capacity explain that variation. In particular, I highlight the relative timing of subnational electoral transitions and demand evolution in organizations. Organizations that sustained an internal organizational capacity model when a party ally assumed the governorship were thrust into a virtuous programmatic cycle. In contrast, organizations that had adopted an external model of generating organizational capacity were prone to look to the electoral victory of an ally as an opportunity to extract patronage from the state.

In a final section, I conduct multi-variate statistical analysis on survey data of ANEC and CCC affiliates from throughout Mexico to more broadly test this relationship. These data lend broader generalizability to case study findings, showing that the ability of organizations to generate organizational capacity internally is a better explanation for demand type, above and beyond pre-existing arguments in the literature—such as the social class of organization members. I identify a number of factors that do relate to higher levels of *both* programmatic and patronage demand-making, including indicators of social capital (number of members and employees) and the strength of the organization network. Yet unlike indicators of internally generated organizational capacity—diversity of resource flows and member services—these variables fail to distinguish between program- and patronage-oriented organizations.

Models of Demand-Making in Rural Mexico: Program and Patronage

In this section I analyze organizations' policy demands, which vary on the basis of the scope of interests that they represent. While some organizations make programmatic demands on behalf of the economic sectors to which they belong (e.g., small-scale grain farmers), others focus their efforts on demanding a larger share of state patronage that accrues only to members. I first describe this overall contrast in demand types with survey data. In the following sections, I trace the sources of this variation with case study evidence. I show that those organizations that sustained an internal model of organizational capacity (ANEC) engaged in programmatic demand-making, while those that were founded with or shifted to an external model (CNC, CCC) narrowed their demands to patronage.

Survey respondents were asked about their organizations' participation in demand-making activities around several types of policies that I have grouped together as programmatic. These policy areas include infrastructure, regulatory policy and trade, and the adoption or modification of rules for sectoral support programs. These are the types of policies that generate benefits that extend beyond the organization and its members, whether related to the local community or to sector-wide policy. Thus, the extent to which an organization engages in these types of demand-making determines the degree to which it can be said to act as a representative of its sector. Programmatic demands for an agricultural organization may include, for instance, calls for the state government to regulate financial institutions in such a way to incentivize them to lend to small-scale producers.

Table 4.1 displays the proportion of organizations in each confederation that have engaged in different modes of programmatic demand-making in the previous year—including contacting elected politicians, contacting ministry personnel, or engaging in extra-institutional strategies (media campaigns or protest). About two-thirds of organizations in this sector reported participating in each of these strategies in the previous year, with 82 percent reporting any of the three. While the common perception is that peasant organizations are saturated by patronage politics

Table 4.1 Programmatic Demand-Making in Peasant Organizations

	Contact Politician	Contact Ministry	Extra-Inst.	Any	Mean, Prog. Demands Index
CCC (*N* = 25)	75.0%	75.0%	75.0%	83.3%	2.3
ANEC (*N* = 10)	60.0%	60.0%	60.0%	80.0%	1.8
All Ag Org's (*N* = 35)	70.6%	72.7%	72.7%	82.4%	2.2

Source: Author's original survey.

to the exclusion of programmatic demand-making, this finding provides evidence to the contrary.[1]

The programmatic demands index, shown in the final column of Table 4.1 is an additive index of these three modes of demand-making around programmatic issues. Organizations in this sector averaged slightly higher than two on this index, suggesting that most organizations levied programmatic demands in multiple ways. Slightly surprisingly, a higher percentage of organizations belonging to the CCC—a partisan organization with a heterogeneous membership—reported engaging in programmatic demand-making than organizations belonging to ANEC—a non-partisan and relatively homogeneous organization of grain farmers. However, similarly to the organizational capacity measures, as discussed Chapter 3, we must interpret these raw numbers with caution, as they do not reflect the degree to which the organization is involved in these activities, only whether they were engaged at all.

Less surprisingly, all peasant organizations in the sample engaged in patronage demand-making in the previous year, with the average organization combining between two and three modes of demand-making, as reflected in the Patronage Demands Index (Table 4.2). As with the Programmatic Demands Index, this index adds a variety of activities—contacting elected politicians, contacting ministry personnel, or engaging

1. In case studies I found that peasant organizations that are centrally patronage-oriented often demonstrate a perfunctory level of programmatic activity. Unfortunately, respondents were not asked about the frequency with which they had engaged in these different strategies around programmatic issues nor the degree of organizational resources that were deployed in these instances of demand-making. Additionally, social-desirability bias may have influenced respondents to falsely report programmatic demand-making.

Table 4.2 Patronage Demand-Making in Peasant Organizations

	Contact Politician	Contact Ministry	Extra-Inst.	Any	Mean, Dist. Demands Index
CCC ($N = 25$)	91.7%	100%	85.7%	100%	2.8
ANEC ($N = 10$)	60.0%	90.0%	70.0%	100%	2.2
All Ag Org's ($N = 35$)	82.4%	97.1%	75.8%	100%	2.6

Source: Author's original survey.

in extra-institutional strategies—but in this case when the respondent reports engaging in such activities to help the organization access a greater share of subsidies or *proyectos productivos*.

The most common venue for levying patronage demands was by contacting the ministry personnel that administer these programs—a tactic employed by thirty-four of the thirty-five organizations. In contrast, there is some variation in the degree to which the electoral arena is used to access these benefits. While all but two of the CCC affiliates reported contacting elected politicians to make demands about patronage, only six out of ten ANEC affiliates reported using this tactic. Perhaps the CCC's party affiliation with the PRD facilitates meetings with elected politicians of this party who wield influence over the allocation of distributive programs.

Overall, from this first glance at data on programmatic and patronage demands, we can glean two provisional conclusions. First, all organizations engage in some form of patronage demand-making, and the vast majority engage in multiple forms. Thus, the variation in demand-making has to do with whether organizations supplement patronage demand-making with programmatic demands, a form that is less universal. Second, while cross-confederation averages are not particularly different, within-confederation variation in programmatic demand-making is much more notable. This conclusion is heartening, as it suggests that a narrow focus on patronage is not the unavoidable fate of organizations representing the rural poor; and individual organizations have leeway to adopt their own goals, independent of trends in their sector or confederation.

The remainder of this chapter is composed of two sections. First, I employ case study evidence of ANEC and CCC affiliates to illustrate how organizational capacity models shape these organizations' modes of demand-making. I then conduct multi-variate analyses of survey data of organizations in these two confederations to test the broader relationship between organizational capacity models and demand-making.

CCC: From Externally Provided Organizational Capacity to Narrow Patronage Demands

Owing to the exhaustion of their organizational capacity model, initially based on helping rural populations negotiate land claims, CCC affiliates have mostly transitioned to an external organizational capacity model. They rely on the brokerage of state patronage benefits—discretionary agricultural subsidies and social programs—to fund organization activities and offer selective benefits to members. In this section I describe two cases of CCC affiliates. In Michoacán, a PRD-governed state for ten years, the CCC grew into the party's most important rural machine. In Jalisco, where the PRD has been much weaker, the CCC has also been patronage-focused, but much smaller and less powerful, depending on a less regular flow of benefits from federal programs. Both organizations, however, rarely engage in programmatic demand-making.

The CCC-Michoacán is a classic example of a patronage-oriented organization that has reproduced the CNC's model of serving as a rural electoral machine for a political party in exchange for preferential access to patronage benefits. The national leadership of the CCC entered into an exclusive alliance with the PRD.[2] The confederation has been inclined toward the PRD (and its forbearer—the FDN) since the CCC was founded in 1988, but this alliance was only formalized and made mandatory for state-level affiliates in the lead-up to the 2012 election. In a national meeting of state-level CCC leaders following the 2012 election, the national president, Max Correa, asserted that this alliance would continue, and asked the state secretaries general to expel members who had supported parties other than the PRD in the election (personal observation, September 25, 2012).

The CCC's Michoacán affiliate is perhaps the most thriving example of a PRD-affiliated patronage organization. While the CCC and other "dissident" organizations had long objected to PRI administrations' practices of

2. In 2017 the CCC defected from the PRD in favor of MORENA, the party of current President López Obrador.

deviating rural development funds to partisan allies, they largely sought the same type of special treatment once their political ally was in office. These linkages yielded significant benefits in the patronage arena during the PRD's two gubernatorial terms. Leonel Godoy, Michoacán's second PRD governor (2006–2011) instituted a practice known as the "carrousel," where leaders of these groups were granted yearly meetings with the Rural Development Secretary to present their projects and request state funding.[3]

As the largest rural organization in Michoacán, with the exception of the CNC, the CCC plays a leadership role among dissident peasant organizations in the state. For instance, the leader of the CCC often meets with rural development ministry personnel to request increased subsidies to members of Michoacán's Peasant Consultative Council (COCOCAM), a body of roughly thirty rural organizations, mainly PRD affiliated while this party was in office. Thus, Carlos González—Secretary General of CCC-Michoacán since 2006—has frequent contact with members of this ministry as well as other state and federal ministries that control funding for application-based subsidies for economic ventures (*proyectos productivos*) or social programs.

As part of the 2012 alliance, González received a nomination from the PRD for the state legislature. Both González and other COCOCAM participants, including the few PRI affiliates, described him as the candidate of the COCOCAM. Perhaps indicative of the low political leverage of peasant organizations, González was posted for a highly competitive seat in the state capital of Morelia, after having been promised nomination to an easily winnable district. González and other COCOCAM members protested this assignment, but eventually relented and González lost to the PRI's candidate.

CCC-Michoacán's success as a patronage-oriented agricultural organization has led the organization into a self-reproducing cycle in which González's position as a broker in the *gestión* process and the ongoing recruitment of patronage-oriented members are reinforced. The capacity of González to mobilize his base in electoral campaigns made him a valuable

3. Interviews, Primitivo Ávalos, Coordinator, El Surco-Michoacán, November 8, 2012; Valerio Celaya, Adviser for Productive Projects, UGOCM-Jacinto López-Michoacán, August 16, 2012; Vicente Estrada Torres, Secretary of Political Operations, CNC-Michoacán, January 26, 2012; Carlos González, Secretary-General, CCC-Michoacán, December 14, 2011.

ally for the Michoacán PRD.[4] He reported more frequent meetings with state ministries of the Godoy administration than any other COCOCAM member organization and experienced relative success in accessing state subsidies. Indicative of the patronage orientation of CCC-Michoacán is that González listed the organization's main demands, all four corresponded to state particularistic benefits: *proyectos productivos*, housing subsidies, subsidized credit, and training programs.

Like CCC-Michoacán, this confederation's affiliate in Jalisco is also centrally patronage-seeking. For CCC-Jalisco, however, affiliation with the PRD presents the drawbacks of party alignment with few of the benefits. The PRD is quite weak in Jalisco, lost by double digits in the 2012 gubernatorial election, and holds very few municipal governments or seats in the state legislature. Lacking allies in government, CCC-Jalisco is excluded from consultative councils and closed out of state and municipal distributive programs that tend to be delivered on a partisan basis. When asked about state-run distributive programs, Miguel Ángel Rodríguez, Secretary General of CCC-Jalisco lamented: "We haven't been able to access those state programs. [The state government] prefers to send it back [to the federal government] than give it to left-wing organizations."[5] Thus, the purported benefit of party alignment—improved access to patronage benefits—has failed to materialize for the state-level affiliate in Jalisco. The CCC's affiliation with the PRD nationally compensates somewhat for the lack of access in Jalisco. Most of the subsidies that the CCC-Jalisco controls come from federal government agencies. The national CCC leadership supports Rodríguez in negotiating for these programs.

Despite the weakness of its party patron in Jalisco, the CCC devotes significant resources to mobilizing electorally on behalf of PRD candidates. Rodríguez enthusiastically extols the ability of the CCC to turn out community members in campaign events and asserts that in several municipalities, his organization commands a greater following in electoral events

4. While the original statutes of the national CCC prohibited party alliances, the confederation had always unofficially supported candidates of this party, beginning with Cuauhtémoc Cárdenas' 1988 presidential campaign. The confederation reformed its statutes in 2011 to permit an electoral alliance with the PRD in that year's election.

5. "No hemos podido acceder a esos apoyos estatales. [El gobierno estatal] prefiere regresarlo [al gobierno federal] que dárselo a organizaciones de la izquierda" (interview, June 6, 2012).

than the rest of the party combined. I attended three campaign events in Tala, the CCC-Jalisco's base of operations, and neighboring municipalities and observed that Rodríguez was not exaggerating. In each of these events, participants displayed at least as many banners and t-shirts for the CCC as for the PRD. Rodríguez's son (also named Miguel Ángel Rodríguez, but known as "Junior") ran for mayor of Tala in 2012, and although he lost the primary election for the PRD candidacy (under questionable circumstances, according to Rodríguez), the CCC organized daily rallies through the streets of the municipality in the month prior to the election to support the PRD candidate who had defeated him.

The elder Rodríguez concedes that he induces members to support the PRD with offers of subsidies, but he views the dynamic through the lens of loyalty, rather than clientelist exchange. When asked if people who support the PRD are privileged in his allocation of subsidies, he replied:

> If you want me to support you with housing or with a subsidy it seems dishonest that you would support the party that punishes us and then come to me to solve a problem. If you say "I'm a PRIista," go to the PRI and see if they solve your problem. If you go with the PAN, it's the same. Because that seems disloyal to me. At the end of the day, you're going to cast your vote. Why not cast it for somebody with whom your organization has an alliance?[6]

CCC's engagement with the state outside of its electoral participation is minimal. Interviewed representatives of the agricultural and economic development ministries in Jalisco said that they were reticent to get involved with the CCC or invite it to participate in consultative councils since it is so strongly associated with partisan tactics (on behalf of an opposition party no less).[7] The organization has engaged in a handful of protests over the past few years, but these have been quite short in duration—typically

6. "Si tú quieres que yo te apoye con vivienda o con un proyecto productivo, me parece deshonesto que apoyes al que nos golpea y vengas aquí a resolver el problema. Si dices 'yo soy priista,' vaya con el PRI y tóquele, resuélveme el problema que yo traigo. Si vas con el PAN, igualmente. Porque me parece una deslealtad. A final de cuenta vas a emitir tu voto. ¿Por qué no emitirlo con alguien en quien tu organización está en un pacto de alianza?" (interview, June 6, 2012).

7. Interviews, Rogelio López Garay, Jalisco delegation of SAGARPA, October 16, 2011; Jorge Urdapilleta, State Economic Development Council, October 28, 2011.

only lasting a single day—and focused on the goal of pressuring the government for subsidies. In short, the CCC in Jalisco has invested heavily in electoral participation in order to comply with the terms of a patronage-based linkage with the PRD, closing off opportunities for other forms of political engagement.

CCC's narrowly partisan mode of political participation has hobbled its ability to engage in productionist demand-making. Sustaining strong ties to the PRD has forced CCC to prioritize electoral mobilization over other forms of political participation and closed off opportunities to engage with state politicians and bureaucrats who belong to the PAN or the PRI. Since the CCC has attained a reputation as a source of patronage, members are quite willing to participate in electoral events if they see it as a means to reap these rewards. However, there is little evidence that the organization helps members attain a consciousness of the structural problems that affect the Mexican countryside and potential government actions that could improve their economic well-being. As a consultant who works with CCC-Jalisco laments, this problem is exacerbated by the fact that CCC's non-discriminating recruitment strategy has created a heterogeneous and opportunistic membership base, composed of small-scale farmers, day laborers, and service-sector workers, who are unable to identify and are uninterested in rallying around shared programmatic goals.[8]

CCC's party dependence also affects its internal governance, generating a leader who acts more as a party broker than as a representative of lower-class rural interests. Rodríguez is the driving force behind this organization's political mobilization and demand-making strategies. Important decisions regarding whether and how to participate in electoral politics and the types of policy goals to pursue are either unilaterally made by Rodríguez or imposed on CCC-Jalisco from the national confederation leadership. This explains why Rodríguez devotes so much of the organization's resources to mobilizing for PRD candidates, even when they are non-competitive. Rodríguez depends on his superiors in the national CCC organization to arrange for the patronage benefits that he relies on to recruit members. While the organization has an intricate leadership structure composed of municipal and regional committees, these bodies engage minimally in deliberation and are unable to hold Rodríguez accountable to long-term goals. Rather, they compete among themselves in recruitment

8. Interview, José Luis Miramontes, Rural Development Consultant, June 25, 2013.

and electoral mobilization, with the knowledge that the most successful committees receive the greatest shares of subsidies. Given that Rodríguez's status among his members, CCC national leadership, and the party patron derives from his ability to control these benefits, he has little incentive to devote resources to programmatic goals.

These two cases trace the trajectory from externally generated organizational capacity to a narrow focus on patronage brokerage in demand-making. In quite different political environments, both CCC affiliates came to rely on state benefits to sustain collective action following the initial spurt of activism and recruitment through the handling of land claims. Once they formalized their ties to the PRD, their modes of state engagement narrowed significantly, as electoral mobilization on behalf of PRD candidates squeezed out other modes of participation such as protests, media campaigns, and lobbying with politicians of other parties.

ANEC: From Internally Generated Organizational Capacity to Programmatic Demands

In this section, I analyze affiliates of ANEC in Michoacán and Jalisco, organizations that sustained an internal organizational capacity strategy, broad modes of state engagement, and a programmatic approach to demand-making. Like the CCC, the size and vibrancy of these organizations still depended in part on the ruling party; the Michoacán PRD administrations were more supportive of that state's ANEC affiliate than were Jalisco PAN administrations supportive of Jalisco's affiliate. However, both organizations persisted as programmatic representatives of small-scale farmers' interests, which is attributable to their internal organizational capacity models.

REDCCAM is ANEC's affiliate in Michoacán. This organization carefully guards its partisan neutrality—this makes the organization quite unique compared with the CNC and the dozens of other "dissident" rural organizations in this state, most of which have formal alliances with the PRD. Like the CCC and others, during Godoy's administration, REDCCAM participated in the "carrousel," the informal meetings between organization leaders and agricultural ministry personnel to negotiate for subsidies. Unlike other dissident organizations, however, REDCCAM refused to provide campaign support to the governor. As a result, meetings with agricultural ministry personnel operated according to official procedures, and requests for subsidies were not given rubber-stamp approval as were those of the governor's allies. Instead, according to Director Omar Lando, REDCCAM has been forced to impress the grant-making authorities with the quality of the projects that it develops and the organization's track record.[9]

REDCCAM's participation in campaign activities resembles the norm for business chambers more than peasant organizations. In the lead-up to state and local elections, REDCCAM invites all candidates to speak to its members. Candidates who accept are given the opportunity to sign a document signaling their agreement with a list of REDCCAM's goals for rural development policy in Michoacán. Also, similarly to business chambers, this organization's non-partisanship does not inhibit its members from pursuing elected office independently: according to Lando, at least five leaders of base-level organizations have run for municipal office since 2004 and have run with each of the three major parties.

Non-partisanship affords REDCCAM the freedom to devote itself to productive rather than electoral issues. Where other organizations allocate time and resources to participating in campaign events, REDCCAM's activities are concerned with issues of organization building and productive projects. By not associating with any given political party, REDCCAM is less vulnerable to changes in government. When the PRI reclaimed the governorship in Michoacán in 2012—after two terms under the PRD—REDCCAM was able to approach the newly elected administration to collaborate on projects with long-term consequences for rural development. For example, REDCCAM representatives have negotiated with the PRI administration to press for improvements to the state's system of crop insurance for small-scale grain farmers and has met with the governor and rural development ministry personnel to voice their demands regarding the state rural development budget.[10] Previously, PRD-affiliated organizations in the state were only granted similar access to these policymaking arenas if they switched alliances to the PRI.

Such engagement in programmatic demand-making reinforces organizational autonomy through both leadership and membership channels. REDCCAM practices internal democracy—electing a new president from among its constituent organizations every three years. Leaders are chosen

9. Interview, Omar Lando Estañol, General Director, REDCCAM, December 9, 2011.

10. Author observation of REDCCAM meetings with representatives of state Rural Development Ministry, July 2013.

on the basis of their commitment to the ideals of the organization and their vision for future projects.[11] Members are motivated by services that the organization offers directly, especially the ability to sell their crops at higher prices through the cooperative and access to technical staff who help improve production techniques. Thus, members are committed to the organization even in periods when the state government is not forthcoming with subsidies and over time, they become socialized to take a concern in the fate of rural development in the state.

Under PRD administrations, there certainly have been temptations to enter into a formal alliance, as did most other dissident peasant organizations At several meetings, members pressed the organization leadership to build an alliance with the PRD or PRI in order to receive more subsidies, as they observed that party linkages reaped rewards for members of other organizations. However, a professional staff and a democratic process of leadership selection allow REDCCAM to remain non-partisan and strengthen its programmatic demands, committed to the long-term goal of improving conditions for small-scale agricultural production.

COMAGRO, the ANEC affiliated in Jalisco, predated REDCCAM by several years. For the majority of its lifespan, COMAGRO operated in Jalisco under PAN governors and was able to sustain a programmatic orientation. According to Antonio Hernández Alarcón, founder and director of COMAGRO from 1992 to 2011, these administrations were ambivalent toward COMAGRO. On the one hand, they applauded the organization's entrepreneurial model and were quite willing to support its activities with subsidies to improve technology and training programs to improve yields. On the other hand, Hernández perceived that the PAN governments—both at the state and federal levels—were unconcerned about the plight of the small-scale farmer and had essentially thrown them to the wolves in the context of the signing of NAFTA. Thus, they consistently found the state government unreceptive to their programmatic demands. Over time, this led COMAGRO leadership to cease lobbying and into contentious activities, limiting their contact to the Rural Development Ministry that provided subsidies and finance for the cooperative.

While it was non-partisan, the leftist bent of the COMAGRO, its participation in contentious anti-neoliberal movements associated with the

11. Interview, José Antonio Valdez Alcanta, President, REDCCAM member organization, July 4, 2013.

PRD, and the fact that its goals conflicted with core PAN actors (large-scale producers such as the CAJ) foreclosed the possibility that it would play an active role in the design of state rural development policy. The Jalisco Rural Development Ministry has not sought to establish a consultative body for small-scale producers to consult in the government process, as in the case of Michoacán.

The lack of an opening for programmatic representation led COMAGRO to concentrate its energy on the business of grain commercializing. If this enterprise has been successful—with ups and downs over the years—it eventually abandoned its social mission of pressing for pro-small-scale rural development policy. As discussed in Chapter 3, COMAGRO eventually transformed into SiCampo, an organization that represents large-scale entrepreneurial grain traders, a core actor for the PAN. In SiCampo, PAN administrations have found a rural organization that conforms to their preferences for societal participation—business minded, formally non-partisan, and non-contentious.

Multivariate Analysis

This final section analyzes survey data to illustrate the relationship between models of organizational capacity and demand-making on a national sample of organizations belonging to the ANEC and CCC confederations. I also introduce a set of additional survey measures to gauge the explanatory power of organizational capacity—my hypothesized variable—versus alternative explanations. In particular, I analyze variables reflecting the class of the organization's members and the density of ties that the organization has with other rural organizations. I analyze the relationship between each of these variables and measures of both programmatic and patronage demand-making. Where a given variable is significantly associated with both of these modes of demand-making, we may surmise that that organizational trait engenders overall organizational dynamism—making the organization more successful at pursuing its chosen ends. However, in other cases, the explanatory variables may be associated with only one or the other of these modes of demand-making.

Table 4.3 displays several measures of organizational traits. These are characteristics that may be thought to produce different demand-making orientations in organizations aside from the dimensions of organizational capacity discussed in Chapter 3 (resource flows and member

Table 4.3 Organizational Traits for Peasant Organizations

Trait	Description	CCC (N = 25)			ANEC (N = 11)		
		Min	Mean	Max	Min	Mean	Max
No. Members	No. of registered members	100	5,988	12,000	129	3,274	15,000
No. Employees	No. of full-time salaried employees	0	5.5	20	2	7.8	25
Percent Micro Members	% members <10 hectares (ag); <10 employees (bus)	10.0%	72.6%	100%	5.0%	50.7%	100%
Org. Contact	No. times contacted org. in same sector in past year	0	15	100	1	28.7	50
Meetings	No. full membership meetings in past three years	1	13	120	2	15.7	60
Attendance	% members attending most recent meeting	2.7%	46.4%	100%	20.0%	71.4%	100%
Leader Tenure	How many years current leader	1	3.8	13	0	2.7	8

Source: Author's original survey.

services). These variables illustrate an overall high degree of similarity between organizations in these two confederations. The first three variables are measures of organizations' human capital. First, the size of the organization—measured as the *Number of Members*—is potentially an indicator of greater organizational dynamism or stability (Bruderl and Schussler 1990; Freeman, Carroll, and Hannan 1983). This could lead us to predict either that larger organizations engage to a greater degree in all modes of demand-making and/or to engage more in programmatic demand-making, as the latter is a less accessible policymaking sphere. The number of paid employees similarly depicts organizational dynamism, while also reflecting the organization's financial position.

Percent Micro Members is a measure of the organization's class composition, depicting the percent of an organization's members that belong to the micro classification for their respective sector—in the agricultural sector this includes those owning fewer than ten hectares of land, including landless rural dwellers. The most consistent prevailing explanation in the literature for programmatic versus patronage demands is that the poor are more vulnerable to patronage politics than other class groups (Calvo and Murillo 2004, 743–45; Dixit and Londregan 1996, 1144; Stokes et al. 2013,

158–71). This account leads to the prediction that *Percent Micro Members* is positively associated with Patronage Demands and negatively associated with Programmatic Demands.

There is not a great deal of variation between the two confederations on these variables. While CCC affiliates tend to have a greater number of members, ANEC affiliates tend to have more employees. Perhaps more importantly, roughly three-fourths of CCC membership on average are "micro" farmers or work outside of agriculture, while only about half of the typical ANEC affiliate pertain to this category. Case study findings point to a more important distinction, as ANEC affiliates have a homogenous membership base—all members are small-to-medium sized grain producers—while many members of CCC affiliates are not agricultural producers at all. Member homogeneity is a predictor for the ability to solve collective action problems, as it makes it easier both to produce selective benefits that appeal to the membership more broadly and to align on a common set of collective goals, in this case demands on the state for a pro-small-scale grain farmer rural development policy.

The remaining variables reflect organizations' internal and external structuration. *Organizational Contacts* measures the number of other peasant organizations that the organization has contacted in the prior year. This variable reflects the size of organizations' networks; wider networks are predicted to avail organizations of greater influence and information (Granovetter 1973; Tarrow 1998, chap. 6). ANEC affiliates on average reported close to twice as many instances of contacting other agricultural organizations as CCC affiliates in the previous year (29 vs. 15), suggesting that affiliates of the former confederation have a more diverse source of information and broader perspective on the conditions in the sector.

The final three variables in Table 4.3 reflect internal structuration. Theories of internal democracy predict that as organizations have greater leadership rotation and more participatory decision-making processes—reflected in more frequent meetings and greater attendance at meetings—they should be more successful at pursuing the goals of membership as opposed to falling prey to oligarchy and narrowing goals to the demands of leadership (Fox 1992a; Michels 1915; Voss and Sherman 2000). It is not altogether obvious that more democratic organizations would necessarily be more programmatic; members certainly have an interest in extracting patronage benefits and thus may push leaders to emphasize patronage politics even in highly democratic organizations. However, as discussed previously, I expect oligarchy to be linked to a patronage orientation, as an entrenched leader often reaches and reinforces their dominant position by acting as a broker for benefits. Here we see signs that ANEC affiliates are more "democratic," with an average attendance of 71 percent at their most recent meeting versus 46 percent for the CCC and an average leader tenure that is a year less than CCC (2.7 years vs. 3.8 years). Both confederations have rules limiting the duration of terms for their affiliates' leaders to eight years. While ANEC affiliates consistently abide by this restriction, several CCC affiliates have been granted exceptions by the national leadership. Three CCC participants in the survey reported that their leaders at the time had been in office for nine, ten, and thirteen years.

How do organizational traits relate to the different demand-making orientations of peasant organizations? The graphs displayed in Figures 4.1 and 4.2 display predicted correlations from multi-variate regression models between several of these variables and the programmatic and patronage demand-making indices presented in this chapter's first section.[12] All variables are standardized—hash marks reflect standard deviations above and below the mean value.

By analyzing the association between these variables and both programmatic and patronage demand-making, I sort between four potential types of traits. First, some traits may bestow *organizational dynamism*, improving organizations' ability to engage in both types of demand-making. Second, traits may be associated with programmatic, but not patronage, demand-making, bolstering the ability of the organization to be representative of their sectors in programmatic policies. Inversely, traits may be related to patronage, but not programmatic demand-making. Finally, some traits may not be associated with greater demand-making of either variety.

Figure 4.1 displays variables associated with human capital—members, employees, and class composition (as measured by percent landless/small-scale producers). Both the number of members and the number of employees are positively associated with both programmatic and patronage demand-making, suggesting that these factors bestow *organizational dynamism*. These two associations are significant at the 90 percent confidence level for both dependent variables, as shown in Appendix A. The magnitude of members and personnel lends itself to all types of demand-making. In contrast, the class composition of organizations appears to have no significant effect on either demand-making index. Taken together, the findings in Figure 4.1 suggest that indicators of human capital, while important, are

12. These graphs reflect the marginal effect of each of the covariates from Model 7 in each set of regressions presented in Appendix A.

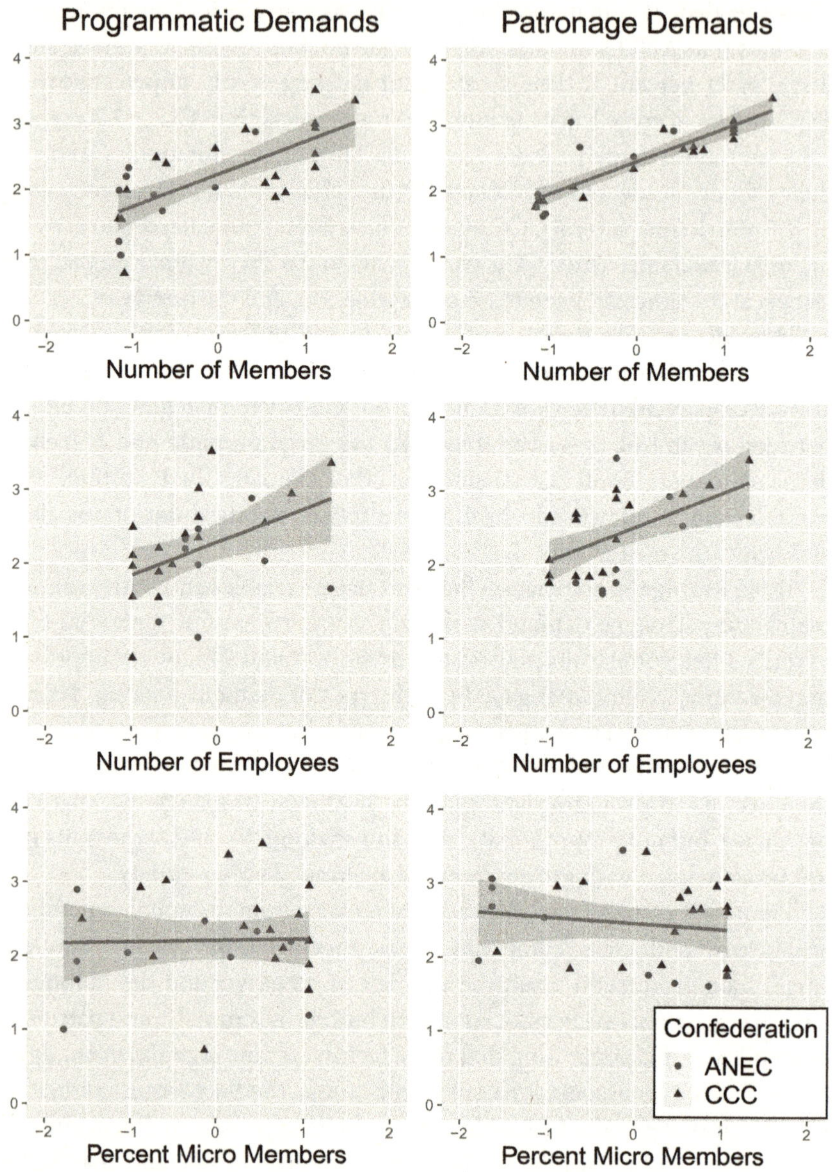

Figure 4.1 Human Capital and Demand-Making, Predicted Values
Source: Author's original survey.
Note: N = 28. Points represent predicted values on Programmatic Demands Index and Patronage Demands Index from Model 7 in regression tables presented in Appendix A and lines depict marginal effects from these same models. Independent variables are standardized with units on the x-axis demonstrating standard deviations from the mean.

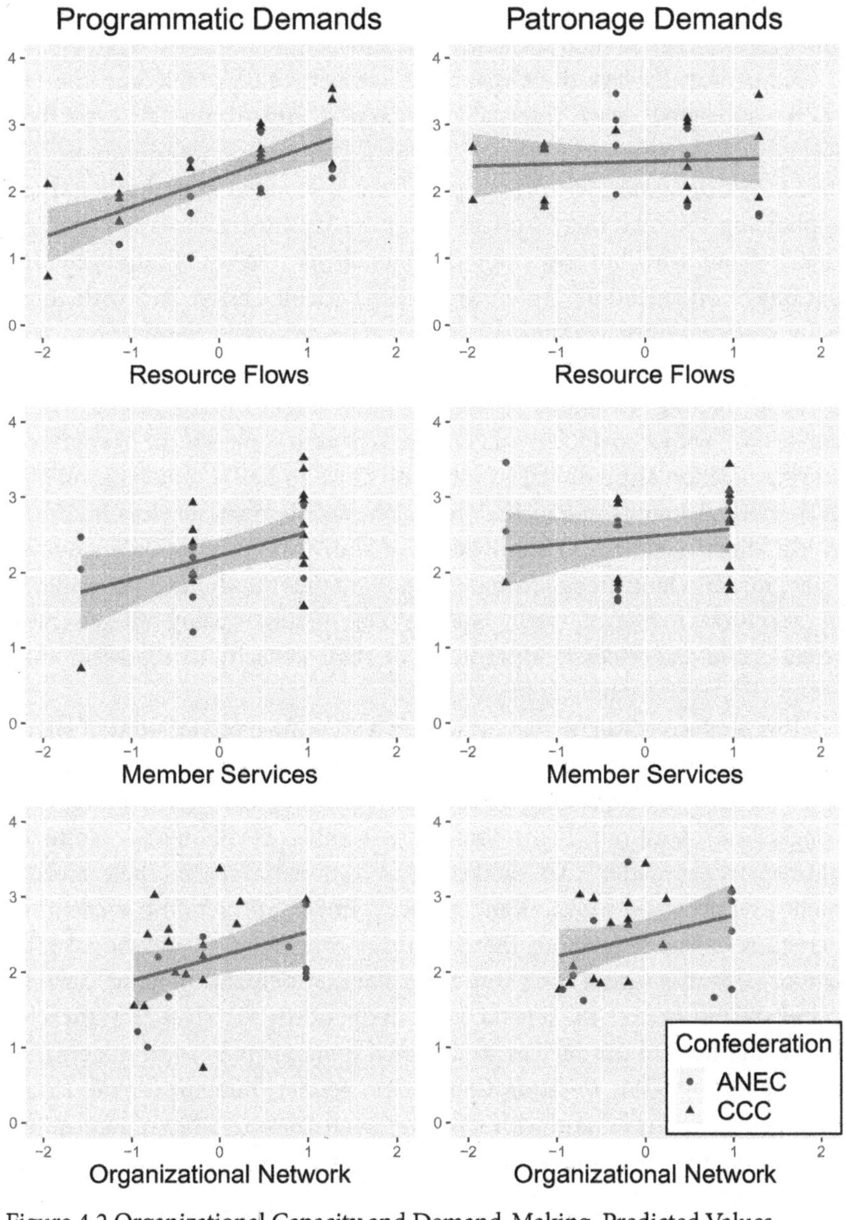

Figure 4.2 Organizational Capacity and Demand-Making, Predicted Values
Source: Author's original survey.
Note: N = 28. Points represent predicted values on Programmatic Demands Index and Patronage Demands Index from Model 7 in regression tables presented in Appendix A and lines depict marginal effects from these same models. Independent variables are standardized with units on the x-axis demonstrating standard deviations from the mean.

not very predictive of why some organizations concentrate on patronage and others integrate programmatic demands.

Figure 4.2 displays the Organizational Network variable and the two traits associated with internally generated organizational capacity—Resource Diversity and Member Services. Like indicators of human capital, Organizational Network is positively associated with both indices, supporting the idea that stronger networks lend themselves to organizational dynamism, but does not distinguish between programmatic and patronage organizations. In contrast, the variables associated with internally generated organizational capacity reflect positive associations with programmatic demand-making, but no notable relationship with patronage demand-making. Resource Flows is significant at the 95-percent confidence level with a coefficient of .40. For each additional source of resources an organization is predicted to move up close to half a point on the programmatic demands index. The coefficient for Member Services is .25 and is just short of statistical significance at the 90-percent confidence level. These findings lend credence to my argument that the ability of agricultural organizations to recruit, retain, and mobilize members using self-generated resources and services is a predictor of their capacity to represent their sectors in programmatic policymaking.

This analysis of survey data provides a window into variation of small-scale agricultural organizations in the present day and the traits that tend to be associated with programmatic and patronage demand-making. Four conclusions stand out. First, despite the significant differences discussed between the broader CCC and ANEC confederations in their recruitment practices and political engagement, important *within-confederation* variation exists, suggesting that the local conditions of individual affiliate organizations go a long way to explaining demand-making. Second, I find strong support for several, but not all, of the variables hypothesized in the literature to produce organizational dynamism, bolstering demand-making in general. Organizations with greater human capital (more members, employees) and with more connectedness to other organizations in their sector are more successful *both in programmatic* and *patronage demand-making.*

Third, the variables associated with internally generated organizational capacity are significant predictors of programmatic, but not patronage, demand-making. This finding suggests that resource autonomy and the ability to attract members with self-generated selective benefits are not so much predictors of organizational dynamism broadly, but rather cross-cutting factors that explain the demand-making orientation of these organizations. Finally, the class of the organizations' members does not predict the degree of either programmatic or patronage demand-making, counter to prevailing expectations in the literature. Whether considered alone or controlling for other traits of organizations related to their strategies for sustaining collective action, the economic status of their members does not do a very good job of predicting demand-making. As I will show in Chapter 5, class is not entirely irrelevant to explaining demand-making. Business chambers—representing middle-class members—evade a narrow patronage orientation to a much greater degree than lower-class agricultural organizations. This advantage is attributable to their ability to generate resources through member dues and a greater disposition by their membership base to participate in an organization for altruistic or civic-minded reasons.

Conclusion

In this chapter I have analyzed demand-making among dissident agricultural organizations operating on the state level in Mexico. I made the argument that the ways in which these organizations generate organizational capacity shapes the degree to which they make demands in the programmatic policymaking sphere. At their founding, these dissident organizations developed either internal or external modes of generating organizational capacity. Those that developed internal models based on the delivery of productive services—and sustained this tactic over the long term—became enmeshed in a programmatic virtuous cycle combining multi-faceted state engagement and demands on behalf of the sector. In contrast, those that sustained organizational capacity through externally provided patronage benefits model entered into dependent relationships with electoral allies, specializing in *gestión* of discretionary distributive programs and losing the ability or interest in levying programmatic demands. These two equilibria are particularly strong when party alternation brings an electoral ally into power.

Evidence from an original survey of dissident agricultural organizations from the CCC and ANEC confederations provides support for the argument that the source of organizational capacity produces different demand-making models. Traits associated with internally generated organizational capacity—a multitude of member services and diverse resources flows—are positively associated with programmatic demand-making, when controlling for other organizational traits in a multi-variate analysis. Other variables predicted to increase organizational dynamism, such as human capital, organizational networks, and internal democracy, either bode in favor of both programmatic and patronage demand-making or are correlated with neither. And social class—the predominant explanation in the party–voter linkage literature for programmatic and patronage demands—surprisingly fails to predict the extent to which organizations extend beyond patronage politics to represent their sectors in programmatic demands.

Process tracing with case studies of dissident peasant organizations in Jalisco and Michoacán depicted the mechanisms through which internal and external models of organizational capacity shape demand-making. In Michoacán, organizations with internally generated organizational capacity when the PRD came into power in 2001 were routed into the programmatic virtuous cycle through an innovative consultative council founded by the new administration. In contrast, organizations that were narrowly patronage-seeking by the time party alternation occurred used this council as a conduit to demand more subsidies as part of an electoral alliance with the PRD. Dissident peasant organizations in Jalisco similarly underwent the solidification of programmatic and patronage politics when party alternation occurred in 1995. However, the fact that the incoming party was the right-wing PAN—not an electoral ally—made both the programmatic and patronage models less conducive to reinforcing organizational capacity.

While this chapter has taken the point of view of the organization, it should be evident to the reader that the process of linkage formation and policy participation is dualistic, and the goals of the partisan actors that hold state power go a long way toward shaping the organizations' representational models. The programmatic virtuous cycle and patronage trap were only so entrenched in Michoacán because the PRD governors from 2001 to 2012 in this state were amenable to incorporating dissident peasants into these two types of policies. In Chapter 6, I analyze the traits of subnational PRD organizations that lead them to incorporate dissident peasant associations into linkages based on programmatic influence or patronage brokerage.

Before moving to the party side of the analysis, however, in Chapter 5 I analyze demand formation for organizations in the small-business sector. These organizations are less likely to succumb to an external model of organizational capacity as they are able to sustain themselves from dues paid by business owners, a more economically advantaged group than peasants.

However, I do observe cases of business chambers that fall prey to the patronage trap through a failure to generate sufficient selective benefits internally. Furthermore, as natural allies of the PAN, a pro-business party, these organizations' demand-making equilibria are reinforced to a greater degree in Jalisco, where the PAN spearheaded party alternation in 1995 and sought programmatic ties to core small-business organizations.

CHAPTER 5

Demand-Making for the Middle Classes

Small-Business Organizations

Historically, collective action for organized business in Mexico has been quite strong compared with other large Latin American economies. As Schneider (2002) noted twenty years ago, this high degree of organization had its roots in the PRI's corporatist system. This system provided formal protection for chambers, most importantly in guaranteeing members—and thus a source of funding in dues—through mandatory membership requirements. At the same time, however, business organizations were intentionally excluded from the PRI's sectoral system, and thus locked out of electoral quotas, which were apportioned to the labor, rural, and popular sectors. As a result, business organizations had strong incentive to generate parallel power structures to serve as a counterweight to administrations that may have favored the interests of labor insiders over business, at least through the 1970s. This chapter focuses on three types of business associations: chambers of commerce, chambers of industry, and COPARMEX (an employers' confederation, always outside the corporatist system) to explain the evolution in their demand-making following the decline of the corporatist system.

Economic and political transitions beginning in the 1980s severely altered the political terrain for business, particularly for the organization of small-business interests. Entry into the GATT in 1985 and the 1994 adoption of NAFTA corresponded with the demise of state protection for domestic business, particularly domestic small industry (Shadlen 2004). And the 1997 reform of the Law of Chambers, revoking mandatory membership, landed a blow to collective action, forcing chambers to devise new types of inducements for members. Post-2000, PAN administrations re-established looser corporatist supports for organized business, in the form of small-business subsidy programs designed to be mediated by organizations (México Emprende, Fondo PyME); and the SIEM—a semi-mandatory registry of firms, which granted a portion of the enrollment fee to chambers. For most small-business organizations, these benefits bolster an already robust set of organizational institutions that sustain organizational capacity internally. However, a subset of business organizations—especially chambers of industry—responded to this challenge by shifting to externally provided organizational capacity, focusing their energies on finances garnered from state programs, to the exclusion of providing self-generated services.

Throughout the twentieth century, COPARMEX was an exceptional case: a business organization intentionally positioned outside (and often in opposition to) the PRI's corporatist system. This organization was founded as a representative of corporate interests in labor disputes with PRI-incorporated unions. The long-standing success of COPARMEX in the absence of state subsidy is attributable in part to this organization's class position. Throughout PRI dominance, dissident *popular-sector* groups—labor and peasants mainly—frequently splintered off from the PRI's corporatist structure or threatened it from the outside. Yet these organizations were routinely co-opted through promises of state benefits and nominations for their leaders.[1] In all likelihood, COPARMEX's ability to resist such co-optation was enabled by its members' privileged economic status. Like early PANistas (often also business leaders), early COPARMEX members are depicted in the literature as ideologically driven activists who derived prestige from their membership in an autonomous organization representing their class interests (Mizrahi 2003).

More broadly, business organizations—in contrast to peasant organizations—benefit from the middle-class nature of their members, which grants freedom from the need to constantly find external sources of funding. Middle-class organizations may collect member dues to fund organization activities. They also can attract members with non-financial selective benefits, such as participation in networking events.

Nonetheless, my research uncovers several examples of business chambers that concentrate their resources and attention on extracting state

1. The "two carrots then a stick" (Smith 1979, 57) practice meant that great pains were taken to co-opt dissident organizations before resorting to outright oppression. However, accounts of state violence against dissident labor and peasant organizations certainly populate historical studies (Handelman 1976; McCormick 2016).

benefits, to the exclusion of programmatic demand-making. Even when these benefits are not delivered explicitly in exchange for electoral support, an organization can be said to have an external organizational capacity model if its economic resources and selective benefits for members overwhelmingly derive from government subsidies. There are two variants of such organizations among business chambers. One variant approaches the common *organización de gestión* model for popular sector organizations, devoting themselves to applying for government benefits, and offering the brokerage of these benefits as the main inducement for members. Others, however, become shells (or fronts) of business chambers, existing mainly to collect SIEM checks and perhaps to receive occasional subsidies from friends in government, but with little of substance to offer to their members and thus a very small or inactive membership. As in the agricultural sector, the failure to generate organizational capacity internally—in either of these two ways—restricts an organization's programmatic demand-making capability.

In contrast, business organizations that do manage to sustain internal organizational capacity models are poised to enter the most prestigious echelon of civil society. Where organizations generate organizational capacity internally, they create spaces for the generation of solidarity among the business community. Members become socialized to think of themselves as invested in the well-being of their city or region's economy and that of their fellow business owners. They also become aware of the major threats and opportunities relevant to their sectors, such as infrastructure, crime, or government corruption, that they may otherwise have been unable to connect to their own firms' profitability. As members align their personal interests with these broader sectoral goals, the organization becomes both more oriented to programmatic demand-making and more influential in these policy areas.

Internally generated organizational capacity also improves the image of the organization in the civic sphere, and thus facilitates broader forms of state engagement. While organizations that rely on state benefits may be apprehensive to criticize sitting politicians, those that generate organizational capacity internally are free to take positions on local policy matters. While contentious mobilization is shunned in the business community, press releases by business leaders often make front page headlines in local newspapers. By evoking a civic non-partisan image and demonstrating their ability to shape public opinion, these organizations become prestigious civil society actors, with politicians eager to curry their favor. Thus, these organizations are among the first to be invited to participate in consultative policy councils and can communicate directly with high-level politicians of all parties. Such business chambers frequently count on the attendance of governors and mayors at their high-profile events. And in the lead-up to elections, chambers invite candidates from all parties to present their platforms or to commit to a set of policy goals established by the chamber. All of these are spaces where organizations can wield disproportionate influence over policy priorities through personal connections to high-level politicians.

The remainder of this chapter parallels the structure of Chapter 4. I first gauge programmatic and patronage demand-making in the small-business sector, combining survey data with qualitative observations. I find that a narrow patronage orientation is rare in the business sector and that business chambers are more likely to limit their inquiries about distributive programs to the ministries that handle these programs, while levying programmatic demands through direct contact with politicians and media campaigns. I then conduct process tracing with case studies of business chambers that are both narrowly patronage-seeking and others that are programmatic. A focus on the state of Jalisco—a historically strong site of business organization and a state governed by the business-friendly PAN for three terms—controls for competing explanations, such as the electoral context and the historical strength of the business community. In the third section, I interpret multi-variate statistical analysis from my survey of business organizations to more broadly test the organizational capacity hypotheses on a dataset of chambers of commerce and industry from across Mexico. As for the rural organizations in Chapter 4, this analysis finds support for the notion that more diverse resource flows and member services—indicators of internally generated organizational capacity—produce organizations that are more capable of programmatic demand-making.

Program and Patronage in the Small-Business Sector

Just as in the agricultural sector, I distinguish between programmatic and patronage-based demands in the small-business sector in terms of the scope of interests. Programmatic demands are for policies that stand to affect a population that extends beyond the organization itself and its members. These may be policies that are specific to the terms of running a business, such as the regulation of piracy and informal commerce, licensing and permitting for new businesses, tax or reforms. However, programmatic demands by business organizations may correspond to much broader civic goals, with a stated or unstated connection to the local economic climate. Thus, it is common to find business organizations participating in policymaking councils and taking public stands about such issues as transportation infrastructure, crime, education, and government corruption.

Patronage demands for small-business organizations are for benefits that accrue only to the organization and its members. For instance, state and municipal governments in Mexico operate substantial small-business subsidy programs that may be intermediated by business organizations (Palmer-Rubin 2016). In contrast to distributive programs operated by the agricultural and social development ministries, where these benefits are formally delivered directly to the individual beneficiaries, with the organizations playing an informal *gestión* role, benefits for small business in Mexico often specify the option (or even the requirement) that business organizations sponsor beneficiaries and play a role in distributing benefits. Under the Fox administration, the Mexico Emprende program was designed to finance small-business support services from inside COPARMEX and chambers. And Fox's small-business subsidy program (Fondo PyME) required that benefits be handled by an intermediating organization, often an affiliate of CONCANACO, CANACINTRA, or COPARMEX.

When business chambers appeal to politicians or bureaucrats to increase their funding through one of these programs, they are making patronage demands. These benefits run a wide gamut. In some cases, benefits are earmarked to develop the organization specifically, such as funds to construct a new building or hire new personnel. In most cases, however, they are smaller and more numerous benefits that the organization delivers to business owners, such as subsidies for consulting or training activities or for small capital investments. The most well-known of these programs was known as Mi Tienda (My Store), a comprehensive package that included training to develop a business plan and a subsidy for small business improvements—such as a meat slicer for a grocery store or a display case for a shoe store.[2] Crucially, organizations that make programmatic demands need not (nor do they typically) abstain from participating in such distributive programs. In fact, the most programmatic organizations discussed below all have México Emprende centers and manage a large number of Fondo PyME projects. Thus, the key distinction is whether the organization

2. For more detail on state supports for small and medium-sized businesses in Mexico, see: Saavedra and Tapia (2012).

depends on these external programs to sustain organizational capacity or rather supplements intermediation of distributive programs with the delivery of self-generated services for members.

As with agricultural organizations, I here analyze programmatic and patronage demands in the survey by gauging the degree to which an organization engages these issues through three modes of participation: contacting elected politicians, contacting government ministries, and outsider tactics (media campaigns and protests). The survey was conducted with 104 business chambers belonging to the CONCANACO and CANACINTRA confederations.[3]

Table 5.1 displays the reported participation of business chambers in programmatic demand-making, including demands about infrastructure, regulatory policy, or public issues such as corruption and crime. The vast majority of organizations report engaging in these modes of demand-making and doing so through multiple channels.[4] The most common modes of programmatic demand-making for these business chambers are direct contact with elected politicians and extra-institutional tactics (typically media campaigns rather than protest). There is not a notable difference in programmatic demand-making between the CONCANACO and CANACINTRA confederations, although members of the latter report programmatic demand-making across all three categories at slightly higher rates. Qualitative evidence in the next sections, however, will suggest the opposite—that industrial chambers are more likely than chambers of commerce to refrain from substantial programmatic demand-making.

Table 5.2 displays rates of reported patronage demand-making for surveyed business chambers. While over 90 percent of chambers in each confederation engaged in at least one mode of patronage demand-making, it was quite rare for chambers to engage in all three. In particular, contact with government ministries was the most common form of patronage demand-making, while only about one in six chambers reported engaging in some form of extra-institutional participation (protest or media campaign) to

3. The survey was conducted online and included several incomplete responses. In this chapter I include the sixty-five surveys with complete responses. See Appendix A for more detail on the survey.

4. As discussed in Chapter 4, it is important to note that the survey did not ask about the intensity or frequency of this participation. Additionally, social desirability bias likely induced some respondents to inflate their reported programmatic participation.

Table 5.1 Programmatic Demand-Making in Business Organizations

	Contact Politician	Contact Ministry	Extra-Inst.	Any	Mean, Prog. Demands Index
CONCANACO (*N* = 50)	72.0%	56.0%	88.0%	94.0%	2.2
CANACINTRA (*N* = 15)	80.0%	73.3%	93.3%	100%	2.5
All Bus. Org's (*N* = 65)	74.2%	60.0%	87.9%	95.5%	2.2

Source: Author's original survey.

Table 5.2 Distributive Demand-Making in Business Organizations

	Contact Politician	Contact Ministry	Extra-Inst.	Any	Mean, Dist. Demands Index
CONCANACO (*N* = 50)	70.0%	82.0%	18.0%	92.0%	1.7
CANACINTRA (*N* = 15)	73.3%	93.3%	13.3%	100%	1.8
All Bus. Org's (*N* = 65)	69.7%	84.6%	16.9%	92.4%	1.7

Source: Author's original survey.

access these programs. In contrast to rural organizations, which frequently use protest to pressure for more patronage benefits, even from an allied party, business chambers reserve pressure politics for programmatic issues. Again, the survey revealed no notable distinction between commercial and industrial chambers.

We may interpret the high degree of direct contact with elected politicians about distributive programs as indicative of patronage politics. Routine procedures for applying for and administering small-business subsidy programs involve close contact with bureaucrats at state and municipal economic development ministries. In contrast, we might only expect a chamber to contact elected politicians about these programs for exceptionally large benefits or when asking for a politician to intercede on their behalf to allocate a greater share of subsidies.

When interpreting these rates of participation, it is important to keep in mind that these chambers' participation does not reflect what we typically associate with big businesses' policy influence. Large corporations hold massive sway over policy owing to their structural power deriving from the threat to disinvest and to elite instrumental power from high-paid lobbyists in the capital. In contrast, the business chambers depicted are mass-based organizations—relying on a large membership for political power—albeit among the most high-brow and well-connected of mass organizations. Lobbying activity by these local chambers is likely to take place through participation in state consultative councils or through activities coordinated by local councils of business chambers. For example, the CCIJ brings together the largest chambers and other business associations in that state. Thus, in cases where business chambers narrow their demand-making to the patronage policy realm, they may still have some degree of perfunctory participation through these external institutions.

In the remainder of this chapter, I use both qualitative and quantitative evidence to further depict the contrast between programmatic and patronage demand-making in the small-business sector and to show how distinct organizational capacity models shape demand-making.

Internally Generated Organizational Capacity and Programmatic Demand-Making in the Small-Business Sector

COPARMEX is the archetype of a programmatic business organization. Founded as an outsider to the PRI's corporatist system, COPARMEX had to persist independently of state subsidy from the very start. Situated in one of the states with the strongest history of business political organization, COPARMEX's Jalisco affiliate is emblematic of the confederation nationwide. The organization is oriented to attracting members through service delivery. Interviewed representatives joked that business owners often mistake the organization for a consultancy firm, as they first hear about COPARMEX through word of mouth of former clients.[5] Members are drawn to COPARMEX because of the classes it offers in developing a business plan, web design, marketing, as well as legal services, in particular regarding labor issues.

This long-standing ability to generate organizational capacity internally has translated into an unparalleled reputation as a voice, not only on behalf of the business community, but in many states as the most respected civil society voice. This is particularly the case in Jalisco, a state with a strong history of business organizing and where the pro-business PAN—a natural ally of COPARMEX—governed from 1995 to 2012. COPARMEX representatives

5. Interview, Juan José González Nuño, Business Manager, COPARMEX-Jalisco, October 26, 2011.

participate in several policy councils at the state and municipal levels and are frequently in the media, applauding or critiquing government action. While vehemently non-partisan, COPARMEX affiliates are active around election time in many states, organizing debates between candidates, get-out-the-vote campaigns, and electoral observation activities. And former presidents of state affiliates often go on to run for elected office.

In short, conversely to the case of the CNC as the stereotypical agricultural organization—party-dependent and patronage-oriented—COPARMEX represents the stereotype of business civil society—autonomous and programmatic. For the remainder of this chapter, however, the focus is less on COPARMEX and more on business chambers—commerce and industry—which reflect greater variation within their confederations in models of demand-making. Between these, chambers of commerce tend to be more consistently programmatic than industrial chambers.

A glaring example is CANACO, the Guadalajara Chamber of Commerce, one of the largest business chambers in the country. Also situated in Jalisco, CANACO-Guadalajara engages meaningfully in programmatic demand-making on behalf of the business community in Mexico's second-most populated urban area. Interviewed organization representatives frequently mentioned policy goals for the chamber that are not related to the distributive realm, such as greater state investment in industrial parks, an industrial policy geared toward attracting foreign investment, and legislation to strengthen municipal and state governments' hands in regulating informal firms. At the same time, this chamber is quite active in the distributive sphere and intermediates both state and federal programs that support small-business capital investment and participation in training programs as well as conventions organized by the chamber.

Recruitment for CANACO-Guadalajara capitalizes more on services and networking opportunities than the organization's role as an intermediary for distributive programs. Thus, owners of small- and medium-sized businesses in Guadalajara have ample reason to join the chamber beyond the promise of state benefits. Membership offers discounts for dozens of training and consulting programs, participation in networking events and meetings with politicians, and the use of the chamber's ample facilities for business meetings or events.[6]

---

6. Interviews, Erick Herrera Ramírez, Consultant, Centro México Emprende; Ana Isabel Solís, Manager of Strategic Analysis, CANACO-Guadalajara, October 31, 2011.

CANACO-Guadalajara's stable membership base enhances its ability to engage state and party actors in a wide variety of forums. The chamber's president and vice presidents have frequent contact with high-level politicians, including close advisers of the governor and members of his cabinet.[7] Chamber representatives also participate in several state and municipal government-sponsored consultative councils, including those concerning economic development, education, and government acquisitions. México Emprende staff members are in constant communication with state and federal development ministries. When I asked a chamber consultant for a recommendation of people to interview in these ministries, he offered the names and telephone numbers of high-level bureaucrats by memory and reported that he is in communication with their offices on a nearly daily basis. CANACO representatives are also quite active in the media, hosting press conferences at least weekly to communicate the chamber's position on such topics as security, infrastructure, and the regulation of informal commerce.[8]

Interviewed representatives of CANACO cited two reasons that politicians and bureaucrats pay such heed to the chamber: first, owing to its prestige and position as the primary representative of commercial business in Jalisco; and second, because of its steadfast non-partisanship. Three separate officials in CANACO offered the same justification for their non-partisanship: the chamber wants to be on a friendly basis with government actors of all parties, so they cannot give the impression that they favor one over another. Interviewed leaders of electoral campaigns for the two major political parties in Jalisco concurred that the strength of CANACO-Guadalajara depends on its partisan neutrality.[9] The PRI's Secretary of Organization in Jalisco described CANACO-Guadalajara and other business organizations in the state thusly: "The business groups are non-partisan, they play with everybody. [CANACO-Guadalajara] plays with the PAN, they play with the PRI, they play with the PRD. They want to be in the good graces of whoever is governor or whoever is governing."[10]

7. Interview, Jorge Barrón, Coordinator of Public and Political Affairs, CANACO-Guadalajara, June 21, 2013.

8. Interviews, Jorge Barrón; Ana Isabel Solís.

9. Interviews, José Mauricio Sandoval Cervantes, Secretary of Relations with Business Organizations, PAN-Jalisco, November 22, 2011; Rafael Soltero Razo, Secretary of Organization, PRI-Jalisco, June 29, 2012.

10. Interview, Rafael Soltero Razo.

The chamber is quite involved in electoral politics, hosting events where politicians of all parties present platforms and interact with the CANACO's executive committee. In the 2012 election, the chamber held meetings with all five candidates for governor and mayoral candidates in three municipalities in the Guadalajara region from the three largest parties. In addition to allowing these members to present their platforms, the chamber presented a document of "proposals and promises," to all candidates, which they were asked to sign as a pledge that they would pursue such policies that the chamber deemed important for the state, including regulating informal firms, addressing security in the state, and avoiding indebtedness of the state government.

Political autonomy allows CANACO-Guadalajara to pursue programmatic demands through both insider strategies, such as direct communication with elected officials and lobbying for legislation; and outsider strategies, including weekly press conferences and press releases, where the president communicates the chamber's positions on legislation and policy. Presidents are replaced every four to six years—as dictated by confederation bylaws—by the chamber's executive committee. Democratic leadership selection motivates presidents to faithfully pursue the interests of the organization and commercial firms broadly and do not fall prey to oligarchic tendencies. The chamber generates many selective benefits independently, and business owners in Jalisco are eager to join to gain access to the chamber's services and professional network. Once members join, they become socialized to the chamber's norms of non-partisanship, internal democracy, and concern for the well-being of their sector.

While CANACO-Guadalajara represents a particularly successful case, chambers of commerce elsewhere in Mexico also tend to reflect this link between internally generated organizational capacity and programmatic demands. The Chamber of Commerce of Morelia—Michoacán's capital city—offers an example of a programmatic business chamber on a smaller scale. Like its Guadalajara counterpart, CANACO-Morelia has internally generated organizational capacity, generating resources and membership through a combination of membership fees and training and consulting services.

However, as discussed in Chapter 3, CANACO-Morelia is much less dynamic than the Guadalajara chamber, offering many fewer services and participating to a lesser degree in policymaking in the state. For instance, the director of this chamber cited as a central policy concern a proposed law to regulate protest, which he views as harmful to the business climate.[11] The chamber helped draft the legislation and lobbied for its approval in Congress, yet the policy ultimately garnered only a very low level of legislative support. The director bemoaned the political climate in the state, which he viewed as more receptive to the concerns of the dissident teachers' unions and constantly striking university students (both aligned with the PRD) than with the interests of ordinary citizens and small businesses. The chamber also participates in a variety of state-level councils, such as the Economic Development Council, but this participation is typically superficial, with little chance of influencing the agenda or policy outcomes. In all, while the chamber is involved in improving the productive capacity of members and has a series of programmatic policy concerns, it is not active in the state's economic policy.

This diminished clout is attributable to two factors. First, Michoacán's business community is much weaker and precarious than Jalisco's, with less of a tradition of organizing and political influence. Business leaders in the state complained about a lack of culture of business collective action, in comparison to Jalisco, Guanajuato, or Monterrey, traditional business strongholds. Second, as explained by this chamber's director, the Michoacán state government has not been particularly interested in supporting the policy participation of non-partisan business chambers. Business organizations were quite critical of PRI administrations in the 1990s; and once alternation took place, it brought PRD governors into power, less interested in incorporating business groups into policymaking. In the end, while the stance of the state government does not fundamentally alter whether an organization has programmatic demands, support from the state can strengthen an internal organizational capacity model and reinforce programmatic representation.

Externally Provided Organizational Capacity and Patronage Demands in the Small-Business Sector

In comparison with the Morelia Chamber of Commerce, this city's industrial chamber (CANACINTRA-Morelia) is considerably more focused on

11. Interview, Agustín Rebollar Cruz, General Director, CANACO-Morelia, December 5, 2011.

distributive demands. The chamber has only superficial interest in local economic policy, instead devoting its efforts to maximizing its returns from SIEM and applying to subsidy programs managed by the state and federal governments. In contrast to patronage-oriented peasant organizations, however, this chamber is formally non-partisan, in line with the Law of Chambers and chamber bylaws. However, CANACINTRA-Morelia is dependent on state distributive benefits to recruit and retain members and pursues these benefits to the exclusion of programmatic goals. This organization's narrow pursuit of state benefits is atypical for a business chamber and is explained by the inability of organization leadership to adopt a service-delivery model in the wake of the revocation of mandatory chamber membership.

Since the 1997 chamber law reform and the reduction of state protections for domestic industry, this organization has seen its membership decline precipitously, with roughly 1,600 members at the time of the interview.[12] Today, the chamber depends on the SIEM both for financial resources and for membership. The main source of financing for the delegation is the commission that they receive for signing firms up to the SIEM. But at least as important is the opportunity that the SIEM process gives the chamber to pitch CANACINTRA to prospective members. The manager of the Morelia CANACINTRA described the process:

> The first people that have contact with business owners are the SIEM staff, those who go out in the streets and go door to door. That's the first contact that a businessperson has with the people from CANACINTRA. They go with their uniforms, with their credentials, they explain to them what the SIEM is and what the chamber is. That's where we get an influx of members.

Compared with highly engaged chambers, such as COPARMEX-Jalisco and CANACO-Guadalajara, CANACINTRA-Morelia has quite little contact with the state government or political processes. Contact with politicians and higher-level cabinet members is isolated mostly to the activity of the president, who has irregular informal conversations with the governor and mayor and participates in only three consultative councils of the state government. According to the director of a business consultative council,

12. Interview, Delia Cárdenas Pedraza, General Manager, CANACINTRA-Morelia, January 26, 2012.

CANACINTRA was only invited in 2010 and its representatives often fail to attend the meetings.[13] Representatives of CANACINTRA were only able to mention one programmatic policy goal pursued with the state government, a law that would have required that the state government allocate one percent of its budget to research and development.[14] This bill eventually failed to pass in the state legislature.

CANACINTRA-Morelia maintains a distance from electoral politics. Chamber leaders do not make a practice of meeting with mayoral and gubernatorial candidates during electoral campaigns, organizing debates, or presenting candidates with proposals. Only once the newly elected governor, Fausto Vallejo, entered office in 2012, CANACINTRA-Morelia would "invite him to get to know the facilities, to see how we are working, our plans, and how he can help us with the federal government."[15] Centrally concerned with accessing federal support, from SIEM, Fondo PyME, and other programs, CANACINTRA looks to the governor in terms for help in accessing these programs, more than as a political actor to lobby for state policies to benefit industrial firms.

Unable to sustain an ample membership base without this support, CANACINTRA devotes much of its attention to the process of recruiting business through the SIEM and intermediating federal programs that provide financial benefits for the organization and its members. Close to half of the delegation's employees are young men and women who drive to businesses in the region on motorcycle, signing the businesses up for the SIEM, and receiving a commission for each firm enrolled. Having tailored its personnel and its recruitment strategy to access federal government programs, CANACINTRA-Morelia is unequipped to play a role in programmatic demand-making. While interviewed personnel could cite programmatic goals—greater state investment in research and technology, improvements in English-language education—the chamber delegation made little effort to further these goals in its state. Rather, they explain that they rely on the federal CANACINTRA chamber and the state business council (CCE) to draft and promote policy proposals.

---

13. Interview, Juán Carlos Vega Solórzano, Executive Director, Consultative Council for Economic Development of Michoacán, January 24, 2012.
14. "Contará Michoacán con nueva Ley de Ciencia, Tecnología e Innovación," *Quadratín Michoacán*, November 17, 2011.
15. Interview, Delia Cárdenas Pedraza.

As with patronage-oriented peasant organizations, CANACINTRA-Morelia has specialized in *gestión* and, since it has established this reputation, firms join with the expectation of receiving these benefits. Staff at the Centro México Emprende help members apply for loans and subsidies through Fondo PyME and to participate in training programs and networking events that are highly subsidized by the federal government and bring commissions to the chamber. For instance, members are often encouraged to participate in an online Harvard business administration course. This month-long course has an "official cost" of 5,500 pesos (about 400 dollars), but CANACINTRA members only have to pay 500 pesos, which accrues to the chamber.

Similarly to CANACINTRA-Morelia, CAREINTRA, the Jalisco Industrial Chamber, has seen its ability to intercede in programmatic policies decay. As described in Chapter 3, this industrial chamber has fallen on hard times over the past two decades, losing a significant portion of its membership and having to rent out most of its headquarters to avoid bankruptcy. Concerned centrally with remaining afloat, CAREINTRA participates little in state economic policy. The chamber has very little direct contract with politicians, as it is not listed among the five peak-level business organizations typically invited to participate in state policy councils. (Instead CAREINTRA defers to the CCIJ, a confederation of twenty-three industrial chambers in the state.)

This is surprising given the volume of industrial activity in Jalisco and the historical position of CAREINTRA. For example, in the 1980s and 1990s—when its membership rivaled that of CANACO-Guadalajara and represented much larger and influential firms—CAREINTRA leaders were commonly nominated to chamber positions and elected office with the PRI and PAN (Arellano Ríos 2009). When asked about the chamber's key policy goals in recent years, however, CAREINTRA's president deferred to the CCIJ, and reported that his central concern is overseeing acquisitions by the state and municipal governments.[16] Given that many of the organizations' members are involved in producing materials purchased by the government—from sewer grates to fiberoptic cables—the ability to understand and potentially influence government purchasing decisions is a quite desirable service for members, yet cannot be characterized as programmatic.

16. Interview, Juan Alberto Porras Brambila, President, CAREINTRA, October 20, 2017.

The absence of a strong voice to advocate on behalf of domestically industrial firms in Jalisco is lamentable, owing to severe deficiencies in infrastructure and state supports, which have disproportionately flowed to transnational firms, without the promised opportunities for domestic small business. Recent studies of Jalisco's industrial policy model have concluded that inducements to large foreign corporations have mostly failed to spur the development of locally run firms capable of export (Gallagher and Zarsky 2007; Samford, Breznitz, and Murphee 2020).

A narrow distributive orientation is also common for business chambers in smaller cities, which, like peasant organizations, are often concerned with remaining alive or with propping up the political or economic status of their leaders.[17] Chambers in smaller cities such as Tlaquepaque, Jalisco; Zamora, Michoacán; or Texcoco, Estado de México are vulnerable economically and fall prey to pressures of oligarchy and dependence on external benefits. One notable set of cases are the Chambers of Small Commerce (Cámaras de Comercio en Pequeño, CANACOPE), forty-five of which exist throughout Mexico. These typically exist in cities with CANACOs, competing with these larger more institutional chambers for members. Most of the CANACOPE affiliates that I visited were practically dormant, collecting rents from SIEM affiliations and doing little else. Interviewed politicians and bureaucrats often could not report recent contact with CANACOPE chambers in their municipalities, if they had heard of them at all. Rival CANACOs in their same cities called them "mafias" and denounced their dirty tricks to undercut them for SIEM memberships, allegedly funneling proceeds to a family that controls the confederation. The two CANACOPE representatives that I interviewed operated out of their houses or personal business and had memberships in the hundreds, yet could not report any recent meetings. They also failed to communicate any specific programmatic demands beyond vague calls for greater government regulation to curb competition from large multinational corporations and the large-firm bias in economic support policies such as Fondo PyME.[18]

17. There certainly are some business chambers in small cities that are active in municipal politics, pushing for improved infrastructure or campaigns to attract tourists. Examples of such programmatic small-city chambers participated in this project are Chambers of Commerce in Puerto Vallarta (a Jalisco beachside resort city) and Tlalnepantla (a Mexico City suburb in Estado de México).

18. Interviews, José Carlos Granados, Director, CANACOPE-Zamora, January 27, 2012; Carlo Iván Gómez Pérez, Director, CANACOPE-Puerto Vallarta, November 18, 2011.

Multi-variate Analysis

In this section I conduct multi-variate analysis on a sample of sixty-five business chambers belonging to the CONCANACO and CANACINTRA confederations that participated in my survey. This analysis allows me to more broadly test the explanatory power of organizational capacity as a determinant of demand type, comparing it to other potential explanatory factors in the literature such as class, overall degree of resources or human capital, and connectedness to other organizations.

Table 5.3 displays summary statistics for the business organizations that participated in the survey. In the multi-variate regressions below I explore the explanatory power of each variable in accordance with two distinct hypotheses. Those factors that are associated with a greater degree of participation in both programmatic and distributive demand-making can be said to foster organizational dynamism. For agricultural associations in Chapter 4 I found that membership size, number of employees and organizational networks were examples of such variables. On the other hand, the main hypothesis to be tested here regards the effect of internally generated organizational capacity—measured in terms of resource flows and member services—on solely programmatic demands. Thus, I hypothesize that internally generated organizational capacity is associated with demand type, producing more programmatic demands, but not fomenting patronage demand-making.

The first three variables reflect organizations' human capital—the total number of members, number of employees, and the percent of their members that are micro-entrepreneurs (business owners with fewer than ten employees, a measure of an organization's class composition). Chambers of commerce are significantly larger (over four times the members) and have on average twice as many employees as industrial chambers, a skewed distribution owing to the Guadalajara CANACO, which has 230 employees. On the other hand, CANACINTRA affiliates tend to have larger businesses as members; on average, fewer than half of their members are micro-entrepreneurs compared with close to 80 percent on average in the small-business chamber.

The remaining variables correspond to organizations' leadership, decision-making, and external ties. Across these three variables, CONCANACO and CANACINTRA affiliates were practically identical on average. Chambers on average contacted other business chambers slightly more than once per year. Chambers of commerce held slightly fewer full-membership meetings, likely attributable to a much larger average size. And

Table 5.3 Organizational Traits for Business Organizations

Trait	Description	CONCANACO (N = 50)			CANACINTRA (N = 15)		
		Min	Mean	Max	Min	Mean	Max
No. Members	No. of registered members	50	1101	9000	75	257	800
No. Employees	No. of full-time salaried employees	1	12	230	2	6	13
Percent Micro Members	% members <10 hectares (ag); <10 employees (bus)	8.0%	79.2%	99.0%	0%	52.3%	98.0%
Org. Contact	No. times contacted org. in same sector in past year	1	25	90	6	44	120
Meetings	No. full membership meetings in past three years	0	8	72	0	13	36
Attendance	% members attending most recent meeting	1%	36%	100%	9%	34%	75%

Source: Author's original survey.

chambers in both sectors report an average attendance of roughly one-third of members at these meetings.

Figures 5.1 and 5.2 display predicted correlations from multi-variate regression analyses for each of these variables with the programmatic demands index and distributive demands index as the dependent variables.[19] The three variables that display a significant positive correlation with programmatic demand-making are resource flows, member services, and organizational network. The first two of these are indicators of internally generated organizational capacity. Just as in the agricultural sector, those organizations that are able to derive financial resources from a variety of sources and offer several different services to members engage to a greater degree in programmatic demand-making. The positive association for organizational networks perhaps reflects organizations that are more active in consultative or business councils and thus regularly interact with other business organizations in venues devoted to programmatic issues. None of the covariates included produce a positive correlation with patronage demand-making. Ultimately, it would appear that business organizations

19. These graphs reflect the marginal effect of each of the covariates from Model 7 in each set of regressions presented in Appendix A.

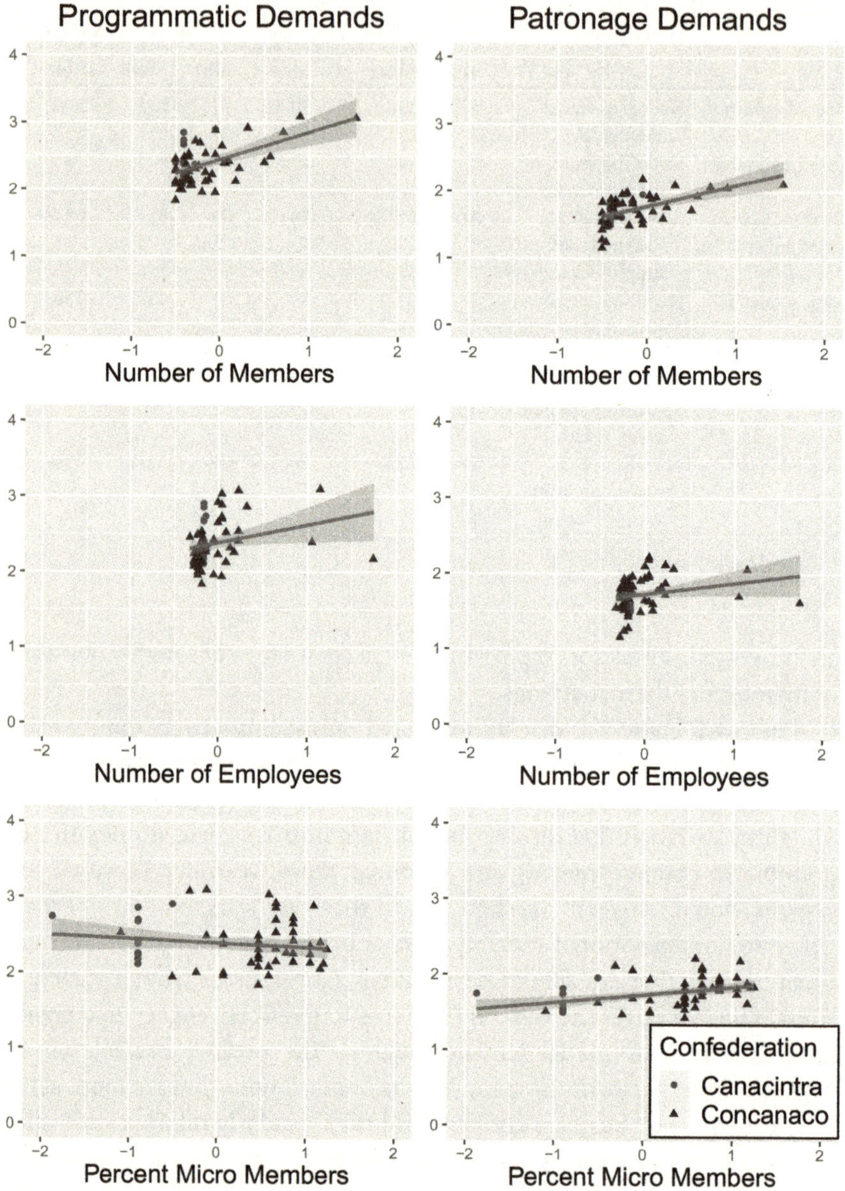

Figure 5.1 Human Capital and Demand-Making, Predicted Values

Source: Author's original survey.

Note: N = 65. Points represent predicted values on Programmatic Demands Index and Distributive Demands Index from Model 7 in regression tables presented in Appendix A and lines depict marginal effects from these same models. Independent variables are standardized with units on the x-axis demonstrating standard deviations from the mean.

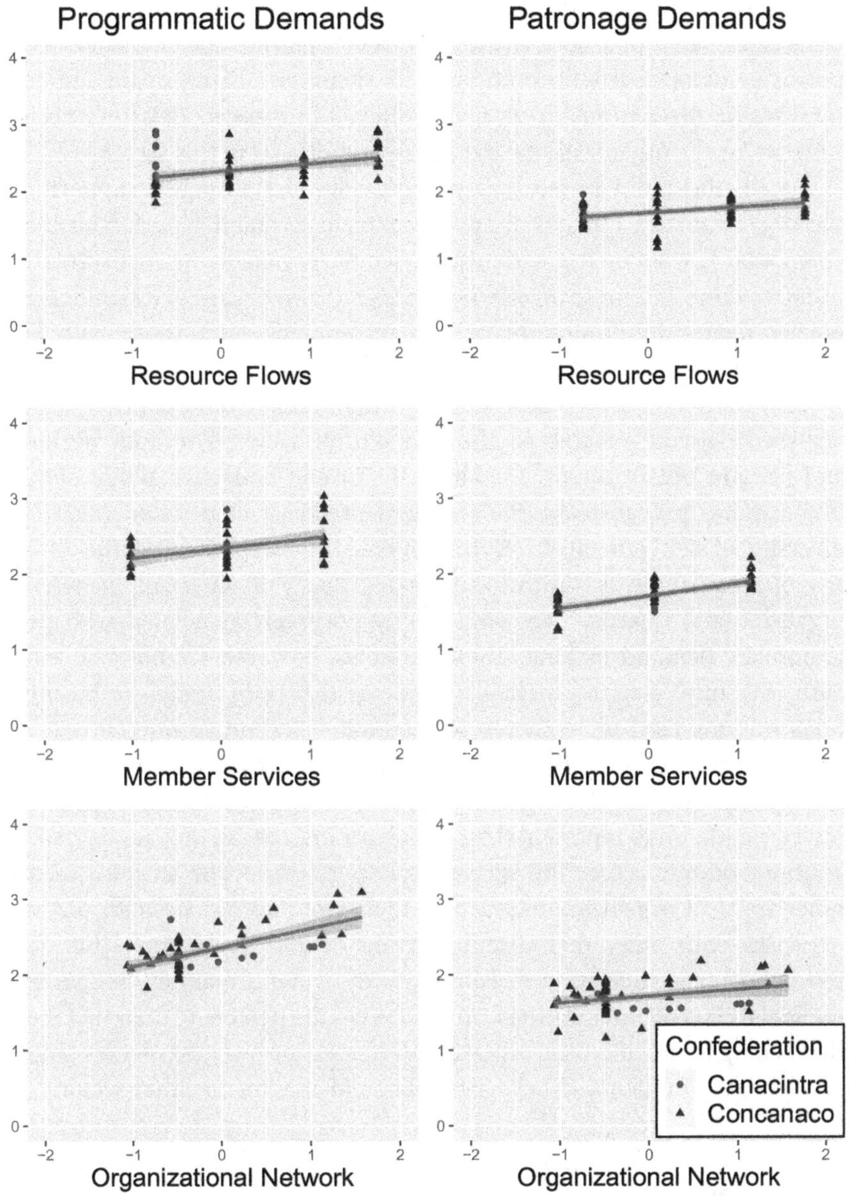

Figure 5.2 Organizational Capacity and Demand-Making, Predicted Values
Source: Author's original survey.
Note: N = 65. Points represent predicted values on Programmatic Demands Index and Distributive Demands Index from Model 7 in regression tables presented in Appendix A and lines depict marginal effects from these same models. Independent variables are standardized with units on the x-axis demonstrating standard deviations from the mean.

are relatively constant in their degree of access to subsidy programs. While traits of human capital such as the number of members and employees were positively associated with both types of demand-making in the agricultural sector, these variables are not significant in these models, offering no support for the organizational dynamism hypothesis in this sector.

In all, the multi-variate analysis provides the strongest support for the organizational capacity model to explain demand type for business chambers. Just as in the agricultural sector, organizations with broader resource flows and more diverse members services engage to a significantly greater degree in programmatic demand-making than those with few sources of financing and fewer services for members.

This analysis of survey data concurs with findings from Chapter 4, which analyzed demand-making in the agricultural sector. For both business and peasant organizations, the ability to sustain collective action autonomously has proven to be the strongest predictor of demand type. The diversity of self-generated services offered to members and the diversity of resource flows—both factors associated with internally generated organizational capacity—are consistently positively associated with programmatic demand-making. These variables, however, are not associated with patronage demand-making. It appears that both models of business organizations tend to be active in pursuing distributive programs from the government. Internally generated organizational capacity, however, strengthens the ability of organizations to extend beyond a narrow distributive orientation to represent their members' interests in policies that affect sectoral conditions. For the agricultural sector, if not the business sector, other traits of organizations, such as their size and the strength of their networks with other organizations, grant overall dynamism—thus fostering higher participation in *both* types of demand-making. In contrast, the social class of organizations—measured in the percent of their members that belong to the micro classification of farmers or business owners—does not appear to influence either type of demand-making in either sector.

Conclusion

This is the last of three chapters analyzing the determinants of demand-making among non-elite economic interest organizations in Mexico. First, in Chapter 3, I reviewed the overall contrast between internally generated organizational capacity and externally provided organizational capacity in the agricultural and small-business sectors. I described the origins of these two models and used case study evidence to elaborate the mechanisms by which organizational capacity models shape demand-making. Organizations that generate organizational capacity internally tend to engender more solidaristic attitudes among members, prevent oligarchic leadership, and retain autonomy from political parties and other political actors that may restrain their demands or mobilization strategies.

These last two chapters have traced how organizational capacity influences demand type in each of the two sectors. In both cases, I found affirmative evidence for the organizational capacity hypothesis. Using survey evidence from roughly 100 organizations across these two sectors, the strongest predictors of programmatic demand-making are the diversity of resource flows and of member services, variables that relate to the ability of an organization to generate collective action autonomously. In contrast, variables associated with alternative explanations either fail to explain programmatic demand-making (such as social class) or are associated with more organizational dynamism (membership size, employees, organizational network) and thus produce higher levels of *both* programmatic and patronage demand-making.

The present chapter has highlighted the potential for the patronage trap to emerge even among organizations that represent a relatively privileged economic class. Patronage-oriented business chambers differ significantly from the *organizaciones de gestión* in the rural sector, as the former sustain (at least the appearance of) non-partisanship and usually rotate their elected leaders, in accordance with chamber bylaws. Nonetheless, examples such as CAREINTRA in Jalisco have affirmed that an inability to sustain an active membership through self-generated resources alone can cause business organizations to narrow their focus to survival. In so doing, these business chambers dedicate a disproportionate amount of their resources and attention to maximizing the state-generated sources of funding that are available to them, in particular enrolling local businesses in the SIEM and applying for Fondo PyME subsidies. In the process, these organizations lose both the institutional fortitude and the public recognition necessary to remain active in local economic policy on behalf of their sectors.

These two chapters have also introduced the specter of the ruling party as an influence on an organization's policy participation. I have sustained throughout that the ability of an organization to sustain programmatic demand-making is a product of the organization's own internal model, and thus we find program-seeking organizations in both scenarios where friendly copartisans govern and in more hostile non-copartisan scenarios. However, the presence of an ally in government does serve to enable and reinforce an organization's chosen demand type. Thus, program-seeking peasant organizations (REDCCAM) flourish in PRD-governed Michoacán and program-seeking business chambers (CANACO-Guadalajara) flourish in PAN-governed Jalisco. In contrast, program-seeking organizations struggle to remain relevant over the long term in states where the governing party is not prone to incorporate them into policymaking—the fate of COMAGRO in Jalisco and CANACO-Morelia in Michoacán.

In the next two chapters, the focus turns to the parties, exploring the factors that shape their strategies to incorporate allied interest organizations into programmatic and patronage policies. Similar to organizations, parties' preferences for programmatic or patronage-based linkages are derived from conditions at their founding. The big picture contrast compares the PAN—an ideologically driven outsider party—to the PRD—a pragmatic electoralist party, and attributes these different party characters to the fact that the PAN was born in opposition to a dominant party and spent several decades as an ideological also-ran, while the PRD was born from a schism in the dominant party and challenged for electoral office from its first days. These different founding trajectories help explain why the PAN has consistently approached core business organizations with the primary goal of organic incorporation in the party structure and recruitment to policy-relevant posts. In contrast, the PRD has typically looked to core peasant organizations as ready-made patronage networks, useful for winning elections, but paying little heed to their programmatic demands. Ultimately the model of sectoral representation—either programmatic or patronage based—is an outcome of the interaction between the organization's demand-type and the ruling party's incorporation strategy.

PART 3

Incorporation Strategies for Ruling Parties

CHAPTER 6

The PRD and Party Incorporation of Peasant Organizations

What interest do political parties have in forming linkages with interest organizations? And under what conditions do party–organization linkages produce programmatic representation for the organizations' membership base? From the previous chapters we saw that organizations approach the political arena with distinct policy goals, deriving principally from whether they generate the resources necessary to sustain collective action internally or depend on external actors for these resources. This dynamic explains whether *organizations* are interested in entering into one of two types of linkages with political parties: dependent patronage-based linkages in which they exchange electoral support for privileged access to discretionary distributive benefits; or autonomous programmatic linkages, in which the organization plays a role in setting sectoral economic policy. However, regardless of the organization's demand-making strategy, *access* to these two policymaking arenas depends on ruling politicians opening channels for organizational participation. In this and the next chapter, I take the party's point of view, interrogating the conditions under which parties ruling at the state level seek to incorporate organizations into programmatic policymaking and patronage brokerage and how these strategies interact with organizations' demands to yield distinct outcomes for policy representation.

This chapter focuses on the linkage strategies of the left-wing PRD with popular-sector organizations, paying particular attention to peasant organizations in the state of Michoacán where this party governed from 2001 to 2012. Chapter 7 analyzes the right-wing PAN and its ties to organized small business. In both cases, I observe ties between these former opposition parties and "core" organizations—those organizations that share programmatic preferences with the party and/or are organizationally embedded into the party, as with the PRI's sectoral organizations. I additionally look at each of these parties' strategies for incorporating non-core organizations into contingent short-term patronage-based linkages.

The PAN and PRD face a dilemma when it comes to mobilizing core organizations. On the one hand, party leaders have incentives to reward these organizations with patronage. During the PRI's one-party dominance, dissident organizations took a risk by opposing the dominant party, foregoing access to state benefits in the process. Thus, leaders of these organizations may view the incoming regime's largesse as their just deserts. Furthermore, organization leaders may make the case that they need these state handouts to remain viable. As the core organization promises to support the party in upcoming elections, providing these patronage benefits can seem like a smart bet for the ruling party.

On the other hand, the long-term sustainability of the party is bolstered by its ability to resist the temptation to deploy organizational allies narrowly as patronage brokers and to rather incorporate them into more durable programmatic linkages. The programmatic incorporation of core organizations yields two benefits. First, it contributes to the long-term goal of party consolidation. Requirements of party building and consolidation are ideological content—or "brand" (Lupu 2013, 2014)—and territorial organizations (Calvo and Murillo 2019; Samuels and Zucco 2015; Tavits 2013), two resources that organizations can provide for parties. First, the organizational linkage signals to members of the organizations' social base (e.g. the rural poor or small-scale business owners) that the party is favorable to that group, allowing the party to establish an ideological brand.[1] And as new parties pivot to the center in an attempt to attract ideologically moderate voters and contest elections, organizational ties can encourage ideological supporters to remain loyal to the party (Rennwald and Pontusson undefined/ed).[2] Second, interest organizations can help parties construct

1. In this way, organizational embeddedness in programmatic policymaking lends credibility to the party's promise to support a given constituency's programmatic goals—a credibility that is often lacking in transitional democracies (Keefer 2007).

2. In this way, organizational linkages ameliorate the dilemma described by Greene (2007, chap. 3) wherein successful party formation in a non-competitive environment attracts ideologues, producing a radical orientation that debilitates the party in competing for moderate voters once consolidated.

and maintain a territorial organization. Parties "outsource" campaign activities—organizing rallies, mobilizing voters, distributing patronage—to the organization prior to an election. Over the long term, organizations may sustain durable base operations, even standing in for party organizations and sustaining ties to voters.

Second, programmatic incorporation of core organizations contributes to the short-term goal of competing in elections by freeing up funds (that otherwise would be spent on core patronage benefits) to be efficiently allocated to swing voters or to public goods likely to have a broader electoral appeal.[3] In this way, the programmatic incorporation of core organizations helps alleviate the need to generate "endogenous loyalty" (Diaz-Cayeros, Estévez, and Magaloni 2016) by continually delivering patronage benefits to the core. Put another way, the degree to which a ruling party resorts to core targeting of patronage is influenced by the degree to which core support depends on patronage. If core supporters remain loyal to the party in the absence of patronage, loyalty is "exogenous" rather than "endogenous" to patronage.[4] The endogenous loyalty assumption is apt for many *voters* in Mexico and other patronage-based democracies, many of whom have been conditioned to view partisanship through the "what have you done for me lately?" logic of patronage (Palmer-Rubin, Garay, and Poertner 2021). On the other hand—as shown in the previous chapters—organizations have proven capable of choosing party alliances programmatically when not in the patronage trap and thus are perhaps more likely than individual voters to remain loyal to a programmatically aligned party in the absence of patronage.

This theory of organizational linkages builds on and modifies existing research on "segmented" linkage strategies, suggesting that a party's ability to form patronage-based linkages with non-core constituencies depends not only on the strength of its activist networks in non-core

3. This strategy for opposition party contrasts with the norm for the PRI, which retained a stranglehold on office for decades despite the fact that it deprived core popular-sector interest organizations of programmatic voice. The PRI's long-term patronage strategy was made possible by its wide organizational networks—constructed during the heyday of popular-sector organizing—and its ideologically nebulous programmatic stance, which positions it as a viable patronage-based linkage partner for organizations across the ideological spectrum.

4. The assumption that party loyalists' support is exogenous to patronage underlies most prominent theories of core targeting (Nichter 2008; Stokes et al. 2013).

communities, but also on the character of its ties to core supporters. Luna (2010, 2014) demonstrates that Chile's conservative Independent Democratic Union (UDI) secured electoral majorities by constructing clientelistic linkages with lower-class voters while retaining middle-class support through programmatic linkages. Thachil (2014) depicts a similar phenomenon in India in which the conservative Bharatiya Janata Party (BJP) courts lower-caste voters through service delivery. As shown by these studies, right-wing parties are able to reach out to poor non-core voters in these ways when they build strong grassroots networks in poor communities and rural areas (a notable weakness for Mexico's PAN). My findings suggest that an additional facilitating factor for segmented linkage strategies is the ability to hold onto core supporters programmatically, therein freeing up patronage benefits for non-core groups. This challenge is more daunting for left-wing parties because their core supporters are more likely to be in the patronage trap than the middle-class core supporters of right-wing parties.

In these two chapters, I also delve into the incorporation strategies of ruling political parties with organizations that do not belong to their core constituencies. Thus, in this chapter, I analyze PRI and PAN governments' engagement with peasant organizations (core for the PRD) and in Chapter 7 I discuss PRI and PRD governments' engagement with small-business organizations (core for the PAN). These non-core linkages are rarely durable and seldom enable programmatic representation, as the policy and electoral goals of both party and organization are at odds. However, absolute exclusion is not the norm either. When confronted with non-core organizations, parties sometimes employ strategies of *co-optation* (constructing short-term patronage accords) or *cherry-picking* (choosing or creating allies with aligned electoral goals within an otherwise non-core sector). Such strategies are particularly appealing when the party faces an electoral threat and seeks to make inroads into the sector in question to broaden its coalition.

Before elaborating on the argument corresponding to parties of the left, I describe what programmatic and patronage incorporation look like for peasant organizations. As conceptualized in Chapter 1, the ideal type of programmatic representing consists of the *routinized* participation of organizational representatives in *high-level* policy discussions, in a way that *exercises legitimate influence* over agenda setting or policy outcomes. In the agricultural sector, such participation therefore deals with the key policy areas that shape the competitiveness of small-scale farmers.[5] While for business leaders such policy access is often reflected in the recruitment of organization leaders for elected office and cabinet posts, leaders of agricultural organizations typically lack the professional profile to enter state or federal administrations. However, several innovative models exist for consultative institutions or participation in the development of party platforms and development plans that grant meaningful programmatic policy access.

A patronage-based incorporation of agricultural organizations occurs through the discretionary allocation of *proyectos productivos* (subsidies for capital investments or training) and social programs favoring the organization. Preferential access to these benefits does not constitute programmatic representation in the sense that the organization sets policy priorities or plays a role in design or implementation of sectoral support policies. Rather, I understand patronage incorporation simply in terms of the organization intermediating discretionary distributive benefits from the state. If such linkages are routinized, the party and organization have a long-standing relationship to the point that the organization acts as a clientelistic network or machine for the party. In contingent patronage ties, on the other hand, the party and organization enter into an alliance in the context of a single election in which the party offers a defined amount of benefits in exchange for support in that election. In either case, the distributive benefits that flow to the organization are typically deployed by the organization leader (acting as a broker), both to recruit and retain members for the organization and to mobilize their members and communities in electoral campaigns (Holland and Palmer-Rubin 2015; Palmer-Rubin 2019).

In this chapter I show how the left-wing PRD's ties to core peasant organizations were more often than not limited to the patronage realm owing to countervailing pressures within the party favoring short-term

5. For instance, a coalition of rural development analysts devised a list of demands that promote the interests of smallholder farmers, including the following policies: allocating a higher share of rural subsidies to small-scale farmers, and tailoring these benefits to increasing profitability rather than consumption; investment in infrastructure for irrigation, storage, and transportation; supporting the formation of cooperative enterprises; constructing market institutions to aid such enterprises to commercialize their products; adoption of regulatory, trade, and government purchasing policies that favor small-scale producers; and sponsoring access to credit and insurance markets (Appendini et al. 2018).

patronage relationships with core dissident organizations. Michoacán, the state where the PRD was founded and was at its most programmatic, is a partial exception. This finding contrasts with the PAN's relationship with small-business organizations (analyzed in Chapter 7), which was more often characterized by programmatic incorporation.

The contrast between the PRD's patronage-based incorporation of peasants and the PAN's programmatic incorporation of business may seem easily explained by the class hypothesis. The PAN's core organizations represent a middle-class constituency and mostly engage in programmatic demand-making, as discussed in Chapter 5. And the PRD's core organizations represent a popular-sector constituency, many of which are oriented to patronage, as shown in Chapter 4. However, experience from elsewhere in Latin America provides examples of new left-wing parties that incorporated core popular-sector organizations into programmatic policymaking, such as Brazil's PT, Bolivia's MAS, and Uruguay's FA. In these cases, the organizations may have been just as predisposed to patronage-based linkages as dissident groups in Mexico, but the parties built institutions to help the organizations sustain organizational capacity autonomously and to institutionalize a programmatic role in the party and in policymaking. The PRD stands alongside these three as the most successful new parties of the left formed in the last fifty years in Latin America (Levitsky and Roberts 2011, 11–16; Van Dyck 2016)—yet is arguably the party that has been least successful at forging programmatic linkages with core popular-sector organizations (Palmer-Rubin 2021).

What explains the PRD's patronage orientation to core organizations? I argue that a party's "genetic traits" (Panebianco 1988) shape the types of linkages that it is equipped to form with core organizations. This argument draws on Shefter (1977), who explains distinct modes of party–voter linkages. Shefter found that "internally mobilized" parties—those founded with access to state resources—would build organizations to engage in patronage politics while "externally mobilized" parties—those formed outside of government—would develop stronger programmatic identities to mobilize ideologically motivated activists. If they survive being exiled from electoral politics, these externally mobilized parties count on strong party brands and extensive territorial organizations made up of committed activists, positioning them to be resilient competitors once the electoral arena opens up. I extend Shefter's logic beyond party–*voter* linkages to explain party–*organization* linkages. Thus, it is the externally mobilized parties that incorporate core organizations in programmatic politics, while the internally mobilized parties deploy these organizations opportunistically with patronage benefits.

Two traits of their party organizations shaped the PAN and PRD's incorporation strategies: the amount of time they spent as electoral outsiders, and the degree to which they incorporate leaders from the patronage-based PRI regime. As I show in Chapter 7, the PAN is a paradigmatic case of an externally mobilized party, having spent decades outside of power, maintaining a principled stance against the incorporation of PRIistas into party leadership or as candidates. In contrast, the PRD had a strong internal current of departing PRIistas and sought to win elections from its very founding. Before even constituting itself as a party, Cuauhtémoc Cárdenas—the party's founder—took up the mantle of constructing an electoral operation to win the presidency in 1988. While in early elections the PRD built alliances with autonomous social movements, particularly in the capital, the party failed to develop the internal structures to guarantee a role for popular-sector organizational allies in party leadership (Bruhn 1997, 214–15). These unconsolidated party–organization ties more often than not yielded patronage incorporation in the long term.

I also analyze here the relationship of the PAN and PRI with peasant associations, which are non-core for these parties. For non-core ties, the linkage outcome has less to do with the party's long-term organizational traits and more to do with the ways in which the organization can contribute to the party's short-term electoral objectives. PAN and PRI approaches to organizations in the rural sector followed one of three patterns: exclusion, co-optation, or cherry-picking. Where the party is electorally dominant, the norm is the exclusion of non-core groups from both policy arenas. However, when facing an electoral threat, ruling parties may *co-opt* non-core organizations with contingent patronage appeals (as observed with the PRI with dissident peasants in Michoacán) or *cherry-pick* organizations within the sector whose programmatic goals are less in conflict with the party's (as with the PAN with agribusiness groups in Jalisco).

The remainder of this chapter proceeds in three parts. First, I describe the PRD's approach to incorporating popular-sector organizations nationwide, showing how the traits of the party at its founding allowed for only a partial and stammering incorporation into the party structure and into programmatic economic policy.

Second, I present a case study of dissident peasants in Michoacán, drawing on field research evidence, including interviews with elected leaders and staff of the most prominent organizations in this sector, representatives of political parties, and staff at ministries charged with carrying out rural development and small-business development policy. I also integrate evidence from newspapers and secondary sources to characterize the relationships between the state and interest organizations over the course of past administrations. I show how the countervailing pressures within the PRD for programmatic and patronage incorporation allowed core dissident peasant organizations to engage this party in either of these modes. Considering that Michoacán is perhaps the state where the PRD most closely resembles an externally mobilized party, REDCCAM is likely one of the few "success cases" of programmatic incorporation of a core ally for this party. In states such as Chiapas and Guerrero, where the incoming PRD administrations were initiated out of splits in the PRI, these governors were more than willing to convert core dissident organizations into patronage networks, but not to nominate organization leaders to important cabinet positions, establish viable institutions for policy consultation, or otherwise grant the organizations spaces apt for programmatic representation.

Table 6.1 shows the representation models for the major agricultural associations in the three states analyzed. As laid out in Chapter 1, for programmatic representation to occur, both organization and party must concur on this mode of linkage. Similarly, for an organization to be mobilized through a strong patronage strategy, both party and organization must be patronage oriented. When party and organizations' preferences diverge, weak patronage representation occurs. In Michoacán, PRD administrations pursued a mixed incorporation strategy toward dissident peasant associations—featuring elements of both programmatic and patronage

Table 6.1 Representation Outcomes for Agricultural Organizations Analyzed

Organization	Organization's Demands	Party Incorporation Strategy	Mode of Representation
Michoacán			
CNC	Patronage	Exclusion	Patronage (weak)
CCC	Patronage	Mixed	Patronage (strong)
ANEC	Programmatic	Mixed	Programmatic
Jalisco	Mixed	Cherry-picking	Patronage (weak)
Estado de México	Mixed	CNC: Patronage Others: Exclusion	CNC: Patronage (strong) Others: Patronage (weak)

incorporation. As a result, these organizations ended up conferring the type of representation that corresponded to their demand type—patronage for the CCC and programmatic for ANEC. However, the Michoacán PRD's posture toward the PRI-affiliated CNC was exclusion, resulting in weak patronage representation. And in Jalisco and Estado de México, the PAN and PRI administrations were uninterested in either programmatic or patronage incorporation of the dissident agricultural organizations studied, producing weak patronage representation. The Jalisco government engaged in cherry-picking, favoring a programmatically aligned group with both policy influence and access to subsidies while excluding dissident groups. And in PRI-dominant Estado de México, the CNC enjoyed strong patronage representation as its preferences aligned with the ruling party, while dissident groups were left to survive with meager distributive benefits.

In the third section, I describe approaches of PRI and PAN governments to incorporating agricultural organizations. For the PRI, this means favoring peasants organized into the party's peasant sector (CNC) with distributive benefits to sustain their role as the party's rural clientelist machine. As a result, in PRI-dominant Estado de México, dissident peasant organizations (such as ANEC and CCC) are excluded from both programmatic and distributive policy. However, where PRI administrations face an electoral threat, they co-opt non-core organizations to woo these organizations away from an opposition party. Therefore, when the PRI took power of Michoacán, it built contingent patronage ties with dissident peasants once loyal to the PRD. The PAN government in Jalisco engaged in cherry-picking in the rural sector. This strategy consisted of selectively incorporating organizations of more highly capitalized entrepreneurial agricultural groups—whose policy demands and partisan stances were less at odds with the party's goals—into both programmatic and patronage politics.

The PRD's Inconsistent Approach to Popular-Sector Linkages

The PRD is unique in Latin America as a left-wing party that formed without access to the dominant strain of popular-sector organizations, as the PRI continued to hold control over labor unions and peasant organizations embedded into its sectoral structure. When the PRD was launched, the PRI had held the presidency continuously for over sixty years and had yet to lose so much as a gubernatorial election. The leftist upstart was formally registered in 1989, after its predecessor—the FDN—was defeated in the surprisingly close 1988 presidential election.[6] The new party was composed of three types of actors: a group of defecting PRIistas, headlined by Cuauhtémoc Cárdenas, the 1988 presidential candidate; small leftist parties that offered the FDN their formal registry to compete in the 1988 elections and merged into the PRD in 1989; and social movements and dissident labor and peasant associations with a left-wing orientation and opposition to the PRI's hegemonic regime. The vast majority of the labor and peasant unions remained firmly entrenched in the PRI's sectoral structure, denying the upstart party with the types of "mobilizing hubs" (Garay 2009) that have lent organizational structure and repertoires of mobilization to other twentieth-century left-wing parties.

However, the 1980s and 1990s featured an upswell of left-wing dissident organizations in both urban and rural areas, which would be the core organizational constituency for the PRD. The PRD's founders were at odds over the types of relationships to build with these organizations. In a departure from the dominant party's authoritarian corporatism, Cárdenas insisted on individual, rather than corporate, membership (Bruhn 1997, 173–74).[7] The organizations that had played a role in building the party in its early years also tended to demand autonomy and adopt norms of formal non-partisanship. Leaders of labor unions that broke with PRI ran for office under the PRD banner, but as "independent" candidates, neglecting to align their unions formally with the party. The most prominent example was Francisco Hernández Juárez, leader of the telephone workers' union and three-time member of the Chamber of Deputies.

There were other figures within the party, however, who saw it as an opportunity to construct a new and more democratic relationship with popular-sector organizations. In their vision, the antidote to the PRI's state corporatism was not the neglect of organizations as a party pillar, but

---

6. The official tally counted 31 percent of the vote for the PRD, compared to 51 percent for the PRI, although the election was roundly criticized for fraud by the PRI-loyal electoral authorities.

7. In the words of Cárdenas, the goal was to "look for people to approach the party, but each person on their own. Since there is a rejection of the way that (the PRI's) corporatism was corrupted, any mode of collective membership was rejected." Interview, April 26, 2010. "buscar que la gente se acerque al partido pero igual cada quien por su lado. Como hay además un rechazo por cómo se corrompió también en la parte corporativa (el PRI), se rechaza cualquier adhesión colectiva."

rather the construction of ties based on a more democratic mode of societal corporatism, where party and organization would be on equal footing. Thus, Cristóbal Arías, a long-time associate of Cárdenas and the PRD's first candidate for governor of Michoacán in 1992, formed the UCD, a peasant confederation designed to promote a smallholder vision in agricultural policy while attracting CNC defectors to the PRD.

The party underwent an abrupt shift in 1997, when (today president) Andrés Manuel López Obrador was elected president of the national party organization, and the party adopted a pragmatic approach to winning subnational elections. Beginning with the 1997 victory in Mexico City's first mayoral election (Mexico City mayors had previously been appointed by the president), PRD candidates eventually claimed the governorship in nine states and have won a total of seventeen gubernatorial elections.[8] However, the prioritization of immediate electoral victories over long-term party building undermined opportunities to recast ties between subnational governments and the dissident popular-sector organizations. Thus, only in states where the PRD had already constructed long-standing ties with these organizations were linkages conducive to programmatic participation.

My analysis partly refutes Van Dyck (2016, 144), who describes the PRD as a classic externally mobilized party, an "opposition party formed under adverse, authoritarian circumstances, [that] built a strong organization with committed activists, survived early electoral crisis, and took root." While the party itself did exist for eight years between its founding (1989) and its first major victory (Mexico City, 1997) the history of the PRD in most states where it was governed more closely resembles an internally mobilized party. Following the initial success of Cárdenas in the 1988 elections, national leaders often sought out local figures—usually departing PRIistas—to challenge for office. This path led the party to enter into instrumental linkages with subnational elites with broad patronage networks and name recognition—useful for winning elections—but weak ideological ties

8. These states include Baja California Sur, Chiapas, Mexico City, Guerrero, Michoacán, Morelos, Tabasco, Tlaxcala, and Zacatecas. The PRD has been part of a victorious coalition with the PAN in an additional eleven elections, across ten states, but in only two of these states (Chiapas and Oaxaca) could the candidate be considered more closely aligned to the PRD than to the PAN. See Appendix B for more details on governors' career trajectories.

to the party or its organizational allies. Thus, in only a couple of subnational units—Mexico City and Michoacán particularly—were long-time party activists central to the PRD's leadership structure.

An instrumental short-term strategy to win elections led the PRD to embrace defectors from the PRI: ten of the seventeen PRD governors held office under PRI administrations at some point prior to running with the PRD, including Cárdenas himself. Six of these held elected office with the PRI *immediately* before assuming the governorship, including the first four states where the PRD won the governorship after Cárdenas' victory in the Distrito Federal—Baja California Sur, Chiapas, Tlaxcala, and Zacatecas. These four candidates were selected during López Obrador's contentious term at the head of the party. In Chiapas and Guerrero, the *second* PRD governors were immediate PRI defectors—after holding the governorship for six years, the PRD neglected to find gubernatorial candidates from among party ranks. In several cases, these candidates were chosen over more ideologically driven PRD stalwarts who were favored by state-level party organizations and social organizations (Cazarín Martínez 2013, 401–04; García Aguilar 2013, 444–46; Solano Ramírez 2013, 365–69). PRI defectors offered the advantages of name recognition, cadres of politicians, and patronage networks. However, they presented little possibility of establishing novel modes of integrating interest organizations into the party framework or policy processes.

In addition to electoral pressure, another challenge for forming organic linkages with organizations was the PRD's factionalized nature. Disparate party factions often failed to coordinate on strategies for incorporating core popular-sector organizations into the party and into policymaking, with significant subnational variation in the types of strategies pursued (Palmer-Rubin 2021). In most cases, these ties are clientelistic in character: In Mexico City, where the PRD won four elections from 1997 until 2012 by large margins, allied urban popular movements have converted into clientelist machines for the ruling party (Bruhn 2013; Hilgers 2008). In Chiapas, indigenous associations have at times formed contingent patronage-based ties with the party, which have generally fallen short of offering autonomous self-rule that these groups aspired to when entering the electoral arena in the 1990s (Cartagena Ticona et al. 2005; Meng and Palmer-Rubin 2017). However, there exist a few notable cases of programmatic incorporation of core dissident groups, such as the peasant associations in Michoacán discussed below.

The PRD and Dissident Agriculture in Michoacán

The PRD's rise to national competitiveness came through a quite sudden emergence from within the PRI. The characteristics of this emergence present three important challenges to programmatic incorporation of popular-sector allies. First, the PRD brought with it a series of repertoires inherited from the PRI—not the least of which was the practice of using organizational allies as patronage machines. Second, the rapidity of the switch precluded the ability to institutionalize programmatic ties with electoral allies: beginning in 1989 these groups—both PRI defectors and dissident outsider organizations—had to be mobilized electorally in a series of tightly contested elections. Third, the party failed to establish a sustainable strategy for power sharing, leading to conflict between factions over the party leadership and little space to grant leadership posts to organizational allies. In Michoacán all three of these obstacles were less acute than elsewhere in Mexico. In this state—perhaps more than anywhere else—the PRD party operation made overtures to establishing a new pattern of party–state linkages with core dissident groups. This owed to the presence of Cárdenas as an ideological leader, a bevy of ideologically committed dissident organizations, and a party base that was more committed to the party's idea of constructing a new model for popular-sector interest representation than in other states.

As the home state of the party's founder, Michoacán is perhaps the state most closely associated with the PRD. Lázaro Cárdenas, the Mexican president who distributed more land than all others, was a Michoacán native, and initiated land reform on a small scale during his term as governor of this state (1928–1932). Lázaro Cárdenas' son, Cuauhtémoc Cárdenas, was the founder of the PRD in 1989. The younger Cárdenas had been governor from 1980 to 1986 as a member of the leftist wing of the PRI, prior to his defection from the party. The PRD claimed the governorship of Michoacán in 2001, with the victory of Lázaro Cárdenas Batel, Cuauhtémoc's son and Lázaro's grandson.[9] After Cárdenas Batel's term, the PRD retained the

9. Cárdenas Batel, only thirty-eight at the time, had previously served in the federal Chamber of Deputies and the Senate for his home state. His victory came after Cristobal Arías, a close collaborator of Cuauhtémoc Cárdenas had unsuccessfully run for the governorship twice (Chávez Gutiérrez 2011).

governorship with the 2007 victory of Leonel Godoy, a long-time associate of Cuauhtémoc Cárdenas. Thus, in contrast to other states where the PRD won gubernatorial elections, the party organization in Michoacán featured a leadership tied to leftist ideological principles, with a greater degree of party discipline, and continuity in its organizational structure.[10]

The PRD's electoral trajectory in Michoacán featured elements of internal and external mobilization. This party's rise to power in the state came after close second-place finishes in 1992 and 1995, elections that featured plausible accusations of fraud by second-place PRD candidates against the victorious PRI candidates (Anderson-Barker 1994). As seen in Figure 6.1, the PRD burst onto the electoral scene in 1992, finishing second with 36.5 percent of the vote in its first opportunity to run for the governorship of the state. Thus, the party expected to challenge for the governorship from its first appearance, a situation that would typically privilege a short-term electoralist strategy. However, the PRD would not win the governorship of Michoacán until 2001, twelve years after the party's founding, forcing the party to consolidate a base organization that could survive without access to state patronage.

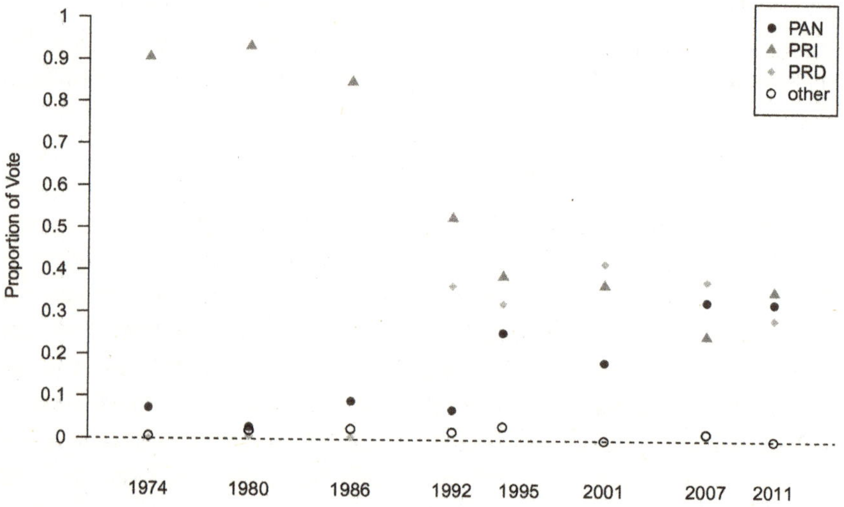

Figure 6.1 Michoacán Governor Races
Source: CIDAC electoral database.

10. After one term of PRI rule (2012–2015), the PRD reclaimed the governorship with the 2015 victory of Silvano Aureoles, the first PRD governor of this state whose political trajectory was not from Cárdenas' *corriente* of the party.

Facing a constant electoral threat, Michoacán PRD governors had the mandate of broadening their electoral coalitions, encouraging a segmented linkage strategy that retained organizational allies while also reaching out to non-core groups. Margins of victory for Cárdenas Batel and his successor, Leonel Godoy, were 5.1 and 4.8 percentage points, respectively, and the PRI retained between thirty-eight and fifty-six of Michoacán's 113 municipalities during the ten-year period of PRD rule.

The PRD inherited a peculiar structure of interest organizations. The party had the sympathies, if not the official backing, of an independent peasant movement that had been revived in the wake of the market-oriented reforms to Mexico's rural development model and the 1994 Zapatista uprising in Chiapas (Zárate Vidal 1998). Michoacán featured a diverse array of rural organizations, some of which had predated by several years the formation of the PRD—UNORCA, CNPA—and others that had come together in the late 1980s and 1990s, when the formation of the PRD had offered a new interlocutor, such as the CCC and ANEC. Only one of these organizations, the UCD, formed in 1988, was formally aligned with the party from its founding. At the same time, however, a prominent faction within the party infrastructure was led by former CNC leaders, loyal to Cuauhtémoc Cárdenas from his previous term as governor, who had defected from the PRI's peasant confederation. These local caciques reproduced practices of clientelism and electoral coercion, tactics that quickly spread to dissident rural organizations that backed the PRD (Gledhill 1995, 73–78; Ramírez Sevilla 1997, 106–10).[11] Thus, in the agricultural realm, the PRD was wrought by countervailing forces—a largely elite-led effort to establish a programmatic partnership with independent peasant movements to promote a pro-smallholder model of rural development and a group of party leaders and rural brokers inclined to reproduce the PRI's rural corporatism under the banner of the PRD.

While popular-sector organizations certainly played an important role in the PRD's rise to power in the state, the state party operation struggled to establish a coherent approach to integrating them into the party.

11. Cristóbal Arías, the founder of UCD and two-time PRD gubernatorial candidate, confirmed that, within a couple of years of its founding, this organization quickly adopted the clientelistic and oligarchic characteristics of the CNC and dissident organizations such as UGOCM, CIOAC, and CNPA (Interview, December 15, 2011).

As with the party's rise to power nationally in the 1980s and 1990s, the PRD's ascendancy in Michoacán featured the enthusiastic participation of organizations and social movements that were eager to displace the PRI and elect a left-wing party. However, these organizations were not organically tied to the party, as are the PRI's sectoral organizations and most in fact rejected formal partisan alignment.[12] Nonetheless, Cárdenas Batel named persons with connections to dissident agricultural organizations as Secretary of Rural Development, first naming Maricruz Campos Díaz, who had broken from the PRI and later founded a local rural organization in the Tierra Caliente region known as Fundación Juan Villarreal. One year later, Campos was replaced with (future governor) Silvano Aureoles, mayor of the city of Zitácuaro and consultant to dissident rural organizations UNORCA and RedMOCAF. Godoy continued the trend, naming Carmen Trejo to this ministry post, a consultant on productive projects for smallholder organizations, having worked with RedMOCAF.

PRD Linkages with Dissident Peasants in Michoacán: Consultative Institutions Serving Double-Duty as Venues for Patronage

The PRD's ambivalence about linkages with core dissident organizations in Michoacán resulted in a flexibility to adapt to the demand-making orientation of the organization in question. Three models emerged. Organizations like the UCD and CCC, formed as party insiders and with a central concern of access to patronage operated as party-embedded clientelist networks. Other organizations—equally patronage-oriented, but less embedded in the party—such as CNPA formed contingent patronage ties with the PRD when it was favored electorally, but flocked to the PRI in 2011 when the PRD's electoral prospects dimmed. Finally, the few programmatically oriented organizations in the state—led by REDCCAM—were granted limited opportunity to participate in programmatic policy.

PRD administrations in Michoacán were interested in enlisting dissident peasant groups to develop a plan to bolster the sustainability of smallholder agriculture. This set of policy prescriptions was outlined in the 2003

12. Perhaps the PRD's most influential organizational ally was the dissident wing of the teachers' union (the Michoacán affiliate of the CNTE), which had taken to disruptive protest in the preceding years to protest the accomodationist posture of the then-PRI affiliated national teaching union—the SNTE.

State Development Plan,[13] whose section on rural development policy *began* with a call to support "free, democratic, plural, and self-governing" organizations of producers. Other elements of the proposal, echoing demands of the programmatic peasant organizations included: investments in infrastructure in the countryside to reduce dependency of small-scale farmers on intermediaries—including roads and storage facilities; subsidies to these farmers to invest in capital to improve crop yields and transition to higher value crops; support for organizations capable of operating cooperative enterprises and lending continued political voice to *campesinos*; and regulations, both against dumping from the United States and genetically modified species.

While interviewed representatives of peasant associations reported an openness on the part of the state government under Cárdenas Batel, attempts at programmatic incorporation really began in earnest during Godoy's governorship (2008–2012). Facing a plethora of dissident peasant organizations, linked to different degrees to varying factions of his party and prone to disruptive protest, Godoy sought to institutionalize the participation of rural interest organizations in agricultural policy through COCOCAM, the Michoacán Peasant Consultative Council. This body brought together over thirty organizations in the state, mostly favoring the PRD, but also including the Michoacán affiliate of the CNC. COCOCAM's mandate was to "promote actions to analyze and construct, with the three levels of government and the congress, the budget and public policy to promote sustainable rural development with a peasant vision."[14] However, the COCOCAM also served as a venue for the routinized negotiation between state rural development authorities and leaders of member organizations regarding their share of yearly subsidies. This process, which became known as "the carrousel," responded to the demands of the majority of organizations in the COCOCAM, which were patronage oriented.

---

13. These plans are put forward by state governments every five years to propose a medium-term strategy for promoting economic development in the state. The development of these plans typically involves the convening of councils with civil society stakeholders over a several month period. The 2003–2008 State Development Plan represents the first such document created in PRD-governed Michoacán.

14. COCOCAM, *Fichas Informativas*. "promover acciones para analizar y construir con los tres niveles de Gobierno y el Congreso, el presupuesto y las políticas públicas que impulsen el desarrollo rural sostenible desde la visión campesina."

The Godoy administration created COCOCAM with two goals. First, this body served as a formal space for core peasant organizations to consolidate electoral ties to the PRD administration. Second, the administration sought to foster regular participation of these organizations in policymaking in a way that would legitimately guide rural development priorities, and obviate the impetus for these organizations to protest. According to interviewed organization representatives in COCOCAM, the availability of this formal structure to make demands on the state reduced the need to turn to protest. As one leader explained the decline in protest activities during the Godoy administration:

> It's not that we've stopped being combative. I think that instead it's that COCOCAM has allowed us to establish a closer working relationship with the government, where we've been able to reach agreements and where there hasn't been so much of a need for protest because there has been permanent, open, frank, and transparent communication. From the moment [that COCOCAM was formed], we have worked with the government on the budget for the countryside.[15]

Shared partisan goals certainly paved the way to this harmony. Of the thirty-two initial members of the COCOCAM, only the CNC and the Coalition of Democratic Urban and Peasant Organizations (Coalición de Organizaciones Democráticas Urbanas y Campesinas, CODUC) were PRI-affiliated.[16] Other organizations were either openly supportive of the PRD or formally non-partisan. However, even organizations in the latter group were open to establishing a working relationship with the Cárdenas Batel and Godoy administrations and many organizations had played an active role in the 2001 and 2007 elections that brought these PRD governors into

15. Interview, Carlos González López, Secretary-General, CCC-Michoacán, December 14, 2011. No es que hayamos dejado de ser más combativas. Yo más bien creo que, que el COCOCAM nos ha permitido establecer una relación de trabajo más estrecha con el gobierno donde hemos construido acuerdos y en donde no ha habido necesidad de la manifestación, porque ha habido una comunicación permanente, abierta, franca, transparente, eso, eso lo creo. Incluso desde el momento mismo [que se formó COCOCAM] junto con el gobierno hemos construido el presupuesto para el campo.

16. Interviews, Omar Lando Estañol, General Director, REDCCAM, December 9, 2011; Marco Rodríguez, Technical Secretary, COCOCAM, January 25, 2012.

office by hosting campaign events in their regions, encouraging members to vote for the PRD, and running for local office under this party's banner.

COCOCAM was granted a formal role in several government processes. Council statutes established that COCOCAM would analyze yearly rural development budgets for the state and suggest modifications to Congress. From its first year, the practice was established that representatives of each of COCOCAM's committees—on finance, commercialization, etc.—would hold meetings at least yearly (and more often several times a year) with the top ministers in several ministries, including not only the Rural Development Ministry, but also the Economic Development and Social Development ministries. Through such outlets, council members generally pushed for larger rural development budgets, more funds for small-scale farmers, and the allocation of programs to the organizations themselves. Citing the precarious nature of the peasant sector, they pushed for a crop insurance program, subsidized fertilizer, and the promotion of smallholder participation in the state's Cruzada por el Maíz (Crusade for Corn) program.[17]

Over time, COCOCAM also integrated activities that extended beyond its formal mandate. For instance, in 2010 the council contracted a line of credit that would be split among member organizations, and in 2011,COCOCAM also initiated the Observatorio Campesino (Peasant Observatory), a first-of-its-kind project to monitor rural development spending in the state in order to track the amount spent on small-scale farmers and detect instances of fraud and electoral bias.

While the COCOCAM experiment can best be described as a partial success in facilitating programmatic engagement of peasant organizations, the PRD administrations proved more successful at facilitating the productive participation of the one organization that was in position to levy programmatic demands—REDCCAM. As discussed in the Chapter 4, the ability of this organization to make programmatic demands was facilitated by its success in recruiting and mobilizing a relatively homogenous and committed membership through a grain commercializing operation that provided farmers with training for production techniques, access to credit, and higher prices for their crops.

17. This eighty-two million peso program, founded in 2009, was focused on improving production yields for corn farmers through subsidies for seeds and other inputs and training programs (Carlos Alonso Cruz, "Contará el programa Cruzada por el Maíz en Michoacán con 82mdp," *Cambio de Michoacán*, March 6, 2009).

Michoacán's rural development ministry was ambivalent towards REDCCAM in a way that reflected the division in the PRD. On the one hand, this organization was the most successful example of a sustainable and democratic model for smallholder production, in line with the programmatic commitments of the party's ideologues. On the other hand, REDCCAM refused to form party alliances and mobilize on behalf of the PRD, a factor that gave it less clout among state party leaders, most of whom were predisposed to a simpler *quid pro quo* mode of patronage politics. REDCCAM personnel would not deny their preference for the PRD, given their opposition to PRI's corporatist mode of rural interest representation privileging the CNC and perceived abandonment of the peasantry.[18] Thus, while REDCCAM pursued a non-partisan mode of demand-making, it came up against a rural development infrastructure that at times (particularly at election time) was more eager to incorporate the organization in patronage exchange rather than programmatic policy.

While his organization must be considered a programmatic success case, Omar Lando, General Director of REDCCAM, lamented that PRD politicians have often been more interested in what REDCCAM can do electorally than its rural development goals. For instance, in the run-up to the 2011 election, COCOCAM invited the three major gubernatorial candidates to an event where they presented a platform for rural development and only the PRI's candidate, Fausto Vallejo attended. The failure of the PRD's candidate, Aureoles, to appear contributed to the perception that he was taking these organizations for granted and was uninterested in including their proposals in his rural development plan.

In contrast, the CCC in Michoacán is a primarily patronage-seeking organization that became involved to some extent in programmatic demand-making through the structure of COCOCAM. Carlos González, the state president of CCC, was one of the leaders in the consultative body, owing in large part to the numerical superiority of his organization—CCC-Michoacán reported having about 6,000 members, the largest among COCOCAM member organization other than the CNC. Thus, González would often be nominated to lead delegations of members in meetings with ministry personnel and was well received by these figures.

18. Furthermore, the president of ANEC, the national confederation to which REDCCAM belonged, had been a federal deputy under the PRD and had been tabbed as the national minister of agriculture under López Obrador if he won the 2012 presidential election.

The capacity of González to mobilize his base in electoral campaigns made him a valuable ally for the Michoacán PRD.[19] He reported more frequent meetings with state ministries of the Godoy administration than any other COCOCAM member organization and experienced relative success in accessing state subsidies.

The fact that other organization leaders viewed the CCC as an ally in pursuing smallholder-friendly policies rather than a competitor in accessing a limited supply of subsidies illustrates how the COCOCAM served to unite these otherwise disparate organizations. When left to their own devices, each organization in COCOCAM—aside from perhaps REDCCAM—was narrowly focused on maximizing their share of patronage benefits, but the process of deliberating over a set of common demands introduced a greater programmatic component, while also consolidating a group of allies for the PRD that did not depend entirely on access to state benefits.

Finally, the CNC represented an outlier in these efforts. As a patronage-oriented organization with firm ties to an opposition party, the CNC did not find Godoy's administration receptive to their demands. According to Vicente Estrada, the CNC's delegate to the COCOCAM, the PRD administrations tried to eradicate the CNC by refusing to fund its members' subsidy applications.[20] The CNC carried out four sit-ins (*plantones*) in 2011 alone, blocking the entrance to state Ministry of Rural Development, but even with this pressure, Estrada estimated that the state government only approves roughly 25 percent of applications from CNC members, a rate much lower than PRD-affiliated organizations. Through the COCOCAM, the CNC's activities were modest, and typically taken in collaboration with dissident organizations. Estrada went so far as to say that he viewed his organization as fighting the same fight as the council's PRD organizations and that he hoped González would win his congressional race (although the CNC would not support this PRD candidate in campaign events).

Unique with its own ample network of state government ties, the CNC did not rely on the COCOCAM as its principal mode of influencing policy.

---

19. While the original statutes of the national CCC prohibited party alliances, the confederation had always unofficially supported candidates of this party, beginning with Cuauhtémoc Cárdenas' 1988 presidential campaign. The confederation reformed its statutes in 2011 to permit an electoral alliance with the PRD in that year's election.

20. Interview, Vicente Estrada Torres, Secretary of Political Operations, CNC-Michoacán, January 26, 2012.

The CNC has representatives charged with outreach to several government ministries, including not only the state and federal agricultural ministries, but also ministries of the economy, health, social development, and others. The CNC has also consistently had several members in the state legislature—five at the time of the interview with Estrada—and often representatives in the federal legislature. As Estrada explained, the organization uses these connections to get legislative attention for its members' concerns: "We have fellow *CNCistas* who are deputies and senators. And they help us open doors, when [executive] governments deny us the chance to look for solutions for our members. Our deputies that are members of the CNC help us negotiate on behalf of the organization."[21]

The PRD's 2011 electoral downturn in Michoacán revealed the contingent nature of many peasant organizations' ties to this party. While during the period of PRD rule, the CNC was one of only two PRI-affiliated organizations in COCOCAM, the electoral composition of the council changed markedly in the lead-up to the 2011 governor's race, where the PRI's candidate was favored, and particularly once Fausto Vallejo came into power in 2012. In the months prior to the 2011 election, several organizations switched affiliations from the PRD to the PRI. Interviewed leaders cited Godoy's poor administration or the quality of the PRI's candidate, but they also acknowledged that the PRI's victory was a likely scenario and that they were promised distributive benefits from Vallejo's administration if they supported his campaign.[22] One year into Vallejo's term, the council split roughly evenly between PRD- and PRI-affiliated organizations and was wrought with infighting as each of these factions sought to take control of the council, which would grant them the power to designate committee leaders who would regularly meet with government ministry personnel.

This experience illustrates the downside of patronage-based linkages with core allies. For those organizations who viewed COCOCAM solely as a

---

21. Interview, Vicente Estrada Torres. "Tenemos compañeros CNCistas que son diputados o senadores. Y ellos no ayudan a abrir las puertas, a veces, cuando los gobiernos también nos niegan la participación de buscar soluciones para nuestros agremiados. Nuestros diputados que son miembros de la CNC nos ayudan a ser gestores, también, de la organización."

22. Interviews, Primitivo Avalos Pérez, Director, Coordinator of Agricultural Producers El Surco, November 8, 2012; Valerio Celaya, Project Consultant, Unión General de Obreros y Campesinos de México-Jacinto López, August 16, 2012; Gilberto González, Dirigente, Coalición de Organizaciones Democráticas y Urbanas, January 25, 2012.

source of patronage, support for the PRD was fleeting. Owing to the lack of consistent commitment on the part of PRD administrations in Michoacán to programmatic engagement and the inability of many dissident peasant organizations to generate organizational capacity internally, patronage politics proliferated as the linkage model for many core organizations in this state. For the organizations, this has the consequence of limiting their capacity to represent small-scale farmers' interests in development policy. For the PRD, this proved to be an electoral liability as it dampened both their ability to consolidate ties to ideologically aligned interest organizations and their ability to mobilize non-core groups in elections with patronage benefits.

PAN and PRI Linkages with Agricultural Organizations

In this section, I analyze the policy of dissident peasant organizations in states governed by the PAN and PRI, parties for whom these organizations fall outside their core constituencies. These parties' programmatic goals contrast with those of dissident agriculture, due in part to their close ties to other organized interests with competing goals—corporate agribusiness in the case of the PAN and the CNC in the case of the PRI. As a result, the prospect of a durable programmatic linkage with these groups is implausible. However, there are reasons for these parties to seek at least contingent short-term linkages with dissident peasants, as their support can be electorally useful.

I observe three approaches of parties to forming linkages with non-core organizations. As a first impulse, parties tend to exclude non-core organizations from both programmatic and distributive policymaking, prioritizing instead the interests of core organizations and voters. This *exclusion* strategy is particularly prevalent in states where the PRI dominates electoral politics—as in Estado de México—and thus has little need to broaden its support base. In contrast, when the party does face an electoral threat, it may pursue a strategy of *co-optation*—allocating patronage benefits to non-core groups in an effort to win their support in an upcoming election. As discussed above, this strategy was implemented by the PRI in the 2011 Michoacán elections, as it promised increased subsidies to rural organizations in COCOCAM if they aided the PRI campaign to defeat the PRD in this state. And as I show in Chapter 7, the PRI would also attempt to co-opt business chambers—typically a core group for the PAN—with distributive benefits in states where it was threated by the PAN, such as Puebla.

A third strategy is to cultivate more durable ties with a programmatically aligned segment of a non-core sector. I refer to this strategy as *cherry-picking*. Reticent to completely neglect organizational linkages in their non-core sectors, these parties seek out groups whose positions conflict less with their programmatic stances. Often, as in the case of the CAJ discussed below, these organizations benefit not only from distributive programs, but are also integrated into authentic spaces for programmatic policymaking.

Peasant Organization Linkages in PRI-Governed Estado de México

The states analyzed in this project offer a glimpse into PRI governments' postures toward linkages with peasant organizations under two distinct scenarios—in Estado de México, where the PRI was electorally dominant; and in Michoacán, where the PRI won a closely contested election over the incumbent PRD and governed from 2012 to 2015. In the former case, the PRI consistently excluded organizations that were not part of their sectoral structure from all types of policymaking. In Michoacán, however, the PRI made attempts at co-optation, offering contingent short-term patronage benefits to dissident organizations in the lead-up to a competitive election.

Dissident organizations are excluded from all types of policymaking in Estado de México and the CNC operates as the main rural patronage machine for the governing party. In agricultural policy, therefore, the main goal of the Estado de México government is to strengthen the mobilization capacity of the CNC. By channeling discretionary distributive benefits through this sectoral organization, the CNC reinforces the "endogenous loyalty" (Diaz-Cayeros, Estévez, and Magaloni 2016) of this state's peasants to the PRI, who might have incentive to defect to another party if they failed to see the PRI as a source of particularistic benefits.

The president of CNC-Estado de México, Edgar Castillo, described agricultural subsidy and rural anti-poverty programs operated by the state government as if they were party benefits, whose criteria for distribution would follow the goal of maximizing votes for the PRI.[23] The CNC in this state is a massive electoral machine, which, according to Castillo, mobilized 230,000 voters in the 2017 elections. The grease of this machine are distributive benefits operated by the state government (and federal government during

23. Interview, Edgar Castillo Martínez, President, CNC-Estado de México, June 28, 2018.

the administration of PRIista Enrique Peña Nieto). Members are recruited through the promise of accessing small-capital subsidies for business, housing benefits, or other distributive programs. According to Castillo, citizens applying to these programs on their own accord have little chance of having their applications approved, but if supported by the CNC their chances are better than 50 percent as the organization controls several thousand rewards. CNC leaders are appointed and promoted as they demonstrate the efficiency with which they convert these benefits into votes for the PRI.

The CNC makes little pretense of engaging in broader rural development policy beyond the brokerage of patronage. Castillo reported that the CNC does not tend to organize contentious events except as a pressure tactic to push the state government to fund more of its members' applications or to make subsidy payments on time. These protests further reinforce the CNC's negotiation power in the PRI's clientelistic system by demonstrating its mobilization capacity, as they bring several thousand members to the state capital in a one-day show of force. On the other hand, when asked about broader issues of rural development, such as trade or regulatory policy, Castillo admitted that he saw little future for the small-scale farmer and that the CNC would be well-served to support the government in the goals of industrializing the countryside.

The Estado de México PRI has little to gain from offering any sort of access to dissident peasant organizations, who constitute for them a non-core group. In contrast to Michoacán, where the Vallejo campaign sought to co-opt dissident peasant organizations, these organizations' counterparts in Estado de México face exclusion from the state government. Dissident groups tend to be small and rely on patronage benefits channeled from representatives of their national-level federations in Mexico City. For example, the CCC-Toluca has 3,500 members and, like other CCC affiliates, was closely linked to the PRD until 2017, when the national-level CCC switched affiliation to MORENA. The leader of CCC-Toluca lamented that the state government is antagonistic to rural organizations that are not PRI-affiliated. Distributive benefits for the CCC are crumbs compared with what flows to the CNC. Of about 350 applications submitted by CCC-Toluca members in 2017, fewer than fifty were funded and only after several days of protest.

Agriculture in PAN-Ruled Jalisco

In contrast to the PRI, whose rural machine was already quite mature, the PAN lacks activist networks in the countryside. In Jalisco, where the

PAN governed for three terms, this party pursued a strategy of cherry-picking: propping up a small segment of the agricultural sector that conformed to its programmatic goals and executing a thorough programmatic incorporation of that group, while also favoring it with distributive benefits. The group that benefitted was the CAJ, a group of medium-and large-sized producers and agribusiness, which operates much more like a business chamber than a peasant association.

This strategy has been much more successful than attempts to create new rural party organizations based on small-scale farmers. In 2004, the federal party organization, with the collaboration of former Jalisco governor and then Secretary of the Environment Alberto Cárdenas, founded the National Council for Rural Action (PLANTAR), however nobody in Jalisco would attest that this organization was still active at the time of research in 2011 and 2012.[24] PAN-Jalisco's Secretary of Rural Affairs, interviewed in 2011, described another rural PAN organization that he and others had formed that year, known as AGROVIVE.[25] However, this project was too little too late—the organization collapsed with the PAN's demise in the 2012 election and I can find no mentions of AGROVIVE in newspapers in the following years.

For the most part, PAN administrations' posture toward dissident peasant associations—most of which are linked to the PRI or PRD—is exclusion, as these organizations are unlikely to contribute to either electoral or policy goals. Government programs that are earmarked for small-scale farmers are managed in a technocratic way, excluding the participation of smallholder organizations. For example, the committee that manages Alianza para el Campo, a subsidy program administered by the state and federal governments, has included only representatives of government ministries at the two levels since the Cárdenas administration.[26] In most states, these committees include representatives from major producer organizations, as required in the program's Rules of Operation.

24. García, Claudia. "Busca PAN ganar voto 'verde'," *Mural*, August 23, 2004; Granados Chapa, Miguel Ángel. "Plaza Pública: Neocorporativismo," *Mural*, June 22, 2004.

25. Interview, José Francisco Flores Martínez, Secretary of Rural Affairs, PAN-Jalisco, November 11, 2011.

26. Interview, Rogelio López Garay, Chief of Information and Statistical Programs, Subdelegation of Planning and Rural Development, SAGARPA-Jalisco, October 31, 2011.

While its participation was not promoted by PAN administrations, the CNC steadily retained significant power during eighteen years with its party patron out of office. The Jalisco CNC is massive, with approximately 300,000 members.[27] As a result the CNC had dozens of its members elected as mayors and local Congress persons during the period of PAN rule. Given the CNC's deep integration into the PRI, it is unlikely that PAN governments could have co-opted base-level CNC affiliates.[28] Rather, the approach of Jalisco's three PAN governors was to isolate the CNC, to the extent possible shutting it out of contact with state ministries and input in the design of rural development policy. Gabriel Ponce, Secretary General of the CNC (2009–2013) and deputy in the state legislature, complained that the executive branch and PAN members of Congress have been unreceptive to his proposed legislation, which sought to establish an inter-ministry task force to make long-term plans for rural competitiveness.

In the distributive realm, CNC representatives interviewed reported that the period of PAN rule in Jalisco had drastically reduced their share of subsidies. Ponce explained that many CNC members have found it impossible to navigate the bureaucratic channels to apply for state programs and that his attempts at *gestión* fall on deaf ears in the state government. The Jalisco CNC has been more successful at receiving federal programs, with ample the support from national CNC leadership.

Lacking the political power enjoyed by the CNC, dissident agricultural organizations such as CCC receive little to no attention from the state government in Jalisco. Interviewed leaders of these organizations explain that they are rebuffed in their attempts to schedule meetings with Rural Development Ministry personnel. When asked how frequently he has contact with the

27. This number is the estimate of former president of CNC-Jalisco, Ricardo Chávez Pérez, cited in Román, Flores, and Govela (2004, 193). Reported membership numbers for the CNC are notoriously inflated. Authorities typically cite the total number of *ejidatarios* registered in the state, although many of these people no longer work on the *ejido*, have migrated, or have died. The interviewed president of the CNC estimated that less than 20 percent of members are active in CNC—at least having attended a meeting of their *ejido* in the last year.

28. The CNC in Jalisco, as elsewhere, resembles a rural party organization more than an organization of agricultural producers. Notably, the state Secretary General of the CNC interviewed in 2011 claimed that he was the first farmer to occupy this post since 1971, having ascended the CNC leadership through *ejido* leadership bodies. He described other leaders over the previous forty years as "políticos" or "técnicos" (Interview, Gabriel Ponce Miranda, Secretary-General, CNC-Jalisco, November 8, 2011).

Jalisco Rural Development Minister, Miguel Angel Rodríguez Castro, Secretary General of the CCC-Jalisco, responded: "Very little because they are very closed off... They work in their jobs very firmly on behalf of their [partisan] colors and since they see that we sympathize with the left, they say 'if we give them support, we are indirectly strengthening the party of the left,' when the truth is that we are autonomous."[29] Perhaps the second most prominent example of a dissident agricultural organization in Jalisco is El Barzón. This organization was formed in 1993 by groups of middle-class farmers marching from the southern Jalisco municipalities of Ameca, Autlán, and Ciudad Guzmán to Guadalajara to protest their untenable debt obligations. El Barzón drew the state and federal governments' attention with a seven-week long occupation of Guadalajara's *centro histórico*, blocking traffic with over 100 tractors and livestock (de Grammont 2001, 81–94; Rodríguez Gómez and Torres 1994, 141–57).[30] The movement quickly took on a national scale, as groups protesting the *cartera vencida* (overdue debt) crisis in the majority of Mexican states joined under the El Barzón banner. After initially taking a sympathetic tone towards the movement, the PRI-led state and federal governments (and affiliated rural organizations such as CNC and CNPR) eventually denounced their obstructive tactics and accused them of having electoral (i.e., anti-PRI) motives. The Jalisco branch of El Barzón agreed to withdraw from the city in exchange for promises that the state government would aid them in resolving their debt obligations on equal terms as farmers in PRI-affiliated organizations. At the same time, the federal government announced a modest increase in the rural finance program replacing BANRURAL, and the formation of PROCAMPO, which offered compensatory payments to farmers in the wake of NAFTA. El Barzón endorsed Cuauhtémoc Cárdenas in the 1994 presidential election and established a formal alliance with the PRD in 1997, running several candidates for congressional and mayoral posts with this party.

---

29. Interview, June 6, 2012. "Muy poco porque están muy cerrados...Toman el puesto muy firmemente con el color [del partido] y como a nosotros nos ven con una simpatía a la izquierda, entonces dicen si les damos el apoyo indirectamente estamos potenciando al partido de la izquierda, cuando la verdad es que somos autónomos."

30. According to a study by the Centro Bancario de Guadalajara (cited in Rodríguez Gómez and Torres 1994, 143), when the El Barzón protest erupted, 7,047 agricultural producers in Jalisco had overdue loan payments, 69 percent of whom owed money to BANRURAL, the federal government's rural finance institution.

PAN administrations in Jalisco have been unreceptive to El Barzón. At the time of field research, producers of agave (the main input in tequila) constituted the most prominent rural faction of El Barzón, with a reported membership of roughly 5,000 producers.[31] Interviewed leaders of El Barzón Agavero echoed CCC leaders' plight, complaining that partisan bias and the privileging of large-scale agribusiness led PAN administrations to deny their demands for debt relief or subsidies.[32] These representatives reported that they had applied for state subsidies several times with no success and have only had one successful case of receiving federal support for the Jalisco agave sector, owing to help from the national El Barzón leadership and affiliated PRD Congress persons. El Barzón's participation in sectoral policymaking is also anemic. Organization leaders in the Consejo Regulador de Tequila (Tequila Regulatory Council), an industrial association of tequila producers centrally concerned with protecting the denomination of origin for tequila from Jalisco and pushing the government to enforce quality standards.[33] Within this body, El Barzón leaders' main goal is to encourage large tequila manufacturers to purchase agave grown locally by small-scale producers. However, they report that this body has not offered an effective space to advocate for broader demands for rural development, concerning most centrally the expansion of credit for small- and medium-sized farmers.

The main organizational beneficiary of PAN rural development policy has been CAJ, an organization representing medium- and large-scale producers.[34] The CAJ participates in several consultative councils alongside major business chambers in the state, has frequent direct contact with state politicians and bureaucrats, and has received millions of pesos in subsidies

31. In the months following the formation of El Barzón, the organization grew to include groups of urban middle-class citizens protesting financial obligations. This faction, under the leadership of Alfonso Ramírez Cuéllar, came to dominate El Barzón and particularly its ties to the PRD (de Grammont 2001, 197–202).

32. Interviews, René Beas Jiménez, former President, El Barzón Agavero, November 9, 2011; Francisco Guzmán de la Torre, President, El Barzón Agavero, November 12, 2011.

33. For more on the Consejo Regulador de Tequila, see Gómez Gómez (2010).

34. Of the 110 members at the time of the interview, CAJ personnel estimate that none would classify as small-scale farmers (owners of fewer than 20 hectares) and that several are large-scale producers, owing over 100 hectares. Roughly half of the members are not involved in primary production, but are rather agro-industry firms, financial institutions, or other firms with an interest in rural development policy.

from the state for its programs. Notably, Francisco Mayorga, Secretary of Rural Development under Cárdenas in Jalisco and then Secretary of SAGARPA (the Ministry of Agriculture, Ranching, Rural Development, Fishing, and Food) in both the Fox and Calderón administrations, was a founding member and first president of the CAJ.[35] The CAJ hosts yearly conventions called the International Agricultural and Food Forum (Foro Internacional Agroalimentario) in a resort in Puerto Vallarta, with financial support from the state rural development ministry, whose secretary attends, often in addition to the governor.

PAN administrations' recognition of the CAJ as the leading organization ("*organización cúpula*") in the agricultural sector has opened space for considerable programmatic influence for this organization. The CAJ is the sole organization of producers that participates in the State Sustainable Rural Development Council (Consejo Estatal de Desarrollo Rural Sustentable), unlike in other states where several representatives of peasant organizations participate. This organization also enjoys direct informal access to politicians and the development ministries that is perhaps only surpassed by the Guadalajara Chamber of Commerce. The president of the CAJ said that he has held meetings roughly once a month with high-level bureaucrats in the state rural development ministry. For example, he has advocated with the state to emphasize the use of hybrid seeds in its subsidies to improve grain yields and to increase support for irrigation infrastructure, which generally benefits large-scale growers with access to credit for such investments.

CAJ also exploits this access for distributive gain. The CAJ worked with the González administration on a project called the Ciudad Agropecuaria (Agricultural City), receiving 6.2 hectares of land from the state and funding to construct facilities for demonstrations. Valdés also explained that his organization is closely involved in helping its members access subsidies from the state and federal governments, assisting in every stage of the process: identifying needs to improve profitability, project design, the application process, and negotiation. In meetings with personnel at each ministry, Valdés advocates for the funding of these projects, identifying the projects by case number. CAJ also supports members in other state issues, such as helping BerryMex, an export-oriented berry-growing

35. Interview, Otilio Valdes, President, Consejo Agropecuario de Jalisco, April 22, 2015.

corporation, work with the Labor Ministry to help resolve labor disputes with day laborers.

In the end, PAN administrations have been successful in the implementation of a new rural development model, based on support for large-scale production, agri-business, and foreign investment. Ideologically opposed both to the concept of forming corporatist ties with rural organizations and to the substance of most dissident organizations' programmatic demands, the PAN in Jalisco made little effort and had little success at incorporating these non-core actors into the party. Rather, the policies (and policymaking practices) of PAN governors served to increase both the size and the representative capacity of organizations representing entrepreneurial agricultural interests that can be described as core for this party.

Conclusion

This chapter has principally analyzed the strategies of the left-wing PRD to incorporate dissident peasant organizations—a core organizational constituency—into rural development policy. While in most of Mexico, this party assumed a patronage-based posture toward core interest organizations, PRD administrations in Michoacán took pains to incorporate popular-sector organizations programmatically. However, conflicting impulses within the party conspired to recreate PRI-style patronage ties to core allies. Thus, COCOCAM, an institution created to support programmatic participation by peasant associations, also served to facilitate patronage exchange between PRD-allied organizations and state ministries. For those organizations that entered into the period of PRD rule with a patronage orientation, this heightened access reinforced the patronage trap, strengthening leaders' hands as brokers by availing them of greater distributive benefits. For REDCCAM, however, a programmatic organization, COCOCAM helped consolidate a programmatic virtuous cycle.

The fate of the PRD is representative of the broader challenges faced by left-wing parties in democracies with high levels of patronage. Oftentimes, the organizations representing these parties' core constituencies—labor unions, peasant associations, neighborhood associations—are so precarious as to place a higher premium on accessing state handouts than on effecting change in structural economic policy. Furthermore, these parties all too often are riddled with internal factions and are driven by short-term electoralist logic, producing temptations to mobilize organizational allies as clientelist machines. However, left-wing parties elsewhere in Latin America have been more successful at overcoming these challenges and producing programmatic representation for popular-sector allies. The Brazilian PT, Bolivian MAS, and Uruguayan FA all offered a more authentic space for programmatic representation of core labor and rural organizations than did the Mexican PRD (Anria 2016; Gómez Bruera 2013; Luna 2007). On the other hand, the PRD was arguably more successful at fostering programmatic representation for organizational allies than personalistic electoral vehicles in Ecuador and Venezuela (Silva 2017).

Chapter 7 depicts how the right-wing PAN confronted this same challenge of programmatically incorporating core organizations—in that case, small-business. Compared to parties of the left, right-wing parties like the PAN have an easier time sustaining programmatic ties to core organizations for several reasons. The organizations are more likely to be program-seeking as they have an easier time generating organizational capacity internally (Chapter 4); the parties themselves tend to face less daunting collective action problems between factions; and a middle-class electoral base that turns its nose up at patronage politics weights against such strategies (Weitz-Shapiro 2012). Mexico's PAN, in particular, offers a best-case scenario for programmatic incorporation as a long-time externally mobilized party boasting a "good governance" brand, paired with like-minded, yet autonomous, business organizations.

Ultimately, this asymmetry between the policy incorporation models of left-and right-wing political parties is what produces a particularly resilient brand of biased pluralism in high-patronage democracies. In the Mexican case, the contrasting electoral trajectories of the PRD and PAN make this representational distortion all the more pronounced.

CHAPTER 7

The PAN and Party Incorporation of Small-Business Organizations

The prospect of policy linkages with the middle-class small-business sector poses distinct challenges to political parties than linkages with the more vulnerable peasant sector analyzed in Chapter 6. Organized business is typically among the most influential societal actors in economic policy, particularly at the local level. Subnational small-business associations exercise remarkable "instrumental power," in which they influence policy through lobbying, direct contact with politicians, and their role in shaping public opinion.[1] The degree of instrumental power over the development priorities of Mexican state governments is shaped by two factors. First, as analyzed in Chapter 5, small-business organizations can focus their demand-making on programmatic or distributive policies. Second, as I analyze in this chapter, governing politicians may adopt diverse institutions to incorporate small-business organizations into policymaking.

Mexican small-business organizations have historically enjoyed remarkable influence in subnational economic policy owing to their high degree of internal coordination, institutionalized roles in state decision-making bodes, and close personal ties with the political elite (González and Alba Vega 1989; Luna 1995; Schneider 2002). As I showed in Chapter 5, whether these organizations translate this instrumental power into programmatic

1. Scholars have attributed businesses' powerful role in agenda setting to their "structural power," derived from an implied threat to disinvest in response to unfavorable policies (Fairfield 2015b; Lindblom 1977). However, the small-business organizations analyzed in this study may not exert considerable structural power as both the size of their investments and the credibility of the disinvestment threat pale in comparison to large corporations, especially multinationals.

demand-making on behalf of the small-business sector depends on the ability of these organizations to sustain organizational capacity internally, a challenge that many Mexican business organizations have met. However, programmatic *demands* do not necessarily yield programmatic *representation*. The latter depends on the actions of the partisan actors that hold state power to incorporate organizations into these policy areas. In the case of organized small business, the relevant state actors are leaders of right-wing political parties, for whom the business organizations constitute a core constituency.

It is common for right-wing parties to encounter a programmatic demand-making strategy among core organizations,[2] as such organizations tend to count on ample resources that allow them to generate organizational capacity and also tend to represent middle-class constituencies that place less value on state handouts than the lower classes. In this context, the challenge for parties of the right is to pursue two interconnected goals—first, sustaining spaces for authentic programmatic participation for these organizations; and second, expanding the electoral coalition beyond the middle-class base, often through the strategic use of patronage benefits. The mandate to expand the electorate in this way is more pronounced for parties of the right, whose core constituency constitutes a small minority of the voting public (Gibson 1996). These two goals reinforce one another. When a party is able to sustain the allegiance of core organizations through programmatic incorporation, the organizations' loyalty to the party is not "endogenous" (Diaz-Cayeros, Estévez, and Magaloni 2016) to the ongoing receipt of private benefits, and the party is thus free to use patronage to appeal to non-core constituencies.

Thus, from a pro-business party's point of view, consolidating programmatic ties with core small-business organizations offers two advantages. First, these ties lock in the support of the influential business community by setting up institutions through which business leaders buy in to the party's economic agenda. Most powerfully, such ties may involve arrangements in which business leaders are nominated for elected office and ministry posts. In the case of the PAN, the nomination of business leaders was commonplace, particularly in its earlier years holding executive office in the 1990s. The second advantage offered by programmatic

2. As defined in Chapter 1, "core" organizations are those that share a programmatic orientation with the party and/or are organizationally embedded into the party.

linkages is that it frees parties to allocate distributive benefits strategically to broaden their short-term electoral coalition. Thus, in the face of competitive elections, the programmatic incorporation of core groups proves to be an advantage, as the party can shift patronage appeals strategically to non-core groups. Lacking an electoral threat, however, parties may prefer to allocate patronage to core allies, less to secure their loyalty to the party than to strengthen these organizations' position in recruiting members, thus growing the party base yet more.

This chapter explains the strategies of ruling parties for incorporating small-business organizations into both programmatic policy and patronage brokerage. First, I analyze the traits of the PAN that positions it to incorporate core small-business organizations into programmatic sectoral policy. Second, I analyze the factors that incentivize ruling parties across the ideological spectrum to allocate distributive benefits to small-business organizations, a strategy that responds to their short-term electoral considerations.

What do programmatic and distributive representation look like in the small-business sector? As conceptualized in Chapter 1, programmatic policies are those that affect the fundamental terms of competitiveness in the organization's sector, such as regulatory policy, infrastructure, and the formulas that govern support programs. At its extreme, programmatic representation consists of the *routinized* participation of organizational representatives in *high-level* policy discussions, in a way that *exercises legitimate influence* over policy priorities or outcomes. Quite often such representation takes place in formally constituted institutions, such as consultative councils. But programmatic representation can be just as genuine when it takes place through informal lobbying or the recruitment of organization leaders to executive office or cabinet positions. Typically, we would only expect to find such programmatic representation when the governing party is ideologically aligned with the organization—as between a pro-business right-wing party and a business association—and thus is prone to incorporate the organization in these policy areas. However, having an ideologically aligned party in office is certainly not *sufficient* for programmatic representation. When programmatic representation is low, organizations participate irregularly, are limited to narrow policy spheres, or lack effective voice, such as when they participate in "rubber-stamp" consultative institutions.

What do patronage-based linkages look like in the small-business sector? As discussed in Chapter 6, the "patronage trap" is a quite common outcome for lower-class organizations such as those representing small-scale farmers, who are prone to converting into clientelist intermediaries for political parties. In contrast, a narrow patronage orientation is rarer for business organizations, and when it occurs it is not so readily apparent. For instance, several small-business organizations observed here devote most or all of the organizations' personnel and resources to applying for subsidy programs that benefit chambers directly or that organizations intermediate for small-business owners, retaining a percentage for themselves. As with the peasant organizations analyzed in Chapter 6, this focus on patronage "squeezes out" programmatic demand-making, attracts a self-selecting membership oriented towards particularistic benefits, and creates oligarchical pressures that strengthen the position of the organization leader—the broker for these state benefits. However, it is extremely rare to find a business organization that declares an overt partisan allegiance or campaigns openly for one party, as do organizational brokers in the peasant sector.

As discussed in Chapter 6, the "genetic traits" (Panebianco 1988) of parties shape their ability to incorporate core organizations in programmatic policy. Those parties that were founded during a period where they were for some reason restricted from competing for elected office tended to build long-standing relationships with organizational allies and a strong ideological character. Once such parties reach a position of competing for office, organizational allies already occupy important spaces in party leadership and parties have constructed institutions to sustain organizational influence in party platforms and candidate selection. Such is the case of Mexico's PAN, an externally mobilized party *par excellence*, but similar traits appear in other right-wing parties in the region, such as the Radical Civic Union (UCR) in Argentina.[3]

In this way, the PAN is distinct from the PRD, which, as analyzed in Chapter 6, exhibits subnational variation in its founding trajectory, but most closely resembles an internally mobilized party, with the objective of winning high-profile elections from its founding. Thus, while over half of the PRD's seventeen governors were defecting PRIistas, only one out of the thirty-one PAN governors have a history within the PRI. In contrast, the PAN has looked to business leaders as candidates. Over a third

3. Given that the authoritarian regimes in the region tended to have a right-wing character, the majority of externally mobilized parties in the region were made up of left-wing opponents, such as the PT in Brazil, FA in Uruguay, and Concertación in Chile. See Van Dyck (2017) for more detail.

of its governors were previously leaders of local business organizations or chambers. Given that PAN administrations have tended to sustain strong programmatic ties to organized business throughout Mexico, they are freer to choose linkage strategies that maximize short-term electoral goals than is the PRD, which is beholden to funneling patronage benefits to its core organizations to keep them in the fold.

The region offers more examples of right-wing parties that emerged from within the governing coalition or on the back of a single politician with immediate electoral aspirations, rather than from an organic societal base. Several of these parties were "authoritarian successors" (Loxton 2016) such as the Chilean Independent Democratic Union and National Renewal parties, and the Brazilian Democratic Social Party. Other prominent right-wing electoral movements were personalistic vehicles, founded for the candidacies of individual politicians with a strong personal following—such as Fujimori in Peru, Uribe in Colombia, and more recently Macri in Argentina. In either of these scenarios, the parties aspire to power in the immediate term and are predicted by my theory to mobilize organized business opportunistically rather than incorporating business organizations into the lifeblood of their electoral organizations.[4]

Secondarily, governments also make decisions about the degree to which they should incorporate core organizations into patronage politics—the discretionary disbursement of private benefits in the form of social programs and sectoral subsidies. In a context where a ruling right-wing party faces electoral competition, it will prefer to use these benefits to appeal to non-core constituencies, either through transfers of particularistic subsidies and social programs or spending on visible public goods, such as a convention center. Only when a right-wing party is electorally dominant do I expect a party to allocate these benefits to allies who are already solidly in the camp of the party through programmatic linkages.

While centrist and left-wing parties are unlikely to pursue a thorough incorporation of business associations in programmatic policy, they may still deploy patronage strategically to woo these organizations to their side in elections. Thus, in the distributive realm, the expectation is that

4. In contrast, these parties commonly incorporate individual business persons into leadership posts, the most prominent example being Macri himself, an heir to his father's fortune built through construction, real estate, and ownership of a major electronics company.

right-wing parties allocate benefits to core small-business organizations when they are electorally strong, but center and left-wing parties act in the opposite fashion, delivering distributive benefits to these organizations when they face an electoral threat, particularly if that threat comes from the right.

The rest of this chapter substantiates this argument through discussion of small-business organizations, with particular attention to PAN governments' strategies for incorporating these into policymaking. The next section of this chapter summarizes the PAN's national rise to power after several decades as a minor opposition party and its national-level strategy to involve small-business organizations in economic policy and party leadership. I then turn to the case of Jalisco, where the PAN governed for three terms and faced a constant electoral threat from the PRI. The PAN administrations that governed Jalisco from 1995 to 2012 constructed formal participatory institutions, recruited business leaders, and sustained powerful informal social ties to make organized small business a centrally important actor in economic policy. These relationships with organized business allowed PAN governors to preserve distributive benefits for non-core groups, investment in visible public works, and attracting multinational corporations to generate employment.

Third, I analyze the strategies pursued by governors of the PRI and PRD, for whom organized small business constitutes a non-core group. In these cases, programmatic participation was either absent or took on a perfunctory character, as these parties attended to the interests of their core groups or to large corporations that exerted greater structural power. I also illustrate the circumstances under which these parties seek to engage small-business organizations in patronage-based linkages, most particularly in the case of PRI governors seeking to forestall their defection to a PAN challenger. Otherwise, these parties see little merit in filtering benefits to an organization prone to support their electoral rival.

Table 7.1 demonstrates the final representation models for business organizations in the three states analyzed. As laid out in Chapter 1, for programmatic representation to occur, both organization and party must concur on this mode of demand-making/incorporation. Similarly, for an organization to be mobilized through a strong patronage strategy, both party and organization must be patronage oriented. When party and organizations' preferences diverge, weak patronage representation occurs. In Jalisco, where

Table 7.1 Representation Outcomes for Business Organizations Analyzed

Organization	Organization's Demands	Party Incorporation Strategy	Mode of Representation
Jalisco			
CANACO-GDL	Programmatic	Programmatic	Programmatic
CAREINTRA	Patronage	Programmatic	Patronage (weak)
COPARMEX	Programmatic	Programmatic	Programmatic
Michoacán	Mixed	Cherry-picking	Patronage (weak)
Estado de México	Mixed	Exclusion	Patronage (weak)

PAN administrations pursued a programmatic incorporation strategy with small-business organizations, the two organizations with mainly programmatic demands were successful in programmatic representation. In contrast, CAREINTRA, which mostly displayed patronage demands, was rebuffed by the Jalisco government with distributive benefits, and thus conferred only weak patronage representation. And in Michoacán and Estado de México, the PAN and PRD administrations were uninterested in either programmatic or patronage incorporation of the major small-business organizations. While business chambers in these states were mixed between those that were oriented to programmatic demands and those that primarily sought patronage, the ultimate models of representation favored weak patronage.

This chapter relies on two sources of data to substantiate these claims. First, in-depth qualitative evidence from the state of Jalisco and shadow cases in non-PAN-governed states (Estado de México and Michoacán) traces how the traits of party organizations shaped incentives for incorporating small-business organizations into policymaking. Second, an analysis of subnational spending on small-business subsidies provides broader evidence of how electoral threat shapes parties' strategies for incorporating small-business organizations into distributive politics. Analyzing Fondo PyME, a state-operated subsidy program targeted to small and medium businesses, I find that PAN governments tend to allocate these benefits to core small-business organizations when they are electorally dominant, but otherwise prefer to use these benefits for programs with broader appeal and potential for job creation. In contrast, PRI governments allocate these programs to small-business organizations, non-core for this party, when facing an electoral threat, but when dominant tend to shut out these organizations from distributive spending.

Construction of Business Linkages by National-Level PAN

The PAN existed for many decades prior to the onset of electoral competition. Unable to challenge for elections during the PRI's one-party dominant regime, the PAN was dominated by ideologically committed activists tied to Catholic thought and local business elites in northern and western Mexico (Loaeza 1999; Mizrahi 2003). When the electoral tides turned in the late 1980s, the PAN pursued an "outside-in" path to electoral competition, first establishing a base by winning subnational elections in a few states and then ramping up to national prominence. This path resulted in a leadership structure centered on subnational ideologues that were wedded to the party's programmatic commitments and held the long-term sustainability of the party organization as a core goal, perhaps even over short-term electoral victory.

In stark contrast to the PRD, which repeatedly embraced ex-PRIistas as candidates, the PAN held party loyalty as a core qualification for party activists and candidates (Greene 2007, 188–89; Mizrahi 2003). Candidates were subjected to a lengthy approval process before being allowed to run under the PAN banner and, until 1996, prospective party members had to be sponsored by a current member, pass an exam, and be approved by a party committee. The party relaxed some of these restrictions in the 1990s in an effort to broaden its appeal and challenge for national office. With a steadfast opposition to "party-jumpers," however, the PAN's early gubernatorial victories in Baja California (1989), Chihuahua (1992), Guanajuato (1995), and Jalisco (1995) were on the backs of "neopanistas," typically prominent business leaders without a political trajectory in any political party, but who pledged their allegiance to the PAN before running for office.[5]

The PAN conquered the presidency in 2000 behind the candidacy of Vicente Fox, former governor of Guanajuato. Once in office, Fox named several former leaders of business associations to his cabinet, including Sergio García de Alba (vice president of CONCAMIN), Secretary of the Economy; Francisco Mayorga (president of Jalisco Agricultural Council), Secretary of Agriculture; Carlos Abascal, (national president

5. These victorious governors include Ernesto Ruffo Appel, Baja California (1989–1995), former president of CCE-Baja California; Francisco Barrio, Chihuahua (1992–1998), former president of COPARMEX-Ciudad Juárez; Vicente Fox, Guanajuato (1995–2000), former president of COPARMEX-Guanajuato, and Alberto Cárdenas, Jalisco (1995–2001).

of COPARMEX, 1995–1997), Secretary of Labor (2000–2005) and of the Interior (2005–2006); and Fernando Canales Clariond (president of CANACO-Monterrey), Secretary of the Economy (2003–2005) and of Energy (2005–2006). Further, the PAN nominated more business organization leaders to congressional posts during Fox's administration than the other parties combined, reaching its peak in the 2006 Chamber of Deputies where twenty-seven out of 206 PAN deputies (13 percent) belonged to business associations, compared to six for the PRI and one for the PRD (Wuhs 2010, 118–19).

This trend of business organization leaders receiving nominations for the PAN responded to two motives. First was the fundamental challenge of filling posts with capable managers. As Mizrahi (2003, 74–75) puts it:

> [Entrepreneurs] brought to the PAN not only much-needed financial resources, leadership styles, organizational capabilities, and new advertising and marketing techniques drawn from their own business experience. More important, entrepreneurs took a leading role in the organization of campaigns and in many cases became the party's candidates. They also organized massive postelection mobilizations when an election was suspected of having been fraudulent.

The nomination of business leaders to executive office and cabinet posts in this way turned a liability—a lack of professional politicians—into a purported strength: the adoption of a new ethos of governance, based on the party's outsider status and the entrepreneurial values of meritocracy, efficiency, and "the new managerialism" (Mizrahi 2003, 91–93). This image had resonance with Mexican voters fed up with the PRI's patronage, corruption, and economic mismanagement. Furthermore, these leaders were uniquely positioned to align economic development goals with those of the business community. The ultra-valuable inducement of nomination to a cabinet post helped overcome wariness business organization leaders may have had to align themselves more closely with the upstart PAN. In contrast, where the PRD built subnational party organizations on the backs of PRI defectors, it handicapped its legitimacy as a democratic alternative to the dominant party and leapfrogged the organization-building process that lends stability to externally mobilized parties.

Thus, when the PAN assumed the presidency small-business organizations already constituted a core constituency—and even a powerful strain—within this party. The Fox and Calderón administrations adopted a series of policies to consolidate these ties. Party-organization affinity had always been most overt for the independent association of employers, COPARMEX, which, while officially non-partisan, played an important role in the PAN's founding in 1939 and has aligned programmatically with the party in confronting PRI administrations in the subsequent decades (Loaeza 1999; Mizrahi, 2003).[6]

Linkages between the associations of business chambers (CONCANACO in the commercial sector and CANACINTRA in the industrial sector) and the PAN was more nuanced and transformed over time. As discussed in Chapter 2, the relationships between these chambers and the PRI had been severely strained in the late twentieth century. In particular, the last pre-transition PRI president, Ernesto Zedillo (1994–2000), delivered a damaging blow to small-business collective action by reforming the Law of Chambers in 1997, removing the mandatory membership requirement, which led to a precipitous decline in chamber membership. Business chambers had clearly become non-core organizations for PRI, given that the party's organizational structure was more closely linked to its labor and peasant sectors and that its programmatic stance favored large corporations over the local firms that make up the backbone of chambers' memberships. The pro-business PAN was the obvious party to which the chambers would be drawn.

Vicente Fox's administration (2000–2006) made concerted efforts to consolidate linkages with organized business and to incorporate business organizations into economic policy, reinvigorating corporatist relationships with business chambers that had decayed during the nadir of PRI rule through the creation of subsidy and training programs that operated through these organizations: the México Emprende program placed small-business support offices in CONCANACO, CANACINTRA, and COPARMEX affiliates and Fondo PyME—Fox's flagship small-business subsidy program—included a provision allowing business organizations to design and implement projects, often retaining a portion of the benefits themselves. These programs empowered PAN governors to consolidate ties with state and local small-business organizations, whose support is coveted in state and municipal electoral campaigns.

---

6. Since its founding, COPARMEX has opposed PRI rule. The COPARMEX website lists among its most important achievements the PRI's loss of its congressional majority in 1997, stating that then "COPARMEX began to have closer ties to the political class and greater influence in national affairs." See: http://www.coparmex.org.mx/.

Despite their non-partisan mandate, these organizations are highly active during campaigns, hosting debates and speeches, presenting proposals to candidates, and organizing election-monitoring initiatives. Interviewed representatives of business organizations said that over the course of a campaign, it is often easy to detect the electoral leanings of the leadership and word can travel fast through the business community about the favored candidate. The PAN's ability to displace the PRI in several states in the 1990s has been attributed to public relations campaigns led by business organizations, denouncing corruption, insecurity, and fiscal irresponsibility and the incoming PAN administrations often included business organization leaders in prominent cabinet positions (Alba Vega, 2002; Arellano Ríos, 2009; Mizrahi, 2003).

PAN and Small Business in Jalisco

Jalisco is a representative case of the PAN's approach to small business nationwide. The Jalisco PAN created durable programmatic linkages with core small-business organizations, helping it retain a brand as a good-government pro-business party, even as it pivoted to the center with the incorporation of "neopanistas" in the 1990s and 2000s. Programmatically oriented business organizations in Jalisco—COPARMEX and CANACO—found a willing linkage partner, while the more patronage-oriented industrial chamber (CAREINTRA) did not find the PAN as receptive to their demands for greater distributive benefits. PAN governors preferred to allocate these benefits to high visibility investments prone to appeal to the electorate and business community at large.

The PAN emerged in Jalisco in 1939, as Efraín González Luna, a prominent Catholic intellectual from Jalisco, was one of the two central founding figures of the party, along with Guanajuato intellectual Manuel Gomez Morín (Loaeza 1999, 155–65). As was the case nationally, the party was a minor electoral figure in Jalisco from its founding until the 1980s. From the 1940s through the 1970s, candidates from the PAN only participated sporadically in municipal and state elections. González Luna was the PAN's first candidate for the presidency, in 1952, finishing a distant second (with 7.8 percent of the vote). However, this candidacy did much to strengthen the profile of the PAN in Jalisco, as the party ran sixty-four candidates for municipal president in the state in 1952 (Lujambio 2001, 66). Despite its lack of electoral competitiveness, the party maintained a loyal nucleus of support among prominent local businessmen, as well as ties with the local church leadership (González and Alba Vega 1989; Hernández Aguila and Morales Márquez 2009, 85–87). After declining to run a candidate for the governorship in the 1970 and 1976 elections, the PAN began its ascendancy in the state in the 1980s, officially winning 22.4 and 27.4 percent of the vote in the gubernatorial elections of 1982 and 1988, elections that were marked by widespread accusations against the PRI of electoral fraud.

The party finally won the governorship in 1995, amassing 52.7 percent of the vote and defeating the PRI by a margin of 15.6 percentage points (Figure 7.1). This victory was aided by the low approval ratings and divisiveness of the PRI in the state, which induced local economic leaders to break ties with the long-time ruling party and support the PAN (Alba Vega 2002, 126–28; Alonso 1995, 58–75; Hernández-Valdez 2000; Lomelí 2001). The collapse was markedly rapid; the PRI went from holding 107 of Jalisco's 125 municipalities in 1994 to only sixty-five in 1995. Among the municipalities that the PRI lost in 1995 were all five composing the Guadalajara Metropolitan Zone. Following the relatively lopsided 1995 victory, the PAN won two more gubernatorial elections, although these were closely contested by the PRI with margins of victory of 2.4 percent in 2000 and 3.8 percent in 2006 and quite low rates of turnout (57.8 percent in 2000 and 60.9 percent in 2006, compared with 71.1 percent in 1995). Despite

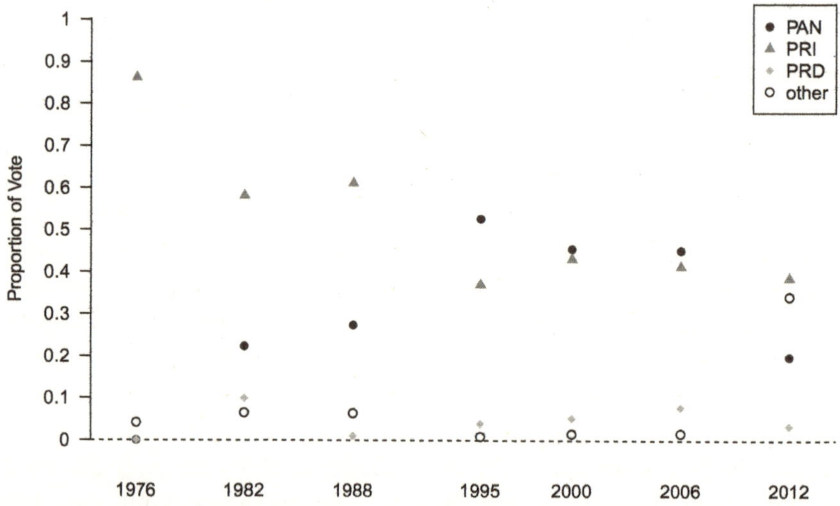

Figure 7.1 Jalisco Governor Races
Source: CIDAC electoral database.

this constant threat by the PRI, the PAN had consolidated Jalisco as one of its strongholds, having elected three consecutive governors, a feat only matched in Guanajuato. The tides turned in the 2012 election, however, as the PAN's candidate came in a distant third place after the PRI and the left-wing Movimiento Ciudadano.[7]

The PAN's first governor in Jalisco, Alberto Cárdenas, represented the "neopanista" wing of the party. He did not come from the long-time PAN community in Guadalajara, but rather had built his career as an engineer and then won the mayoral election in 1992 in the southern-Jalisco municipality of Ciudad Guzmán. Cárdenas' candidacy had been supported by the business community and broader neopanismo movement in Jalisco and inaugurated a period during which leaders of business organizations were centrally involved in governing Jalisco (Alonso 1995, 152–54). During PRI administrations, business associations had remained officially non-partisan, although the leaders of the state PAN organization frequently were elected to posts in the largest business chambers and COPARMEX (González and Alba Vega 1989). Beginning with the elections of 1994 and 1995, however, the organized business community began to play a coordinated and overt role in electoral politics.

In 1992, leaders of several business organizations in the state published an advertisement in a Jalisco newspaper criticizing Governor Guillermo Cosío Vidaurri for failings in the provision of security (Arellano Ríos 2009, 46).[8] This was only the most prominent of several instances of veiled or not-so-veiled criticisms of the Cosío administration by business organizations that ramped up in the early 1990s and likely contributed to his being deposed by Carlos Salinas in 1992. Dissatisfaction continued under Cosío's successor, Carlos Rivera Aceves (1992–1995), whose administration was wrought with its own security scandals, coming to a head in the 1993 assassination of a prominent Catholic cardinal at Guadalajara

7. The prospects of the PRI in Jalisco have mirrored the national party, which experienced a decline in popularity related to poor economic performance and corruption and violence scandals beginning during the Calderón administration. The 2015 election saw the rise of Movimiento Ciudadano as the second electoral force in the state, as Enrique Álfaro won the election for municipal president in Guadalajara. Álfaro was elected governor in 2018 with the backing of a coalition that included the PAN.

8. This episode had similar significance as the famous article taken out by the CCE criticizing national policies of President López Mateos, declaring "¿Por Cual Camino Señor Presidente?" (Which path Mr. President?).

airport. The president of CAREINTRA from 1993 to 1995 (and later Minister of Economic Promotion under Alberto Cárdenas) recounts his organization's discontent with the PRI administrations of the 1990s: "We were very critical of the actions of the government [in Jalisco the governor was Carlos Rivera Aceves] and that got us in the media. We spoke out against corruption, inefficiency, overregulation, both of the Jalisco government and the federal government under Carlos Salinas de Gortari."[9] Once in office Alberto Cárdenas made immediate arrangements to secure the participation of business organization leaders at an unprecedented rate in the state's economic policymaking. According to Arellano Ríos (2009, 54), six of Cárdenas' cabinet members were businessmen, five of whom had held elected leadership positions in peak-level business organizations in Jalisco, including previous presidents of COPARMEX-Jalisco, CANACO-Guadalajara, CAREINTRA, the CAJ, and the Jalisco Chamber of Shoe Manufacturers (CICEJ).[10] Cárdenas' successors followed suit, each naming five businessmen to cabinet posts, among them former presidents of COPARMEX, CANACO, and CICEJ. This presence of business leaders was notable, following three PRI administrations that had had no more than three business owners in their cabinets, none of whom had served in the leadership of business organizations.

During its sixteen-year period of holding the state government, the PAN consolidated its ties to organized business. This does not mean that Cárdenas and his successors were able to entirely entice organized business away from the PRI. The chambers took a publicly non-partisan stance (a legal mandate) and they have always had members loyal to the PRI, particularly within CAREINTRA.[11] However, after the 2000 elections, when the PAN secured a second term as governor of Jalisco and also

9. Taken from: Pedro Mellado, "Memoria Viva: Carlos García de Alba," *Mural*. November 17, 2013. "Fuimos muy críticos de las acciones de Gobierno [en Jalisco era Mandatario estatal Carlos Rivera Aceves] y eso nos puso en los medios de comunicación. Hablábamos sobre la corrupción, las ineficiencias, la sobrerregulación, tanto del Gobierno de Jalisco como el Gobierno federal que encabezaba Carlos Salinas de Gortari (periodo 1988–1994)."

10. Two of these figures went on to hold national cabinet positions: Sergio García de Alba, Secretary of Economic Promotion in Jalisco and then federal Secretary of the Economy (2005–2006) and Francisco Mayorga, Secretary of Rural Development in Jalisco and then federal Secretary of Agriculture (2005–2006, 2009–2012).

11. Interviews, Jorge Barrón, Coordinator of Public and Political Affairs, CANACO-Guadalajara, June 21, 2013; Luis del Valle, Councilmember COPARMEX-CESJAL, March 7, 2013.

toppled the PRI in the presidential race, the Jalisco business community had greater incentive to associate itself with the PAN.

Beginning in 2009, the PRI began an electoral comeback in the state, winning forty-five out of 125 municipalities, including four of the five municipalities in the Guadalajara metropolitan area. Finally, the PRI retook the governorship of Jalisco in 2012, with the victory of Jorge Aristóteles Sandoval Díaz, former mayor of Guadalajara. Like the decline of the PRI in the early 1990s, the PAN's downfall in these years must be understood in the context of national economic strife, low approval ratings for the sitting president, internal rifts in the party, and a national movement favoring the opposition party, in this case the PRI's trajectory that culminated in the election of Enrique Peña Nieto to the presidency.

In the next section, I show how the electoral context in Jalisco, and particularly the constant threat from the PRI, shaped the last PAN administration's (Emilio González, 2007–2012) strategies to incorporate core small-business organizations in programmatic policymaking. I show that business organizations were granted substantial access to programmatic policymaking and acted as pseudo-governmental agencies in setting economic development policy. This administration was less eager to incorporate business organizations into patronage, preferring to channel the state's business support programs to broadly appealing projects such as building industrial parks, attracting foreign businesses, and setting up consultancy centers at universities.

This restraint in the use of patronage originated in the PAN's longstanding organic ties with organized business, which allowed it to retain the support of these groups despite abstaining from constantly funneling distributive benefits to them. For organizations that came into the period of PAN rule with a commitment to programmatic demands, the PAN governments' receptiveness to their incorporation reinforced a programmatic virtuous cycle. These organizations—COPARMEX and CANACO-Guadalajara particularly—attained prestige as top representatives of the business community, attracted members that were civic minded, and found it easy to gain an audience with politicians of all parties, including the governor himself. For Jalisco's industrial chamber, CAREINTRA, the programmatic virtuous cycle was not so prevalent, as the organization was less successful at achieving organizational capacity on its own. A greater reliance on patronage benefits to mobilize an increasingly precarious small industrial membership base led this chamber to hedge its bets to a greater degree, retaining ties to PRI politicians prone to reward this organization with subsidies.

Jalisco Business: Programmatic Incorporation of Core Allies

The PAN administrations in Jalisco from 1995 to 2012 reflect a successful case of the programmatic incorporation of core organizations. Small-business organizations—particularly COPARMEX, CANACO-Guadalajara, and the umbrella organization CCIJ—engaged in several venues, both formal and informal, to shape the direction of economic policy in the state.[12] PAN governors of Jalisco proved not only to be receptive to listening to the demands of business leaders, but eager to integrate them into the party infrastructure. As a result, in collaboration with organized business, PAN administrations in Jalisco have placed small-business development at the center of their economic development agenda. On the one hand, these administrations have delivered benefits to local businesses, spurring entrepreneurship and conditions for traditional firms ranging from small industry in Guadalajara to the tourist industry in Puerto Vallarta. On the other hand, PAN governments have made overtures to attract foreign investment and to position Jalisco as an epicenter of Mexico's nascent position in global information technology.

PAN administrations were able and motivated to build these ties with organized business because of three reasons. First, business organizations in Jalisco were predisposed to programmatic participation, as shown in Chapter 5. The largest associations, CANACO-Guadalajara and COPARMEX, were willing to forgo access to patronage in pursuit of larger economic goals and extraordinary access to the state government. (The exception is the industrial chamber, CAREINTRA, which is more oriented to distributive demands and has been less successful at exploiting spaces for programmatic participation.) Second, the leadership of the PAN in Jalisco exhibited a long-standing commitment to a programmatically distinct form of government and a new way of relating to core organizations than their

---

12. In addition to the Guadalajara Chamber of Commerce, Jalisco has over a dozen other Chambers of Commerce. I interviewed CANACO representatives in Puerto Vallarta and Tlaquepaque as well as an affiliate of the National Chamber of Small Commerce (CANACOPE) in Puerto Vallarta. These chambers tend to engage primarily with municipal governments and have little interaction in state-level business policy (Interviews, Carlo Iván Gómez Pérez, General Director, CANACOPE-Puerto Vallarta, November 18, 2011; Sheila Hernández, General Director, CANACO-Puerto Vallarta, November 18, 2011; Rafael Lara López, General Director, CANACO-Tlaquepaque, November 16, 2011).

predecessors. And third, constant electoral pressure from the PRI sustained the incentive to use development budgets for spending that appealed to non-core populations, reducing temptations to substitute programmatic access of the small-business core with patronage ties.

González has largely followed in the pattern established by his party's predecessors in the governorship: Alberto Cárdenas (1995–2001) and Francisco Ramírez Acuña (2001–2006). Coming into power in the wake of the 1994 economic crisis and entry into NAFTA, Cárdenas focused on attracting foreign investment, particularly in high-tech sectors, by offering tax breaks, training programs for local labor, infrastructure investments, direct subsidies, and reducing red tape (Chapa García 2009, 130–40). This approach has yielded results; firms such as Hewlett Packard, Intel, Motorola, IBM, and Flextronics have moved to the Guadalajara Metropolitan Zone, as well as international industrial giants such as Continental Tires. PAN administrations and the largest business organizations—those based in the capital city of Guadalajara—have coincided in the position that such foreign investment bodes well for local small firms, while also spearheading improvements in education and infrastructure that benefit the population more broadly.[13]

Agreements on economic development priorities have been reinforced by the fact that the Ministry of Economic Promotion (SEPROE), the state ministry charged with setting business policy in the state and disbursing business subsidies, was typically led by business organization leaders. Cárdenas drastically strengthened this ministry, charging it with carrying out the ambitious employment-generating plan laid out in his proposed Law for the Economic Development of the State of Jalisco,[14] and increasing its budget from 6.6 million pesos in 1995 to 122.3 million pesos in 2000 (Alba Vega 2002, 128–31). Sergio García de Alba, a former president of CAREINTRA and Secretary of SEPROE under Cárdenas, oversaw a process

13. Jorge Urdapilleta, director of the State Economic Support Council (CEPE), a state government agency that manages small-business support programs explained that the González administration had placed a high priority on attracting foreign investment and creating high-paying jobs, particularly by allocating state business subsidies to incentivize medium- and large-sized businesses through tax breaks and space in government-owned industrial parks rather than allocating these funds directly to small-business development (Interview, Jorge Urdapilleta Núñez, October 28, 2011).

14. The Ley para el Fomento Económico del Estado de Jalisco was proposed by the Cárdenas administration in 1997, but not finally ratified until 2001 under the governorship of Francisco Ramírez Acuña.

of reorganizing and broadening the ministry's mandate, creating the State Council for Economic Promotion, a body charged with promoting investment in Jalisco.[15]

Throughout the PAN administrations in Jalisco, organized business was integrated into the life of the party and economic policymaking through nominations of business leaders to elected and cabinet positions, the establishment of authentic consultative institutions, and substantial informal access to policymakers. These formal and informal spaces were dedicated to a variety of issues of governance that affect the local business community broadly—government acquisitions, infrastructure, security, and especially regulation of informal commerce. This incorporation was made possible by the programmatic orientation of business chambers and COPARMEX. The patronage temptation—to divert economic development spending to less efficient subsidies for domestic business—was forestalled by the ongoing electoral threat of the PRI and the business organizations' support for the foreign investment maximizing approach to regional development. In a list of eight priorities that composed the "Agenda Única del Sector Privado," a document delivered to the candidates for governor in 2012, subsidies for domestic business was absent, while competitiveness in attracting foreign investment, infrastructure, and reforms to education, telecommunications and other structural policies were present.[16]

The most direct line of influence for business chambers has been the nomination of business leaders to executive and bureaucratic office. Once the PAN proved to be electorally competitive, the tendency in Jalisco, as in other states, was to integrate local entrepreneurs into the party as candidates or to name them to cabinet posts. As mentioned above, all three PAN governors named business organization leaders as heads of state ministries. González Márquez named four members of CANACO-Guadalajara and COPARMEX-Jalisco to ministry posts, including Guillermo Martínez Mora, former president of COPARMEX, who became Secretary of SEPROE. Having prominent businessmen, and particularly former business organization leaders in office both facilitates the organization's ability to lobby the state government and the ability of PAN candidates to appeal to the chamber electorally. A representative of CANACO-Guadalajara explained how members of PAN administrations

15. Pedro Mellado, "Memoria Viva: Carlos García de Alba," *Mural*. November 17, 2013.
16. "Presentan agenda del sector privado," *Mural*, June 17, 2012.

use these ties in their campaigns for other posts: "The candidates try to capitalize on [having a former CANACO president in the administration]. They say 'here as part of the government there is one of your representatives, ex-president so-and-so.' This sends signals, it sends the signal of closeness, that 'of course I'll attend to your sector, so much so that I have (one of your people) there.' "[17] While PAN administrations were wary about establishing patronage channels or overt corporatist alliances, the administrations' posture towards business organizations was to create formal institutions for consultation. These spaces serve the dual goals of channeling policy preferences of the business community to policymakers and sustaining electorally advantageous personal relationships between business leaders and elected politicians. According to an analysis by a Jalisco newspaper in 2001, business leaders were present on thirteen of the seventeen consultative councils in Ramírez Acuña's administration that allowed citizen participation, compared with only four councils in which university representatives participated.[18] Four councils, including the Acquisitions Council of the Ministry of Administration, which included several members from COPARMEX and CANACO, were made up entirely of business leaders. Expanding to include municipal councils and specialized committees, COPARMEX in Jalisco lists on its website 135 councils, committees, and boards that it belongs to at the state and municipal level and CANACO lists fifty-five such councils (placing a particular emphasis on government contracting committees).[19] While these councils lack veto power or formally vested authority over budgets, they provide these organizations with important resources: regular access to high-level politicians and bureaucrats, important information about government programs and policies to share with their members, and a mouthpiece from which to make public statements regarding policy proposals.

---

17. Interview, Antonio Guzmán, Coordinator of Public and Political Affairs, CANACO-Guadalajara, June 12, 2012. "Los candidatos solamente tratan de capitalizarlo. Dicen, 'aquí como parte del gobierno está un representante suyo, el expresidente fulano de tal.' Eso manda señales, manda una señal de cercanía, de 'claro que atiendo a su sector y tan lo atiendo que tengo a alguien aquí.' "

18. "Privilegian a empresarios en consejos ciudadanos," *Mural*, August 6, 2001. Of particular note, a former president of CANACO, Alejandro Elizondo was the head of the Electoral Council.

19. See: http://www.coparmexjal.org.mx; https://www.camaradecomerciogdl.mx/

In addition to these ministry-specific councils, which proliferate (at least on the books) across Mexico, Jalisco was the first state in Mexico to establish a Social and Economic Council, patterned after European consultative bodies, the Economic and Social Council of the State of Jalisco for Development and Competitiveness (CESJAL). This council, founded in 2004, brings together representatives of several societal organizations, including economic sectors (business, agriculture, labor), non-profits and universities. CESJAL makes non-binding recommendations to the state government regarding legislation and other policies related to economic development. The council also conducts research on the Jalisco economy, recommending strategic projects, and reaching consensus between business, labor, and other stakeholders on industrial policy.[20] While the participation of major business organizations in CESJAL can be seen as formalizing core organizations' input in state development policy, several sectoral organizations of the PRI—the CNC, CTM, Revolutionary Confederation of Workers and Peasants (CROC), Regional Ranchers Union of Jalisco, and State Federation of Small Landholders—also participate.

Another example of formalized consultation is the participation of these core business organizations in the drafting of the State Development Plan (Plan Estatal de Desarrollo) under the González Márquez administration. Interviewed leaders of COPARMEX and CANACO-Guadalajara said that they participated officially in the process of drafting the document in 2007.[21] (Many of the planning meetings took place in the headquarters of CANACO-Guadalajara.) The presidents of CESJAL and the CAJ were members of official planning committee. The document itself specified several specific roles for business organizations in state business-promotion efforts including working with the state government to build a network of business incubators.[22] This important role of organized business was not continued with PRI governor Sandóval, who drafted a new State

20. Ley del Consejo Económico y Social del Estado de Jalisco para el Desarrollo y la Competitividad, 2004. See: https://info.jalisco.gob.mx/gobierno/documentos/3124.

21. Interviews, Luis del Valle, Ana Isabel Solís. Elizabeth Ortiz, "Revisará COPARMEX avances del PED," *Mural*, December 4, 2007.

22. "En el sector empresarial, las cámaras y asociaciones tienen un papel trascendente en este proceso, ya que pueden consolidar la cadena productiva de cada sector" (106).

Development Plan upon entering office in 2013. Leaders of business organizations in the state reported less participation in this process than in 2010, and a general disinclination on the part of Sandóval's administration to engage organized business in planning and spending.[23]

Through these formal institutions—as well as personal relationships—communication between business organization leaders and PAN government figures is constant and nearly effortless. At the level of operations, staff at the México Emprende offices in COPARMEX and CANACO reported practically daily communication with their counterparts in SEPROE and the Jalisco delegation of the federal Ministry of the Economy.[24] When asked for a recommendation of a contact at these offices, the interviewed staff member at CANACO-Guadalajara listed off names and telephone numbers from memory.

At the elite level, presidents and vice presidents of the chambers and COPARMEX engage in regular communication with the governor and cabinet ministers. A CANACO staffer who had previously worked at COPARMEX explains the utility of this informal contact that generates from the friendly ties between business leaders and politicians:

> "When we want to invite a politician or minister to an event, we go through the whole protocol—sending letters, making phone calls. If we're unsuccessful, we ask the president of CANACO to call him. He calls him on his cell phone and he always blames his secretary—'I never got the message. I always attend these events.'—and he comes."[25]

Perhaps the most frequent topic of discussion between organized commercial firms and the municipal governments in the Guadalajara Metropolitan Zone is informal commerce. CANACO-Guadalajara has been centrally

---

23. Luis Duran, Jorge Velazco and Mariana Alvarado, "Ven paralizado al gobierno de Jalisco," *Mural*. June 10, 2013. "Va Fojal de reversa," *Mural*. November 29, 2013.
24. Interviews, Juán José González Nuño, Business Manager, COPARMEX-Jalisco, October 26, 2011; Erick Herrera Ramírez, Centro México Emprende Consultant, CANACO-Guadalajara, October 31, 2011.
25. Interview, Jorge Barrón. "Cuando queremos convocar a un politico o secretario a algún evento, hacemos todo el protocol—mandar cartas, llamar. Si no tenemos exito, decimos al presidente de CANACO que lo llame. Lo llama a su celular y él siempre culpa a su secretaria—'no me llego el mensaje. siempre asisto a esos eventos.'—y viene."

involved in pressing the state and municipal governments to toughen enforcement of policies prohibiting informal-sector business activity and the sale of pirated merchandise. A political analyst at CANACO-Guadalajara connected the issue of the informal sector to broader issues of governance and rule of law in the Guadalajara area:

> "In the chamber...we have on our agenda the reconversion of the informal sector. That is, a frontal attack on informal commerce and then to reconvert them [to formal businesses], because [the goal] is not just to combat them and that's it. This requires initiatives to improve efficiency in public administration: that [politicians] don't spend too much, that there's no corruption, proper functioning of the justice system."[26]

Under the González Márquez administration, CANACO-Guadalajara made numerous public statements and held at least five meetings with members of the state government, some in cooperation with other member organizations of the CCIJ, to explore possibilities for improving enforcement. This collaboration resulted in the creation of the Subprocuraduría de Apoyo a la Investigación de Delitos Federales, a special state prosecutor to help investigate federal crimes—most centrally tax evasion and piracy related to the informal sector; and the Consejo Metropolitano de Prácticas de Comercio, a task force made up of federal, state, and municipal politicians, as well as representatives of CANACO and street vendors associations to encourage legal activities in street vending.[27]

CAREINTRA, Jalisco's main industrial chamber has not been integrated to the same degree into programmatic policymaking. This can be attributed to two main factors. First—as established in Chapter 5—CAREINTRA is preoccupied with keeping afloat and thus tends to come to the state with distributive demands, which are rarely paid much heed by the state

---

26. "En la cámara, por ejemplo, en la agenda tenemos lo de reconversión del comercio informal. Es decir, combate frontal al comercio informal y aparte después reconvertirlos, porque no solo es combatirlos y ya. Esto require iniciativas-el manejo de la gestión pública eficiente: que no gasten de más, que no haya corrupción, manejo correcto de la justicia" (Interview, Antonio Guzmán).
27. "Refuerzan Lucha contra Piratería," *Mural*, February 25, 2010; "Integran Bloque contra Informalidad," *Mural*, March 1, 2012. The special prosecutor's office has been a point of acrimony in state politics. Soon after its creation, the CCIJ alleged that it was not pursuing many cases, and González placed the blame on the Congress (then with a PRI majority) for not approving budgets and staff ("Pasan bolita al Congreso," *Mural*, July 30, 2008). Perhaps because the PRI has a relationship with

government. As a result, CAREINTRA leaders themselves have quite infrequent contact with high-level politicians and tend not to have seats on consultative councils, instead delegating these tasks to the overarching CCIJ.[28] Second, the backwards-looking nature of the organization makes it less compatible with pro-globalization PAN administrations. And while the PAN governments have been open to include CAREINTRA representatives in consultative institutions, they have tended to attribute less importance to often protectionist economic demands of domestic small industry that clash with the goal of attracting foreign investment.

When it came to spending on business promotion, the González Márquez administration prioritized big-ticket investments that present an image to the general public of economic dynamism, forgoing spending on subsidies for local small business. This strategy has had the blessing of the COPARMEX, and CANACO, while it has ruffled feathers at CAREINTRA, the association that most depends on state subsidies for survival.

The largest chambers in Jalisco have pushed for the government to set up infrastructure projects to facilitate "clusters," such as industrial and technology parks where local firms can provide inputs or complementary services to large firms. These clusters place demands on the state in terms of urban planning, infrastructure, and subsidies. The most prominent initiative undertaken by the González Márquez administration in this regard was the Ciudad Creativa Digital (Creative Digital City), a project promoted by the state government and co-financed with municipal, state, and federal funds. This multi-year urban redevelopment initiative features significant investments in infrastructure and the building or renovation of several buildings in the *centro histórico* of Guadalajara. The government claimed that by 2023 this project would create space for 550 firms working in the "creative high-tech sectors, such as film, television, video games, digital animation, interactive media, mobile apps, internet, and other creative industries."[29]

---

many street vendors, the Sandóval administration has been more reticent to come to the table to discuss the issue with the CANACO or CCIJ, although it has named a new special prosecutor ("Reciclan plan contra piratas," *Mural*, March 21, 2014).

28. Interview, Juán Alberto Porras Brambila, President, CAREINTRA, October 20, 2017.

29. See: http://www.ciudadcreativadigital.mx/. "La ciudad creativa digital busca posicionar a México como un referente en la producción creative al nivel global. Un centro de negocios de esta industria y como el cluster más significativo de habla hispana." (video on website). "Un espacio para albergar el sector productive, impulsando el crecimiento de empresas locales y dando espacio para las compañías globales."

Representatives of the CCIJ and National Chamber of the Electronic Telecommunications Industry and Information Technologies (CANIETI) participated in the advisory board. And CANACO and other chambers have consistently supported the project in the media and in public events.[30]

In the commercial sector, the largest initiative undertaken by González was bringing the Pan-American Games to Jalisco in 2011. This event—similar to the Olympic Games, but featuring only delegations of athletes from the Western Hemisphere—was promised to boost the state's tourism industry. Preparing for the games required investments in roads, hotels, and security, and sports facilities. The state government delegated several of these responsibilities to CANACO-Guadalajara and COPARMEX and allocated millions of pesos to these organizations to train small commercial firms in customer service (approximately 700 for CANACO, 250 for COPARMEX, with capital subsidies of up to 5,000 pesos per beneficiary firm), promote tourism for the games, and to establish a branding campaign for local commercial firms to bear symbols of the Pan-American Games on their establishments.[31]

Despite a clear affinity between organized business and PAN administrations on economic policy and the close contact during periods of governance, I found no evidence of organizations overtly supporting a candidate or receiving preferential access to state benefits in exchange for electoral resources. On the side of the organizations, this stance is the result of a steadfast commitment to non-partisanship—a legal requirement in the case of the chambers of commerce and industry and a long-standing organizational statute for COPARMEX. Organization leaders were consistent in citing their non-partisanship as an important tool in maintaining good relations with politicians of all parties—a goal that increased their access to

30. Although this project was initiated under the gubernatorial administration of González, successor Sandoval continued it, although chambers have become more critical under the current administration, criticizing the Sandoval administration for being behind schedule, cutting the budget, and for keeping the public in the dark about the status of the project ("Difieren por apoyos a Cumbre de Negocios," *Mural*, June 27, 2013; "Cámaras critican opacidad en CCD," *Mural*, September 4, 2014).

31. "Crean operador de Panamericanos," *Mural*, June 17, 2010; "Capacitarán a comercios para JP," *Mural*, September 23, 2010; "Se Suman Comerciantes a Panamericanos," *Mural*, October 3, 2011. Interviews, Juan José González Nuño, Erick Herrera.

the programmatic policies that most shape their sectors' competitiveness. CAREINTRA, however, does rely on its brokerage role for state and federal subsidies and has made public pronouncements criticizing administrations when these benefits subside or celebrating large projects funded by Fondo PyME and other programs.[32]

A non-partisan stance does not prevent business associations from active participation in electoral campaigns. The chambers organize events where gubernatorial and mayoral candidates from the major parties meet with executive committees. In the weeks before the 2012 election, the Council of Industrial Chambers of Jalisco (CCIJ) invited gubernatorial candidates to public forums where they presented policy recommendations. (While PAN candidate Fernando Guzmán and Movimiento Ciudadano candidate Enrique Álfaro attended both of these events, PRI candidate Aristóles Sandóval was absent.) At the event, this council bringing together the largest business organizations in the state presented to candidates for governor, municipal presidents, and legislature their Sole Agenda for the Private Sector (Agenda Única del Sector Privado), including eight main programmatic goals: macroeconomic stability, crusade for competitiveness, economic growth and employment, structural reforms, education, social security, public security, and rule of law and democracy.[33] CANACO also held meetings with the candidates individually, where the candidates spoke with the chamber's executive council. In this same election, COPARMEX led a monitoring operation, aimed at uncovering fraud and vote buying. In a context where the PRI is the party best positioned to benefit from these electoral crimes (Nichter and Palmer-Rubin 2015), this can be seen as a way of putting the finger on the scale in favor of the other parties.

Distributive Strategies in PAN-Governed Jalisco vs. Other PAN-Governed States

As explained above, programmatic linkages with core small-business organizations have liberated PAN governments in Jalisco to use patronage strategically to maximize votes, in a context where this party has consistently

32. "Sin recursos...y sin respuesta," *Mural*, November 5, 2013; "Traen más recursos de la federación," *Mural*, February 11, 2014.

33. Marylú Vallejo, "Presentan agenda del sector privado," *Mural*. June 17, 2012; Luis Durán, "Establecen ejes para la economía," *Mural*. June 15, 2012.

faced electoral threats from the PRI. Under González Márquez, the state government allocated a very small portion of distributive programs for small businesses to these organizations, instead preferring to use these funds for visible infrastructure investments and to reach out to other societal actors, such as universities and NGOs. Data from Fondo PyME, a federal small-business subsidy program that grants discretion to state governments to determine which projects to find, is illustrative. From 2004 to 2011, small-business organizations intermediated only three out of 157 projects, totaling less than five million pesos (about 400,000 dollars)—less than 1 percent of total Fondo PyME spending in the state. Instead, 153 of the 157 total Fondo PyME projects in Jalisco had government agencies as intermediating organizations. 329 million pesos (68 percent of all spending in Jalisco) was concentrated into five large infrastructure projects, including an industrial park, a research institute, and a small-business incubator.[34]

In the distributive realm, PAN administrations in Jalisco are representative of other PAN administrations that faced an electoral threat.[35] While small-business organizations are core for these subnational party organizations, they prefer to allocate distributive benefits to non-core groups or to highly visible public goods that appeal to the population at large or generate employment. As shown in Figure 7.2, only when PAN governments exceed vote margins of roughly 15 percentage points do they allocate more Fondo PyME to projects mediated by small-business organizations than do PRI governments. Even when controlling for several other factors, such as level of economic development and including state-level fixed effects, the best predictor of the amount of subsidies funneled through small-business associations by PAN governments is the degree of electoral competition.

The opposite in this regard is the state of Guanajuato—the only state where the PAN has consistently won gubernatorial elections by margins exceeding 10 percent. Guanajuato—the home state of former president Vicente Fox—is the national stronghold for the PAN, which wrested control of this state from the PRI in 1995 and won the two subsequent gubernatorial elections by margins exceeding 20 percentage points. With a firm hold on power, PAN administrations have been free to allocate distributive benefits

34. "Jalisco va por el centro de inovación, diseño y desarrollo industrial," *El Informador*, March 14, 2012; "Jalisco es innovator," *El Empresario.mx*, August 15, 2011; "Destacan apoyos en economía," *Reforma*, November 27, 2012.

35. See Appendix C and Palmer-Rubin (2016) for a more detailed analysis of Fondo PyME spending.

to reward their allies. Fondo PyME spending in this state demonstrates a strong allegiance between the state government and organized business. Small-business organizations intermediated thirty-three of the 159 projects from 2004 to 2011, representing 14 percent of Fondo PyME spending in the state. Ties with the PAN government have been particularly strong in the Guanajuato textile and leather industries, which played an important role in this party's founding in 1939. From 2004 to 2011, the Guanajuato government funded twenty-nine projects for which the Chamber of the Footwear Industry of the State of Guanajuato (CICEG) was the intermediating organization, totaling approximately 120 million pesos (about 10 million US dollars). In most years, CICEG participated in several Fondo PyME projects, which funded conventions, advertising campaigns, and consulting services for footwear manufacturers. The Guanajuato footwear industry has historically been a core group for the PAN and CICEG has a high degree of organizational overlap with the PAN. For example, José Abugaber Andonie,

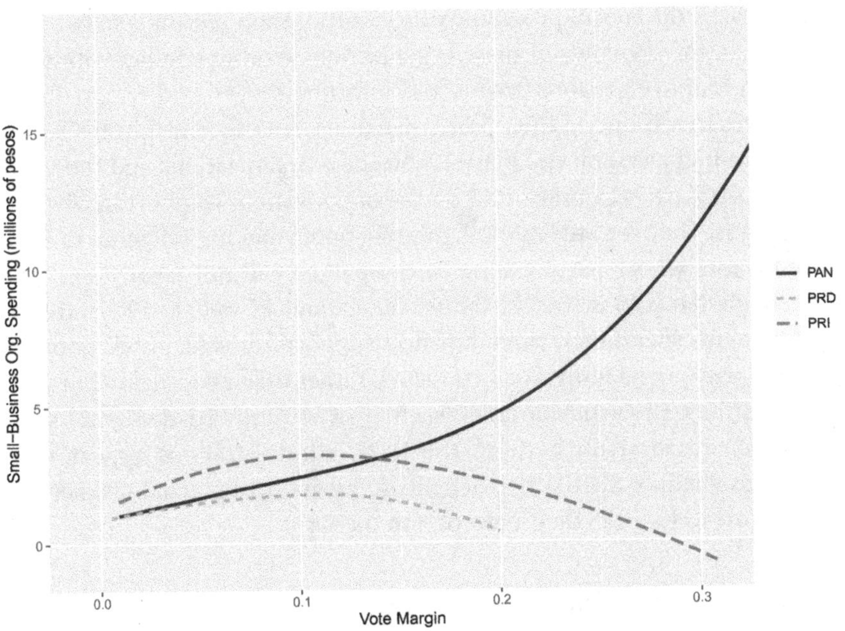

Figure 7.2 Vote Margin and Small-Business Organization Spending by Governing Party

Note: $N = 199$. Data reflects federalized Fondo PyME spending from 2004 to 2011 for all states that participated in the program. Curves created with loess to reflect overall trends.

Source: Author's calculations based on program data received in response to public information request.

former president of CICEG and president of CCE-Guanajuato, an umbrella organization for all business organizations in the state, is the brother-in-law of the PAN's 2012 candidate for mayor of León, Guanajuato's largest city. The state PAN committee offered Abugaber a federal congressional candidacy in the same year.[36]

PRD and PRI Linkages with Small Business Organizations

Qualitative findings from states governed by the PRI and PRD, for whom small-business organizations are a non-core constituency, demonstrate a lack of incorporation of these organizations into programmatic policymaking. Rather than an overt exclusion of these interests, these administrations typically adopt perfunctory participatory institutions—small in number and weak in impact—that fail to effectively offer voice to organizational participants but grant a symbolic level of access. From the perspective of the ruling party, the lack of programmatic incorporation responds to two realities. First, the demands of these organizations tend to conflict with those of core groups (e.g., labor unions and informal-sector workers), reducing incentives to respond to their policy demands. And second, given a lack of long-standing electoral ties between business organizations and these two parties, the parties cannot count on the organizations' support in electoral campaigns. They see little merit in offering policymaking influence to organized actors whose participation in campaigns will not favor them. This same logic tends to drive distributive allocations as well, as PRI and PRD governments spend their small-business support funds on public goods or projects that can be individually targeted, rather than allocated in blocks to organizations. In particular cases, such as in waning PRI-dominant states facing an electoral threat from the PAN, administrations appear more willing to channel distributive benefits to business organizations, perhaps in an effort to forestall their defection to the PAN.

Business in PRI-Dominated Estado de México

Business organizations in Estado de México exhibit an overall tendency of exclusion from both programmatic and distributive policy on the state level.

---

36. "En los zapatos del liderazgo," *El Economista*, April 25, 2012.

Consultative councils are less prevalent than in the other states studied, and those that do convene organized business are less functional and less inclusive of the broader business community. Small-business subsidies are managed by a "semi-autonomous" government agency that allows the state government to circumvent the requirement to allocate funds through intermediary organizations. Where business leaders have access to the state government, it occurs because they (wisely, given the circumstances) elect leaders with personal ties to PRI politicians.

This exclusion of non-partisan small-business organizations can be explained by the electoral circumstances of the ruling party in this state. At the time of research, Estado de México was one of a few remaining PRI-dominant states. This party has never lost an election in the state, and until 2017 had won every election by at least a 20-point margin over the second-place finisher, but one.[37] This control reduces the incentives for the state government to incorporate non-core groups—such as organized business—into policymaking. Rather, in programmatic politics, the party favors the interests of core allies, while "insourcing" small-business subsidies—which in other states are mediated by organizations—through state agencies. These agencies exercise discretion in the allocation of such benefits—either spending on allies to sustain their "endogenous loyalty" (Diaz-Cayeros, Estévez, and Magaloni 2016) or spending on large public projects.

The difficulty of achieving voice in state economic policy is exacerbated by the unique political geography of Estado de México. Mexico's most populous state, Estado de México wraps around the national capital in an upside-down U shape in such a way that traveling from one region of the state to another typically implies passing through the interminable traffic of Mexico City. The state capital, Toluca, lies to the west of Mexico City and has historically been the center of political power in state government, and perhaps the most important nucleus of power for the PRI nationwide as the heart of the Carlos Hank González political dynasty in the municipality of Atlacomulco, which spawned the political careers of presidents Carlos Salinas de Gortari and Enrique Peña Nieto. In recent decades, however,

37. In 1999 the PRI won with only a 6.8 percentage-point margin over the second-place PAN. In the next two elections—2005 and 2011—the PRI won by margins of 22.8 and 41.0 percentage points. During the latter half of Peña Nieto's presidency, the PRI's electoral dominance has unraveled. The PRI's candidate in the 2017 election, a cousin of Peña Nieto's named Alfredo del Mazo, won with only a 2.8 percentage-point margin over MORENA candidate Delfina Gómez.

the northern region of the state (the Valle de México), including exurbs of Mexico City such as Tlalnepantla, Naucalpan, and Ecatepec, has become an important power center. Eruviel Ávila (2011–2017) was the first governor who built his career in this region, having twice served as mayor of Ecatepec prior to running for the governorship.

With both political and economic power split between these two poles, business organizations have typically had difficulty articulating their power statewide. Leaders of small-business associations have thus focused their energies either on influencing municipal economic policy or have looked to the federal government (when under the control of the PAN) for benefits. The director of the CANACINTRA delegation in Toluca—the only in the state—asserted that it is difficult to organize industry in the Valle de México, as these businesses are more closely tied to economic networks in Mexico City. Reflecting the low degree of collaboration among business organizations to influence state politics, the CANACINTRA director was unable to even conjure the names of the directors or presidents of CANACO and COPARMEX affiliates in the state.[38] The director of the COPARMEX delegation in Toluca also reported minimal coordination with COPARMEX affiliates in the north and east of the state. There are three CANACO affiliates in the state, two in the Valle de México (Naucalpan and Tlalnepantla) and one in Toluca. Leaders of these chambers reported very little contact with each other, and political strategies focused much more on their immediate regions than on business issues statewide.

The lack of coordinated demand-making by the organized business community in state economic policy is not solely attributable to geography, however. Were these governments eager to foment such coordination, they may have created consultative institutions as illustrated earlier in this chapter with the case of CESJAL in Jalisco and in Chapter 6 with COCOCAM—the peasant consultative council—in Michoacán. However, no interviewed representative of a business organization in the state reported regular participation in consultative councils convened by the state government. According to Romero, CANACINTA does not participate in state-level councils on its own, instead delegating the representative function to the umbrella organization for organized business in the state. The leader of CANACO-Tlalnepantla reported very little contact with

38. Interview, Guadalupe Romero, Director, CANACINTRA-Estado de México, April 16, 2012.

the state government, but frequent participation in municipal Economic Development Councils in the three municipalities to which his chamber pertains, and in Tlalnepantla's Planning Committee (COPLADEMUN).[39] Given the much more competitive electoral climate in the Valle de México—PAN, PRD, and MORENA all have their strongest organizations in the state in this region—mayors in these municipalities likely felt greater pressure to make overtures to the business community than did state government figures, for fear that they would support opposition parties.

Business chambers and COPARMEX do certainly have demands regarding publicly relevant issues, such as security, corruption, and informal commerce, but they tend to resort to going through the press to influence public opinion or autonomous coordination rather than participating in formal participatory institutions or direct contact with the administration. COPARMEX in particular was active in the press during this period to criticize the state's inability to address insecurity, which had led to the kidnapping of several prominent business persons in the state.[40] In 2008, COPARMEX went against its typical distaste for contentious action, helping organize a protest about insecurity in Toluca.[41] In 2011, the Toluca delegations of COPARMEX and CANACO—with the backing of PAN and PRD members of the state legislature—joined a citizen-led Citizen Observatory to oversee the state governments' security forces.[42] And CANACO regularly takes to the press to denounce the proliferation of informal commerce and excessive paperwork to open and operate formal firms, with little sign of collaboration as took place between the Guadalajara CANACO and the Jalisco government.[43]

Given the mandate of remaining non-partisan, no representative of the major business chambers or COPARMEX reported an overtly oppositional stance to the state government or to the PRI. They did, however, lament the

39. Interview, Raúl Avilés, Director, CANACO-Tlalnepantla, April 24, 2012.

40. "Crece extorsión a empresarios en Edomex," *Reforma*, July 21, 2009.

41. "Marcha Toluca por la seguridad," *Reforma*, August 20, 2008.

42. "Propone PAN observatorio ciudadano," *Reforma*, December 2, 2009; "Promueve el PRD Observatorios Ciudadanos," *Reforma*, October 27, 2011; "Cuida Observatorio Ciudadano a empresas," *Reforma*, April 11, 2012.

43. "Piden agilizar apertura de empresas," *Reforma*, August 11, 2009; "Critican tramitología en Atlacomulco," *Reforma*, September 7, 2010; "Piden mano dura contra piratería," *Reforma*, January 31, 2011; "Crece 300% ambulantaje en Toluca," *Reforma*, August 2, 2011.

absence of entry points into state politics. The director of CANACINTRA complained that the PRI would not send their gubernatorial candidate to meet with members during the 2011 campaign unless the chamber was able to organize an event with at least 1,000 participants, which was financially unfeasible.[44] Similarly, CANACO affiliates held events with mayoral candidates in their respective municipalities and with congressional candidates, but not with gubernatorial candidates, and have expressed frustration, both in print and in interviews over the reticence of candidates to meet with their chambers.[45] As in other states, COPARMEX has insisted on its non-partisanship, but has held campaigns to encourage turnout and informed voting and to denounce vote buying.[46] In the 2011 election, CANACO-Toluca offered discounts and prizes to citizens who showed evidence of voting.[47] In a context where state politics are dominated by a single party famous for mobilizing voters clientelistically, these efforts to modify the terms of electoral competition likely favor opposition party candidates.

The nomination of business leaders to elected office in Estado de México constitutes an important exception to the overall lack of access to policymaking by business organizations. Multiple heads of business chambers have gone on to receive nominations for the federal legislature with the PRI or its coalition partners, including José Luis Velasco Lino, former President of COPARMEX-Toluca who is the cousin of the personal secretary to President Peña Nieto, former governor of Estado de México.[48] The seeping of electoral politics into the organized business community has sowed divisiveness—elections of the head of the CCE have led to recriminations in the press and accusations of manipulation.[49] This threat to the organizations'

44. Interview, Guadalupe Romero.
45. "Busca Canaco acercamiento con candidatos," *Reforma*, April 9, 2012; "Se reunen empresarios con candidatos," *Reforma*, June 12, 2012; Interviews, Raul Avilés; Claudia Serrano, Director, Coparmex-Toluca, April 26, 2012.
46. "Llaman a ignorar campaña de voto nulo," *Reforma*, July 3, 2009; "Desgrada posible alianza AN y PRD," *Reforma*, January 25, 2010; "Llaman empresarios a votar razonadamente," *Reforma*, January 31, 2011; "Alerta IFE por compra de votos en Edomex," *Reforma*, June 28, 2012.
47. "Desea Canaco motivar votación en Edomex," *Reforma*, May 25, 2011.
48. "Callejón Informativo," *EdoMex Al Día*, December 13, 2011; "Funtanet, de CONCAMIN a diputado," *Milenio*, March 9, 2015.
49. "Cervantes quiere ser líder de empresarios," *Poder EdoMex*, May 8, 2011; "Divide a empresarios sucesión en CCE," *Reforma*, August 1, 2011; "Impuso Francisco Funtanet al Presidente del Consejo Empresarial," *MVT*, August 11, 2011.

non-partisanship and the typical disinclination toward the PRI is likely attributable to the monopoly that this party holds over economic policy in the state. As shown in Chapter 6, in the case of agricultural organizations, where the PRI dominates, it is uninterested in incorporating actors in policymaking if they are not aligned with the party. And where the state government fails to open space for institutional participation, it behooves organizations to elect leaders who can get policymakers' attention through informal channels, even if such access fails to consolidate into institutionalized spaces for participation in policymaking on behalf of the business community.

The PRI's secure hold on power in the state has also led Estado de México governors to exclude organized business from distributive spending. As discussed in the introduction to this chapter, governments are predicted to allocate distributive benefits to non-core groups (as organized business is for the PRI) when facing an electoral threat and seeking to form short-term alliances for an upcoming election. Without the need to attract these organizations' support, the state government uses its benefits instead to reinforce the loyalty of its party base or, as alleged by critics, to funnel money to friends and family of ruling politicians.

Rather than engaging business organizations as the executors of small capital subsidies, training programs, conventions, and other state-funded benefits for small-business, the Estado de México government established a "semi-autonomous" agency to receive applications and allocate such benefits. The Estado de México Institute for the Entrepreneur (Instituto Mexiquense del Emprendedor) served as a model for other PRI-governed states and later for the federal government's Mexican Institute for the Entrepreneur (INADEM) under Peña Nieto. These bodies allow government agencies to "insource" small-business benefits that previously had been mandated to be intermediated by civil society actors under the PAN administrations. In the words of the head of training for INADEM , "all of the intermediary organizations have to find their own resources. It's unlikely that I would get resources for somebody else to do another program that I cannot control."[50]

50. Interview, Ricardo Mayer Téllez, Head of Training Programs, Estado de México Institute for the Entrepreneur, April 26, 2012. "Todos los organismos intermedios bajan sus propios recursos. Difícilmente yo voy a estar bajando para que hagan otro programa que yo no voy a tener el control, porque tengo aquí una situación, que si yo bajo recursos para una cámara, no quiero decir ninguna, bajo recursos para una cámara y no me lo empiezan a aplicar, y no me comprueban bien, me atoran todo el procedimiento para el siguiente año."

Interviewed representatives of CANACO, CANACINTRA, and COPARMEX all reported a near complete exclusion from state-controlled small-business subsidies and have taken to the press to complain about unclear rules of operation and opacity and discretion in the state government's management of small-business subsidies.[51] Instead, these organizations report more success applying for benefits directly from the federal government.

Data from Fondo PyME reflect this exclusion of business organizations. From 2004 to 2011, the state government allocated only six projects to small-business organizations, totaling 6.3 million pesos (about 500,000 dollars), approximately 0.5 percent of all Fondo PyME spending in the state. Ninety-one percent of Fondo PyME spending in Mexico State, over one billion pesos (about eighty million dollars), was granted to Ford Motor Company as an inducement to situate a factory in the state in 2006.[52] Of the sixty-three remaining projects, thirty were mediated by government agencies, most commonly the Estado de México Institute for the Entrepreneur. The most prominent of these projects were the construction of a technology park and several projects funding consultancy services for small businesses.[53]

While PRI governments nationwide appear not to be particularly warm to organized business, given these organizations affinity to the PAN, the exclusion from distributive benefits in Estado de México is an extreme case. As shown in Figure 7.3 (derived from models presented in Appendix C), the degree to which PRI governments allocate Fondo PyME benefits to projects intermediated by small-business organizations increases as vote margins become narrower. Where the PRI wins by margins of over 20 percentage points, as in Estado de México, the money it spends on such programs

51. Interviews, Claudia Serrano; Raúl Avilés; Damián Flores Pérez, President, ANIT-Valle de Chalco, April 17, 2012. "Impulsan economía," *Reforma*, May 27, 2009.

52. "Secretaría de Economía entrega recursos públicos a transnacionales," *Fortuna*, September 15, 2008. Obviously, Ford does not classify as a small business. Fondo PyME includes a category of projects for "tractor" businesses—large firms whose activities are expected to generate economic activity for smaller firms that provide complementary services. Oddly, the administrators of this project did not classify it under the tractor category, but rather as a benefit for micro-enterprises.

53. "Inauguran 'Tecnopolo Esmeralda Bicentenario'," *Heraldo Estado de México*, January 24, 2013.

diminishes to less than half of what is spent in states where the PRI wins by lower than 10-percentage point margins.

Puebla in the pre-2011 period is an example of a PRI-governed state under threat. The former dominant party governed this state continuously until 2010, when it was finally defeated by PAN Senator Rafael Moreno Valle. While the PRI enjoyed a 14-percentage point margin of victory in the 2004 gubernatorial race, this party was losing ground in the capital city, which concentrates 30 percent of the state population and half of its GDP,[54] and where the PAN won mayoral elections in 1996 and 2002. The PRI government in Puebla, facing a significant electoral threat from the pro-business PAN, involved small-business organizations frequently in Fondo PyME projects. These organizations mediated twenty-two projects over the eight-year period, totaling fifty million pesos (about four million dollars), 23 percent of total spending in this state. The most common recipients were affiliates of CONCANACO, CANACINTRA, and COPARMEX, all based in the capital city, which each received between twelve and twenty-three million pesos. The largest of these projects was the construction of a meat-processing plant, intermediated by CANACINTRA, which received eight million pesos of Fondo PyME funding. Also, between 2008 and 2011 the Puebla CANACO received yearly projects ranging from 2.4 to 4.9 million pesos to fund a week-long promotional and networking event for small businesses, Puebla Region PyME Week (Semana Regional PyME Puebla).

Business in Michoacán: Exclusion and Cherry-picking

Similarly to Estado de México, the Michoacán government's approach to business development is notable for its exclusion of the organized business community, along with a cherry-picking approach to managing small-business support programs. As shown in Chapter 5, the prime business organizations in the state are not as large nor did they have the same history of closeness with the state government as their sister organizations in Jalisco. The administrations of Cárdenas and Godoy gave clear signs of avoiding chambers in the operation of business support programs and the PRD party organization in Michoacán did

54. Source: Sistema Nacional de Información Municipal. http://www.snim.rami.gob.mx/.

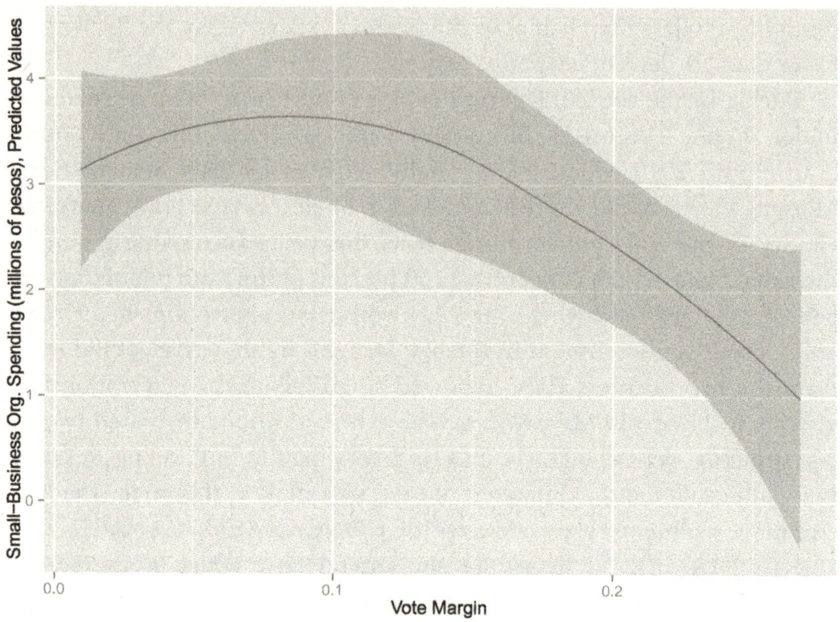

Figure 7.3 Vote Margin and Small-Business Organization Spending, PRI-Governed States

Note: $N = 102$. Values on the vertical axis represent predicted values from Model 3 in Appendix C. Band shows 95 percent confidence intervals.

Source: Author's calculations based on program data received in response to public information request.

not pay much heed to integrating business leaders into its electoral or policymaking processes.

The business organizations are also wary of PRD leaders. Representatives of both CANACO and COPARMEX in the state mentioned that a central programmatic goal that they had was the approval of a law to regulate protest in the state, claiming that disruptive protests adversely affect business. Given that the PRD is aligned with groups that engage frequently in protest activities, such as the dissident teachers' union and peasant organizations, there is a clear clash of programmatic interests.

Business promotion in Michoacán has combined support for micro and small businesses with occasional strategic projects to attract large-scale foreign investment. In both areas, prominent business organizations have largely been excluded from planning or implementation, while the state government seeks out allied groups to favor with these benefits. For instance, state-government-funded business incubators are situated exclusively at universities whose leadership is PRD-affiliated, and not in business organization headquarters as in other states. State economic development ministry personnel have developed a suite of programs for micro-enterprise promotion that operate outside the structure of Fondo PyME and target them to municipal governments and local groups of family-run businesses. This strategy resembles the PAN's approach of cherry-picking a friendly middle-class agricultural organization amidst a hostile group of dissident peasant associations.

This state created the program @Tienda in 2004, targeted to five types of businesses—convenience stores (*tiendas de abarrotes*), bakeries (*panaderías*), auto mechanics (*talleres*), office supply stores (*papelerías*), and tortilla vendors (*tortillerías*). This program, which the federal government later replicated as a subprogram within Fondo PyME, provides training and resources to help these businesses remain competitive in the face of proliferating chain stores. According to a consultant for @Tienda, most potential beneficiaries approach the program seeking credit or subsidies, but benefit most substantially from the consulting provided to develop a business plan and improve the image and layout of their stores.[55]

The Michoacán Ministry of Economic Development (SEDECO) also operates a variety of services to help micro-entrepreneurs place their products in local stores, including a networking service to promote locally produced foodstuffs in convenience stores and the operation of an *artesanía* store to promote locally produced crafts. Finally, the state operates a small-business loan program called Sí Financia. None of these programs centrally involve the collaboration of business organizations in the state. State business organizations instead work as intermediaries for federal Fondo PyME projects and, at times refer small business owners to SEDECO if they mention the programs by name.[56] The head of programs for PyME promotion at this ministry reported that they prefer to work with groups of business owners from a given community—often at the request of a municipal president—rather than limit beneficiaries to those who have approached chambers requesting support.[57]

55. Interview, Janitzio Piña, Consultant, FUNDES-México, November 16, 2011.
56. Interviews, Delia Cárdenas Pedraza, Manager of Social Communication and Training, CANACINTRA-Morelia, January 26, 2012; Humberto Ortega, Centro México Emprende Consultant, CANACO-Morelia, December 5, 2011.
57. Interview, Gabriel Gutiérrez, Director of Programs for Micro, Small, and Medium Firms, Michoacán Ministry of Economic Development, December 8, 2011.

In the realm of large-scale infrastructure, the state government has pursued a handful of strategic projects, such as the creation of industrial parks or improvements in the transportation infrastructure in the port city of Lázaro Cárdenas. Again, these projects have operated without much input from organized business. Tellingly, the entrepreneurial interests in Cárdenas and Godoy's cabinets did not have ties to organized business, but rather were owners or managers of large corporations based in the state. Heads of SEDECO and have been executives at Organización Ramírez, Michoacán's largest corporation and owner of the dominant movie theater chain in the country and other corporations, without direct ties to organized business (Chávez Gutiérrez 2011, 264–69).

The PRD administrations' impassivity toward organized business is further illustrated in the perfunctory attempts to create consultative institutions for this sector. Representatives of the major business organizations located in Morelia report participating in only a handful of committees. The Consultative Council for Economic Development of Michoacán (Consejo Consultivo para el Desarrollo Económico de Michoacán) was founded in 1997, prior to Cárdenas' entry into state government. This council, whose members are named directly by the governor, includes several state ministry leaders and eight representatives of business associations in the state. While COPARMEX and the Consejo Coordinador Empresarial of Michoacán were included from the beginning, CANACINTRA and CANACO-Morelia were not integrated into this council until 2010. The council is quite inactive, holding meetings irregularly roughly every four months, with many absences. The business organization leaders interviewed reported no important initiatives that they had pursued through this council,[58] and the council's director described the council as "rubber-stamping" projects that have already been approved by SEDECO or other agencies and that votes are almost always unanimously in favor: "This is not a body where there's much confrontation or disagreement. In reality, projects are presented, and more than anything the process is an issue of form, not really substance."[59]

58. Interview, Eduardo Sánchez Mártinez, Ex-President, COPARMEX-Michoacán, February 2, 2012. "Ese Consejo de Desarrollo Económico si es un consejo creado por el gobierno para respaldar también al gobierno y que el gobierno invita a participar de muchas cosas. Es un consejo consultivo que lo propone el gobierno y es estrictamente consultivo, no es vinculatorio."

59. Interview, Juan Carlos Vega Solórzano, Executive Director, Consultative Council for Economic Development of Michoacán, January 24, 2012. "No es un

Instead, the technical director of this council said that the most important project that it has undertaken is building economic ties between Michoacán and China through participation in international forums and scholarships for students travel to China.

The Chamber of Commerce of Morelia is the largest business organization in the state with roughly 4,000 active members, and 32,000 affiliates through the SIEM. As discussed in Chapter 5, this organization has been particularly enterprising with a high-intensity recruitment program, which also yields impressive financial resources through the federal SIEM program. These tactics position the CANACO to be active in the state's programmatic business development agenda. However, the economic development apparatus in Michoacán has typically not opened doors to CANACO's participation. Staff of the training area of the CANACO reported that state employees frequently attend training sessions, often with the cost covered by their employers, but the state does not otherwise support the routine programming of the chamber. According to CANACO's director, the most important instance of state–chamber collaboration is the Semana PyME, a yearly week-long event providing training activities, keynote speakers, and networking opportunities for business owners and any citizens in the state interested in entrepreneurial activity.[60] This program is subsidized both by SEDECO and the federal Fondo PyME program, but most of the funds come from entry fees.

The other large business organizations in Morelia report even less engagement in state business-development programming. Founded in 1940, the Morelia CANACINTRA is the oldest state delegation of this chamber and certainly was an important political actor in the mid-century period. However, since the revocation of mandatory chamber membership and the decline of the manufacturing industry in Michoacán, this organization has seen its membership decline, with roughly 1,600 members at the time of the interview and today is primarily patronage seeking.[61] The head of training for CANACINTRA reported that in 2011, the organization helped get funding from Fondo PyME for over 400 local businesspersons

organismo en el cual haya mucha confrontación, donde haya polémica. En realidad se presentan los proyectos, es más que nada para atender una cuestión de forma, no así de fondo."

60. Interview, Agustín Rebollar Cruz, General Director, CANACO-Morelia, July 5, 2013.

61. Interview, Delia Cárdenas Pedraza.

to take part in an online business management course. Like CANACO, CANACINTRA has minimal participation in state programs, instead accessing programs offered by the federal Ministry of the Economy through its México Emprende Center.

The Michoacán COPARMEX affiliate is quite small, with only roughly 320 active members.[62] Like CANACINTRA and CANACO, COPARMEX operates a Centro México Emprende, through which it manages federal small-business support programs, primarily Fondo PyME programs that offer finance or training such as Mi Tienda. The interviewed consultant of this center said that their office does not apply for these benefits directly, but that instead they are negotiated by the federal COPARMEX headquarters and allotted to each state delegation. In 2006, COPARMEX also received funds from the federal Ministry of the Economy through Fondo PyME to buy land to build a new headquarters and industrial park. According to a former president of COPARMEX and PAN state legislator, the federal government under the PAN presidencies of Fox and Calderón turned to organizations like COPARMEX to avoid providing benefits to a state government that was under the control of an opposition party and had allies in the business sector that were not connected to the long-standing business organizations:

> "Since the state government has its friends in the business sector, [COPARMEX and other business organizations] were drawn to Fox, we saw his as a force for change. SEDECO had lots of conflicts with the federal Ministry of the Economy because they come from different parties and have different interests. So, naturally, the Ministry of the Economy looked to COPARMEX, or somebody coming from COPARMEX to be in charge of the committees supervising Fondo PyME for example."[63]

---

62. Interview, Julia Sánchez Sarabia, Centro México Emprende Consultant, COPARMEX-Michoacán, December 13, 2011.

63. Interview, Eduardo Sánchez Martínez. "Como el gobierno del estado tiene sus empresas afines, digamos, organismos empresariales, nosotros, nosotros veíamos al gobierno de Fox como un cambio, entonces había mucha empatía. El gobierno estatal, la Sedeco, chocaba mucho con con la federal, por ser de diferente partido y de distinto interés. Chocaban mucho. Entonces, naturalmente la Secretaría de Economía buscaba la COPARMEX, o para que fuera alguien de COPARMEX el que tuviera los comités de supervisión del Fondo Pyme, por ejemplo."

Outside of its administration of distributive programs, COPARMEX in Michoacán has been active in promoting democracy-strengthening programs, such as electoral monitoring, transparency reforms, and co-organizing a March for Peace to protest the insecurity crisis in the state.

Given its decentralized nature, the state of Michoacán has business chambers in several cities outside of Michoacán, including fifteen chambers of commerce and six CANACINTRA delegations throughout the state. These organizations typically are small in size and report very limited interaction with the state government. Instead, their political engagement is largely limited to the municipal level—each interacting with several municipal governments in their surroundings. In these smaller outlying chambers, the nomination of chamber leaders to municipal government posts is common, and leaders were less reluctant to express their partisan leanings (mostly with the PAN) than fervently non-partisan chambers in the big cities, although they were clear to state that these preferences were personal inclinations of the presidents and not the position of the chambers.[64] Of the four outlying chambers studied, all but one (CANACOPE-Zamora) had México Emprende modules and used them with the goal of accessing Fondo PyME programs. Yet these chambers all reported fewer than ten proposals per year and most had not had a single project approved.

Conclusion

As I have shown in this chapter, programmatic *representation* of middle-class groups, such as small business, presents more challenges than programmatic *demand-making* in the first place. When it comes to incorporating these organizations into policy decisions around regulatory policy, the allocation of infrastructure funds, or other highly contentious issues of economic policy, political leaders need to carefully manage their competing goals and constituencies. I presented a series of expectations about ruling parties' incorporation strategies for small-business organizations that

64. Interviews, Isabel Fuentes Salomón, Manager, CANACINTRA-Uruapan, February 3, 2012; José García Velázquez, President, CANACO-Zamora, January 27, 2012; José Carlos Granados Garnica, President, CANACOPE-Zamora, January 27, 2012; Jorge Jiménez Casillas, Consultant, CANACINTRA-Zamora, January 27, 2012; Pedro Plancarte Molina, President, CANACO-Uruapan, February 3, 2012.

differentiates between right-wing parties—for whom these organizations are a core constituency—and left-wing or centrist parties—for whom the organizations are non-core.

Findings from the state of Jalisco, governed for three terms by the PAN—an externally mobilized right-wing party—substantiated the argument that parties that count on long-standing organic ties with core organizations are equipped to incorporate these organizations into the programmatic elements of governing, reserving patronage benefits for short-term electoral strategies to appeal to non-core groups. Analysis of budgetary data for small-business subsidy programs across many PAN-governed states more broadly illustrated this tendency: PAN administrations typically exclude core small-business organizations from distributive spending when they face an electoral threat.

Further evidence from the states of Michoacán and Estado de México—states governed by parties for whom small-business organizations are a non-core constituency—tells a quite different story. These administrations lack a motivation to incorporate small-business organizations into either programmatic policymaking or patronage. First, the programmatic goals of small-business organizations tend to conflict with those of the parties' core constituencies, such as informal-sector vendors for the PRD and organized labor for the PRI. Second, clientelistic strategies are not so effective with these organizations, as they avoid overt partisanship and might alienate their members by supporting a non-traditional ally. Ultimately, these non-core cases reproduce findings from the previous chapter as the PRI and PRD either completely exclude the non-core groups, or cherry-pick a small segment of the sector for incorporation while excluding the major sectoral organizations.

With this chapter, I conclude the contrast between the two economic sectors (peasants and small business) and two political parties (PAN and PRD) that constitute the empirical base of this study. I have shown that the ways that non-elite interest organizations participate in economic policy is the result of an interaction between two dynamics. First, processes internal to the organizations determine whether the organizations approach the state with the primary goal of extracting selective benefits for organizational maintenance or influencing policies to generate more favorable conditions for the sectors that they purport to represent. Second, processes inherent to the political parties that hold state power determine whether ruling administrations are interested in sustaining institutions to channel the programmatic demands of interest organizations. Only where both organization and party coincide in a desire for programmatic participation does this mode of representation prevail.

In the Mexican case at least, such a convergence is typical for the middle-class small-business associations and right-wing PAN, and much rarer for lower-class small-scale farmers and left-wing PRD. In Chapter 8, I analyze the external validity of these findings, probing whether my explanations for representational bias in Mexico extend to other contexts. The heightened pressures of patronage politics among popular-sector organizing is a widespread phenomenon. It is common for organizations representing the poor to struggle to sustain collective action and to turn to state patronage for solutions to their membership challenges. And it is also common for left-wing parties to encounter pressure to deploy organizational allies through clientelist mobilization strategies, prioritizing short-term electoral goals over long-term goals of economic transformation and party consolidation.

While class bias in interest representation is widespread, however, I will show that class is not destiny. The region offers examples of popular-sector organizations that have evaded the patronage trap and left-wing parties willing and able to incorporate them in programmatic policy. And, conversely, we find cases of patronage-oriented business groups and right-wing political parties that fail to incorporate core business organizations into programmatic politics.

Conclusion

Can Organizations Confront Latin American Oligarchy?

This book has explained why some small-business and peasant associations lend voice to their sectors in the policies that shape sectoral competitiveness, while others focus their efforts on extracting patronage benefits from the state. While existing research stresses the effect of poverty on demand for patronage, I have uncovered factors that explain how even organizations representing poor rural population can evade the "patronage trap" and how organizations representing middle-class small-business owners can fall prey to it. I found that organizations and political parties must converge on a preference for programmatic linkages for programmatic representation to prevail. Thus, this book has traced two distinct causal processes: one producing organizational demand type and another to explain parties' incorporation strategies.

First, I have argued that the mode in which an organization generates organizational capacity—the ability to recruit, retain, and mobilize members—is an important determinant of the types of policy demands that organizations levy on the state. Some organizations were founded with an *internal* organizational capacity model, based on the provision of services or collective economic ventures. Where organizations were able to sustain this model until the moment that an electoral ally assumed power, they retained the autonomy necessary to levy programmatic demands. Other organizations were founded with an *external* organizational capacity model or slipped into this model when the productive services that they offered were exhausted. These organizations prioritized patronage demands after the electoral transition in an attempt to maximize benefits that the leader could allocate selectively to incentivize member participation.

Second, I showed how political parties' founding traits shape their strategies for incorporating core and non-core organizations into policymaking. In an electorally competitive context, the optimal approach is a "segmented" (Luna 2014) linkage strategy, incorporating core organizations into long-term programmatic linkages and allocating patronage benefits efficiently to attract non-core groups at election time. The ability of parties to execute this multi-faceted strategy, however, requires organizational structures within the party that are conducive to long-term programmatic linkages with core organizations. Externally mobilized parties—those formed out of power—are more prone to have such structures, as they spent a significant amount of time outside of office, relying on allied organizations to retain a ground presence. Internally mobilized parties—those formed with access to state benefits—are more prone to place immediate electoral victory over long-term party building, preventing these parties from forming programmatic linkages with core organizations.

Where party and organization converge on preferences for programmatic or patronage linkages, the organizations enter into self-reproducing cycles of policy representation. The most robust of these cycles is the one that is patronage-based. While patronage linkages offer particularistic goods that organization leaders can repurpose as selective benefits to spur collective action, they route organizations into *the patronage trap*, a vicious cycle in which organizations become specialized for patronage intermediation. These linkages convert leaders into electoral brokers and force organizations to forgo protest, lobbying, and other forms of political participation in favor of electoral mobilization on behalf of the party patron. The parallel programmatic equilibrium occurs when party and organization converge on a preference for long-term linkages based on programmatic representation. In these cases, the organization avoids becoming dependent on the party, allowing it to engage in diverse modes of political participation to maximize its influence over policies that most affect its sector.

Re-evaluating the Class Hypothesis

My main foil throughout this book has been the class hypothesis: the conventional wisdom that patronage politics is the realm of the poor, while programmatic linkages are the norm for middle-class voters and organizations.

To be clear, a central finding is that class matters an awful lot for representation, and that patronage-based models of representation are much more prevalent as one moves down the socio-economic spectrum. This tendency is a root cause of biased pluralism—and ultimately of structural inequalities—in patronage-ridden democracies such as Mexico's. However, understanding the mechanisms through which class influences representation models is important, as it helps us explain the organizations that contravene class-based explanations, such as REDCCAM, the programmatic peasant organization and CANACINTRA-Morelia, the patronage-based business chamber. My account both shows how class status tilts the playing field against organizations representing the poor, but also how lower-class organizations can evade the patronage trap.

I have offered two addenda to theories of class and representation. First, I have developed a theory that takes seriously the *demand side* of programmatic and patronage politics. Existing theories linking class to patronage politics mostly focus on supply, analyzing the strategic decisions made by partisan actors in deciding *whether* to base their electoral appeals on patronage (Hagopian forthcoming; Shefter 1977; Weitz-Shapiro 2012) and *which* segments of the electorate to target with patronage appeals (Calvo and Murillo 2004, 743–45; Stokes et al. 2013, 161–71). In my focus on interest organizations—actors that specialize in levying policy demands on behalf of citizens—I develop a model that incorporates the logic not only of political representatives, but also of those who are being represented. I draw a contrast between organizations that generate organizational capacity internally—and thus are positioned to levy programmatic demands—and those that rely on patronage benefits to sustain organizational capacity. This contrast offers a lesson for organizations seeking to sustain a programmatic representation model.

My second addendum to the class hypothesis highlights subnational variation on both the supply and the demand-side. By analyzing state-level interest organizations nested within national confederations and political parties' subnational organizational structures, I found that the determinants of programmatic and patronage representation can operate below the national level. For example, the PRD in Chiapas pursues purely patronage-based linkages with rural organizations, while the Michoacán PRD pursues programmatic linkages. At the same time, I found some structures that were homogenous across Mexican states, such as the programmatic orientation of the PAN and COPARMEX, and the patronage-based orientation of the PRI and its peasant sector, the CNC. While scholarship on Latin America has a tendency to label entire parties or party systems as programmatic or patronage-based (Hagopian forthcoming; Kitschelt et al. 2010), future research should account for subnational variation in representation models

Broader Contributions

More broadly, in constructing a theoretical model to understand interest representation in post-neoliberal states, this book has made three main contributions. First, I have argued that we should pay more attention to organizations to explain democratic representation. After the neoliberal turn in Latin America, scholars often assume that organized interests—once so central to policymaking and to electoral politics under statist corporatist systems—are less relevant today.[1] My findings have shown that in Mexico organizations continue to play a central role in linking citizens to the state through either programmatic or patronage politics. Organizational mediation may be a necessary condition for programmatic representation given that citizens acting independently lack tools to influence policy, beyond the blunt and ephemeral instrument of voting in elections (Walker 1991, 20–23). Organizations are designed to engage in a wide variety of modes of demand-making between elections, including mobilizing protests, communicating through the press, and lobbying politicians. Participation in organizations offers citizens their best chance at influencing the most important and contentious of policy areas. If countries like Mexico are to move beyond oligarchic development models (Cameron 2021), non-elite interest organizations will play an important role articulating demands and shaping policy outcomes.

Second, I have shown that political parties continue to rely on organizations. Research on Mexico and other Latin American democracies has argued that transitions in both economic models and electoral campaign technology favor individual party–voter linkages rather than collective mobilization through labor unions and other mass organizations

1. This neglect also has disciplinary roots. The analysis of organized interests was once central to political science and public policy research, both in studies of the United States (Key 1942; Lipset, Trow, and Coleman 1956; Schattschneider 1935; Wilson 1974) and in comparative politics (Bates 1981; Schmitter 1974; Verba 1961). However, research on organizations has been marginalized in the wake of the behavioral revolution. See Baumgartner and Leech (2001, chap. 3) and Pierson and Skocpol (2002) for extended critiques.

(Langston 2017; Levitsky 2003; Roberts 2015). My findings suggest that this transition may have been overstated. This is not to deny that parties have shifted away from organizations as the *main* organizational component (if they ever were). Yet I have documented how all three major parties in Mexico rely on organizations to recruit candidates, mobilize in campaigns, establish an ideological brand, socialize partisans, and sustain a presence on the ground between elections. The PAN turns to business organizations to recruit gubernatorial candidates and cabinet appointees and to carry out election monitoring initiatives against its clientelist-prone competition (Luna 1995; Wuhs 2010). The PRD's ideological credibility was derived from linkages to urban popular movements and today employs interest organizations in both urban and rural areas for its campaign machinery and clientelist networks (Bruhn 2013; Hilgers 2008). And the PRI continues to funnel patronage benefits through its sectoral organizations (Larreguy 2013; Larreguy, Olea, and Querubin 2017), which also are responsible for organizing campaign events.

A second contribution is to highlight the importance of productionist economic policy and the institutions constructed to incorporate organized interests in policies aiming to generate economic opportunity. Under import-substitution industrialization, party-linked interest organizations in countries such as Brazil and Mexico were closely involved in shaping industrial policies by interventionist states, including labor policy, development finance, research and development, and trade protection (Schneider 1999). In the neoliberal period, however, interventionist industrial policies were replaced by the mandate to attract foreign investment combined with piecemeal efforts to support domestic firms capable of competing in the open economy (Hochstetler and Montero 2013; Schrank and Kurtz 2005). Along the way, the interest arena for non-elite interest organizations has shifted from a site of bargaining for *productionist* policies (wages and benefits for unionized workers; subsidies and guaranteed prices for farmers; finance and trade protection for business) to intermediating and demanding *consumptionist* benefits, such as social policy and neighborhood infrastructure (Collier and Handlin 2009b, 86–87). It has become increasingly clear, however, that anemic and disorganized productionist policies today are largely to blame for poor economic growth and an inability to create good jobs for all but the most privileged citizens. The ongoing economic malaise by commodity exporters and *maquila* economies, such as Mexico, suggests that these societies might consider a more vigorous and coherent approach to "industrial policy for the twenty-first-century" (Rodrik 2008, chap. 4) in an effort to generate economic opportunity for globalization's losers. And as observers of twentieth-century industrial transformation noted decades ago (Evans 1995; Johnson 1982), the success of such a model depends on the continued involvement of societal stakeholders in policy design and implementation.

Future work may zoom in on specific economic sectors that have been the target of state promotion, as well as the roles played by organized economic actors in these efforts. For instance, in my analysis of the grain farmers' cooperatives belonging to ANEC, I found a virtuous cycle between the provision of productive services to members and the lodging of demands for rural development policies that favor small-scale farmers. While the future prospects for small-scale grain farmers are grim, higher value export crops such as avocados, coffee, and berries offer greater potential for sustainable smallholder production (World Bank 2007, 58–61). Policies to promote these sectors vary considerably, and as Snyder (2001a) observed in the case of coffee, patterns of producer organization and state efforts to incorporate these organizations in policymaking go a long way to explain whether rural development models offer economic opportunity to small-scale producers.

Another promising venue for a fine-grained sectoral analysis is the creation of high-tech "hubs" or "clusters." In recent decades, local and regional governments in the Global South have courted foreign investment by offering tax breaks to attract multinational tech firms and investing in education and infrastructure to support them. While results have been underwhelming in Mexico (Gallagher and Zarsky 2007; Pacheco-Vega 2007; Samford, Breznitz, and Murphee 2020), the hope is that these "anchor" firms will spur innovation by domestic firms through transfers of technology, skills, and an entrepreneurial culture. For example, in Chapter 7, I described efforts to promote the Guadalajara region as "Mexico's Silicon Valley,"[2] by investing in the Creative Digital City. The degree and type of participation of local stakeholders—including firms, universities, financial institutions, and tech workers—may explain variation in these sectoral promotion models and their level of success.

The third contribution of this book is to suggest that the subnational level is a promising venue to identify novel models for interest representation in post-neoliberal states. Given limits on federal governments' efforts at sectoral promotion and obstacles to "scaling" (Collier and Handlin 2009b, 63–66)

2. Wikipedia lists over 200 Silicon Valley-inspired technology centers around the world, from Silicon Savannah in Nairobi to Silicon Fjord in Norway. See: https://en.wikipedia.org/wiki/List_of_technology_centers.

by producer organizations, meaningful peak-level corporatist institutions did not survive the neoliberal transition. However, in some subnational governments, specialization in certain economic sectors and legacies of active organizing help preserve spaces for programmatic interest representation. For example, in his study of subnational regulatory models for coffee production, Snyder (2001a, 201–4) concluded that success cases of post-neoliberal "neo-corporatism" are easier to find on the subnational than national level, especially in federal systems. The main example from this study was COCOCAM, the Consultative Council of Peasant Organizations in Michoacán, which was possible only because of the rare programmatic character of the PRD administrations and the density of rural organizations in this state.

The decentralization of interest representation offers both advantages and disadvantages, reminiscent of the tradeoffs to decentralization more broadly. On the positive side of the ledger, subnational institutions offer greater potential for experimentation and also capitalize on personal relationships between societal and state actors (Faguet 2012; Oates 1972; Ostrom 1996). It is notable that the most programmatic organizations analyzed in both sectors were those that belonged to the most decentralized structures—ANEC and COPARMEX—which offered considerably more autonomy to state-level affiliates than the other sectoral confederations. Where subnational governments were open to programmatic incorporation—in Michoacán for ANEC and Jalisco for COPARMEX—these affiliates could capitalize on their autonomy to make the most of local spaces for representation. Decentralized interest representation has its downsides, however. First, many important elements of economic policy—such as trade agreements—operate only at the federal level. Where organizations fail to scale up to wield influence with the federal government, they cannot access these policy areas. Second, just as decentralization offers venues for exemplary models in some states, it also abandons other laggard states. For example, in Chiapas, where PRD administrations were patronage-oriented, the ANEC affiliate enjoyed much less policy influence than did ANEC's Michoacán affiliate and was only able to sustain a weak patronage model of representation.

Evaluating the Generalizability of the Argument

The subnational comparative method has offered the advantage of comparing cases—organizations, parties, and states—that vary on key variables of interest, while holding constant other traits of the institutional environment that otherwise may have confounded results. The drawback to this approach, however, is that Mexican states and sectoral associations do not represent the full variation encountered in a broader universe of economic sectors and transitional democracies. In particular, a critic may speculate that the argument generated and tested here is contingent on two traits unique to Mexico. First, this country has a deeply embedded history of state corporatism, which left a legacy of oligarchical interest organizations, prone to reliance on state patronage. Perhaps in countries without such a built-up organizational environment or with pluralist (rather than corporatist) legacies of interest representation, organizations would not be so vulnerable to the patronage trap. Second, at the time of research, Mexico had a stable party system with three organizationally consolidated and ideologically differentiated parties (Rosas 2010).[3] While this setting has permitted a comparison between three stable party types, the dynamics at play may differ from those in a fragmented or volatile system, which I would expect to impede organic programmatic linkages by shortening parties' time frames (Mainwaring 2018, chap. 3).

In this section, I draw on secondary literature to probe the extent to which the hypothesized explanations for organizational participation extend to cases that do not share these traits. While I cannot do justice to the details in each case, I seek to show how the main variables uncovered in this book—the source of organizational capacity and parties' founding traits—shaped the ability of organizations to offer programmatic representation. First, I look at organizations in Mexico without such a strong history of incorporation into the PRI's sectoral system—neighborhood and indigenous associations. For these organizations—core for the PRD—I assess the degree to which the source of organizational capacity and the PRD's party organizations in Mexico City and Chiapas shaped their mode of participation. I then analyze rural and business associations outside of Mexico, to explore whether alternate trajectories of sectoral representation and party

3. In the past several years, this party system has unraveled with the rise of MORENA and formation of ideologically nebulous coalitions between the three traditional parties to confront it (Bautista Lucca 2019; Espinoza Toledo and Navarrete Vela 2016). Mexico's party system scores quite low on "issue congruence" and "policy convergence" between parties and their supporters (Luna and Zechmeister 2010), likely due to the large number of self-identifying left-wing voters mobilized clientelistically on behalf of a neoliberal party (the PRI) or who vote strategically for the PAN where the PRD is non-competitive (Klesner 2005).

systems contravene my explanatory model. In the rural sector, I look at the Brazilian Movement of Landless Rural Workers (MST), an association formed with ties to the externally mobilized PT. In the business sector, I analyze Chilean business chambers, closely aligned with the conservative UDI party.

Urban Popular Organizations in Mexico City

Urban popular movements (movimientos urbanos populares, MUPs) in Mexico City offer an opportunity to observe PRD linkages with a quite different mode of popular-sector organizations than the rural associations discussed in linkage with the PRD in Michoacán. Compared to dissident peasant organizations, MUPs in Mexico City were less bureaucratized. Many of these associations formed as social movements in the 1980s and formalized their structures along with the PRD in the 1990s. The neighborhood groups thus lacked a history in the PRI's corporatist system. On the one hand, since these organizations were formed outside the corporatist system, we may expect them to lack the patronage-based culture of demand-making characteristic of peasant interest representation during twentieth-century PRI hegemony. On the other hand, my theory predicts that these organizations would be particularly prone to the patronage trap, as they are made up of heterogeneous, popular-sector actors without a shared condition in economic production. Mexico City constitutes a good venue to address this variation on the social side because it holds the PRD's electoral trajectory relatively constant. Michoacán and Mexico City are probably the two states where the PRD is most "externally mobilized" as these were the states with the largest contingent of *cardenista* organizing in the early years of the PRD. The first PRD executives in each of these states were Cárdenas' (Cuauhtémoc Cárdenas in 1997 Mexico City and Lázaro Cárdenas Batel in 2001 Michoacán) and the party held onto power for multiple terms in both cases.

During the nadir of the PRI's one-party dominance, MUPs in Mexico City were at the forefront of the left-wing opposition. Organizational capacity was based neither in service provision nor in patronage brokerage as much as it was in the "structural crisis" (Piven and Cloward 1979), stemming from a 1982 peso devaluation and 1985 earthquake, producing a "protest wave" (Tarrow 1998) that wrapped up participants through appeals to emotion and solidarity. While the enthusiasm for mobilization extended into the 1988 elections, these urban movements—based on a heterogeneous and vulnerable population—would have to devise strategies to sustain organizational capacity. Much as in Michoacán, PRD administrations in Mexico City after 1997 offered opportunities for both programmatic incorporation and patronage mobilization. Given the inability to generate organizational capacity internally, the vast majority of urban associations fell into the patronage trap. These organizations operated as a clientelistic machine for the PRD, which dominated politics in the capital from 1997 to 2018.

Mexico City was the epicenter of Cárdenas' social base in the 1988 campaign, which counted on the support of a variety of popular-sector social movements, neighborhood associations, and student groups. Since the 1968 Tlaltelolco student movement, Mexico City had been a base of activism against the authoritarian PRI regime, and MUPs revived in protest of the state's failure to provide needed services to displaced residents following the 1985 earthquake.[4] These social movement structures, which in 1985 had reached a consensus to stay outside of electoral politics, found an electoral ally in Cárdenas—a major politician who shared their disdain for the PRI's neoliberal turn. An initial rapprochement between MUPs and Cárdenas occurred during late-1987 protests against the Economic Solidarity Pact, an anti-inflation accord implementing wage and price freezes, which was accomplished through the cooperation of the PRI's corporatist labor sector (López Leyva 2007, 185–86). Without committing

4. Prominent groups included the Asamblea de Barrios, Unión Popular Nueva Tenochtitlán, Unión Popular Revolucionaria Emiliano Zapata, Organización Independiente Revolucionaria Línea de Masas, and Movimiento Revolucionario del Pueblo, all of which are often referred to jointly as the Urban Popular Movement (MUP). For a longer list of MUPs and other social movements that participated in the 1988 Cárdenas campaign see López Leyva (2007, 34). The Asamblea de Barrios—a transformation of the Coordinadora Única de Damnificados, an organization formed in relation to the earthquake—participated in the creation of the FDN, but the majority of others were non-partisan, only joining the electoral realm in the 1988 election (Tavera Fenolloso 2013). The Frente Popular Francisco Villa (FPFV) a radical alliance of UNAM students and squatters opted to preserve its autonomy, refusing to support Cárdenas in 1988. In following years, however, the FPFV broke into two factions, over the question of whether to participate in Cárdenas' 1997 bid for the head of government of Mexico City. Fragmentation was a common fate for MUP organizations; at last count the Asamblea de Barrios had broken into nine separate structures (Bruhn 2013, 141–44).

to formal party affiliation, MUPs endorsed Cárdenas' economic model of *nacionalismo revolucionario* and in the months before the July 1988 election mobilized their communities in rallies on behalf of Cárdenas' electoral vehicle, the FDN. When Cárdenas launched his presidential campaign, he counted on the support of roughly fifty organizations, which also presented candidates for local office under the FDN (Tavera Fenolloso 2013, 106–7).

After this initial collaboration in the 1988 campaign, ties between MUP factions and the PRD were formalized in a model designed to protect organizational autonomy and institute a loose "movement–party" model. PRD candidacies for neighborhood leadership posts were granted to several MUP leaders as "external" candidates, who saw in the party a route to power, but a minority of MUP organizations declared exclusive alliances with the PRD and several realigned with the PRI, which continued to control the federal and Mexico City governments (Bruhn 2013, 138–42). As the 1985–1988 cycle of protest drew to a close, social movements either disintegrated or transformed into neighborhood associations with the mandate of *gestión*, negotiating with the government for housing and services. While protest declined significantly when the PRD came into power in Mexico City, organizations still would turn periodically to manifestations, usually to pressure the state to deliver benefits (Bruhn 2008, 123–35).

By the time Cárdenas won and became Jefe de Gobierno in 1997, the PRD had taken on a highly factionalized internal structure. While its deep roots in Mexico City neighborhoods curtailed the impulse to integrate PRI defectors as occurred in other states, the inability of party leaders to coordinate on a model for incorporating neighborhood groups produced organizational linkages that took on the character of machine politics. The Cárdenas (1997–2000) and López Obrador administrations (2000–2005) set up novel participatory structures and methods for electing local party leaders, although these institutions generated conflict between faction leaders over control over candidacies and public resources (Harbers 2007; Hilgers 2008, 135–36; Montambeault 2011). Given the power that MUP organizations exercised within the party, citizen participatory institutions were designed to cede policy authority to these territorial networks, locking out issue-based civil society organizations and sectoral organizations (Álvarez Enríquez 2013). As with the COCOCAM for the patronage-oriented peasant organizations in Michoacán, these institutions served as venues for patronage brokerage for urban associations in Mexico

City. PRD governments have consistently granted MUP leaders control over public housing and other subsidies in exchange for candidacies and party leadership posts.[5] This authority proved indispensable for solidifying brokerage roles; leaders typically grant housing only to organization members who are active in meetings and protests (Bruhn 2013, 150–52; Hilgers 2008, 142–47).

The case of the Mexico City MUPs illustrates that the patronage trap is not limited to organizations with a history in the PRI's sectoral corporatist system. Even in comparison to highly precarious economic groups such as small-scale farmers, urban social movements face extremely high barriers to sustaining organizational capacity over the long run. After mobilizing in mass protests, these groups shifted to a patronage brokerage strategy to sustain collective action. And while the PRD in Mexico City was at its most programmatic—as in Michoacán—it still lacked a consistent commitment to constructing programmatic ties with these core organizations. Once PRD candidates began to reach elected office in the city government, MUP leaders faced no difficulty in finding selective benefits that would strengthen their hands as brokers, yet did struggle to translate their close party ties into effective voice in city planning.

Two alternative electoral scenarios may have lent themselves more to the proliferation of programmatic demand-making by the MUP. First, a context of weak parties or party volatility reduces the threat of co-optation, as research on urban popular movements in Colombia, Ecuador, and Peru has shown (Dosh 2009; Holland and Palmer-Rubin 2015). Where parties lack the institutionalization to convert these organizations into clientelist machines, the organizations are forced to devise internal organizational capacity models, based on the communal provision of security or services. At the same time, lacking constant state subsidy, organizations in these environments are much more vulnerable to extinction. Another scenario emerges in countries where new parties of the left were more externally mobilized (the Brazilian PT and Bolivian MAS). While certainly prone to mobilize their urban support bases clientelistically, these parties were much more successful than the PRD at building and maintaining

5. René Bejarano and Dolores Padierna are perhaps the most successful political entrepreneurs to have built careers in the PRD out of their leadership of an urban association—the Unión Popular Nueva Tenochtitlán (Bruhn 2013, 145). The husband and wife have both held state and federal congressional posts and Bejarano led a prominent PRD *corriente*, the National Democratic Left until 2017.

participatory institutions for the urban popular sectors (Anria 2013; Baiocchi 2005).

Indigenous Organizations in Chiapas

Indigenous organizations in Chiapas bear many similarities to dissident peasants in Michoacán, while varying the traits of the PRD party organization. The PRD in Chiapas is at the internally mobilized extreme for this party. As with organizations that participated in Michoacán's Peasant Consultative Council, some but not all of the indigenous associations in Chiapas were programmatically oriented at the time of party alternation in 2000. However, as I illustrate using original field research evidence,[6] a complete disinterest in programmatic incorporation on the part of the factions of the state party organization that controlled the government led to the exclusion of programmatically oriented organizations, and a privileging of those indigenous organizations inclined to broker patronage benefits.

While the PRD had been founded in Chiapas by diverse groups of activists—including dissident peasant and indigenous organizations—in support of Cárdenas' presidential candidacy in 1988, it first posed a serious threat for the governorship with the successful campaign of Pablo Salazar in 2000. Like PRD governors who had overturned PRI rule before him in Zacatecas, Baja California Sur, and Tlaxcala, Salazar had defected from the PRI immediately before running with the PRD. Salazar's main base of support was in Chiapas' three largest cities, where he won 65 percent of the vote in the 2000 election (García Aguilar 2013). In a highly rural state with an indigenous population of over 40 percent, the PRI candidate won over 54 percent of votes in the state's indigenous regions. Salazar embarked on a strategy to attract indigenous support by nominating local indigenous leaders for elected office and government posts. The PRD penetrated communities that had previously voted overwhelming for the PRI by forming alliances with leaders of indigenous associations, who often wield substantial power in their communities as brokers in patronage networks and kingmakers in local elections. These organizations—such as ARIC (Rural Collective Interest Association), CIOAC, and UNORCA—originated in

6. For a more detailed discussion of the PRD alliances with indigenous associations in Chiapas, see Meng and Palmer-Rubin (2017).

land invasions and rifts in the CNC in the 1970s and were reinvigorated during the 1994 Zapatista movement.[7]

The Salazar project was oriented to convert indigenous communities—once PRI bastions—into machines aligned with the new PRD faction controlled by the sitting governor, who had just completed a term as PRI senator. Indigenous organizations became channels through which the state government provided patronage benefits, including agricultural subsidies and social programs, which often exceeded the inducements that these communities had received from PRI administrations. For example, an interviewed leader of CIOAC in the municipality of Comitán explained that he was drawn to the PRD because the Salazar administration channeled dozens of housing subsidies to its members, a benefit that had not been afforded under the PRI.[8] One of the main attractions of aligning with the PRD was the guarantee of a nomination for mayor, yet indigenous leaders found it easier to receive PRD nominations for state and federal legislature prior to the Salazar administration than during. Controlling municipal government availed indigenous organizations of patronage resources, such as job posts and discretionary infrastructure spending.

While indigenous organizations found an administration eager to enlist them in patronage-based electoral mobilization, Salazar proved less willing to open space for their programmatic participation. He refused to discuss modifying state institutions to open space for institutions of indigenous governance, as the neighboring state of Oaxaca had done by adopting the *usos y costumbres* system (Benton 2012; Díaz-Cayeros, Magaloni, and Ruiz-Euler 2014). A former president of CIOAC and PRD Congressman in the 1990s attested that the Salazar administration refused to participate in a roundtable discussion organized by indigenous leaders and the state legislature to discuss modifying the state constitution.[9] The electoral involvement also prompted a shift in the orientation of the indigenous organizations. A local PRD committee president lamented that the CIOAC—the most prominent of Chiapas' indigenous associations—lost its representative character when it became immersed in the party alliance: "Before 2000,

7. The organization that spearheaded the Zapatista rebellion, the Ejercito Zapatista de Liberación Nacional (National Zapatista Liberation Army) withheld from forming party alliances.

8. Interview, Antonio Hernández Cruz, Secretary-General, CIOAC-Regional, July 5, 2012.

9. Interview, Margarito Ruíz Hernández, ex-President, CIOAC, July 4, 2012.

CIOAC was a bastion of the social struggle, for social groups and leaders of the left in Chiapas. It initiated the defense of indigenous issues and all that. But once they became part of the government the leaders became corrupt, they turned into functionaries, they were granted government positions... So they forget about the indigenous struggle."[10]

PRD linkages with these organizations failed to institutionalize during Salazar's term, owing largely to a power struggle over control of the party's state-level organization and internal divisions in the organizations over candidacies and control of patronage benefits. Fragmentation was exacerbated under the party's second governor, Juan Sabines, who, like Salazar, defected from the PRI immediately before the running with the PRD in 2006. A political rival of Salazar,[11] Sabines cleaned house upon assuming the governorship, favoring alternate indigenous factions. Conflicting ties to the Sabines and Salazar machines led to rifts within indigenous organizations. For instance, CIOAC has splintered into at least four factions with adjectives differentiating them, such as CIOAC-Histórico, CIOAC-Independiente, and CIOAC-Regional, linked to different factions of the PRD and other parties. The contingent nature of PRD incorporation of the indigenous came back to haunt the party in 2012, when Sabines—still in office—urged his allies to support the successful gubernatorial bid of Manuel Velasco, a candidate running with Mexico's Green Party, a PRI coalition partner.[12]

The case of indigenous organizations in Chiapas provides more evidence in favor of the patronage trap model for poor rural populations in Mexico. In particular, here we have seen the prominence of the supply side in determining the terms of party–organization linkages. While Chiapas counted on a highly organized and activated network of programmatically oriented indigenous associations, the instrumental approach to incorporation on the part of the Salazar and Sabines administrations trumped these programmatic demands. In the next section, I discuss a similarly activated

10. Interview, Mariano Medina López, President, PRD Municipal Committee, San Cristóbal de las Casas, Chiapas, July 6, 2012. "Antes del 2000 la CIOAC era un bastión de luchas sociales, de grupos sociales y de líderes sociales de la izquierda en Chiapas. Abrió la defensa las cuestiones indígenas y todo eso. Pero a raíz de que se hacen del gobierno los líderes se corrompen, los hacen funcionarios, les dan puestos en gobierno...Entonces ellos se olvidan de la lucha indígena."

11. Accusing his predecessor of money laundering, Sabines had Salazar imprisoned on corruption charges soon upon entering office.

12. Interview, Gabriel Gutiérrez Ávila, PRD State Council member, July 9, 2012.

rural movement in Brazil as it engaged with the PT, a party with a more distinct externally mobilized trajectory.

Landless Workers' Movement in Brazil

The Movement of Landless Rural Workers in Brazil (MST) is quite similar to dissident peasants in Mexico, yet with ties to a political party more fully in the externally mobilized model than the PRD. Like the CCC, the MST was founded alongside a new political party on the left (the PT) and its initial appeal to members was help in accessing land. Also like the CCC's rejection of the CNC, the MST sought to break with oligarchic and clientelistic practices of a prior rural structure, the National Confederation of Agricultural Workers (CONTAG), that had become co-opted and controlled under authoritarianism (Houtzager 1998). The party environment was quite different from Mexico's one-party dominance, however. The MST was founded prior to the end of Brazil's military dictatorship, and would inherit a volatile, fragmented party system, one that would not appear conducive to organic programmatic ties.[13] However, unlike the CCC, by the time the PT took power on the national level in 2003, the MST had developed a self-sustaining model to recruit and mobilize members and was prepared to enter into programmatic politics with the ascendant leftist party.

The MST emerged in 1984 in the Brazilian south, around the drawdown of this country's period of military dictatorship, with the central demand of accessing land for the rural poor. The organization persisted as an autonomous and oppositional political force for over a decade as it led land invasions and pushed the state to redistribute land, a demand that led to a resounding victory as President Fernando Henrique Cardoso (1995–2003) implemented the largest land distribution in Brazilian history (Ondetti 2008, 140–78). As discussed in the case of the CCC, however, land reform represents a "one-shot" demand that, upon delivery, leaves beneficiaries without a reason to continue participating in the organization. Thus, when the cycle of land reform drew to a close by the end of Cardoso's presidency,

---

13. Gay (1990) describes organization-mediated clientelism under extreme party system volatility in 1980s Rio de Janeiro. The lack of consistency in party organizations leads the leader of a neighborhood association to bargain with multiple parties each election for local club benefits, but the lack of consistent ties to any one political movement thwarts attempts at representation in more transformative policy areas. On the persistence of rural clientelism in Brazil, see Hagopian (2007).

the MST was left with a structure that appeared poised for social movement decline: a poor, dispersed membership engaged in diverse modes of economic production and a lack of direct ties to the state that would deliver benefits. This second trait would change once the PT took power in 2003 with strong support from the MST.

Yet, the MST insured against a transition to patronage brokerage by innovating in new modes of internally generated services—based on "Education for the Countryside" (Educação do Campo), a model of rural education that combined agricultural extension services with ideological study based on Liberation Theology and Paulo Freire's *Pedagogy of the Oppressed* (Meek 2015; Tarlau 2013). Organizational survival was further bolstered by the MST's long-standing ties to church networks, which provided funding and an organizational infrastructure during the long period without allies in power (Ondetti 2008, chap. 2). The MST certainly represented a uniquely successful case of social movement institutionalization while mostly avoiding the pitfalls of oligarchy. What is notable about the scholarship on the MST is this movement's success in imparting a collective consciousness, socializing peasants to a new understanding of the rural struggle and constructing an "imagined community" that would hold members together, and loyal to the organization (Wolford 2003). Like the ANEC affiliates in Mexico, this socialization is achieved through joint participation in cooperative production practices that respond to members' economic motives (Navarro 2006; Pahnke 2015).

These strategies to sustain organizational capacity internally have bolstered the MST's ability to levy programmatic demands, which it has done through protests for a reinstatement of land reform, state limits on monocropping, restrictions on genetically modified organisms, and environmental activism under PT administrations post-2003 (Klein 2015; Motta 2016, 723–25; Ondetti 2008, 200–19). These contentious mobilizations, which have drawn the opprobrium of otherwise sympathetic Presidents Luis Inácio Lula da Silva and Dilma Rousseff, were accompanied by authentic spaces for participation in local and national rural development policies facilitated by PT governments. Owing somewhat to the absence of state institutions in remote areas where the MST established settlements, PT state and national governments delegated a good deal of policy to these groups, including the implementation of local services and land reform (Wolford 2010). The MST has been a central participant in national consultative councils on agricultural and environmental policy. And the PT has granted dozens of candidacies to MST leaders in mayoral and state and national legislative elections. Thus, despite increasing tensions between these linkage partners, MST–PT alliances exhibit programmatic incorporation with organizational autonomy.

The explanation for this success in evading the patronage trap does not lie solely with the organization; the PT's commitment to programmatic incorporation of allies is the important counterpart. The PT was much more externally mobilized than the Mexican PRD, combining several elements conducive to an innovative approach to programmatic incorporation of core organizational allies at its founding. Perhaps more akin to the Mexican PAN, the PT was founded as an ideological opposition to the authoritarian regime, removing the temptation of patronage linkages and cementing ties to ideologically committed activists (Keck 1992, chap. 4; Van Dyck 2016). The founding core—including Lula himself—belonged to a democratic union movement that prized internal democracy and autonomy from the state in a rejection of officialist *pelego* unions (the Brazilian analog to Mexican *charrismo*), while securing an organizational backbone that would persist through the party's arduous beginnings. A vacuum on the left of the Brazilian party system following the military regime created an opportunity for the party to appeal to voters on the basis of redistributive appeals.

While the MST touts its autonomy, scholars disagree about the degree to which the MST depends on the state for its continued organizational capacity. The movement certainly reaped financial and organizational rewards from allied politicians in power. Through Education for the Countryside, the federal government delegated the operation of over 2,000 rural schools to the MST (Tarlau 2013, 398). This was a response to one of the MST's core demands post-land conquest—the provision of rural education—but also offered a space through which MST leaders could recruit new members, gain community prestige, and socialize community members to organizational norms and demands. The MST received millions of dollars in state resources, beginning with PT subnational victories in the early 1990s (Navarro 2006). These benefits complemented the MST's internal organizational capacity model, as they were primarily allocated to strengthen affiliated agricultural cooperatives. The distinction between state benefits that generate dependence and those that bolster organizational autonomy ultimately has to do with the degree of politicians' discretion over these resources and the organization's ability to subsist without them. There certainly was some variation in the degree to which MST affiliates were able to sustain collective action autonomously through their self-generated services and community-building activities alone. And in line with the patronage trap model, it was those places where the MST struggled to sustain collective action autonomously or where the PT exhibited a clientelistic rather than a programmatic orientation that coproduction broke down, producing shorter-term transactional politics (Tarlau 2013).

In sum, the case of the Brazilian MST resembles dissident peasants in Michoacán on a much larger scale, and if the PRD were closer to the externally mobilized pole on the party organization spectrum. Here, an organization fiercely committed to an autonomous ideological position and a party eager to incorporate that organization produced a programmatic virtuous cycle for an extremely poor rural population. This cycle has not been without its downturns and its strain of patronage politics. However, the MST was also quite successful at devising strategies to sustain organizational capacity internally, both through the operation of productive enterprises and community-building activities. The PT underwent a transition from a movement–party organization to an electoral-professional party after conquering national power (Gómez Bruera 2015; Hunter 2010). This shift certainly introduced co-optative pressures on the MST. Yet the tension between the MST and PT during the Lula and Dilma administrations is evidence of the organization's autonomy and continued programmatic orientation.

Organized Business in Chile

Organized business in Chile is similar in power to Mexico's yet operates in an even friendlier electoral and institutional environment. Mexico and Chile shared two factors that lend themselves to high levels of business organization under ISI in the 1930s to 1960s: corporatist systems that offered significant organizational resources; and an ascendant labor movement that posed a threat to capital, offering incentive to organize (Drake 1978; Schneider 2004, 152–72; Silva and Durand 1998, 10–14). The Chilean case, however, contains two main contrasts with Mexican organized business. First, business organization under ISI and authoritarianism left a legacy of a greater centralization, elitism, and state involvement than in Mexico. While Mexico's cross-sectoral business council (the CCE) includes representatives of small and medium-sized businesses—CONCANACO and CANACINTRA—Chile's Confederation for Production and Commerce

(CPC) is mostly limited to large business owners.[14] And while the PRI's one-party dominant regime balanced commitments to business with those to labor and other sectoral associations, Chile's government—before, during and after the dictatorship—retained extremely close ties to the CPC, privileging business over labor. These two factors bode in favor of programmatic incorporation, as Chile's business sector is more homogenous and encounters a less daunting collective action problem, and began the neoliberal period embedded in institutions for programmatic representation.

The second main contrast between Mexico and Chile is the party ally of business, which produces an opposite prediction for programmatic representation in the Chilean case. Mexico's PAN was an externally mobilized party *par excellence*, producing long-standing programmatic ties with core small-business organizations decades before this party held elected office. In contrast, the two main parties in Chile's conservative electoral coalition—National Renovation (RN) and Independent Democratic Union (UDI)—are "authoritarian successor parties" (Loxton 2015), led by *Pinochetista* insiders. In line with Shefter (1977), I have argued that parties that generate from within a governing coalition, with immediate electoral ambitions, will tend not to invest in party structures to grant space for organizational allies in party leadership and policymaking. I illustrated this tendency in the case of the PRD, which mostly failed to produce institutions for programmatic incorporation of organizational allies (dissident peasants, neighborhood associations), instead preferring to broker short-term patronage-based linkages to mobilize voters in closely contested elections. In this regard, Chile presents an opportunity to evaluate whether the electoral expediency of an internally mobilized party can swamp an otherwise programmatic-oriented organization.

Literature on organized business in Chile resoundingly depicts programmatic representation under democracy, reflecting continuity from the authoritarian period. While the military regime initially closed off avenues for business influence, Pinochet pivoted after the 1982 economic crisis, relying on organized business to design a plan for economic recovery (Silva

---

14. The Chilean CPC is the business-wide confederation, comparable to Mexico's CCE. Members of the CPC include the National Chamber of Commerce (CNC), Society for Industrial Promotion (SFF), National Agricultural Society (SNA), National Mining Society (SONAMI), and Chilean Chamber of Construction (CChC).

1996, chap. 7). This offered business greater incentive to retain a peak-level organization.[15] After the ouster of Pinochet, business associations remained unified and led the charge to stay true to the market-led model established during the dictatorship. Even under center-left governments of Aylwyn (1990–1994), Frei (1994–2000), Lagos (2000–2006), and Bachelet (2006–2010, 2014–2018), business remained powerful due to two institutional bequests from the dictatorship: "an extensive system of consultation between business peak associations and key economic ministries" and constitutional rules protecting conservative majorities in the Senate (Silva 1998, 238). To this day, business corporatism in Chile is alive and well—reflective of Chile's stagnant democratization process more broadly, which protects Pinochet-era elite. Leaders of CPC-affiliated associations are central to this oligarchy and overtly align with RN and UDI in elections (Fisse and Thomas 2014; Pribble 2013, 126–28).

Organized business wields their remarkable instrumental power to influence every important area of economic policy, during both Concertación (left-wing) and Alianza (right-wing) administrations. Labor reforms, including efforts to expand collective bargaining rights, by Aylwin, Frei, and Lagos were quickly abandoned or watered down in the face of direct or implied threats by the CPC to destabilize the nascent democracy (Cook 2007, 127–33). Attempts under the Lagos administration to raise Chile's corporate tax rate in line with regional standards were swept off the agenda by influential business leaders, working in coalition with conservative party allies (Fairfield 2015a, 73–78). Agenda setting by organized business limited the expansion of the welfare state (health, pensions) to incremental reforms, even under left-wing administrations (Ewig and Kay 2011; Garay 2016, chap. 7; Pribble 2013). And at the behest of organized business, Chile has retained an orthodox market-led industrial policy, while other countries in the region have ramped up state intervention (Bril-Mascarenhas and Madariaga 2019). Business associations' programmatic

15. Chile represents one end of the spectrum for programmatic incorporation of organized business in neoliberal restructuring. The opposite extreme is the Brazilian case, where the military regime compensated individual businesses in a particularistic fashion, undercutting sectoral coordination (Weyland 1998, 76–79). Mexico represents an intermediate case, where the CCE maintained a loose coordination between the distinct sectoral confederations and alternated between active engagement with the state in economic restructuring and defensive pressure against policies that disrupted sectoral stability (Collier 1992, 93–97; Schneider 2004, 81–84).

influence is amplified under the conservative rule of Sebastián Piñera (2010–2014, 2018–present), whose perceived elite-favoring policies led to mass protests.

Given their internally mobilized character, my argument would predict the RN and UDI to pursue patronage-based ties with organizational allies. However, conservative party ties to organized business instead reflect continuity from the extreme programmatic incorporation under Pinochet. I could find no mention of distributive policies in Chile oriented to provide particularistic benefits or organizational funding for business organizations, along the lines of Fondo PyME, México Emprende, or the SIEM in Mexico. The need to deliver services or broker patronage for organizational maintenance was perhaps ameliorated by the predominance of large firms in Chile's major business organizations. Unlike Mexico throughout the twentieth century, where all private-sector firms were dues-paying chamber members, Chile never had mandatory chamber membership rules; as a result, these organizations tilted toward large firms. According to Schneider (2004, 156–57), in the 1960s, the CPC's member organizations constituted roughly 30 percent of all entrepreneurs yet represented 80 percent of total production.

Chile simply does not have a mass-based business organization on the scale of CONCANACO, CANACINTRA, or COPARMEX, and therefore organized business does not rely on ongoing selective benefits to retain an active membership. The collective action challenge for organized business is reduced in Chile because of these organizations' small size and interest homogeneity, two traits that lend themselves to reproduction through purposive or solidary incentives, rather than selective material benefits. In this context, the state supports organizational capacity by reinforcing the programmatic prestige and policy influence of organized business, not through financial subsidies or mandatory membership requirements.

The programmatic incorporation of organized business has proven to be electorally convenient, particularly for the UDI, as it frees this party to build patronage ties to popular sector non-core constituencies. Luna (2014, 202–24) describes this "segmented" strategy as the unique strength of the UDI. Business leaders and wealthy citizens allied with the UDI donate money to the party, which it uses to construct clientelist machines that deliver services and particularistic benefits in poor urban communities. As a result, the UDI has been more successful than other right-wing parties in the region, such as Mexico's PAN or Argentina's Radical Party, at building clientelistic linkages with poor voters (Nichter and Palmer-Rubin 2015; Weitz-Shapiro 2012). Here, the UDI's internally mobilized founding has proven to be as asset, enabling the party to draw on clientelist networks created under the dictatorship (Luna 2014, 213–14).

Ultimately, the Chilean case may signal a limit on the external validity of findings, illustrating that the patronage trap is not a risk for organizations unless their survival depends on mass recruitment. In contrast to nonpartisanship in Mexico, the main Chilean business associations have aligned overtly with conservative rulers, beginning with Pinochet in the 1980s and extending through Piñera today. Yet unlike the organizations in the Mexican case that established open linkages with internally mobilized political parties (the PRI and PRD), Chilean business organizations have sustained ample programmatic representation as the elite character of Chilean associations reduces the need to deliver a constant flow of selective benefits.

Organizing in the Twenty-First Century: Implications for Interest Representation

The skeptic may contend that this book has dedicated excessive attention to explaining political actors in extinction. The primacy of sectoral organizations and mass-based political parties as the drivers of electoral politics and economic policy was the story of twentieth-century Latin America. In the last few decades, however, the social bases of organized labor and peasants have dissolved. Union membership in Latin America's "labor mobilizing" systems has plummeted to less than half of its peak twentieth-century level (Roberts 2015, 100)[16] and unions have increasingly come to represent middle-class rather than popular-sectors interests as public-sector employees unions predominate. Rural population shares have decreased from 60 percent of the region to less than 20 percent, and a minority of those that remain in the countryside depend on agriculture as their primary source of income (World Bank 2007, 29). And political parties rely more on mass media appeals and clientelist exchanges with individual

16. Calculated using mostly ILO data, Roberts reports trade union density declining by close to half from its twentieth-century peak to the 1990s in Argentina (50.1 to 22.3 percent), Chile (35.0 to 13.1), Peru (25.0 to 5.7), and Venezuela (26.4 to 13.5). Brazil had the smallest change, declining only half a percent from its peak of 24.3. Mexico represents an intermediate case, declining from 32.1 to 22.3 percent over this period.

voters than ground mobilization through mass organizations (Burgess and Levitsky 2003; Katz and Mair 1995; Roberts 2015). So why devote so much attention to understanding how organized economic interests engage in electoral politics and policymaking?

Given that the skeptic has made it this far in the book, I shall offer three responses. First, the last century's would-be antiquated mode of interest representation is more resilient than some analysts acknowledge. The most successful parties on the left continue to rely on organized popular-sector bases, both with previous corporatist insiders (e.g., labor unions) and previous outsiders (e.g., neighborhood associations). Unions may be on their heels, but they are the backbone of the left, often serving as coordinating hubs for popular-sector associations (Garay 2009). Rural populations may be dwindling, but agricultural markets have become increasingly central to development models given Chinese demand for soy and other commodities, generating contestation between revitalized organizations representing agribusiness, smallholder farmers, indigenous communities, and environmentalists (Appendini 2014; Lapegna 2016; Oliveira and Schneider 2016). And while right-wing parties have never been centered on mass economic interests,[17] peak-level business associations have proven to be key allies for advancing the electoral ambitions and economic goals of conservative politicians. In short, corporatism may not be at the center of politics as it was during the mid-twentieth century, but the organized interests constructed during and after this period continue to exercise considerable clout.

Second, programmatic non-elite interest organizations are *needed* if Latin American economies are going to become more inclusive. Technocracy—rule by experts protected from the influence of societal interests—has lent coherence to several policy areas, such as macroeconomic management and cash transfers to the poor. But it has also proven quite limited in other areas, both in the capacity to excise patronage politics from distributive policy and in generating economic opportunity for the lower classes (Babb 2001, chap. 7; Dargent 2014). Alongside the growing ranks of governmental technocrats, this century has witnessed a boom in "elite civil society," NGOs and thinktanks—often with international funding—claiming to represent

17. As in Europe, some right-wing parties in Latin America have capitalized on the reach of the Catholic Church, most successfully the Mexican PAN and Chilean Christian Democratic Party. See Mainwaring and Scully (2003).

broad societal interests in pushing for the rule of law, monitoring elections, or evaluating government programs. However, these organizations' elite character and non-partisan mandate stand in the way of representing specific and often counterposed interests (e.g., labor and capital). Brazilian experiments in deliberative institutions have proven to empower marginalized citizens (Baiocchi, Heller, and Silva 2011; Touchton, Sugiyama, and Wampler 2017), but are better suited to local *decision-making* about spending than to scaled-up *demand-making* about regulatory or redistributive policy. In the end, we are left with interest organizations, the only agents with the mandate and the capacity to represent non-elite interests in the design of national development models.

Finally, the organizational and party traits that I have shown to shape the ability of non-elite interests to garner effective policy voice will be similarly influential for "new" types of organizations. Latin America's contemporary interest arena contains novel organizing models, including groups that channel demands of ethnic minorities, the urban poor, and "post-material" issues such as environmental policy or the rights of sexual minorities and women (Collier and Handlin 2009a). In the economic realm, organizations representing labor-market "outsiders," particularly informal sector workers and the unemployed, have taken on increased importance (Garay 2016; Holland 2017; Rossi 2017). Given their more fragmented and marginal character, the patronage trap is at least an acute a risk for these organizations as the sectoral interests that I have studied. Those that develop the ability to sustain organizational capacity internally will be at an advantage in sustaining programmatic representation.

If the skeptic is convinced about the plausibility and the importance of non-elite interest organizations' participation in programmatic policies, I would conclude by offering three policy recommendations to make this a reality. First, states, parties, and donor institutions interested in fomenting programmatic representation should take steps to help organizations offer productive services. In particular, states may regulate credit markets and productive chains in a way that facilitates the involvement of agricultural cooperatives, business chambers, and other organized interests, permitting them to generate organizational capacity by offering training programs and managing formula-based sectoral supports. Second, further progress must be made in eliminating discretion in the allocation of distributive programs. Mexico offers a cautionary tale in this regard. This country has been lauded for its landmark programmatic anti-poverty program PROSPERA (previously PROGRESA and Oportunidades). Simultaneously, however, demand-based social programs and subsidies have proliferated, which offer a veneer of technocratic management but in practice typically favor applications backed by the best-connected intermediary (Cejudo, Michel, and Sobrino 2017; Garay, Palmer-Rubin, and Poertner 2020; Rizzo 2019). Without these programs, many patronage-oriented organizations would likely expire, opening space for new models of representation. Third, consultative institutions should be designed not only to bring individual citizens together in local decision-making, but also to bring representatives of organized interests together to deliberate and make binding recommendations on the policies that affect sectoral competitiveness. Brazil's policy councils offer a notable example (Mayka 2019).

Over a half century ago, Schattschneider (1960, 35) sardonically poked a hole in the myth of majoritarian pluralism, observing that "the flaw in the pluralist heaven is that the heavenly chorus sings with a strong upper-class accent." All these years later, across world regions, these words ring truer than ever. Elite and corporate interests have a more direct line to influence policies than do those of the lower and middle classes. This book has sought to interrogate the traits of organizations that cause them to be more or less representative of non-elites, lowering the socio-economic status of that chorus singing the tune of economic policy in middle- and low-income democracies. And while the path to programmatic representation is narrow and full of trapdoors, particularly for the poor, success cases exist. My hope is that this analysis offers hope and a glimpse of the path forward for scholars, activists, and policymakers interested in building on this success.

Appendices

Appendix A

Mexican Organizational Survey

The National Survey of Economic Interest Organizations in Mexico was carried out between September and December 2012 and applied to elected presidents or hired directors of organizations belonging to Mexico's two largest confederations of business chambers—the Confederation of the National Chambers of Commerce (CONCANACO) and the National Chamber of the Manufacturing Industry (CANACINTRA)—and two prominent confederations of "dissident" agricultural organizations—Cardenista Peasant Central (CCC) and National Association of Commercializing Firms of Rural Producers (ANEC). I used three criteria to choose these confederations. First, all members organizations are primarily made up of micro- and small-scale farmers or business owners, and thus classify as "non-elite." Second, the confederations are all national in scope and have state-level affiliates in the majority of Mexican states. And third, the confederations exhibit internal variation in the political orientation of composite organizations (in contrast with CNC, the National Peasant Confederation, Mexico's largest rural organization, which is formally incorporated into the PRI). Response rates and state coverage for the survey are reported in Table A.1. Mexico has thirty-one states, plus the Federal District (Mexico City). As shown, participants in the survey came from all thirty-one states.

The survey for business organizations was implemented online; all member organizations of these two confederations were emailed a link from confederation staff to an online survey that I designed using Qualtrics. Agricultural organizations were surveyed using a printed questionnaire that I distributed to leaders of these organizations at periodic national meetings. As top elected officials and directors of operations, these figures were uniquely positioned to serve as informants about their organizations although, as discussed below, the division of labor between

Table A.1 Survey Response Rate by Confederation and Sector

Confederation	Total Org's in Confed.	Sample (w/ inc.)	Response Rate	States	Sample (complete)	Response Rate	States
CONCANACO	250	74	29.6%	28	45	18.0%	21
CANACINTRA	79	30	38.0%	18	9	11.4%	7
Total Business	*329*	*104*	*31.6%*	*29*	*54*	*16.4%*	*22*
CCC	31	24	77.4%	19	21	67.7%	17
ANEC	16	11	68.8%	9	10	62.5%	8
Total Ag.	47	35	74.5%	23	31	66.0%	21
Total Orgs	*379*	*139*	*36.7%*	*31*	*85*	*22.4%*	*28*

Note: "Sample (w/ inc.)" refers to all organizations that participated in the survey, including those with incomplete responses. "Sample (complete)" refers to organizations with complete responses to all items in multi-variate analysis.

Source: Author's original survey.

executive leadership and day-to-day operations likely led to non-response to several survey items. The different modes were implemented to maximize response rates: while business organization leaders frequently use the internet in their daily operations, many leaders of agriculture organizations are less comfortable with this medium. The agricultural and business survey instruments included thirty-nine and fifty-four items, respectively. The median response time for completed online surveys was approximately eighteen minutes. The surveys were divided into three sections: (1) organizational traits, such as membership, revenue sources, services, and leadership; (2) political participation, including frequency and goals of engaging in electoral politics, protest, media campaigns, and contacting politicians and bureaucrats; (3) access to distributive programs, including frequency of applying for and receiving subsidies and social benefits from different government entities.

Several respondents did not complete the entire survey. In particular, this occurred for many business organizations when the respondent was an elected leader who was able to answer questions about political participation and demand-making, but less aware of organizational statistics (e.g., number of members, sources of income). Multi-variate models in Chapters 4 and 5 impute missing values for the four organizational traits (Resource Flows, Member Services, Percent Micro Members, Number of Members, Number of Employees, and Organizational Network), using confederation medians. I did not impute values for any component measures of outcomes (demand-making indices).

Table A.2 Summary Statistics of Organizational Traits

Variable	Measures Used	Agricultural Orgs					Business Orgs				
		Min	Mean	Max	SD	N	Min	Mean	Max	SD	N
Independent Variables, Control											
Resource Flows	Diversity of funding; count of: (1) membership fees; (2) donations from the confederation; (3) commission for subsidies; (4) payments for services; (5) other lucrative activity	0	2.4	5	1.2	32	0	2.6	5	1.2	57
Member Services	Number of services offered to members; count of: (1) consulting or project design; (2) access to credit; (3) helping access government programs; (4) providing information about market conditions or politics; (5) other service	2	4.2	5	0.9	34	1	3.0	5	1.1	64
Class Composition	% of members that belong to the "micro" classification (agriculture: <10 hectares; business: <10 employees)	5.0%	65.3%	100%	33.2%	33	0%	75.2%	99.0%	23.1%	68
No. Members	No. of registered members	100	5,190	15,000	4,377	34	50	930	9,000	1,584	74
Other Variables											
Member Fee %	% of members that pay membership fees	1.0%	31.8%	80.0%	26.0%	18	4.3%	57.8%	100%	29.2%	71
No. Employees	No. of full-time employees that receive a salary	0	6.3	25	6.5	32	1	11.2	230	30.8	56
Org. Contact	No. of times contacted orgs in the same sector in past year	0	24.9	100	25.6	32	0	21.6	100	27.3	70
Meetings	No. of full-membership meetings held in the last three years	1	14.2	120	25.3	33	0	8.8	72	11.9	64
Attendance	% of members attended most recent meeting	2.7%	54.5%	100%	29.3%	34	1.0%	36.1%	100%	27.5%	56

Note: *N*'s report number of respondents from each sector with valid responses. Multivariate analyses in main text use imputed sectoral medians for units with missing values on organizational traits.

Source: Author's original survey.

Non-response bias is potentially an issue, as sampling of respondents was not random. Non-participants in the survey include those who either did not respond to the email from the confederation (business) or did not attend national confederation meetings (agriculture). Thus, we might expect non-participants to have lower organizational capacity or looser ties to the confederations than participants. However, it is difficult to venture a prediction of how non-response may have produced bias in outcome measures (participation and demand-making indices). If anything, I might speculate that those who responded are more participatory overall, and thus would score higher across all the participation indices than non-responders. Given that the model's predictions have less to do with how much participation than with what kind of participation (institutional, electoral, or extra-institutional), it is unlikely that the internal validity of the main findings is threatened by non-response bias among organizations in these four sectors. On the other hand, it is important to keep in mind the non-random nature of sampling when interpreting the generalizability of results. As shown in summary statistics (Table A.2), however, the respondents included exhibit quite high variation across measured organizational traits such as number of members, number of employees, class composition, and frequency of holding meetings.

Tables A.3, A.4, A.5, and A.6 display bivariate and multi-variate models predicting programmatic and distributive demand-making for agriculture and business organizations. Marginal effects plots in Chapters 4 and 5 correspond to Model 7 in each table.

Table A.3 Regression Models of Programmatic Demand-Making (Agriculture)

	Model 1	Model 2	Model 3	Model 4	Model 5	Model 6	Model 7
No. Members	0.44**						0.35*
	(0.18)						(0.18)
No. Employees		0.24					-0.10
		(0.21)					(0.23)
% Micro Members			0.02				-0.05
			(0.20)				(0.21)
Resources. Flows				0.43**			0.40**
				(0.19)			(0.18)
Member Services					0.34*		0.25
					(0.19)		(0.19)
Org. Network						0.26	0.07
						(0.19)	(0.18)
R^2	0.19	0.05	0.00	0.20	0.11	0.07	0.42
Num. obs.	28	28	28	28	28	28	28

Note: ***p < 0.01, **p < 0.05, * p < 0.1.
Source: Author's original survey.

Table A.4 Regression Models of Distributive Demand-Making (Agriculture)

	Model 1	Model 2	Model 3	Model 4	Model 5	Model 6	Model 7
No. Members	0.49**						0.48*
	(0.10)						(0.11)
No. Employees		0.33**					0.24*
		(0.14)					(0.14)
% Micro Members			-0.08				-0.11
			(0.15)				(0.13)
Resources. Flows				0.06			-0.11
				(0.14)			(0.06)
Member Services					0.13		0.06
					(0.14)		(0.11)
Org. Network						0.17	-0.01
						(0.14)	(0.11)
R^2	0.47	0.18	0.01	0.01	0.03	0.05	0.60
Num. obs.	28	28	28	28	28	28	28

Note: ***p < 0.01, **p < 0.05, * p < 0.1.
Source: Author's original survey.

Table A.5 Regression Models of Programmatic Demand-Making (Business)

	Model 1	Model 2	Model 3	Model 4	Model 5	Model 6	Model 7
No. Members	0.05						-0.08
	(0.11)						(0.12)
No. Employees		0.24					-0.09
		(0.29)					(0.33)
% Micro Members			-0.01				-0.01
			(0.10)				(0.10)
Resources. Flows				0.16*			0.20*
				(0.09)			(0.11)
Member Services					0.14*		0.08
					(0.08)		(0.08)
Org. Network						0.20**	0.20**
						(0.09)	(0.10)
R^2	0.00	0.01	0.00	0.04	0.05	0.08	0.15
Num. obs.	65	65	65	65	65	65	65

Note: ***p < 0.01, **p < 0.05, * p < 0.1.
Source: Author's original survey.

Table A.6 Regression Models of Distributive Demand-Making (Business)

	Model 1	Model 2	Model 3	Model 4	Model 5	Model 6	Model 7
No. Members	0.07						-0.00
	(0.11)						(0.13)
No. Employees		0.14					-0.12
		(0.30)					(0.37)
% Micro Members			0.13				0.12
			(0.10)				(0.11)
Resources. Flows				0.11			0.08
				(0.10)			(0.12)
Member Services					0.13		0.09
					(0.08)		(0.09)
Org. Network						0.08	0.09
						(0.09)	(0.10)
R^2	0.01	0.01	0.02	0.02	0.03	0.01	0.07
Num. obs.	65	65	65	65	65	65	65

Note: ***p < 0.01, **p < 0.05, * p < 0.1.
Source: Author's original survey.

Appendix B

Career Trajectories for Mexican Governors

Table A.7 shows the career trajectories of the six most recent chief executives in all thirty-two of Mexico's federal entities (thirty-one states plus Mexico City). I report whether each governor had previously held elected office as a member of the PRI or had served in the cabinet of a PRI administration. I also show whether online searches uncovered evidence that governors had previously held leadership positions in interest organizations, such as business chambers, peasant associations, labor unions, or professional groups.

Ten of the seventeen PRD governors had held elected office as PRIistas at some point prior to running with the PRD, including Cárdenas himself. Six of these held elected office with the PRI *immediately* before assuming the governorship, including the first four states where the PRD won the governorship after Cárdenas' victory in Mexico City—Baja California Sur, Chiapas, Tlaxcala, and Zacatecas. These four candidates were selected during current President Andrés Manuel López Obrador's contentious term at the head of the party. In several cases, these candidates were chosen over others favored by state-level party organizations and social organizations (Cazarín Martínez 2013:401–04; García Aguilar 2013:444–46; Solano Ramírez 2013:365–69). In Chiapas and Guerrero, the *second* PRD governors were immediate PRI defectors. After holding the governorship for six years, the PRD was still unable to find gubernatorial candidates from among party ranks. An additional eleven governors have been elected through a coalition of the PAN and PRD, and the majority of these had held office with the PRI previously. Of all of these twenty-eight governors elected with the backing of the PRD, I could only identify three (11 percent) that had a background as leaders of interest organizations.

Table A.7 Career Trajectories for Mexican Governors

	Total No. Governors	PRI History	Organization Leadership History
PRD	17	10 (59%)	3 (24%)
PAN	31	1 (3%)	11 (35%)
PRI	127	127 (100%)	37 (29%)
PAN/PRD	11	7 (64%)	0 (0%)
Other	6	3 (50%)	1 (17%)

Note: *N* = 192. Data include the six most recent heads of government through 2020 in all thirty-two federal units (thirty-one states plus Mexico City).

Source: Author's online research.

This trajectory contrasts markedly with PAN governors. I only identified one PAN governor who had previously held elected office with the PRI—Héctor Ortiz of Tlaxcala (2005–2011). On the other hand, as shown in the last column, over one-third of PAN governors had previously held leadership posts in organizations; ten out of these eleven had been leaders of business organizations. In short, the PAN is the archetype of an externally mobilized party, recruiting candidates from ideologically aligned interest organizations, while the PRD marginalized organizational allies in favor of professional politicians defecting from the PRI.

Appendix C

Analysis of Small-Business Subsidies

In this appendix, I describe the analysis conducted of small-business subsidies that is reported in Chapter 7.

PAN-Governed States: Allocations to Core Organizations

I begin by analyzing the allocation of Fondo PyME projects in states governed by the PAN, for which small-business organizations are core. My theory predicts that governors of this party will engage these organizations less in distributive spending when elections are closely contested because they have a greater need to build linkages with non-core groups, but that when they enjoy larger margins of victory, PAN administrations will reward these core groups to bolster recruitment efforts and consolidate their position in the party base.

As shown in Table A.8, PAN administrations' spending on projects mediated by small-business organizations is positively associated with Vote Margin, in line with my prediction. Coefficients and significance levels for Vote Margin are quite stable across all models, with the exception of Model 5, which uses state-level fixed effects. There does not appear to be any consistent change in spending over time relative to election years, as shown in the lack of significant findings for Election Distance and Election Year. While PAN governors under threat deviate money away from core business organizations, this strategy is reflected in spending over the course of a governor's term and not solely at election time.

Table A.8 Correlates of Business Organization-Mediated Spending, PAN-Governed States

	Model 1	Model 2	Model 3	Model 4	Model 5
Vote Margin	41.14***	41.02***	42.10***	49.20**	32.88
	(13.04)	(11.71)	(9.91)	(21.53)	(29.08)
Election Distance		-0.75	-0.85	-0.87	-0.90
		(0.51)	(0.77)	(0.80)	(0.57)
Election Year		-4.14	-6.10	-5.88	-5.77
		(3.36)	(5.96)	(6.02)	(4.80)
GDP (logged)		-14.27*	-14.00	0.85	-8.74
		(8.26)	(8.92)	(12.09)	(27.62)
Population (logged)		26.11**	25.87**	16.11	-10.82
		(10.61)	(11.72)	(14.54)	(47.13)
Percent Poverty		-0.16	-0.17	0.10	-0.35
		(0.16)	(0.19)	(0.30)	(0.82)
No. Firms (logged)		-9.99***	-10.21**	-15.29***	31.40
		(3.51)	(3.89)	(3.17)	(43.84)
SIEM Rate		5.81	5.98	3.57	-31.85
		(4.67)	(4.46)	(3.06)	(50.14)
Year Fixed Effects	No	No	Yes	Yes	Yes
Region Fixed Effects	No	No	No	Yes	No
State Fixed Effects	No	No	No	No	Yes
R^2	0.16	0.24	0.33	0.34	0.36
Num. obs.	65	65	65	65	65

Note: ***p < 0.01, **p < 0.05, * p < 0.1.
Source: Author's calculations based on program data received in response to public information request.

PRI-Governed States: Allocations to Non-Core Organizations

I now turn to spending in states governed by the centrist PRI, for which small-business organizations are a non-core constituency. In contrast to the PAN, which engages these organizations more when vote margins are high, my theory predicts that PRI administrations will increase allocations to these organizations when facing an electoral threat. Thus, I expect to find negative associations between Vote Margin and small-business organization mediation in PRI-governed states.

However, I also explore additional dynamics for the PRI, given this party's unique position in Mexico's party system. In states where the PRI retains a stranglehold on elected office, distributive spending operates under a machine-party logic, which differs considerably from the logic of distribution in states where opposition parties pose a realistic electoral threat to the PRI. In these models I thus include the squared value of Vote

Margin to capture a potential non-linear relationship (or threshold effect) between Vote Margin and PRI governments' incorporation of SBOs. I also include a categorical variable reflecting the challenger party, coded as the party that finished in second place in the immediately prior gubernatorial election. This variable allows me to gauge whether the PRI makes different decisions about the distribution of small-business subsidies when opposed by the PAN—for whom business organizations are a core group—or the PRD—for whom business organizations are also a non-core group.[1]

As shown in the Table A.9, the associations between Vote Margin and small-business-organization-mediated spending is positive in most models, against my main hypothesis, but more consistently I find significant negative estimates for the square of Vote Margin. I find no significant association for Challenger Party, suggesting that PRI governments base their distributional decisions on their degree of electoral threat, but not on the type of party that poses the threat. These results are robust to the inclusion of controls and fixed effects at the year and region, but not state levels. As with the PAN, I find no association for Election Distance, but do find a significant negative coefficient for Election Year in some models. Thus, if the PRI is entering into short-term linkages with SBOs in competitive states, the benefits that accrue to organizations do not appear to be more likely to be delivered at election time.

1. Neither of these analyses were possible for PAN-governed states, given that it is extremely rare that the PAN enjoys subnational dominance (vote margins only exceed 13 percentage points for nine state-years in the PAN dataset) or that the PAN faces a party other than the PRI as its main challenger party (the PRD classifies as the challenger party for only five state-years in the PAN dataset).

Table A.9 Correlates of Business Organization-Mediated Spending, PRI-Governed States

	Model 1	Model 2	Model 3	Model 4	Model 5
Vote Margin	33.74*	39.78*	30.54	15.47	-20.51
	(18.90)	(21.75)	(19.13)	(9.78)	(29.00)
Vote Margin^2	-146.42**	-180.49*	-141.84*	-95.84**	-7.49
	(73.06)	(92.20)	(76.97)	(42.08)	(102.54)
Challenger Party (PRD)	-0.89	-0.06	0.07	0.04	-3.45
	(0.81)	(0.85)	(0.98)	(0.88)	(2.50)
Election Distance		0.00	-0.03	-0.02	-0.03
		(0.16)	(0.13)	(0.14)	(0.15)
Election Year		-1.41*	-1.31	-1.35*	-1.08
		(0.76)	(0.80)	(0.74)	(0.88)
GDP (logged)		0.16	0.36	-0.17	-77.01**
		(0.77)	(0.73)	(0.55)	(33.64)
Population (logged)		1.91	1.69	5.30***	165.05**
		(2.80)	(2.69)	(1.92)	(63.80)
Percent Poverty		-0.06	-0.06	-0.07	-1.28*
		(0.06)	(0.06)	(0.05)	(0.65)
No. Firms (logged)		-1.54	-1.11	-4.96**	-104.4***
		(2.85)	(2.84)	(1.95)	(36.05)
SIEM Rate		-4.17	-5.62**	-5.75***	83.70**
		(2.62)	(2.75)	(1.99)	(33.53)
Year Fixed Effects	No	No	Yes	Yes	Yes
Region Fixed Effects	No	No	No	Yes	No
State Fixed Effects	No	No	No	No	Yes
R^2	0.05	0.12	0.27	0.35	0.48
Num. obs.	140	140	140	140	140

Note: ***$p < 0.01$, **$p < 0.05$, * $p < 0.1$.

Source: Author's calculations based on program data received in response to public information request.

BIBLIOGRAPHY

Acemoglu, Daron, Simon Johnson, and James A. Robinson. 2005. "Chapter 6: Institutions as a Fundamental Cause of Long-Run Growth." Pp. 385–472 in *Handbook of Economic Growth*. Vol. 1, edited by P. Aghion and S. N. Durlauf. Amsterdam: Elsevier.

Ackerman, Edwin F. 2018. "El PRI y la sociedad civil." *Nexos*, January 9. https://redaccion.nexos.com.mx/?p=8491.

Ahlquist, John S., and Margaret Levi. 2011. "Leadership: What It Means, What It Does, and What We Want to Know About It." *Annual Review of Political Science* 14(1):1–24. doi: 10.1146/annurev-polisci-042409-152654.

Alba Vega, Carlos. 2002. "Regional Policy Under NAFTA: The Case of Jalisco." Pp. 125–45 in *NAFTA in the New Millennium*, edited by E. J. Chambers and P. H. Smith. San Diego, CA: Center for US–Mexican Studies, University of California, San Diego.

Alcázar, Marco Antonio. 1970. *Las Agrupaciones Patronales en México*. Mexico City: Colegio de México.

Alonso, Jorge. 1995. *El Cambio en Jalisco: Las Elecciones de 1994 y 1995*. Guadalajara, Mexico: Universidad de Guadalajara.

Álvarez Enríquez, Lucía. 2013. "La Participación Ciudadana en los Gobiernos Perredistas del DF." Pp. 319–39 in *El PRD: orígenes, itinerario, retos*, edited by J. Cadena-Roa and M. A. López Leyva. Mexico City: Universidad Nacional Autónoma de México, Instituto de Investigaciones Sociales.

Amengual, Matthew. 2016. *Politicized Enforcement in Argentina: Labor and Environmental Regulation*. New York, NY: Cambridge University Press.

Anderson-Barker, Cynthia. 1994. "A Case Study of Elections in the State of Michoacan on July 12, 1992." *Loyola of Los Angeles International and Comparative Law Review* 16:307–50.

Andrews, Kenneth T., Marshall Ganz, Matthew Baggetta, Hahrie Han, and Chaeyoon Lim. 2010. "Leadership, Membership, and Voice: Civic Associations That Work." *American Journal of Sociology* 115(4):1191–242.

Anria, Santiago. 2013. "Social Movements, Party Organization, and Populism: Insights from the Bolivian MAS." *Latin American Politics and Society* 55(3):19–46. doi: 10.1111/j.1548-2456.2013.00201.x.

Anria, Santiago. 2016. "Democratizing Democracy? Civil Society and Party Organization in Bolivia." *Comparative Politics* 48(4):459–78.

Anria, Santiago, and Jennifer Cyr. 2017. "Inside Revolutionary Parties: Coalition-Building and Maintenance in Reformist Bolivia." *Comparative Political Studies* 50(9):1255–87.

Appendini, Kirsten. 2003. "The Challenges to Rural Mexico in an Open Economy." Pp. 255–75 in *Mexico's Politics and Society in Transition*, edited by J. S. Tulchin and A. D. Selee. Boulder, CO: Lynne Rienner Publishers.

Appendini, Kirsten. 2014. "Reconstructing the Maize Market in Rural Mexico." *Journal of Agrarian Change* 14(1):1–25. doi: 10.1111/joac.12013.

Appendini, Kirsten, Julia Carabias, Alfonso Cebreros, Max Correa, Isabel Cruz, Jaime De la Mora, Enrique Del Val, Margarita Flores, Gustavo Gordillo, Sergio Madrid, Francisco Mayorga, Héctor Robles, José Sarukhán, John Scott, and Antonio Yunes. 2018. *La Nueva Sociedad Rural: Grupo de Agenda Rural*. Mexico City: Centro Latinoamericano para el Desarrollo Rural.

Arellano Ríos, Alberto. 2009. "Empresarios y Cambio Político En Jalisco." *Acta Republicana: Política y Sociedad* 8(8):41–54.

Arnold, Jason Ross, and David J. Samuels. 2011. "Evidence from Public Opinion." Pp. 31–51 in *The Resurgence of the Latin American Left*, edited by S. Levitsky and K. M. Roberts. Baltimore, MD: Johns Hopkins University Press.

Auerbach, Adam Michael. 2017. "Neighborhood Associations and the Urban Poor: India's Slum Development Committees." *World Development* 96:119–35. doi: 10.1016/j.worlddev.2017.03.002.

Babb, Sarah. 2001. *Managing Mexico: Economists from Nationalism to Neoliberalism*. Princeton, NJ: Princeton University Press.

Baiocchi, Gianpaolo. 2005. *Militants and Citizens: The Politics of Participatory Democracy In Porto Alegre*. Stanford, CA: Stanford University Press.

Baiocchi, Gianpaolo, Patrick Heller, and Marcelo K. Silva. 2011. *Bootstrapping Democracy: Transforming Local Governance and Civil Society in Brazil*. Stanford, CA: Stanford University Press.

Baker, Andy. 2003. "Why Is Trade Reform So Popular in Latin America? A Consumption-Based Theory of Trade Policy Preferences." *World Politics* 55(3):423–55.

Baker, Andy, and Kenneth F. Greene. 2015. "Positional Issue Voting in Latin America." Pp. 173–94 in *The Latin American Voter: Pursuing Representation and Accountability in Challenging Contexts*, edited by R. E. Carlin, M. M. Singer, and E. J. Zechmeister. Ann Arbor, MI: University of Michigan Press.

Bartels, Larry M. 1996. "Uninformed Votes: Information Effects in Presidential Elections." *American Journal of Political Science* 40(1):194–230.

Bartra, Armando. 2007. "El Gobierno No Cumple Con El Acuerdo Nacional Para El Campo...y Se Hicieron Pactos." Pp. 69–79 in *El Campo No Aguanta Más*, edited by A. Sánchez Albarrán. Mexico City: Miguel Angel Porrúa.

Bates, Robert H. 1981. *Markets and States in Tropical Africa: The Political Basis of Agricultural Policies*. Berkeley, CA: University of California Press.

Baumgartner, Frank R., Jeffrey M. Berry, Marie Hojnacki, David C. Kimball, and Beth L. Leech. 2009. *Lobbying and Policy Change: Who Wins, Who Loses, and Why*. Chicago, IL: University of Chicago Press.

Baumgartner, Frank R., and Beth L. Leech. 2001. *Basic Interests: The Importance of Groups in Politics and in Political Science*. Princeton, NJ: Princeton University Press.

Bautista Lucca, Juan. 2019. "Teoría y política en la génesis de MORENA como nuevo partido." *Estudios Políticos* 49. doi:http://dx.doi.org/10.22201/fcpys.24484903e.2020.49.72396.

Bentancur, Verónica Pérez, Rafael Piñeiro Rodríguez, and Fernando Rosenblatt. 2019. "Efficacy and the Reproduction of Political Activism: Evidence From the Broad Front in Uruguay." *Comparative Political Studies* 52(6):838–67.

Benton, Allyson L. 2012. "Bottom-Up Challenges to National Democracy: Mexico's (Legal) Subnational Authoritarian Enclaves." *Comparative Politics* 44(3): 253–71. doi: 10.5129/001041512800078931.

Bersch, Katherine, Sérgio Praça, and Matthew M. Taylor. 2017. "State Capacity, Bureaucratic Politicization, and Corruption in the Brazilian State." *Governance* 30(1):105–24. doi: 10.1111/gove.12196.

Blofield, Merike. 2011. "Introduction: Inequality and Politics in Latin America." Pp. 1–18 in *The Great Gap: Inequality and the Politics of Redistribution in Latin America*, edited by M. Blofield. University Park, PA: Penn State University Press.

Boulding, Carew, and Claudio Holzner. 2021. *Voice and Inequality: Political Participation in Latin American Democracies*. New York, NY: Oxford University Press.

Bril-Mascarenhas, Tomás, and Aldo Madariaga. 2019. "Business Power and the Minimal State: The Defeat of Industrial Policy in Chile." *The Journal of Development Studies* 55(6):1047–66. doi: 10.1080/00220388.2017.1417587.

Bruderl, Josef, and Rudolf Schussler. 1990. "Organizational Mortality: The Liabilities of Newness and Adolescence." *Administrative Science Quarterly* 35(3):530–47. doi: 10.2307/2393316.

Bruhn, Kathleen. 1997. *Taking on Goliath: The Emergence of a New Left Party and the Struggle for Democracy in Mexico*. University Park, PA: Penn State University Press.

Bruhn, Kathleen. 2008. *Urban Protest in Mexico and Brazil*. New York, NY: Cambridge University Press.

Bruhn, Kathleen. 2013. "El PRD y Los Movimientos Urbanos Populares En El Distrito Federal." Pp. 133–54 in *El PRD: orígenes, itinerario, retos*, edited by J. Cadena-Roa and M. A. López Leyva. Mexico City: Universidad Nacional Autónoma de México, Instituto de Investigaciones Sociales.

Bueno, Natália S. 2018. "Bypassing the Enemy: Distributive Politics, Credit Claiming, and Nonstate Organizations in Brazil." Comparative Political Studies 51(3):304–40.

Burgess, Katrina. 2004. *Parties and Unions in the New Global Economy*. Pittsburgh, PA: University of Pittsburgh Press.

Burgess, Katrina, and Steven Levitsky. 2003. "Explaining Populist Party Adaptation in Latin America: Environmental and Organizational Determinants of Party Change in Argentina, Mexico, Peru, and Venezuela." *Comparative Political Studies* 36(8):881–911. doi: 10.1177/0010414003256112.

Calvo, Ernesto, and Maria Victoria Murillo. 2004. "Who Delivers? Partisan Clients in the Argentine Electoral Market." *American Journal of Political Science* 48(4):742–57.

Calvo, Ernesto, and Maria Victoria Murillo. 2019. *Non-Policy Politics: Richer Voters, Poorer Voters, and the Diversification of Electoral Strategies*. New York, NY: Cambridge University Press.

Camp, Roderic A. 1989. *Entrepreneurs and Politics in Twentieth-Century Mexico*. New York, NY: Oxford University Press.

Cameron, Maxwell A. "The Return of Oligarchy? Threats to Representative Democracy in Latin America." *Third World Quarterly* 42(4):775–92.

Cartagena Ticona, Ruth Pamela, Manuel Roberto Parra Vázquez, Araceli Burguete Cal y Mayor, and Antonio López Meza. 2005. "Participación Social y Toma de Decisiones en los Consejos Municipales de Desarrollo Rural Sustentable de los Altos de Chiapas." *Gestión y Política Pública* 14(2):341–402.

Castells, Manuel, and Alejandro Portes. 1989. "World Underneath: The Origins, Dynamics, and Effects of the Informal Economy." Pp. 11–40 in *The Informal Economy: Studies in Advanced and Less Developed Counties*, edited by M. Castells, A. Portes, and L. Benton. Baltimore, MD: Johns Hopkins University Press.

Cazarín Martínez, Angélica. 2013. "El PRD en Tlaxcala." Pp. 399–412 in *El PRD: orígenes, itinerario, retos*, edited by J. Cadena-Roa and M. A. López Leyva. Mexico City: Universidad Nacional Autónoma de México, Instituto de Investigaciones Sociales.

Cejudo, Guillermo M. 2012. "Evidence for Change: The Case of Subsidios al Campo in Mexico." *SSRN Electronic Journal*. 10.2139/ssrn.2333675.

Cejudo, Guillermo M., Damian I. Lugo, and Cynthia Michel. 2018. *Hacia Una Política Social Integral*. Mexico City: Centro de Investigación y Docencia Económicas.

Cejudo, Guillermo M., Cynthia Michel, and Armando Sobrino. 2017. "La Política Social en los Estados: Un Análisis de Integración." 10.13140/RG.2.2.31406.61762.

Cejudo, Guillermo M., and Roberto Zedillo Ortega. 2015. "Accountability, Electoral Competition, and Discretionary Policy-Making: Social Policy in the Mexican States." *International Congress of Latin American Studies Association*.

Chandra, Kanchan. 2004. *Why Ethnic Parties Succeed: Patronage and Ethnic Head Counts in India*. New York, NY: Cambridge University Press.

Chapa García, José Benjamín. 2009. "Proyectos Gubernamentales de Desarollo Económico y su Influencia en la Zona Metropolitana de Guadalajara." Pp. 121–52 in *El Desarrollo Económico de la Zona Metropolitana de Guadalajara*, edited by C. E. Barba Solano and E. de la P. Hernández Aguila. Guadalajara, Mexico: Universidad de Guadalajara, Centro Universitario de Ciencias Sociales y Humanidades.

Chartock, Sarah. 2013. " 'Corporatism with Adjectives'? Conceptualizing Civil Society Incorporation and Indigenous Participation in Latin America." *Latin American Politics and Society* 55(2):52–76. doi: 10.1111/j.1548-2456.2013.00193.x.

Chávez Gutiérrez, Héctor. 2011. *Se Asomo el Sol: El Proceso de Formación del PRD en Michoacán (1986–2001)*. Morelia, Mexico: Universidad Michoacana San Nicolás de Hidalgo.

Clark, Peter B., and James Q. Wilson. 1961. "Incentive Systems: A Theory of Organizations." *Administrative Science Quarterly* 6(2):129–66.

Collier, Ruth Berins. 1992. *The Contradictory Alliance: State–Labor Relations and Regime Change in Mexico*. Berkeley, CA: International and Area Studies, University of California, Berkeley.

Collier, Ruth Berins. 2015. "The High-Tech Economy, Work, and Democracy 2.0: A Research Agenda." IRLE Working Paper No.114–15. http://irle.berkeley.edu/workingpapers/114-15.pdf.

Collier, Ruth Berins, and David Collier. 1979. "Inducements versus Constraints: Disaggregating 'Corporatism.'" *American Political Science Review* 73(4):967–86.

Collier, Ruth Berins, and David Collier. 1991. *Shaping the Political Arena: Critical Junctures, the Labor Movement, and Regime Dynamics in Latin America*. Princeton, NJ: Princeton University Press.

Collier, Ruth Berins, and Samuel Handlin. 2009a. "Introduction: Popular Representation in the Interest Arena." Pp. 3–31 in *Reorganizing Popular Politics: Participation and the New Interest Regime in Latin America*, edited by R. B. Collier and S. Handlin. University Park, PA: Penn State University Press.

Collier, Ruth Berins, and Samuel Handlin. 2009b. "Logics of Collective Action, State Linkages, and Aggregate Traits: The UP-Hub Versus the A-Net." Pp. 61–92 in *Reorganizing Popular Politics: Participation and the New Interest Regime in Latin America*, edited by R. B. Collier and S. Handlin. University Park, PA: Penn State University Press.

Cook, Maria Lorena. 2007. *The Politics of Labor Reform in Latin America: Between Flexibility and Rights*. University Park, PA: Penn State University Press.

Cornelius, Wayne A., Ann L. Craig, and Jonathan Fox. 1994. *Transforming State–Society Relations in Mexico: The National Solidarity Strategy*. San Diego, CA: Center for US–Mexican Studies, University of California, San Diego.

Cornelius, Wayne A., and David Myhre. 1998. "Introduction." Pp. 1–20 in *The Transformation of Rural Mexico: Reforming the Ejido Sector*, edited by W. A. Cornelius and D. Myhre. San Diego, CA: Center for US–Mexican Studies, University of California, San Diego.

Cress, Daniel M., and David A. Snow. 1996. "Mobilization at the Margins: Resources, Benefactors, and the Viability of Homeless Social Movement Organizations." *American Sociological Review* 61(6):1089–1109. doi: 10.2307/2096310.

Dahl, Robert A. 1961. *Who Governs?: Democracy and Power in an American City*. New Haven, CT: Yale University Press.

Dahl, Robert A. 1982. *Dilemmas of Pluralist Democracy: Autonomy vs. Control*. New Haven, CT: Yale University Press.

Dargent, Eduardo. 2014. *Technocracy and Democracy in Latin America: The Experts Running Government*. New York, NY: Cambridge University Press.

De La O, Ana Lorena. 2015. *Crafting Policies to End Poverty in Latin America: The Quiet Transformation*. New York, NY: Cambridge University Press.

Diaz-Cayeros, Alberto, Federico Estévez, and Beatriz Magaloni. 2016. *The Political Logic of Poverty Relief: Electoral Strategies and Social Policy in Mexico*. New York, NY: Cambridge University Press.

Díaz-Cayeros, Alberto, Beatriz Magaloni, and Alexander Ruiz-Euler. 2014. "Traditional Governance, Citizen Engagement, and Local Public Goods: Evidence from Mexico." *World Development* 53:80–93. doi: 10.1016/j.worlddev.2013.01.008.

Dixit, Avinash, and John Londregan. 1996. "The Determinants of Success of Special Interests in Redistributive Politics." *Journal of Politics* 58(4):1132–55.

Dosh, Paul. 2009. "Tactical Innovation, Democratic Governance, and Mixed Motives: Popular Movement Resilience in Peru and Ecuador." *Latin American Politics and Society* 51(1):87–118.

Drake, Paul W. 1978. "Corporatism and Functionalism in Modern Chilean Politics." *Journal of Latin American Studies* 10(1):83–116. doi: 10.1017/S0022216X00019751.

Dunning, Thad. 2009. "Direct Action and Representational Distortion: Problem-Solving Repertoires of Individuals." Pp. 95–131 in *Reorganizing Popular Politics: Participation and the New Interest Regime in Latin America*, edited by R. B. Collier and S. Handlin. University Park, PA: Penn State University Press.

Emerson, Richard M. 1962. "Power-Dependence Relations." *American Sociological Review* 27(1):31–41.

Esping-Andersen, Gøsta. 1990. *The Three Worlds of Welfare Capitalism*. Princeton, NJ: Princeton University Press.

Espinoza Toledo, Ricardo, and Juan Pablo Navarrete Vela. 2016. "MORENA en la reconfiguración del sistema de partidos en México." *Estudios Políticos* 37: 81–109. doi: 10.1016/j.espol.2016.02.004.

Estevez, D. 2017. "Better Year For Mexico's Billionaires, As Fortunes Climbed 17%, Carlos Slim $4.5 Billion Richer." *Forbes*, March 20. https://www.forbes.com/sites/doliaestevez/2017/03/20/better-year-for-mexicos-billionaires-as-fortunes-climbed-17-carlos-slim-4-5-billion-richer/#17409b35740b.

Etchemendy, Sebastián. 2019. "The Rise of Segmented Neo-Corporatism in South America: Wage Coordination in Argentina and Uruguay (2005–2015)." *Comparative Political Studies* 52(10):1427–65. https://doi.org/10.1177/0010414019830729.

Evans, Peter. 1995. *Embedded Autonomy: States and Industrial Transformation*. Princeton, NJ: Princeton University Press.

Evans, Peter. 1999. "Bureaucracy and Growth: A Cross-National Analysis of the Effects of 'Weberian' State Structures on Economic Growth." *American Sociological Review* 64(5):748–65. doi: 10.2307/2657374.

Ewig, Christina, and Stephen J. Kay. 2011. "Postretrenchment Politics: Policy Feedback in Chile's Health and Pension Reforms." *Latin American Politics and Society* 53(4):67–99. doi: 10.1111/j.1548-2456.2011.00134.x.

Faguet, Jean-Paul. 2012. *Decentralization and Popular Democracy: Governance from Below in Bolivia*. Ann Arbor, MI: University of Michigan Press.

Fairfield, Tasha. 2015a. *Private Wealth and Public Revenue in Latin America: Business Power and Tax Politics*. New York, NY: Cambridge University Press.

Fairfield, Tasha. 2015b. "Structural Power in Comparative Political Economy: Perspectives from Policy Formulation in Latin America." *Business and Politics* 17(3):411–41.

Ferreira, Francisco HG, and Michael Walton. 2005. *World Development Report 2006: Equity and Development*. Vol. 28. New York, NY: World Bank Publications.

Fisse, Hernán Rodríguez, and Clive S. Thomas. 2014. "The Chilean Big Business Lobby: A Long-Standing and Major Influence on Public Policy." *Journal of Public Affairs* 14(3–4):310–30. doi: 10.1002/pa.1520.

Fox, Jonathan A. 1992a. "Democratic Rural Development: Leadership Accountability in Regional Peasant Organizations." *Development and Change* 23(2):1–36.

Fox, Jonathan A. 1992b. *The Politics of Food in Mexico: State Power and Social Mobilization*. Ithaca, NY: Cornell University Press.

Fox, Jonathan A. 1994. "The Difficult Transition from Clientelism to Citizenship: Lessons from Mexico." *World Politics* 46(2):151–84.

Fox, Jonathan A., and Josefina Aranda. 1996. "Los Fondos Municipales de Solidaridad y La Participación Comunitaria En Oaxaca." *Revista Mexicana de Sociología* 58(3).

Fox, Jonathan A., and Libby Haight. 2010a. "Farm Subsidy Recipient Lists: A Case of Clear or Opaque Transparency?" Pp. 127–43 in *Subsidizing Inequality: Mexican Corn Policy Since NAFTA*, edited by J. A. Fox and L. Haight. Washington, DC: Woodrow Wilson International Center for Scholars.

Fox, Jonathan A., and Libby Haight. 2010b. "Mexican Agricultural Policy: Multiple Goals and Conflicting Interests." Pp. 9–50 in *Subsidizing Inequality: Mexican Corn Policy Since NAFTA*, edited by J. A. Fox and L. Haight. Washington, DC: Woodrow Wilson International Center for Scholars.

Freeman, John, Glenn R. Carroll, and Michael T. Hannan. 1983. "The Liability of Newness: Age Dependence in Organizational Death Rates." *American Sociological Review* 48(5):692–710. doi: 10.2307/2094928.

de la Fuente Hernández, Juan, and Joaquín Morales Valderrama. 1996. "Crisis Rural y Respuesta Campesina: La Comercializadora Agropecuaria de Occidente." Pp. 283–353 in *Neoliberalismo y Organización Social en el Campo Mexicano*, edited by H. C. de Grammont. Mexico City: Plaza y Valdés.

Fukuyama, Francis. 2001. "Social Capital, Civil Society and Development." *Third World Quarterly* 22(1):7–20.

Fung, Archon, and Eric Olin Wright. 2003. *Deepening Democracy: Institutional Innovations in Empowered Participatory Governance*. London: Verso.

Gallagher, Kevin P., and Lyuba Zarsky. 2007. *The Enclave Economy: Foreign Investment and Sustainable Development in Mexico's Silicon Valley*. Cambridge, MA: MIT Press.

Ganuza, Ernesto, and Gianpaolo Baiocchi. 2012. "The Power of Ambiguity: How Participatory Budgeting Travels the Globe." *Journal of Public Deliberation* 8(2). doi: https://doi.org/10.16997/jdd.142.

Garay, Candelaria. 2009. "Associational Linkages to Labor Unions and Political Parties." Pp. 260–90 in *Reorganizing Popular Politics: Participation and the New Interest Regime in Latin America*, edited by R. B. Collier and S. Handlin. University Park, PA: Penn State University Press.

Garay, Candelaria. 2016. *Social Policy Expansion in Latin America*. New York, NY: Cambridge University Press.

Garay, Candelaria, Brian Palmer-Rubin, and Mathias Poertner. 2020. "Organizational and Partisan Brokerage of Social Benefits: Social Policy Linkages in Mexico." *World Development* 136. DOI: 10.1016/j.worlddev.2020.105103.

García Aguilar, María del Carmen. 2013. "De La Oposición al Gobierno: Luces y Sombras Del PRD En Chiapas." Pp. 437–63 in *El PRD: orígenes, ininerario, retos*, edited by J. Cadena-Roa and M. A. López Leyva. Mexico City: Universidad Nacional Autónoma de México, Instituto de Investigaciones Sociales.

García Ponce, Jorge Ignacio. 2009. *Los Pasos De La Tierra: Campo y Movimiento Campesino En México a Través De La Trayectoria Y Perspectiva De La Central Campesina Cardenista, 1973–2009*. Mexico City: Ediciones Eón.

Gay, Robert. 1990. "Community Organization and Clientelist Politics in Contemporary Brazil: A Case Study from Suburban Rio de Janeiro." *International Journal of Urban and Regional Research* 14(4):648–66.

Geddes, Barbara. 1994. *Politician's Dilemma: Building State Capacity in Latin America*. Berkeley, CA: University of California Press.

George, Alexander L., and Andrew Bennett. 2005. *Case Studies and Theory Development in the Social Sciences*. Cambridge, MA: MIT Press.

Gibson, Edward L. 1996. *Class and Conservative Parties: Argentina in Comparative Perspective*. Baltimore, MD: Johns Hopkins University Press.

Gilens, Martin. 2012. *Affluence and Influence: Economic Inequality and Political Power in America*. Princeton, NJ: Princeton University Press.

Gilens, Martin, and Benjamin I. Page. 2014. "Testing Theories of American Politics: Elites, Interest Groups, and Average Citizens." *Perspectives on Politics* 12(3):564–81. doi: 10.1017/S1537592714001595.

Gledhill, John. 1995. *Neoliberalism, Transnationalization, and Rural Poverty: A Case Study of Michoacán, Mexico*. Boulder, CO: Westview Press.

Golden, Miriam, and Brian Min. 2013. "Distributive Politics Around the World." *Annual Review of Political Science* 16:73–99.

Gómez Bruera, Hernán F. 2013. *Lula, the Workers' Party and the Governability Dilemma in Brazil*. New York, NY: Routledge.

Gómez Bruera, Hernán F. 2015. "Participation Under Lula: Between Electoral Politics and Governability." *Latin American Politics and Society* 57(2):1–20. doi: 10.1111/j.1548-2456.2015.00265.x.

Gómez Gómez, Claudia Verónica. 2010. *Aprendizaje Individual y Colectivo en Asociaciones Profesionales: El Caso del Consejo Regulador del Tequila, Jalisco, México*. Guadalajara, Mexico: Universidad de Guadalajara.

Gómez López, Alicia. 1992. "Los Empresarios y Estado En Jalisco." Pp. 61–70 in *Los empresarios mexicanos, ayer y hoy*, edited by C. Puga and R. Tirado. Mexico City: Ediciones el Caballito.

González, Fernando, and Carlos Alba Vega. 1989. *Cúpulas Empresariales y Poderes Regionales en Jalisco*. Guadalajara, Mexico: Universidad de Guadalajara.

Gordillo, Gustavo. 1988. *Campesinos al Asalto del Cielo: Una Reforma Agraria con Autonomía*. Mexico City: Siglo XXI.

de Grammont, Hubert C. 1996. "La Organización Gremial de Los Agricultores Frente a Los Procesos de Globalización En La Agricultura." Pp. 21–67 in

Neoliberalismo y Organización Social en el Campo Mexicano, edited by H. C. de Grammont. Mexico City: Plaza y Valdés.

de Grammont, Hubert C. 2001. *El Barzón: Clase Media, Ciudadanía y Democracia*. Mexico City: Plaza y Valdés.

de Grammont, Hubert C., and Horacio Mackinlay. 2006. "Las Organizaciones Sociales Campesinas e Indígenas Frente a Los Partidos Políticos y el Estado, México 1938–2006 / Peasant and Indigenous Social Organizations Vis-à-Vis Parties and the State, Mexico 1938–2006." *Revista Mexicana de Sociología* 68(4):693–729.

de Grammont, Hubert C., and Horacio Mackinlay. 2009. "Campesino and Indigenous Social Organizations Facing Democratic Transition in Mexico, 1938–2006." *Latin American Perspectives* 36(4):21–40.

Granovetter, Mark S. 1973. "The Strength of Weak Ties." *American Journal of Sociology* 78:1360–80.

Greene, Kenneth F. 2007. *Why Dominant Parties Lose: Mexico's Democratization in Comparative Perspective*. New York, NY: Cambridge University Press.

Grindle, Merilee S. 1977. *Bureaucrats, Politicians, and Peasants in Mexico: A Case Study in Public Policy*. Berkeley, CA: University of California Press.

Grindle, Merilee S. 2007. *Going Local: Decentralization, Democratization, and the Promise of Good Governance*. Princeton, NJ: Princeton University Press.

Grossmann, Matt. 2012. *The Not-So-Special Interests: Interest Groups, Public Representation, and American Governance*. Stanford, CA: Stanford University Press.

Guerrero Anaya, Francisco Javier. 1999. "Four Responses to Neoliberalism: Peasant Organizations in Western Mexico." Pp. 135–60 in *Institutional Adaptation and Innovation in Rural Mexico*, edited by R. Snyder. San Diego, CA: Center for US–Mexican Studies, University of California, San Diego.

Haber, Paul L. 2013. "Las Relaciones Entre Movimientos Sociales y Partidos Políticos en México." Pp. 41–57 in *El PRD: orígenes, itinerario, retos*, edited by J. Cadena-Roa and M. A. López Leyva. Mexico City: Universidad Nacional Autónoma de México, Instituto de Investigaciones Sociales.

Hacker, Jacob S., and Paul Pierson. 2002. "Business Power and Social Policy: Employers and the Formation of the American Welfare State." *Politics & Society* 30(2):277–325.

Hacker, Jacob S., and Paul Pierson. 2010. *Winner-Take-All Politics: How Washington Made the Rich Richer--and Turned Its Back on the Middle Class*. New York, NY: Simon and Schuster.

Hagopian, Frances. 2007. *Traditional Politics and Regime Change in Brazil*. New York, NY: Cambridge University Press.

Hagopian, Frances. forthcoming. *Reorganizing Political Representation in Latin America: Parties, Program, and Patronage in Argentina, Brazil, Chile, and Mexico*. New York, NY: Cambridge University Press.

Han, Hahrie. 2014. *How Organizations Develop Activists: Civic Associations and Leadership in the 21st Century*. New York, NY: Oxford University Press.

Handelman, Howard. 1976. "The Politics of Labor Protest in Mexico: Two Case Studies." *Journal of Interamerican Studies and World Affairs* 18(3):267–94. doi: 10.2307/174959.

Hanson, Gordon H. 2003. "What Has Happened to Wages in Mexico Since NAFTA?" *SSRN ELibrary*.

Harbers, Imke. 2007. "Democratic Deepening in Third Wave Democracies: Experiments with Participation in Mexico City." *Political Studies* 55(1):38–58. doi: 10.1111/j.1467-9248.2007.00644.x.

Hardy, Clarisa. 1984. *El Estado y Los Campesinos: La Confederación Nacional Campesina (CNC)*. Mexico City: Editorial Nueva Imagen.

Harrison, Ann, and Gordon Hanson. 1999. "Who Gains from Trade Reform? Some Remaining Puzzles." *Journal of Development Economics* 59(1):125–54. doi: 10.1016/S0304-3878(99)00008-5.

Hernández, Gerardo Esquicel. 2015 "Concentración del Poder Económico y Político." *Iguales*. https://www.oxfammexico.org/sites/default/files/desigualdad extrema_informe.pdf.

Hernández Aguila, Elena de la Paz, and Juan José Morales Márquez. 2009. "Metrópolis en Transición. La Zona Metropolitana de Guadalajara: Su Desarrollo Económico y sus Empresarios." Pp. 69–97 in *El Desarrollo Económico de la Zona Metropolitana de Guadalajara*, edited by C. E. Barba Solano and E. de la P. Hernández Aguila. Guadalajara, Mexico: Universidad de Guadalajara, Centro Universitario de Ciencias Sociales y Humanidades.

Hernández-Valdez, Alfonso. 2000. "La Caída Priista en Jalisco: Análisis de la Rupturas Internas y la Pérdida de la Disciplina Partidista a Partir de las Elecciones Locales." *Renglones* 46:44–47.

Hevia de la Jara, Felipe J. 2009. "De Progresa a Oportunidades: Efectos y Límites de la Corriente Cívica en el Gobierno de Vicente Fox." *Sociológica* 24(70): 43–81.

Hevia de la Jara, Felipe J., and Ernesto Isunza Vera. 2012. "Constrained Participation: The Impact of Consultative Councils on National-Level Policy in Mexico." Pp. 75–98 in *New Institutions for Participatory Democracy in Latin America: Voice and Consequence*, edited by M. A. Cameron, E. Hershberg, and K. E. Sharpe. New York, NY: Palgrave Macmillan.

Hewitt de Alcántara, Cynthia. 2007. "Ensayo sobre los obstáculos al desarrollo rural en México: Retrospectiva y prospectiva." *Desacatos* 25:79–100.

Hidalgo, F. Daniel, and Simeon Nichter. 2016. "Voter Buying: Shaping the Electorate through Clientelism." *American Journal of Political Science* 60(2):436–55. doi: 10.1111/ajps.12214.

Hilgers, Tina. 2008. "Causes and Consequences of Political Clientelism: Mexico's PRD in Comparative Perspective." *Latin American Politics and Society* 50(4): 123–53.

Hilgers, Tina. 2018. "Gestión" edited by A. Ledeneva. *Global Encyclopaedia of Informality* 2:216–19.

Hochstetler, Kathryn. 2011. "The Politics of Environmental Licensing: Energy Projects of the Past and Future in Brazil." *Studies in Comparative International Development* 46(4):349–71. doi: 10.1007/s12116-011-9092-1.

Hochstetler, Kathryn, and Alfred P. Montero. 2013. "The Renewed Developmental State: The National Development Bank and the Brazil Model." *The Journal of Development Studies* 49(11):1484–99. doi: 10.1080/00220388.2013.807503.

Holland, Alisha C. 2015. "The Distributive Politics of Enforcement." *American Journal of Political Science* 59(2):357–71. doi: 10.1111/ajps.12125.

Holland, Alisha C. 2017. *Forbearance as Redistribution: The Politics of Informal Welfare in Latin America*. New York, NY: Cambridge University Press.

Holland, Alisha C., and Brian Palmer-Rubin. 2015. "Beyond the Machine: Clientelist Brokers and Interest Organizations in Latin America." *Comparative Political Studies* 48(9):1186–1223.

Holzner, Claudio A. 2007. "The Poverty of Democracy: Neoliberal Reforms and Political Participation of the Poor in Mexico." *Latin American Politics & Society* 49(2):87–122. doi: 10.1353/lap.2007.0021.

Houtzager, Peter P. 1998. "State and Unions in the Transformation of the Brazilian Countryside, 1964–1979." *Latin American Research Review* 33(2):103–42.

Huber, Evelyne, and John D. Stephens. 2012. *Democracy and the Left: Social Policy and Inequality in Latin America*. Chicago, IL: University of Chicago Press.

Huffstutter, P.J. and Barrera, A. 2018. "Exclusive: As Trump trashes NAFTA, Mexico turns to Brazilian corn." *Reuters*, February 22. https://www.reuters.com/article/us-trump-effect-corn-exclusive/exclusive-as-trump-trashes-nafta-mexico-turns-to-brazilian-corn-idUSKCN1G61J4.

Hummel, Calla. 2017. "Disobedient Markets: Street Vendors, Enforcement, and State Intervention in Collective Action." *Comparative Political Studies* 50(11):1524–55. doi: 10.1177/0010414016679177.

Hunter, Wendy. 2010. *The Transformation of the Workers' Party in Brazil, 1989–2009*. New York, NY: Cambridge University Press.

Hunter, Wendy, and Natasha Borges Sugiyama. 2014. "Transforming Subjects into Citizens: Insights from Brazil's Bolsa Família." *Perspectives on Politics* 12(4): 829–45. doi: 10.1017/S1537592714002151.

Hylton, Forrest, and Sinclair Thomson. 2007. *Revolutionary Horizons: Past and Present in Bolivian Politics*. London: Verso.

ILO. 2018. "Panorama Laboral 2018: América Latina y El Caribe." International Labour Organization. https://www.ilo.org/wcmsp5/groups/public/---americas/---ro-lima/documents/publication/wcms_654969.pdf.

Iversen, Torben. 1999. *Contested Economic Institutions: The Politics of Macroeconomics and Wage Bargaining in Advanced Democracies*. New York, NY: Cambridge University Press.

de Janvry, Alain, Kyle Emerick, Marco Gonzalez-Navarro, and Elisabeth Sadoulet. 2015. "Delinking Land Rights from Land Use: Certification and Migration in Mexico." *American Economic Review* 105(10):3125–49. doi: 10.1257/aer.20130853.

de Janvry, Alain, Gustavo Gordillo, and Elisabeth Sadoulet. 1997. *Mexico's Second Agrarian Reform: Household and Community Responses, 1990–1994*. San Diego, CA: Center for US–Mexican Studies, University of California, San Diego.

Johnson Ceva, Kristin. 1998. "Business–Government Relations in Mexico Since 1990: NAFTA, Economic Crisis, and the Reorganization of Business Interests." Pp. 125–57 in *Mexico's Private Sector: Recent History, Future Challenges*, edited by R. Roett. Boulder, CO: Lynne Rienner Publishers.

Johnson, Chalmers. 1982. *MITI and the Japanese Miracle: The Growth of Industrial Policy: 1925–1975*. Stanford, CA: Stanford University Press.

Juárez González, Leticia. 1989. "Una Década de la Organización y Participación Empresarial: 1928–1938." Pp. 251–91 in *Las Empresas y los Empresarios en el México Contemporáneo*, edited by R. Pozas and M. Luna. Mexico City: Editorial Grijalbo.

Katsiaficas, George N. 2006. *The Subversion of Politics: European Autonomous Social Movements and the Decolonization of Everyday Life*. Oakland, CA: AK Press.

Katz, Richard S., and Peter Mair. 1995. "Changing Models of Party Organization and Party Democracy: The Emergence of the Cartel Party." *Party Politics* 1(1): 5–28. doi: 10.1177/1354068895001001001.

Katznelson, Ira. 1986. "Working-Class Formation: Constructing Cases and Comparisons." Pp. 3–41 in *Working-class Formation: Nineteenth-century Patterns in Western Europe and the United States*, edited by I. Katznelson and A. R. Zolberg. Princeton, NJ: Princeton University Press.

Katznelson, Ira, and Aristide R. Zolberg. 1986. *Working-Class Formation: Nineteenth-Century Patterns in Western Europe and the United States*. Princeton, NJ: Princeton University Press.

Keck, Margaret E. 1992. *The Workers' Party and Democratization in Brazil*. New Haven, CT: Yale University Press.

Keefer, Philip. 2007. "Clientelism, Credibility, and the Policy Choices of Young Democracies." *American Journal of Political Science* 51(4):804–21. doi: 10.1111/j.1540-5907.2007.00282.x.

Key, Valdimer Orlando. 1942. *Politics, Parties and Pressure Groups*. New York, NY: Thomas Y. Crowell Company.

King, Timothy. 1970. *Mexico: Industrialization and Trade Policies Since 1940*. London: Development Centre of the Organization for Economic Co-operation and Development.

Kitschelt, Herbert. 2000. "Linkages between Citizens and Politicians in Democratic Polities." *Comparative Political Studies* 33(6–7):845–79.

Kitschelt, Herbert, Kirk A. Hawkins, Juan Pablo Luna, Guillermo Rosas, and Elizabeth J. Zechmeister. 2010. *Latin American Party Systems*. New York, NY: Cambridge University Press.

Kitschelt, Herbert, and Steven I. Wilkinson. 2007. *Patrons, Clients and Policies: Patterns of Democratic Accountability and Political Competition*. New York, NY: Cambridge University Press.

Klein, Peter Taylor. 2015. "Engaging the Brazilian State: The Belo Monte Dam and the Struggle for Political Voice." *The Journal of Peasant Studies* 42(6):1137–56. doi: 10.1080/03066150.2014.991719.

Klesner, Joseph L. 2005. "Electoral Competition and the New Party System in Mexico." *Latin American Politics and Society* 47(2):103–42. doi: 10.1111/j.1548-2456.2005.tb00311.x.

Korpi, Walter. 1983. *The Democratic Class Struggle*. London: Routledge.

Kurtz, Marcus J. 2004a. *Free Market Democracy and the Chilean and Mexican Countryside*. New York, NY: Cambridge University Press.

Kurtz, Marcus J. 2004b. "The Dilemmas of Democracy in the Open Economy: Lessons from Latin America." *World Politics* 56(2):262–302.

Langston, Joy. 2001. "Why Rules Matter: Changes in Candidate Selection in Mexico's PRI, 1988–2000." *Journal of Latin American Studies* 33(3):485–511.

Langston, Joy. 2017. *Democratization and Authoritarian Party Survival: Mexico's PRI*. New York, NY: Oxford University Press.

Lapegna, Pablo. 2016. *Soybeans and Power: Genetically Modified Crops, Environmental Politics, and Social Movements in Argentina*. New York, NY: Oxford University Press.

Larreguy, Horacio. 2013. "Monitoring Political Brokers: Evidence from Clientelist Networks in Mexico." https://papers.ssrn.com/sol3/papers.cfm?abstract_id=2225027.

Larreguy, Horacio, John Marshall, and Pablo Querubín. 2016. "Parties, Brokers and Voter Mobilization: How Turnout Buying Depends Upon the Party's Capacity to Monitor Brokers." *American Political Science Review* 110(1):160–79.

Larreguy, Horacio, Cesar E. Montiel Olea, and Pablo Querubin. 2017. "Political Brokers: Partisans or Agents? Evidence from the Mexican Teachers' Union." *American Journal of Political Science* 61(4):877–91. doi: 10.1111/ajps.12322.

Lawder, D. 2018. "U.S., Mexico unions file NAFTA labor complaint to influence talks." *Reuters*, January 25. https://www.reuters.com/article/us-trade-nafta-labor-exclusive/u-s-mexico-unions-file-nafta-labor-complaint-to-influence-talks-idUSKBN1FE1ZE.

Lawson, Chappell. 2000. "Mexico's Unfinished Transition: Democratization and Authoritarian Enclaves in Mexico." *Mexican Studies/Estudios Mexicanos* 16(2):267–87. doi: 10.2307/1052198.

Lehmbruch, Gerhard, and Philippe C. Schmitter. 1982. *Patterns of Corporatist Policy-Making*. London: Sage.

Levitsky, Steven. 2003. *Transforming Labor-Based Parties in Latin America: Argentine Peronism in Comparative Perspective*. New York, NY: Cambridge University Press.

Levitsky, Steven, and María Victoria Murillo. 2013. "Lessons from Latin America: Building Institutions on Weak Foundations." *Journal of Democracy* 24(2):93–107. doi: 10.1353/jod.2013.0031.

Levitsky, Steven, and Kenneth M. Roberts. 2011. "Introduction: Latin America's 'Left Turn': A Framework for Analysis." Pp. 1–28 in *The Resurgence of the Latin American Left*, edited by S. Levitsky and K. M. Roberts. Baltimore, MD: Johns Hopkins University Press.

Levy, Santiago. 2010. *Good Intentions, Bad Outcomes: Social Policy, Informality, and Economic Growth in Mexico*. Washington, DC: Brookings Institution Press.

Levy, Santiago, and Dani Rodrik. 2017. "The Mexican Paradox." *Project Syndicate*, August 10. https://www.project-syndicate.org/commentary/mexican-paradox-economic-orthodoxy-low-productivity-by-santiago-levy-and-dani-rodrik-2017-08.

Lindblom, Charles E. 1977. *Politics and Markets: The World's Political Economic Systems*. New York, NY: Basic Books.

Lipset, Seymour Martin, Martin A. Trow, and James S. Coleman. 1956. *Union Democracy: The Internal Politics of the International Typographical Union*. Glencoe, IL: Free Press.

Loaeza, Soledad. 1999. *El Partido Acción Nacional, La Larga Marcha, 1939–1994: Oposición Leal y Partido De Protesta*. Mexico City: Fondo de Cultura Económica.

Loaeza, Soledad. 2010. *Acción Nacional: El Apetito y Las Responsabilidades Del Triunfo*. Mexico City: El Colegio de México, Centro de Estudios Internacionales.

Lomelí, Luz. 2001. *El Sentido Del Voto: Electores, Votos y Sistema de Partidos een Jalisco*. Guadalajara, Mexico: Instituto Tecnológico de Estudios Superiores de Occidente.

López Leyva, Miguel Armando. 2007. *La Encrucijada: Entre la Protesta Social y la Participación Electoral (1988)*. Mexico City: FLACSO Mexico.

Lowi, Theodore J. 1964. "American Business, Public Policy, Case-Studies, and Political Theory." *World Politics* 16(4):677–715.

Loxton, James. 2015. "Authoritarian Successor Parties." *Journal of Democracy* 26(3):157–70. doi: 10.1353/jod.2015.0052.

Loxton, James. 2016. "Authoritarian Successor Parties and the New Right." Pp. 245–72 in *Challenges of Party-Building in Latin America*, edited by S. Levitsky, J. Loxton, B. Van Dyck, and J. I. Domínguez. New York, NY: Cambridge University Press.

Lujambio, Alonso. 2001. "Democratization through Federalism? The National Action Party Strategy, 1939–2000." Pp. 47–94 in *Party Politics and the Struggle for Democracy in Mexico: National and State-Level Analyses of the Partido Acción Nacional*, edited by K. J. Middlebrook. San Diego, CA: Center for US–Mexican Studies, University of California, San Diego.

Luna, Juan Pablo. 2007. "Frente Amplio and the Crafting of a Social Democratic Alternative in Uruguay." *Latin American Politics & Society* 49(4):1–30.

Luna, Juan Pablo. 2010. "Segmented Party Voter Linkages in Latin America: The Case of the UDI." *Journal of Latin American Studies* 42(2):325–56.

Luna, Juan Pablo. 2014. *Segmented Representation: Political Party Strategies in Unequal Democracies*. New York, NY: Oxford University Press.

Luna, Juan Pablo, and Elizabeth J. Zechmeister. 2010. "Political Representation in Latin America." Pp. 119–44 in *Latin American Party Systems*, edited by H. Kitschelt, K. A. Hawkins, J. P. Luna, G. Rosas, and E. J. Zechmeister. New York: Cambridge University Press.

Luna, Matilde. 1995. "Entrepreneurial Interests and Political Action in Mexico: Facing the Demands of Economic Modernization." Pp. 77–94 in *The Challenge of Institutional Reform in Mexico*, edited by R. Roett. Boulder, CO: Lynne Rienner Publishers.

Lupu, Noam. 2013. "Party Brands and Partisanship: Theory with Evidence from a Survey Experiment in Argentina." *American Journal of Political Science* 57(1):49–64.

Lupu, Noam. 2014. "Brand Dilution and the Breakdown of Political Parties in Latin America." *World Politics* 66(4):561–602.

Lustig, Nora. 1998. *Mexico: The Remaking of an Economy*. Second edition. Washington, DC: Brookings Institution Press.

Lustig, Nora. 2020. "Inequality and Social Policy in Latin America." Commitment to Equity (CEQ) Working Paper Series 94, Tulane University, Department of Economics. https://ideas.repec.org/p/tul/ceqwps/94.html.

Mackinlay, Horacio. 1996. "La CNC y El 'Nuevo Movimiento Campesino' (1989–1994)." Pp. 165–238 in *Neoliberalismo y Organización Social en el Campo Mexicano*, edited by H. C. de Grammont. Mexico City: Plaza y Valdés.

Magaloni, Beatriz. 2006. *Voting for Autocracy: Hegemonic Party Survival and Its Demise in Mexico*. New York, NY: Cambridge University Press.

Mainwaring, Scott. 2018. *Party Systems in Latin America: Institutionalization, Decay, and Collapse*. New York, NY: Cambridge University Press.

Mainwaring, Scott, and Timothy R. Scully, eds. 2003. *Christian Democracy in Latin America: Electoral Competition and Regime Conflicts*. Stanford, CA: Stanford University Press.

Mainwaring, Scott, Timothy R. Scully, and Jorge Vargas Cullell. 2010. "Measuring Success in Democratic Governance." Pp. 11–51 in *Democratic Governance in Latin America*, edited by S. Mainwaring and T. R. Scully. Stanford, CA: Stanford University Press.

Mair, Peter. 1994. "Party Organizations: From Civil Society to the State." Pp. 1–22 in *How Parties Organize: Change and Adaptation in Party Organizations in Western Democracies*, edited by R. S. Katz and P. Mair. London: Sage.

Malloy, James M. 1977. "Authoritarianism and Corporatism in Latin America: The Modal Pattern." Pp. 3–22 in *Authoritarianism and Corporatism in Latin America*, edited by J. M. Malloy. Pittsburgh, PA: University of Pittsburgh Press.

Mansuri, Ghazala, and Vijayendra Rao. 2013. *Localizing Development: Does Participation Work?* Washington, DC: World Bank.

Mares, Isabela. 2006. *Taxation, Wage Bargaining, and Unemployment*. New York, NY: Cambridge University Press.

Marichal, Carlos. 2013. *Nueva historia de las grandes crisis financieras: Una perspectiva global, 1873–2008*. Buenos Aires: Penguin Random House Grupo Editorial Argentina.

Markus, Stanislav. 2015. *Property, Predation, and Protection: Piranha Capitalism in Russia and Ukraine*. New York, NY: Cambridge University Press.

Mayka, Lindsay. 2019. *Building Participatory Institutions in Latin America: Reform Coalitions and Institutional Change*. New York, NY: Cambridge University Press.

McCarthy, John D., and Mayer N. Zald. 1977. "Resource Mobilization and Social Movements: A Partial Theory." *American Journal of Sociology* 1212–41.

McCormick, Gladys I. 2016. *The Logic of Compromise in Mexico: How the Countryside Was Key to the Emergence of Authoritarianism*. Chapel Hill, NC: UNC Press Books.

Meek, David. 2015. "Learning as Territoriality: The Political Ecology of Education in the Brazilian Landless Workers' Movement." *The Journal of Peasant Studies* 42(6):1179–1200. doi: 10.1080/03066150.2014.978299.

Meng, Anne, and Brian Palmer-Rubin. 2017. "Gerrymandering Opposition: Minority-Concentrated Districts and Electoral Competition in Mexico." *Studies in Comparative International Development* 52(1):64–86. doi: 10.1007/s12116-015-9206-2.

Merino, Mauricio. 2010. "Agricultural Subsidy Programs: The Rationale and Irrationality of a Poorly-Designed Policy." In *Subsidizing Inequality: Mexican*

Corn Policy Since NAFTA, edited by Jonathan A. Fox and Libby Haight, 51–66. Washington, DC: Woodrow Wilson International Center for Scholars.

Mestries Benquet, Francis. 2007. "El Movimiento El Campo No Aguanta Más: Hacia Un Proyecto Campesino De Desarrollo Agrícola Nacional." Pp. 189–230 in *El Campo No Aguanta Más*, edited by A. Sánchez Albarrán. Mexico City: Miguel Angel Porrúa.

Michels, Robert. 1915. *Political Parties*. New York, NY: Taylor & Francis.

Middlebrook, Kevin J. 2001. "Party Politics and Democratization in Mexico: The Partido Acción Nacional in Comparative Perspective." Pp. 3–44 in *Party Politics and the Struggle for Democracy in Mexico: National and State-Level Analyses of the Partido Acción Nacional*, edited by K. J. Middlebrook. San Diego, CA: Center for US–Mexican Studies, University of California, San Diego.

Mizrahi, Yemile. 2003. *From Martyrdom to Power: The Partido Acción Nacional in Mexico*. Notre Dame, IN: University of Notre Dame Press.

Moe, Terry M. 1981. "Toward a Broader View of Interest Groups." *The Journal of Politics* 43(2):531–43. doi: 10.2307/2130382.

Molinar Horcasitas, Juan, and Jeffrey A. Weldon. 1994. "Electoral Determinants and Consequences of National Solidarity." Pp. 123–41 in *Transforming State-Society Relations in Mexico: The National Solidarity Strategy*, edited by W. A. Cornelius, A. L. Craig, and J. Fox. San Diego, CA: Center for US–Mexican Studies, University of California, San Diego.

Montambeault, Françoise. 2011. "Overcoming Clientelism Through Local Participatory Institutions in Mexico: What Type of Participation?" *Latin American Politics and Society* 53(1):91–124.

Morales, César. 2018. "La sociedad civil fifí: una defensa del término." *Nexos*, November 26. https://redaccion.nexos.com.mx/la-sociedad-civil-fifi-una-defensa-del-termino/.

Motta, Renata. 2016. "Global Capitalism and the Nation State in the Struggles over GM Crops in Brazil." *Journal of Agrarian Change* 16(4):720–27. doi: 10.1111/joac.12165.

Muñoz, Paula. 2014. "An Informational Theory of Campaign Clientelism: The Case of Peru." *Comparative Politics* 47(1):79–98. doi: 10.5129/001041514813623155.

Murillo, Maria Victoria. 2001. *Labor Unions, Partisan Coalitions, and Market Reforms in Latin America*. New York, NY: Cambridge University Press.

Naseemullah, Adnan. 2016. *Development after Statism: Industrial Firms and the Political Economy of South Asia*. New York, NY: Cambridge University Press.

Navarro, Zander. 2006. "'Mobilization without Emancipation': Social Struggles of the Landless in Brazil." Pp. 146–78 in *Another Production is Possible: Beyond the Capitalist Canon*, edited by B. de S. Santos. London: Verso.

Nichter, Simeon. 2008. "Vote Buying or Turnout Buying? Machine Politics and the Secret Ballot." *American Political Science Review* 102(1):19–31.

Nichter, Simeon, and Brian Palmer-Rubin. 2015. "Clientelism, Declared Support, and Mexico's 2012 Campaign." Pp. 200–226 in *Mexico's Evolving Democracy: A Comparative Study of the 2012 Elections*, edited by J. I. Domínguez,

K. F. Greene, C. H. Lawson, and A. Moreno. Baltimore, MD: Johns Hopkins University Press.

Novaes, Lucas M. 2018. "Disloyal Brokers and Weak Parties." *American Journal of Political Science* 62(1):84–98. doi: 10.1111/ajps.12331.

Oates, Wallace E. 1972. *Fiscal Federalism*. New York, NY: Harcourt Brace Jovanovich.

Offe, Claus, and Helmut Wiesenthal. 1980. "Two Logics of Collective Action: Theoretical Notes on Social Class and Organizational Form." *Political Power and Social Theory* 1(1):67–115.

Oliveira, Gustavo de L. T., and Mindi Schneider. 2016. "The Politics of Flexing Soybeans: China, Brazil and Global Agroindustrial Restructuring." *The Journal of Peasant Studies* 43(1):167–94. doi: 10.1080/03066150.2014.993625.

Olson, Mancur. 1965. *The Logic of Collective Action: Public Goods and the Theory of Collective Action*. Cambridge, MA: Harvard University Press.

Ondetti, Gabriel. 2008. *Land, Protest, and Politics: The Landless Movement and the Struggle for Agrarian Reform in Brazil*. University Park, PA: Penn State University Press.

Ostrom, Elinor. 1996. "Crossing the Great Divide: Coproduction, Synergy, and Development." *World Development* 24(6):1073–87.

Pacheco-Vega, Raúl. 2007. "Una Crítica al Paradigma de Desarrollo Regional Mediante Clusters Industriales Forzados." *Estudios Sociológicos* 25(75):683–707.

Pahnke, Anthony. 2015. "Institutionalizing Economies of Opposition: Explaining and Evaluating the Success of the MST's Cooperatives and Agroecological Repeasantization." *The Journal of Peasant Studies* 42(6):1087–107. doi: 10.1080/03066150.2014.991720.

Palmer-Rubin, Brian. 2010a. "Is Decentralization the Answer? Lessons from Alianza Para El Campo." Pp. 153–61 in *Subsidizing Inequality: Mexican Corn Policy Since NAFTA*, edited by J. A. Fox and L. Haight. Washington, DC: Woodrow Wilson International Center for Scholars.

Palmer-Rubin, Brian. 2010b. "Small Producer Access to Decentralized Agricultural Subsidies in Mexico: Alianza Para El Campo." *Mexican Rural Development Research Reports*.

Palmer-Rubin, Brian. 2016. "Interest Organizations and Distributive Politics: Small-Business Subsidies in Mexico." *World Development* 84:97–117. doi: 10.1016/j.worlddev.2016.03.019.

Palmer-Rubin, Brian. 2019. "Evading the Patronage Trap: Organizational Capacity and Demand Making in Mexico." *Comparative Political Studies* 52(13–14):2097–134. doi: 10.1177/0010414019830745.

Palmer-Rubin, Brian. 2021. "After Corporatism: Party Linkages with Popular-Sector Organizations in Neoliberal Latin America." Pp. 327–61 in *The Inclusionary Turn in Latin American Democracies*, edited by D. Kapiszewski, S. Levitsky, and D. Yashar. New York, NY: Cambridge University Press.

Palmer-Rubin, Brian, and Ruth Berins Collier. forthcoming. "Work and Demand Making: Productionist and Consumptionist Politics in Latin America." *Comparative Political Studies*. doi: 10.1177/00104140211060282.

Palmer-Rubin, Brian, Candelaria Garay, and Mathias Poertner. 2021. "Incentives for Organizational Participation: A Recruitment Experiment in Mexico." *Comparative Political Studies* 54(1):110–43. doi: 10.1177/0010414020919927.

Panebianco, Angelo. 1988. *Political Parties: Organization and Power*. New York, NY: Cambridge University Press.

Paschel, Tianna S. 2016. *Becoming Black Political Subjects: Movements and Ethno-Racial Rights in Colombia and Brazil*. Princeton, NJ: Princeton University Press.

Persson, Torsten, and Guido Enrico Tabellini. 2002. *Political Economics: Explaining Economic Policy*. Cambridge, MA: MIT Press.

Pfeffer, Jeffrey, and Gerald R. Salancik. 2003. *The External Control of Organizations: A Resource Dependence Perspective*. Stanford, CA: Stanford University Press.

Pierson, Paul. 2000. "Increasing Returns, Path Dependence, and the Study of Politics." *American Political Science Review* 94(2):251–67. doi: 10.2307/2586011.

Pierson, Paul, and Theda Skocpol. 2002. "Historical Institutionalism in Contemporary Political Science." *Political Science: The State of the Discipline* 3:693–721.

Pilar Martínez, Maria del. 2017. "CTM quiere "proteger" la contratación con renegociación del TLCAN." *El Economista*, August 7. https://www.eleconomista.com.mx/empresas/CTM-quiere-proteger-la-contratacion-con-renegociacion-del-TLCAN--20170807-0052.html.

Piven, Frances Fox, and Richard A. Cloward. 1979. *Poor People's Movements: Why They Succeed, How They Fail*. New York, NY: Vintage Books.

Poertner, Mathias. 2021. "The Organizational Voter: Support for New Parties in Young Democracies." *American Journal of Political Science* 65(3): 634–51. doi: 10.1111/ajps.12546.

Portes, Alejandro, and Kelly Hoffman. 2003. "Latin American Class Structures: Their Composition and Change During the Neoliberal Era." *Latin American Research Review* 38(1):41–82.

Pribble, Jennifer. 2013. *Welfare and Party Politics in Latin America*. New York, NY: Cambridge University Press.

Przeworski, Adam. 1986. *Capitalism and Social Democracy*. New York, NY: Cambridge University Press.

Przeworski, Adam, and John Sprague. 1986. *Paper Stones: A History of Electoral Socialism*. Chicago, IL: University of Chicago Press.

Puga, Cristina. 2004. *Los Empresarios Organizados y el Tratado de Libre Comercio de América Del Norte*. Mexico City: Miguel Angel Porrúa.

Putnam, Robert D., Robert Leonardi, and Raffaella Y. Nanetti. 1994. *Making Democracy Work: Civic Traditions in Modern Italy*. Princeton, NJ: Princeton University Press.

Ramírez Sevilla, Luis. 1997. *Dibujo de Sol con Nubes: Una Aproximación a los Límites y Potencialidades del PRD en un Municipio Michoacano (Historia de una Utopía Nonata)*. Zamora, Mexico: Colegio de Michoacán.

Rennwald, Line, and Jonas Pontusson. 2021. "Paper Stones Revisited: Class Voting, Unionization and the Electoral Decline of the Mainstream Left." *Perspectives on Politics* 19(1): 36-54. doi: 10.1017/S1537592720000067.

Rich, Jessica. 2019. *State-Sponsored Activism: Bureaucrats and Social Movements in Democratic Brazil.* New York, NY: Cambridge University Press.

Rich, Jessica, Lindsay Mayka, and Alfred P. Montero. 2019. "The Politics of Participation in Latin America: New Actors and Institutions." *Latin American Politics and Society* 61(2):1–20. doi: 10.1017/lap.2018.74.

Riedl, Rachel Beatty. 2014. *Authoritarian Origins of Democratic Party Systems in Africa.* New York, NY: Cambridge University Press.

Rizzo, Tesalia. 2020. "Intermediaries of the State: Bureaucratic Transaction Costs of Claiming Welfare in Mexico." PhD diss., Massachusetts Institute of Technology, Department of Political Science.

Roberts, Kenneth M. 2015. *Changing Course in Latin America: Party Systems in the Neoliberal Era.* New York, NY: Cambridge University Press.

Robles Berlanga, Héctor M. 2014. "Ejercicio Del Presupuesto 2011 del Programa Especial Concurrente Para El Desarrollo Rural." Subsidios al Campo en México Working Paper. http://subsidiosalcampo.org.mx/wp-includes/textos_pdf/subsidios-pdf/15PEC2011.pdf.

Robles Berlanga, Héctor M., and Ana Joaquina Ruiz Guerra. 2012. "Presupuestos Para la Agricultura Familiar y Campesina en México." https://www2.congreso.gob.pe/sicr/cendocbib/con4_uibd.nsf/13CF8B3A72F6423005257D120058643A/$FILE/resumen_presupuestos_agricultura_mexico.pdf.

Rodriguez, Estaban David. 2017. "Mercado de lealtades para 2018 : Tejen red clientelar con fines proselitistas: experto; unimoss, CNC y CCC, organizaciones vinculadas." *El Universal*, December 26. https://www.eluniversal.com.mx/periodismo-de-investigacion/millonaria-bolsa-para-asociaciones-ligadas-partidos-politicos.

Rodríguez Gómez, Guadalupe, and Gabriel Torres. 1994. "Los agroproductores frente a las políticas neoliberales: El Barzón y COMAGRO." *Espiral* 1(1):129–76.

Rodrik, Dani. 2008. *One Economics, Many Recipes: Globalization, Institutions, and Economic Growth.* Princeton, NJ: Princeton University Press.

Román, Luis Ignacio, Rodrigo Flores, and Roberto Govela. 2004. *Planes, Políticas y Actores Económicos en Jalisco en el Marco de la Liberalización Económica.* Guadalajara, Mexico: Instituto Tecnológico de Estudios Superiores de Occidente.

Rosas, Guillermo. 2010. "Issues, Ideologies, and Partisan Divides: Imprints of Programmatic Structure on Latin American Legislatures." Pp. 70–95 in *Latin American Party Systems*, edited by H. Kitschelt, K. A. Hawkins, J. P. Luna, G. Rosas, and E. J. Zechmeister. New York, NY: Cambridge University Press.

Rossi, Federico M. 2017. *The Poor's Struggle for Political Incorporation: The Piquetero Movement in Argentina.* New York, NY: Cambridge University Press.

Rossi, Federico M., and Eduardo Silva. 2018. "Introduction: Reshaping the Political Arena in Latin America." Pp. 23–31 in *Reshaping the Political Arena in Latin America: From Resisting Neoliberalism to the Second Incorporation*, edited by F. M. Rossi and E. Silva. Pittsburgh, PA: University of Pittsburgh Press.

Saavedra, María Luisa, and Blanca Tapia. 2012. "El Entorno Sociocultural y La Competitividad de La PYME En México." *Panorama Socioeconómico* 30(44):4–24.

Samford, Steven, Dan Breznitz, and Michael Murphee. 2020. "Business Networks and Enclave Formation: Why Foreign Investment Fails to Transfer Technology." *Academy of Management Proceedings* 2020(1).

Samuels, David, and Cesar Zucco. 2015. "Crafting Mass Partisanship at the Grass Roots." *British Journal of Political Science* 45(4):755–75. doi: 10.1017/S0007123413000549.

Schattschneider, Elmer Eric. 1935. *Politics, Pressures and the Tariff*. New York, NY: Prentice Hall.

Schattschneider, Elmer Eric. 1960. *The Semisovereign People: A Realist's View of Democracy in America*. New York, NY: Holt, Rinehart and Winston.

Schlozman, Kay Lehman, Sidney Verba, and Henry E. Brady. 2012. *The Unheavenly Chorus: Unequal Political Voice and the Broken Promise of American Democracy*. Princeton, NJ: Princeton University Press.

Schmitter, Philippe C. 1974. "Still the Century of Corporatism?" *The Review of Politics* 36(1):85–131.

Schneider, Ben Ross. 1999. "The Desarrollista State in Brazil and Mexico." Pp. 276–305 in *The Developmental State*, edited by M. Woo-Cumings. Ithaca, NY: Cornell University Press.

Schneider, Ben Ross. 2002. "Why Is Mexican Business So Organized?" *Latin American Research Review* 37(1):77–118.

Schneider, Ben Ross. 2004. *Business Politics and the State in Twentieth-Century Latin America*. New York, NY: Cambridge University Press.

Schneider, Ben Ross. 2013. *Hierarchical Capitalism in Latin America: Business, Labor, and the Challenges of Equitable Development*. New York, NY: Cambridge University Press.

Schrank, Andrew, and Marcus J. Kurtz. 2005. "Credit Where Credit Is Due: Open Economy Industrial Policy and Export Diversification in Latin America and the Caribbean." *Politics & Society* 33(4):671–702. doi: 10.1177/0032329205280927.

Scott, James C. 1977. *The Moral Economy of the Peasant: Rebellion and Subsistence in Southeast Asia*. New Haven, CT: Yale University Press.

Scott, John. 2010. "Agricultural Subsidies in Mexico: Who Gets What?" Pp. 67–118 in *Subsidizing Inequality: Mexican Corn Policy Since NAFTA*, edited by J. A. Fox and L. Haight. Washington, DC: Woodrow Wilson International Center for Scholars.

Shadlen, Kenneth C. 2000. "Neoliberalism, Corporatism, and Small Business Political Activism in Contemporary Mexico." *Latin American Research Review* 35(2):73–106.

Shadlen, Kenneth C. 2004. *Democratization Without Representation: The Politics of Small Industry in Mexico*. University Park, PA: Penn State University Press.

Shefter, Martin. 1977. "Party and Patronage: Germany, England, and Italy." *Politics & Society* 7(4):403–51.

Shefter, Martin. 1994. *Political Parties and the State: The American Historical Experience*. Princeton, NJ: Princeton University Press.

Shirk, David A. 2005. *Mexico's New Politics: The PAN and Democratic Change*. Boulder, CO: Lynne Rienner Publishers.

Silva, Eduardo. 1996. *The State and Capital in Chile: Business Elites, Technocrats, and Market Economics*. Boulder, CO: Westview Press.

Silva, Eduardo. 1998. "Organized Business, Neoliberal Economic Restructuring, and Redemocratization in Chile." Pp. 217–52 in *Organized Business, Economic Change, and Democracy in Latin America*, edited by F. Durand and E. Silva. Coral Gables, FL: North-South Center Press.

Silva, Eduardo. 2017. "Reorganizing Popular Sector Incorporation: Propositions from Bolivia, Ecuador, and Venezuela." *Politics & Society* 45(1):91–122.

Silva, Eduardo, and Francisco Durand. 1998. "Organized Business and Politics in Latin America." Pp. 1–50 in *Organized Business, Economic Change, and Democracy in Latin America*. Coral Gables, FL: North-South Center Press.

Skocpol, Theda, and Alexander Hertel-Fernandez. 2016. "The Koch Network and Republican Party Extremism." *Perspectives on Politics* 14(3):681–99. doi: 10.1017/S1537592716001122.

Smith, Peter H. 1979. *Labyrinths of Power: Political Recruitment in Twentieth-Century Mexico*. Princeton, NJ: Princeton University Press.

Snodgrass, Michael. 2014. "The Golden Age of Charrismo: Workers, Braceros, and the Political Machinery of Postrevolutionary Mexico." Pp. 175–95 in *Dictablanda: Politics, Work, and Culture in Mexico, 1938–1968*. Durham, NC: Duke University Press Books.

Snyder, Richard. 2001a. *Politics After Neoliberalism: Reregulation in Mexico*. New York, NY: Cambridge University Press.

Snyder, Richard. 2001b. "Scaling Down: The Subnational Comparative Method." *Studies in Comparative International Development* 36(1):93–110.

Solano Ramírez, Gabino. 2013. "¿Fracaso de Una Utopía? El PRD En Guerrero." Pp. 361–79 in *El PRD: orígenes, itinerarios, retos*, edited by J. Cadena-Roa and M. A. López Leyva. Mexico City: Universidad Nacional Autónoma de México, Instituto de Investigaciones Sociales.

Staggenborg, Suzanne. 1988. "The Consequences of Professionalization and Formalization in the Pro-Choice Movement." *American Sociological Review* 53(4):585–605.

Stevens, Evelyn P. 1977. "Mexico's PRI: The Institutionalization of Corporatism." Pp. 227–58 in *Authoritarianism and Corporatism in Latin America*, edited by J. M. Malloy. Pittsburgh, PA: University of Pittsburgh Press.

Stokes, Susan C. 2005. "Perverse Accountability: A Formal Model of Machine Politics with Evidence from Argentina." *American Political Science Review* 99(3):315–25.

Stokes, Susan C., Thad Dunning, Marcelo Nazareno, and Valeria Brusco. 2013. *Brokers, Voters, and Clientelism: The Puzzle of Distributive Politics*. New York, NY: Cambridge University Press.

Story, Dale. 2014. *Industry, the State, and Public Policy in Mexico*. Austin, TX: University of Texas Press.

Streeck, Wolfgang, and Anke Hassel. 2003. "Trade Unions as Political Actors." *International Handbook of Trade Unions* 335–65.

Suárez Carrera, Víctor. 2011. *Políticas Públicas Para La Agricultura Mexicana*. Mexico City: Editorial Itaca.

Tarlau, Rebecca. 2013. "Coproducing Rural Public Schools in Brazil Contestation, Clientelism, and the Landless Workers' Movement." *Politics & Society* 41(3):395–424.

Tarrow, Sidney. 1998. *Power in Movement: Social Movements and Contentious Politics*. New York, NY: Cambridge University Press.

Tavera Fenolloso, Ligia. 2013. "El Movimiento Urbano Popular y El Frente Democrático Nacional: Campo Organizacional y Liderazgos." Pp. 105–31 in *El PRD: orígenes, itinerario, retos*, edited by J. Cadena-Roa and M. A. López Leyva. Mexico City: Universidad Nacional Autónoma de México, Instituto de Investigaciones Sociales.

Tavits, Margit. 2013. *Post-Communist Democracies and Party Organization*. New York, NY: Cambridge University Press.

Thachil, Tariq. 2014. *Elite Parties, Poor Voters: How Social Services Win Votes in India*. New York, NY: Cambridge University Press.

Touchton, Michael, Natasha Borges Sugiyama, and Brian Wampler. 2017. "Democracy at Work: Moving Beyond Elections to Improve Well-Being." *American Political Science Review* 111(1):68–82. doi: 10.1017/S000305541600068X.

Touchton, Michael, and Brian Wampler. 2014. "Improving Social Well-Being through New Democratic Institutions." *Comparative Political Studies* 47(10):1442–69.

Truett, Lila J., and Dale B. Truett. 2010. "Globalization Challenges for the Mexican Textile Industry." *International Review of Economics & Finance* 19(4):733–41. doi: 10.1016/j.iref.2010.04.003.

Truman, David Bicknell. 1951. *The Governmental Process: Political Interests and Public Opinion*. New York, NY: Knopf.

Unda Gutiérrez, Mónica. 2015. "La Reforma Tributaria de 2013: Los Problemas de La Hacienda Pública y La Desigualdad En México." *Espiral (Guadalajara)* 22(64):69–99.

Van Dyck, Brandon. 2016. "The Paradox of Adversity: New Left Party Survival and Collapse in Brazil, Mexico, and Argentina." Pp. 133–58 in *Challenges of Party-Building in Latin America*, edited by S. Levitsky, J. Loxton, B. Van Dyck, and J. I. Domínguez. New York: Cambridge University Press.

Van Dyck, Brandon. 2017. "The Paradox of Adversity: The Contrasting Fates of Latin America's New Left Parties." *Comparative Politics* 49(2):169–92.

Verba, Sidney. 1961. *Small Groups and Political Behavior: A Study of Leadership*. Princeton, NJ: Princeton University Press.

Verba, Sidney, Kay Lehman Schlozman, and Henry E. Brady. 1995. *Voice and Equality: Civic Voluntarism in American Politics*. Cambridge, MA: Harvard University Press.

Voss, Kim, and Rachel Sherman. 2000. "Breaking the Iron Law of Oligarchy: Union Revitalization in the American Labor Movement." *American Journal of Sociology* 106(2):303–49.

Walker, Jack L. 1991. *Mobilizing Interest Groups in America: Patrons, Professions, and Social Movements*. Ann Arbor, MI: University of Michigan Press.

Weitz-Shapiro, Rebecca. 2012. "What Wins Votes: Why Some Politicians Opt Out of Clientelism." *American Journal of Political Science* 56(3):568–83. doi: 10.1111/j.1540-5907.2011.00578.x.

Weyland, Kurt. 1998. "The Fragmentation of Business in Brazil." Pp. 73–97 in *Organized Business, Economic Change, and Democracy in Latin America*, edited by F. Durand and E. Silva. Coral Gables, FL: North-South Center Press.

Wilson, James Q. 1974. *Political Organizations*. New York, NY: Basic Books.

Wise, Timothy A. 2009. "Agricultural Dumping under NAFTA: Estimating the Costs of U.S. Agricultural Policies to Mexican Producers." 10.22004/ag.econ.179078.

Wolford, Wendy. 2003. "Producing Community: The MST and Land Reform Settlements in Brazil." *Journal of Agrarian Change* 3(4):500–520. doi: 10.1111/1471-0366.00064.

Wolford, Wendy. 2010. "Participatory Democracy by Default: Land Reform, Social Movements and the State in Brazil." *The Journal of Peasant Studies* 37(1):91–109. doi: 10.1080/03066150903498770.

World Bank. 2007. *World Development Report 2008: Agriculture for Development*. Washington, DC: The World Bank.

Wuhs, Steve T. 2010. "From the Boardroom to the Chamber: Business Interests and Party Politics in Mexico." *Journal of Politics in Latin America* 2(1):107–30.

Yashar, Deborah J. 2005. *Contesting Citizenship in Latin America: The Rise of Indigenous Movements and the Postliberal Challenge*. New York, NY: Cambridge University Press.

Zárate Vidal, Margarita. 1998. *En Busca de La Comunidad. Identidades Recreadas y Organización Campesina En Michoacán*. Zamora, Mexico: Colegio de Michoacán.

Zaremberg, Gisela. 2012. "'We're Either Burned or Frozen Out': Society and Party Systems in Latin American Municipal Development Councils (Nicaragua, Venezuela, Mexico, and Brazil)." Pp. 21–51 in *New Institutions for Participatory Democracy in Latin America: Voice and Consequence*. New York, NY: Palgrave Macmillan.

INDEX